Extending Oracle Application Express with Oracle Cloud Features

A Guide to Enhancing APEX Web Applications with Cloud-Native and Machine Learning Technologies

Adrian Png
Heli Helskyaho

Apress®

Extending Oracle Application Express with Oracle Cloud Features: A Guide to Enhancing APEX Web Applications with Cloud-Native and Machine Learning Technologies

Adrian Png
Whitehorse, YT, Canada

Heli Helskyaho
Helsinki, Finland

ISBN-13 (pbk): 978-1-4842-8169-7
https://doi.org/10.1007/978-1-4842-8170-3

ISBN-13 (electronic): 978-1-4842-8170-3

Managing Director, Apress Media LLC: Welmoed Spahr
Acquisitions Editor: Jonathan Gennick
Development Editor: Laura Berendson
Coordinating Editor: Jill Balzano

Cover image designed by Freepik (www.freepik.com)

Distributed to the book trade worldwide by Springer Science+Business Media LLC, 1 New York Plaza, Suite 4600, New York, NY 10004. Phone 1-800-SPRINGER, fax (201) 348-4505, e-mail orders-ny@springer-sbm.com, or visit www.springeronline.com. Apress Media, LLC is a California LLC and the sole member (owner) is Springer Science + Business Media Finance Inc (SSBM Finance Inc). SSBM Finance Inc is a **Delaware** corporation.

For information on translations, please e-mail booktranslations@springernature.com; for reprint, paperback, or audio rights, please e-mail bookpermissions@springernature.com.

Apress titles may be purchased in bulk for academic, corporate, or promotional use. eBook versions and licenses are also available for most titles. For more information, reference our Print and eBook Bulk Sales web page at http://www.apress.com/bulk-sales.

Any source code or other supplementary material referenced by the author in this book is available to readers on GitHub (https://github.com/Apress). For more detailed information, please visit http://www.apress.com/source-code.

Printed on acid-free paper

Dedicated to Joel R. Kallman.

Thank you for showing us what angels look like.

Table of Contents

About the Authors.. xi

About the Technical Reviewer xiii

Acknowledgments..xv

Introduction xvii

Chapter 1: Architecting a Secure Infrastructure for APEX................................ 1

Network Components 2

    Virtual Cloud Network... 3

    Network Security Groups.. 7

    Bastion 11

Infrastructure as Code 17

    Terraform and the Resource Manager.. 18

    The OCI Designer Toolkit... 19

Deploying APEX to a Database System 20

    Oracle Autonomous Linux.. 20

    Load Balancer... 21

APEX on an Autonomous Database... 21

    Private Endpoint 22

    Vanity URL 24

Web Application Firewall... 25

Vulnerability Scanning 28

Logs, Metrics, and Alarms.. 31

Summary... 33

Chapter 2: Storing Large Objects Using Object Storage **35**

Oracle Cloud Infrastructure.. 36

Storing Files in the Oracle Database... 37

The OCI Object Storage Alternative 37

Using OCI Object Storage with APEX.. 39

    Create a Compartment 39

    Create an OCI Object Storage Bucket.. 40

    Create an Oracle Autonomous Database (Optional).. 41

    Create Identity and Access Management Resources 42

    The APEX Application... 48

    Considerations... 62

Summary... 63

Chapter 3: Using Oracle Cloud Functions **65**

Image Processing 65

    Processing Images on the Client Browser.. 68

    Custom Image Processing REST API... 68

    Using Third-Party REST APIs.. 68

Oracle Cloud Functions 69

    Required Software and Tools.. 70

    Virtual Cloud Network.. 72

    Identity and Access Management 74

    Set Up Fn Project CLI... 82

    Oracle Cloud Infrastructure Container Registry... 85

    Validate Setup 85

Thumbnail Generator Function... 86

    Approach to Development 93

    Configuration Parameters.. 97

Triggering Functions with Oracle Events 97

Resource Principals 100

Complete Function and Deploy 103

Troubleshooting and Logging... 105

Thumbnails Applied...107

Summary...110

Chapter 4: Exposing Functionality with API Gateway...........................**111**

Use Case Definition...112

Deploy the Language Translation Engine...115

Oracle Functions for Language Translation 123

API Gateway for Language Translation 124

Calling the API Gateway from APEX...132

Security and Logging 136

Summary...138

Chapter 5: Oracle Machine Learning in Autonomous Database **139**

Setting Up the Oracle Machine Learning Environment 139

Creating an Autonomous Database 139

Obtaining the URLs Needed for Using the OML Service 145

Creating an OML User...146

Oracle Machine Learning...151

An Introduction to Oracle Machine Learning User Interface.................................151

Administration 154

Notebooks 158

AutoML 167

Models..177

Oracle Machine Learning for SQL (OML4SQL)...181

Oracle Machine Learning for Python (OML4Py)..184

In-Database Machine Learning and APEX...190

Summary...191

Chapter 6: Oracle Machine Learning REST Services............................**193**

A Short Introduction to REST APIs..193

Introduction to OML REST Services 196

REST API for Oracle Machine Learning Services 196

REST API for Embedded Python Execution 198

Using OML REST Services 200

    Installing and Setting Up a REST Client (cURL) 200

    Creating an Access Token 201

    Examples of Using OML REST Services 203

Using OML REST Services from APEX 213

Summary 232

Chapter 7: Data Labeling 233

Setting Up the Service 233

Datasets, Records, and Labeling 243

    Creating a Dataset and Records 244

    Labeling Records in a Dataset 249

    Adding New Records to the Dataset 252

    Data Labeling Errors 252

Data Labeling with APEX Using OCI APIs 255

    Data Labeling APIs 255

    Setting Up APEX for Data Labeling APIs 255

    Using Data Labeling APIs with APEX 261

Summary 268

Chapter 8: Anomaly Detection 269

Setting Up the Anomaly Detection Service 270

    Compartment, Policies, User Groups, and a User 270

    Vault, Keys, and Secrets 280

Anomaly Detection Service 289

    Requirements for the Data 289

    Creating a Machine Learning Model and Detecting Anomalies 293

    Metrics 310

Anomaly Detection with APEX Using the OCI API 313

    Anomaly Detection API 313

    Setting Up APEX for Anomaly Detection API 313

    Using Anomaly Detection APIs with APEX 315

Summary 317

Chapter 9: Language.. **319**

Different Use Cases for Language Service.. 319

Language Detection.. 320

Text Classification.. 321

Key Phrase Extraction... 321

Named Entity Recognition 322

Sentiment Analysis 323

Setting Up the Service 324

Analyzing Text with the OCI Console 329

Analyzing Text with the OCI Language API and APEX... 334

Language API... 334

Setting Up APEX for Language API.. 335

Using Language API with APEX... 339

Summary... 344

Chapter 10: Vision **345**

Working with OCI REST APIs 346

OCI Object Storage 347

OCI Vision 349

Summary... 366

Chapter 11: Email Delivery Services **367**

Setting Up OCI Resources 368

Identity and Access Management 368

Regions, Availability, and Server Information 376

Email Domains... 377

Approved Senders 386

Suppression List.. 388

Configure APEX Instance for OCI Email Delivery Service 389

Email Deliverability 393

Testing Deliverability 394

Troubleshooting Deliverability 396

Other Essentials 400

Summary.. 401

Index... **403**

About the Authors

Adrian Png is a seasoned solutions architect with over 20 years of experience working with clients to design and implement state-of-the-art infrastructure and applications. He earned a Master of Technology (Knowledge Engineering) degree from the National University of Singapore and is always eager to apply his knowledge and skills in machine learning. Adrian is also trained and certified in several Oracle technologies, including Oracle Cloud Infrastructure, Oracle Autonomous Database, Oracle Cloud-Native Services, Oracle Database, and Oracle Application Express. He is an Oracle ACE and a recognized contributor in the Oracle community. Most recently, he co-authored the Apress book *Getting Started with Oracle Cloud Free Tier*. In his spare time, Adrian enjoys tinkering with electronics projects and 3D printing.

Heli Helskyaho is the CEO of Miracle Finland Oy. She holds a master's degree in Computer Science from the University of Helsinki and specializes in databases. At the moment, she is working on her doctoral studies at the University of Helsinki.

Heli has been working in IT since 1990. She has held several positions, but every role has included databases and data. She believes that understanding your data makes using the data much easier. She is an Oracle ACE Director and a frequent speaker at many conferences. She is the author of several books and has been listed as one of the top 100 influencers in the ICT sector in Finland for each year from 2015 to 2021.

About the Technical Reviewer

 **Karen Cannell** is President of TH Technology, a consulting firm providing Oracle technology services. A mechanical engineer, she has analyzed, designed, developed, converted, upgraded, enhanced, and otherwise implemented database applications for over 30 years, concentrating on Oracle technologies. She has worked with Oracle APEX since its beginnings and continues to leverage Oracle tools to build solutions in government, health care, and engineering industries. Karen is ODTUG Vice President, an Oracle ACE Director, editor emeritus of the *ODTUG Technical Journal*, an Oracle Developer's Choice finalist, an ODTUG Volunteer of the Year, and co-author of *Expert Oracle Application Express*, *Agile Oracle Application Express*, and *Beginning Oracle Application Express 4.2*. She is an active member of ODTUG and other local and regional user groups. She may be contacted at kcannell@thtechnology.com and @thtechnology.

Acknowledgments

We would like to thank Jonathan Gennick and Jill Balzano for believing in us and guiding us through the process of getting this book published. We also want to express our deep gratitude to Guillermo Ruiz and Bo English-Wiczling from Oracle for supporting us during the development of the book contents. And, finally, our heartfelt thanks to Karen Cannell for taking time out of her busy schedule to review our book.

—Adrian Png and Heli Helskyaho

I would like to thank my wife once again for supporting and encouraging me to complete this project. My thanks also to Heli, my co-author, without whom this book would not be possible.

—Adrian Png

I would like to thank my husband Marko and my two sons, Patrik and Matias, for their continuous support and encouragement. And thank you to my parents for always being there to support me. Adrian Png, thank you! Thank you for being such a great friend and such a fun colleague to work with. And a very special thank you for inviting me to this project.

—Heli Helskyaho

Introduction

There are three topics many people are interested in: cloud solutions, low-code/no-code development, and machine learning/artificial intelligence (AI). Oftentimes, the reason is that we all need to achieve more with less money and as fast as possible. The competition is hard, and we need to use our time and resources more efficiently than our competitors to make correct decisions faster. We need to understand the business, the data, and the information it holds. And, we do not want to spend our working hours on basic maintenance tasks because that time is away from more important and more business-critical work. And, being very honest, many of us are on Information and Communications Technology (ICT) to be able to learn new, interesting things every day.

In this book, we talk about all these three topics, plus more. We talk about the Oracle Cloud Infrastructure (OCI) and the Oracle Autonomous Database (ADB) available in OCI. ADB automatically includes the Oracle Application Express (APEX) low-code environment and the Oracle Machine Learning (OML) functionalities for both SQL and Python. APEX and OML are both pre-installed and cost-free features of the database. APEX lets you build applications for any enterprise for as little work and time as possible, including the possibility to build proof of concepts very easily. But that is probably something you already knew and you are probably equally excited about APEX as we are. What you might not know is that in OCI, the APEX in ADB is also maintained by Oracle: both ADB and APEX are automatically patched by Oracle. OML and other machine learning/data science capabilities of OCI make it easy to use existing machine learning models and AI solutions or to build new ones.

OCI also offers Oracle Cloud Functions, several AI services, and much more.

OCI is evolving all the time and new or improved features are added. In this book, we have a chance to take a look at some of the features, including very recently added features, but we hope this book shares our excitement for OCI so that you will continue to learn about all the possible new features we are yet to know and to use to make APEX even better.

## CHAPTER 1

Architecting a Secure Infrastructure for APEX

The role of *Oracle Application Express* (APEX) in Oracle's huge portfolio of technology products has grown significantly in the past few years. It has transformed from its humble beginnings as a no-cost, rapid application development environment that came with all editions of the Oracle Database, to become a core component of Oracle's flagship product, the *Autonomous Database* (ADB).

The ADB is a fully managed database service that is powered by state-of-the-art machine learning capabilities. Subscribers of the service do not have to manage the underlying hardware, operating systems (OS), and software that power the database. Oracle is responsible for ensuring that the database is configured for availability and scalability. These databases are also automatically patched for security and feature enhancements. The ML-powered algorithms allow the database to automatically create table indexes and tune execution plans to ensure optimal performance of database queries and code.

ADBs are offered with four workload types:

- Autonomous Transaction Processing

- Autonomous Data Warehouse

- Autonomous JSON Database

- APEX Service

All workload types come with APEX preinstalled and configured, including a fully managed *Java Enterprise Edition* (EE) application server that hosts the *Oracle REST Data Services* (ORDS). Except for the APEX Service, the ADBs also come with the *Oracle Machine Learning Notebooks* (OML Notebooks) and the *Oracle Graph Studio*.

1

A. Png and H. Helskyaho, *Extending Oracle Application Express with Oracle Cloud Features*, https://doi.org/10.1007/978-1-4842-8170-3_1

Note   Also missing from the APEX Service is support for *Oracle Net Services* (SQL*Net). This limits development activities to the *APEX App Builder* and *Database Actions*.

However, as APEX can be installed on any database edition, it is possible to deploy an instance without an ADB. Among the several data management products the Oracle Cloud Infrastructure (OCI) offers, there are Oracle Database (DB) Systems that can be deployed on either a virtual machine or bare metal servers. Databases provisioned as a DB System come with the necessary software preinstalled and configured using best practices. The amount of allocated virtual CPUs, memory, and storage is easily managed using the OCI Console. Backups and patches can also be managed and applied through the console. Unlike the ADBs though, APEX and ORDS are not installed by default.

Note   As of Oracle Database 19c, the standard edition now allows you to create up to three pluggable databases (PDBs) without needing to purchase additional licenses. This opens the opportunity to create more than one APEX environment for non-production purposes such as development and testing.

In this chapter, we will look at both approaches for provisioning an APEX instance and how we can prepare and secure the instance for production rollout.

Network Components

APEX is fundamentally a web application and, as such, relies on the Internet or intranet to provide access to the beautiful functionalities that developers can create. Today, there are many options on where one could host an APEX instance. Here are few examples:

- Hosting a server on premises

- Hosting a server at a shared data center

- Hosting on virtual computing resources through an Infrastructure-as-a-Service (IaaS) vendor

- Subscribing to APEX as a Platform as a Service (PaaS)

There are, of course, pros and cons of each approach. Hosting a server on premises requires significant investments in real estate for the data center, providing uninterruptible power and cooling, monitoring physical server access, and so much more. However, it does provide absolute control of both hardware and software and, more importantly, guarantees that data sovereignty is maintained.

Subscribing to a PaaS service is probably the most straightforward method for hosting an APEX application on the Internet. Simply obtain a workspace and dedicated database schema and deploy your application. However, the PaaS provider determines all other aspects of the APEX environment. For example, the vendor would determine the Oracle Database version installed, edition and features enabled, and software patch levels. They are also responsible and decide on infrastructure issues such as systems architecture and network security.

A good middle ground is to host the APEX instance on a server that is hosted by a third-party vendor. In the early days of the Internet, server colocation provided independent software providers (ISPs) the ability to host a server, install the necessary software, and deploy web applications. However, these were costly as the hosting provider takes on the responsibility and costs associated with hosting any data center.

With the advent of server virtualization and software-defined networks, it became possible for IaaS vendors to provide computing and networking resources at much lower prices. These allow ISPs to have the "best of both worlds," that is, managing their own infrastructure and at a more palatable price.

However, as the proverbial saying goes, "With great power comes great responsibility." When hosting APEX on the OCI, cloud architects need to consider what OCI resources to use, how they interact, and, more importantly, how to maintain an environment that is robust and secure for both application and data.

Virtual Cloud Network

The OCI offers a wide range of network components, and the *Virtual Cloud Network* (VCN) is the core to building up our virtual infrastructure for APEX. A VCN is made up of several subcomponents, such as

- Subnets
- Routes
- Security lists

- DHCP options

- Internet, Network Address Translation (NAT), and service gateways

There are many considerations and ways to design a VCN. For example, a VCN can contain one or more subnets, so what is the ideal number to create? And as usual, the answer is: "It depends!" Fortunately, Oracle provides some guidance through their *Oracle Architecture Center* website (`https://docs.oracle.com/solutions/`), where you can find several reference architectures, solution playbooks, and customer-published solutions. And on *GitHub*, Oracle lists several repositories (`https://github.com/oracle-quickstart`) containing *Terraform* (`https://terraform.io/`) scripts for building different types of environments that you can use to deploy through the *Resource Manager*.

In this chapter, we will design and deploy a simple VCN (see Figure 1-1) in a compartment *ch01*. It will consist of three subnets. One subnet will be public. OCI resources in this subnet can be assigned publicly accessible IP addresses. The Internet gateway provides two-way communications between the resource and Internet clients. Two subnets will be private, and though the OCI components can access Internet-based resources through the NAT gateway, they are isolated and not addressable outside of the VCN. This network topology helps minimize the exposure of critical assets like database and application servers to external threats on the Internet, which are otherwise not accessed directly by users.

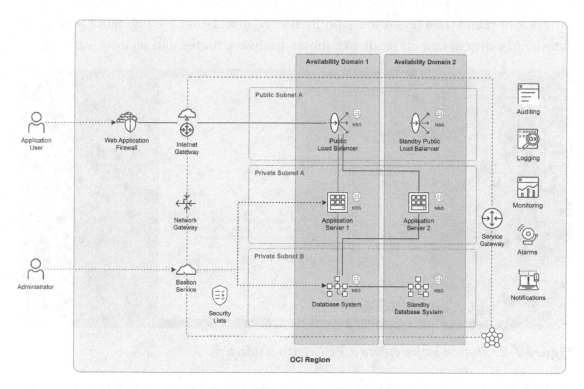

Figure 1-1. *A simple topology for APEX on a DB System*

VCNs can be created through the OCI Console, and an option to use the wizard (Figure 1-2) is available. The latter gets you started with a viable VCN in a few mouse clicks. To access the wizard, click the navigation menu on the top left of the OCI Console, click *Networking*, and then click *Virtual Cloud Networks*. Next, click *Start VCN Wizard*, and in the first step, provide the following details:

- **VCN name**: vcn-ch01

- **Compartment**: ch01

- **VCN CIDR block**: 10.0.0.0/16

- **Public Subnet CIDR Block**: 10.0.0.0/24

- **Private Subnet CIDR Block**: 10.0.1.0/24

Click *Next* and then review the submitted VCN information. Finally, click *Create* and the wizard will generate the required subnets, gateways, routes, and security lists.

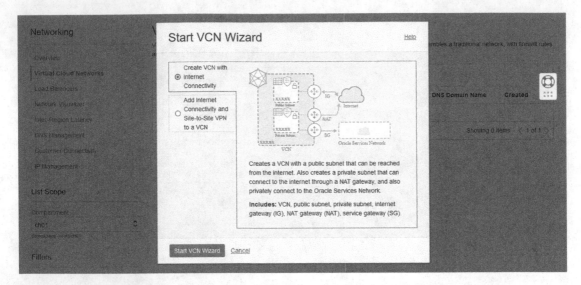

Figure 1-2. *In two steps, create a VCN with a wizard*

Unfortunately, the wizard only creates two subnets, one public and the other private. An additional subnet must be created to build the target network topology in Figure 1-1.

Note   The wizard does not give you the opportunity to name the subnets. After the VCN is created, go to the subnet's details page, and rename the public and private subnets to *Public Subnet A* and *Private Subnet A*, respectively.

---

1.   From the VCN's details page, click *Create Subnet*.

2.   Provide the following information (Figure 1-3):

   a.   **Name**: Private Subnet B

   b.   **Create in Compartment**: ch01

   c.   **Subnet Type**: Regional

   d.   **CIDR Block**: 10.0.2.0/24

   e.   **Route Table**: Route Table for Private Subnet-vcn-ch01

  f. **Subnet Access**: Private Subnet

  g. **DNS Resolution**: Checked

  h. **DNS Label**: Leave blank

  i. **Dhcp Options**: Default DHCP Options for vcn-ch01

  j. **Security Lists**: Security List for Private Subnet-vcn-ch01

 3. Click *Create*.

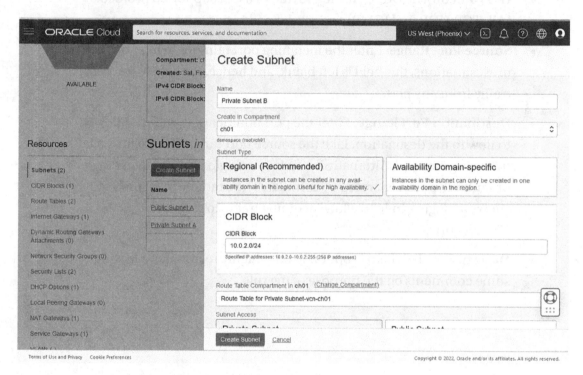

Figure 1-3. *Create a second private subnet*

Network Security Groups

The OCI now offers administrators two methods of adding security rules to manage access to networked resources. All subnets should already have a security list defined and associated with it. When the security list is created, it will be empty, and hence, all traffic to every component is blocked, regardless of the source.

There are two types of security rules, one each for managing ingress and egress traffic. Both require similar types of information.

- **Source/Destination Type**: This can be either CIDR, Service, or Network Service Group. Most rules rely on CIDR.

- **Source/Destination CIDR**: The IPv4 of the originating source or destination.

- **IP Protocol**: The OCI Console provides a list of supported protocols (All, TCP, UDP, and ICMP) and predefined services.

- **Source Port Range**: Enter the incoming port number to filter on. In most situations, this field is left blank, and hence, the rule will accept traffic from any port.

- **Destination Port Range**: Enter the port number that traffic is allowed to flow to the destination. Like the source port range, if left blank, all traffic is permitted. Alternatively, specify a single port number, range, or multiple ports separated by commas. The example in Figure 1-4 shows an ingress rule to allow incoming traffic to standard HTTP/ HTTPS ports.

- **Description**: This field is optional, but I highly recommend leaving some comments on the purpose of the rule.

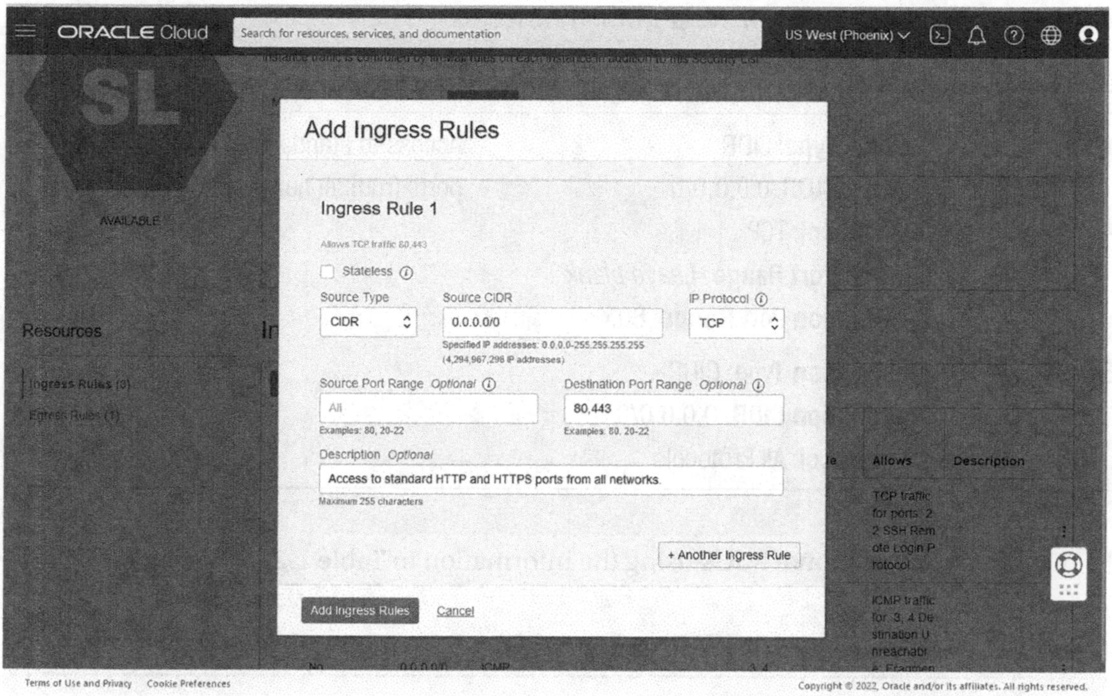

Figure 1-4. *An ingress rule that allows access to standard ports used on web servers*

Once a security list is associated with a subnet, all its rules apply for any resource that attaches to the subnet. *Network Security Groups* (NSGs) are a more recent feature that allows more fine-grained control on what rules to apply against each network resource. As opposed to security lists, NSGs are associated with the OCI component, rather than the subnet that they belong to.

To create an NSG, perform the following tasks:

1. Go to the VCN's details page and click *Network Security Groups*.

2. Click *Create Network Security Group*.

3. Enter a name for the NSG, for example, *NsgPublicWebAccess*.

4. Add two security rules using the information in Table 1-1. Click *Another Rule* if necessary.

5. Click *Create*.

Table 1-1. *Security rules for NsgPublicWebAccess*

Direction	Details	Description
Ingress	**Source Type**: CIDR **Source CIDR**: 0.0.0.0/0 **IP Protocol**: TCP **Source Port Range**: *Leave blank* **Destination Port Range**: 80,443	Access to standard HTTP and HTTPS ports from all network sources
Egress	**Destination Type**: CIDR **Destination CIDR**: 0.0.0.0/0 **IP Protocol**: All Protocols	

Create three additional NSGs using the information in Table 1-2.

Table 1-2. *Security rules for three other NSGs*

NSG Name	Details	Description
NsgPrivateWebAccess	**Direction**: Ingress **Source Type**: CIDR **Source CIDR**: 0.0.0.0/0 **IP Protocol**: TCP **Source Port Range**: *Leave blank* **Destination Port Range**: 80,443	Access to standard HTTP and HTTPS ports from all network sources
NsgPrivateWebAccess	**Direction**: Egress **Destination Type**: CIDR **Destination CIDR**: 0.0.0.0/0 **IP Protocol**: All Protocols	
NsgPrivateJavaEEAccess	**Direction**: Ingress **Source Type**: CIDR **Source CIDR**: 10.0.0.0/24 **IP Protocol**: TCP **Source Port Range**: *Leave blank* **Destination Port Range**: 80,443	Access to standard HTTP and HTTPS ports from all *Public Subnet A*

(continued)

Table 1-2. (*continued*)

NSG Name	Details	Description
NsgPrivateJavaEEAccess	**Direction**: Egress **Destination Type**: CIDR **Destination CIDR**: 0.0.0.0/0 **IP Protocol**: All Protocols	
NsgPrivateDatabaseAccess	**Direction**: Ingress **Source Type**: CIDR **Source CIDR**: 10.0.0.0/16 **IP Protocol**: TCP **Source Port Range**: *Leave blank* **Destination Port Range**: 1521–1522	Access to database ports from any VCN subnets
NsgPrivateDatabaseAccess	**Direction**: Egress **Destination Type**: CIDR **Destination CIDR**: 0.0.0.0/0 **IP Protocol**: All Protocols	

Bastion

Today, the risk of cyberattacks is extremely high. Regardless of how small or large your organization's web application is, it is pertinent that we limit the surface of attack and secure access to data and code. In the proposed architecture, all application and database servers are placed in private subnets that are not accessible *via* the Internet. The load balancers are OCI-managed services, have very specific functionality, and do not retain any code or data. They can be placed in a public subnet that is sometimes referred to as a demilitarized zone (DMZ).

For most organizations, these private subnets are accessed using a site-to-site Virtual Private Network (VPN) between the VCN and the on-premises network. Employees working remotely can then connect to the corporate network using a separate VPN and then through the secure IPsec tunnels, onward to the servers.

Oracle provides an alternate solution, the *Bastion* service, to securely tunnel into the VCN and connect to servers on private subnets. Like load balancers, this is a managed service provided by the OCI. Bastions can be assigned to public subnets, and their access can be managed through *Identity and Access Management* (IAM) groups and policies.

Create a bastion using the following steps:

1. Open the navigation menu, click *Identity & Security*, and then click *Bastion* (you may have to scroll down the page a little).

2. Click *Create bastion*.

3. Enter a name (Figure 1-5). Specify the target VCN and subnet (a public subnet since our goal is to access the servers *via* the Internet), updating the selected compartment if necessary. If you need to limit connections to a predefined range of IP addresses, then add them to the *CIDR block allowlist* field.

4. Click *Create bastion*.

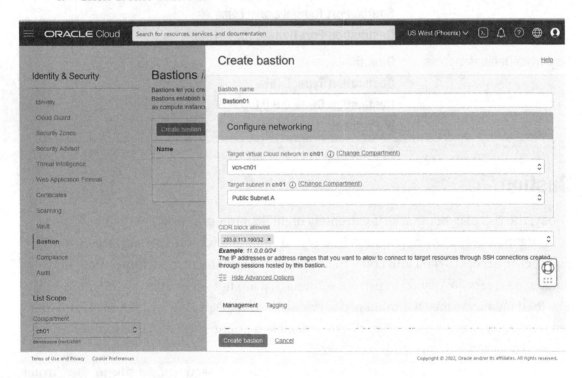

Figure 1-5. *Create a bastion and place it on the public subnet*

Two types of sessions are available through a bastion, depending on what you wish to connect to on the private subnets. If a compute instance was created using one of Oracle's provided Linux images, users can create *managed SSH sessions* to connect to the servers using SSH. In addition, these hosts need to have OpenSSH installed and running, must have the Oracle Cloud Agent installed, and the Bastion plug-in enabled (Figure 1-6). The VCN that the hosts are on must also have a service gateway and a rule for all OCI services to route through it.

Note   SSH is a secure protocol for communicating with servers running Unix-based operating systems, typically over Transmission Control Protocol (TCP) port number 22. The most common application for clients to communicate with the servers is OpenSSH. This software is available to install with current versions of Microsoft Windows, Mac, and Linux. Users will require an OS user account and can authenticate using various methods such as a password or an SSH key pair. To perform the latter, OpenSSH provides tools to manage these keys that are, by default, stored in the subdirectory .ssh, under the user's home directory. To generate a key pair, run the command:

```
ssh-keygen -t rsa
```

A passphrase is optional, so leave it blank to use the keys without one. Once the private and public keys are generated, you will find them in the files ~/.ssh/id_rsa and ~/.ssh/id_rsa.pub, respectively. Keep the private key secure, but provide the contents of the public key to systems that you require access to. The public key is added to a file (~/.ssh/authorized_keys) in the user's home directory that is then used for authentication.

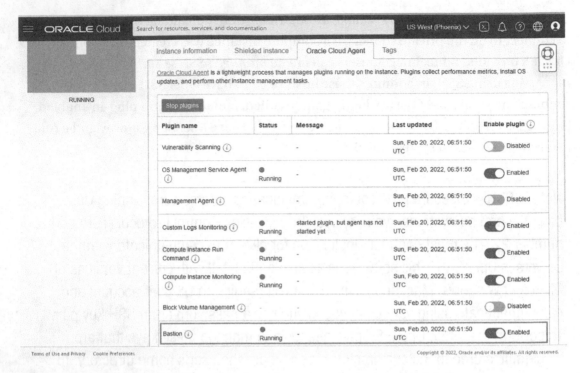

Figure 1-6. *Ensure that instance has the Bastion plug-in enabled*

Let us assume that there is a compute instance named *appsrv01* that meets these requirements and has been deployed in *Private Subnet A*. Create a managed SSH session to access the server using the following steps:

1. Go to the bastion's details page.

2. Click Create session.

3. Select or provide the following details (Figure 1-7):

    a. **Session type**: Managed SSH session

    b. **Session name**: BastionSession_appsrv01

    c. **Username**: opc *(or any other Linux user that has a SSH public key added)*

    d. **Compute instance**: appsrv01

    e. **Add SSH key**: *Provide your SSH public key*

4. Click *Create session.*

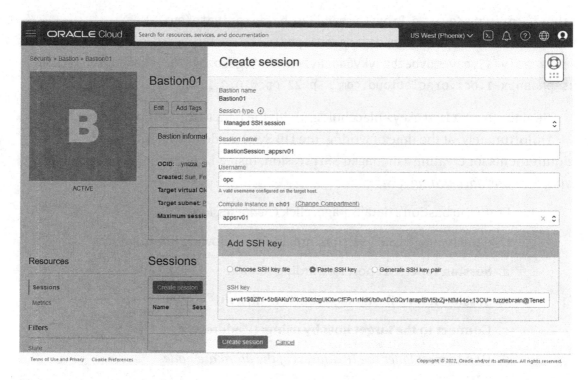

Figure 1-7. *Create a bastion managed SSH session to access a compute instance securely*

After the session has been created, return to the bastion's details page where you will find it listed. Click the three vertical dots to access additional options (Figure 1-8). Click *Copy SSH command.*

Resources	Sessions							
Sessions	Create session							
Metrics	Name	Session type	Target resource	Target port	Username	State	Session TTL	
Filters	BastionSession_appsrv01	Managed SSH	appsrv01	22	opc	● Active	3 hours, 00 minutes	
State All								

Edit session name
View SSH command
Copy SSH command
Copy OCID
Delete session
Open support request

Figure 1-8. *Copy the SSH command to connect to the server*

The following is an example of the SSH command:

```
ssh -i <privateKey> -o ProxyCommand="ssh -i <privateKey> -W
%h:%p -p 22 ocid1.bastionsession.oc1.phx.
amaaaaaafy4s5yqavemdvoezbztyky6djzuyznny2km5egdzozbys2ncftka@host.bastion.
us-phoenix-1.oci.oraclecloud.com" -p 22 opc@10.0.1.246
```

Replace the `<privateKey>` placeholders with the path to the SSH private key.

Unfortunately, at the time of writing, the DB Systems do not yet meet the requirements for creating a managed SSH session. Instead, create the second session type: *SSH port forwarding session*.

1. From the bastion's details page, click *Create session*.

2. Like the managed SSH session, provide the following information:

   a. **Session type**: SSH port forwarding session

   b. **Session name**: BastionSession_Ssh_dbsrv01

   c. **Connect to the target host by using**: IP address

   d. **IP address**: *Enter the IP address of the database node*

   e. **Port**: 22

   f. **Add SSH key**: *Provide SSH public key*

3. Click *Create session*.

Back on the bastion's details page, copy the SSH command that should look somewhat like the following:

```
ssh -i <privateKey> -N -L <localPort>:10.0.2.90:22 -p
22 ocid1.bastionsession.oc1.phx.
amaaaaaafy4s5yqajaqf5gmoiqdly5ttccf3ks4qnmifvkk3dhe3izs5h5ba@host.bastion.
us-phoenix-1.oci.oraclecloud.com
```

Replace the placeholders `<privateKey>` and `<localPort>` with the SSH private key path and the local port number to be mapped. For example:

```
ssh -i ~/.ssh/id_rsa -N -L 2222:10.0.2.90:22 -p 22 ocid1.bastionsession.
oc1.phx.amaaaaaafy4s5yqajaqf5gmoiqdly5ttccf3ks4qnmifvkk3dhe3izs5h5ba@host.
bastion.us-phoenix-1.oci.oraclecloud.com
```

Execute the command to create the SSH tunnel. From another terminal on the same workstation, log in to the DB System via SSH and connect to the localhost using the local port number. For example:

```
ssh -p 2222 -i ~/.ssh/id_rsa opc@localhost
```

To connect to the database from the workstation, for example, using either *SQL Developer* or *SQLcl*, create a second SSH tunnel using the database port number 1521. Run the SSH command and specify a local port number to map to, and then set up the database connection (Figure 1-9).

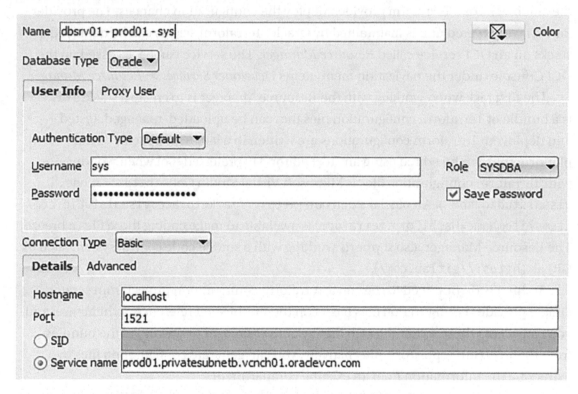

Figure 1-9. *Example database connection in SQL Developer*

Infrastructure as Code

Earlier in this chapter, we had created the base VCN using the wizard that created the necessary network subcomponents and configurations. This greatly reduced the number of manual steps performed to create the base environment. However, the template does not always meet our operational requirements. After the VCN was provisioned, we had to rename resources and add some new ones.

A common risk or disadvantage associated with any type of manual intervention is reproducibility. Should we need to restore the same VCN configuration due to either some failure or new requirements, it is not easy to guarantee that the setup can be repeated accurately. Is there a way to document the infrastructure with code?

Terraform and the Resource Manager

Yes, and the answer to this very common challenge is Terraform. Terraform allows architects to define the infrastructure using configuration files and, then with the help of the cloud vendor's Terraform provider, deploy the configuration changes. The provider for OCI was created and is maintained by Oracle. Terraform scripts can be deployed as stacks on an OCI service called *Resource Manager*. The service can be accessed on the OCI Console under the navigation menu items *Developer Services* ➤ *Resource Manager*.

The first task when working with the Resource Manager is to create a stack. This is a bundle of Terraform configuration files that can be uploaded, managed, tested, and deployed. Terraform configurations are written in a language specific to the platform that can be edited using any text editor. My preferred tool when working with Terraform configuration files is Microsoft Visual Studio Code (`https://code.visualstudio.com/`). An official extension (`https://marketplace.visualstudio.com/items?itemName=HashiCorp.terraform`) is available to make coding these files a breeze. The Resource Manager also supports working with a source code control system such as GitLab (`https://gitlab.com/`).

Architects do not need to start on a Terraform configuration project from scratch. Oracle provides configuration files based on their published reference architecture, and you can access these either through the Resource Manager or download the bundles from their GitHub repository. Alternatively, you can generate configuration files by extracting the information from an existing compartment.

Terraform configuration often relies on information that is only available when a deployment is required. These are exposed as variables and the console provides a user interface that allows architects to set and/or modify them.

Once the stack is ready, architects should validate the configuration files using the *Plan* action and, then after careful inspection of the outcomes, deploy the stack using the *Apply* action. All resources linked to a stack deployment can also be deleted by executing the *Destroy* action.

The OCI Designer Toolkit

It is also worthwhile mentioning that Oracle has a nifty visual tool (Figure 1-10) for designing your tenancy's architecture, the *OCI Designer Toolkit* (OKIT). At the time of writing, OKIT is still under active development, but it already supports many OCI services, sufficient to create the network topology we have described earlier.

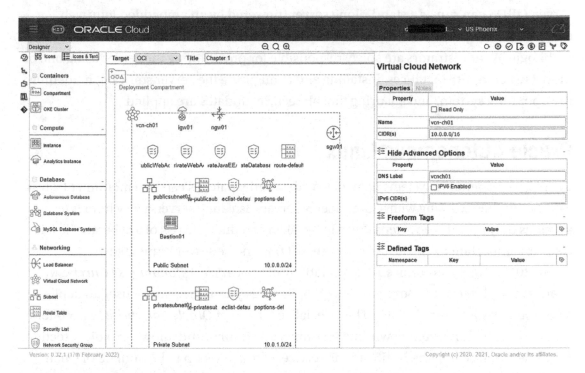

Figure 1-10. *OKIT that defines the desired network topology described in this chapter*

OKIT is a web application tool that runs within a Docker container. If you are interested in using the tool, install Docker or any other *Open Container Initiative* runtime, and then follow the instructions available on the GitHub repository (`https://github.com/oracle/oci-designer-toolkit`) to build and run the container.

After configuring the workstation and container to support OCI REST API access, OKIT can then work seamlessly with the tenancy. Architects can export the design as Terraform configuration files and even deploy them as stacks on the Resource Manager from within the tool.

Deploying APEX to a Database System

When deploying APEX to an OCI DB System, administrators are fully responsible for installing APEX. They are also responsible for all aspects of database performance tuning, security patching, and planning for database backups and recovery.

Similarly, ORDS is a Java web application and runs inside a Java EE application server. ORDS can run as a stand-alone server (powered by an embedded Jetty web container) or deployed to a supported container such as Apache Tomcat or Oracle WebLogic. Administrators are solely responsible for provisioning the server using one or more OCI compute instances, installing and configuring the server software, hardening the operating system, and ensuring that all security updates are applied.

Oracle Autonomous Linux

Keeping the operating systems up to date with security patches can be a monumental task especially when working with a large fleet of servers. Isolating servers away from Internet access is only one of many steps that can be taken to reduce the risk of a cyberattack. It is also very important to ensure the software that powers the server is updated.

In 2019, Oracle announced the availability of the *Oracle Autonomous Linux* (`www.oracle.com/linux/autonomous-linux/`) operating system that can be used to deploy a compute instance on the OCI. This specialized flavor of *Oracle Enterprise Linux* offers automated patching, zero downtime planning, self-tuning, and known exploit detection. Administrators, using the Notifications service, can also set up to be notified of when the operating system is patched. These features make Oracle Autonomous Linux a great operating system to host ORDS.

Note   ORDS is available to install through the Oracle Enterprise Linux software package repositories when deployed on OCI compute instances. When ORDS is installed through the repository, it runs as a stand-alone server. In Oracle Autonomous Linux, the ORDS software is automatically updated, but administrators will need to ensure that the `ords.conf` configuration file is correct, the configuration directory location is set in the `ords.war` file, and the installation procedure is performed to ensure that any ORDS schema changes are applied. Do these three steps before restarting the ORDS *systemd* service.

Load Balancer

Ideally, both the database and application servers should be deployed in private subnets. In the proposed architecture (Figure 1-1), servers that play different roles in the stack are further isolated in separate networks. This allows administrators to define fine-grained security and access control policies. With these servers deeply entrenched in a private network, how do we expose APEX applications on the Internet securely?

The OCI provides load balancers as a managed service which are great companions to the Java application servers. As a highly specialized resource, load balancers proxy web traffic between browser or REST clients and the application servers to deliver web content, without exposing any additional attack surface to the public network. Oracle manages, monitors, and updates the hardware and software that are responsible for delivering the service. In OCI *regions* where there are more than one *availability domain* (AD), the load balancer service also offers automatic failovers should an AD goes down.

APEX on an Autonomous Database

The Oracle Autonomous Database provides a complete stack for running APEX. Unlike in the previous deployment strategy, the APEX runtime comes preinstalled with the database. There is no need to install any software or create additional compute instances. The ADB service includes a managed and resilient environment for hosting ORDS.

In this next section, we will propose an architecture (Figure 1-11) that isolates the ADB in a private network but allows APEX applications to be accessed from the external network.

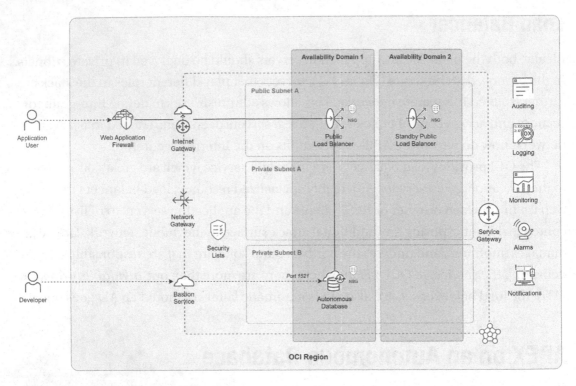

Figure 1-11. *A secure APEX stack powered by an Autonomous Database*

The ADB will be configured with an endpoint that provides private network access only. A load balancer placed in a public subnet is then configured not only to make the ADB tool suite available on the Internet but also to support *vanity URLs* that are more user-friendly and representative of the organization that owns the applications.

Private Endpoint

A paid instance of the ADB, regardless of the workload type, will allow administrators to choose between any of the following network access types:

1.   Secure access from everywhere

2.   Secure access from allowed IPs and VCNs only

3.   Private endpoint access only

You can choose the access type when creating the instance or change it even after the ADB has been created. Figure 1-12 illustrates the choice to restrict access through a private endpoint, where administrators must assign the target VCN, subnet, and NSGs.

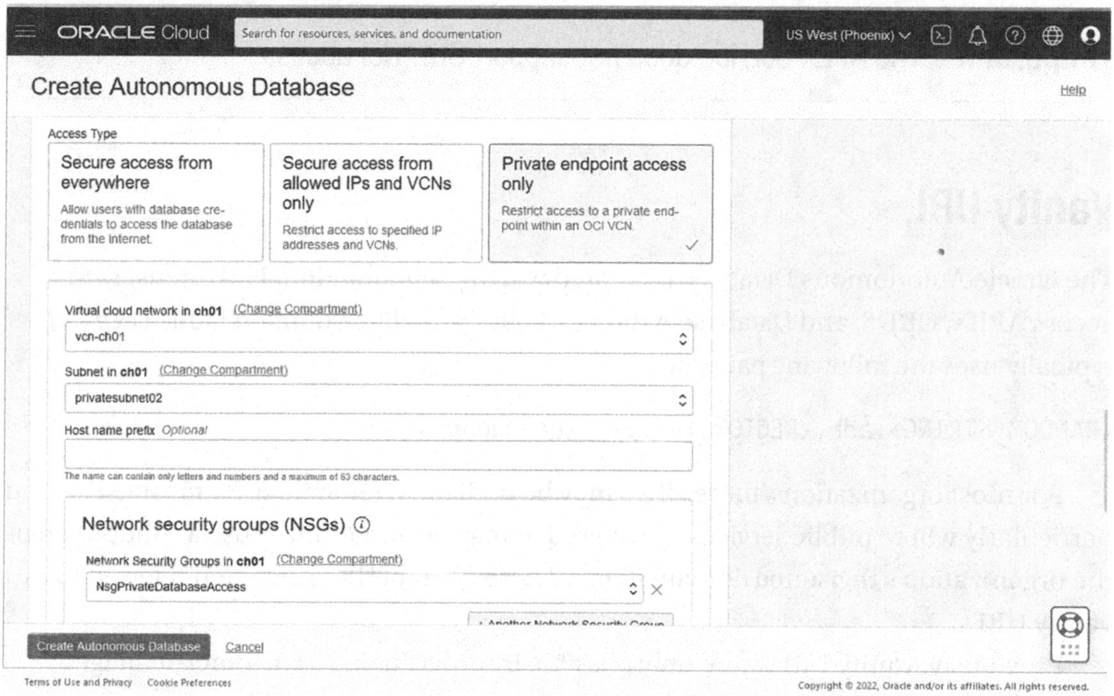

Figure 1-12. *Choosing a network access type when creating an ADB*

By default, ADBs are created to be accessed from everywhere. Users can access all the features of the ADB from the Internet, including APEX, Database Actions, Graph Studio, and connecting to the database using SQL*Net and the downloadable database wallet. Any security list rules that were defined in a VCN do not apply as the endpoint exists outside of the tenancy and its VCNs. If restricted access is desired, they must be specified through an access control list after switching to the second network access type. The alternative is to restrict access to the ADB through a private endpoint (option 3). Incidentally, this configuration is a requirement for ADBs to support vanity URLs without the need to host an instance of the customer-managed ORDS.

An ADB with a private endpoint can only be accessed through the VCN and any on-premises network that is linked by either a site-to-site VPN or *FastConnect*. Like any other OCI resources that are associated with the VCN, access is governed by rules defined in either security lists or NSGs. Administrators can also disable mutual TLS authentication, thus allowing SQL*Net access to the database without needing a database wallet.

Important   The APEX Service does not support SQL*Net access.

Vanity URL

The Oracle Autonomous Database is created with a pseudorandom URL for users to access APEX, ORDS, and Database Actions. The fully qualified domain name (FQDN) typically uses the following pattern:

```
<RANDOM_STRING>.adb.<REGION_ID>.oraclecloudapps.com
```

For most organizations, these URLs may be difficult to remember for most users. And particularly where public services are offered, it may be important to use a subdomain of the organization's registered domain name. These types of URLs are often referred to as vanity URLs.

Previously, vanity URLs were only possible by provisioning a customer-managed ORDS that connects to the ADB using a special database account. This approach required a separate compute instance, and customers are expected to keep the version of the hosted ORDS in sync with what has been installed in the ADB. Thankfully, direct support for vanity URLs is now possible since 2021.

Supporting vanity URLs requires the following:

- A private endpoint for the ADB

- Security rules defined using either security lists or NSGs

- An SSL/TLS certificate that is signed by a Certificate Authority (CA)

- A load balancer on the public subnet

If you have not already done so, configure the ADB with a private endpoint assigned in a private subnet, as described earlier. Next, using the NSGs created earlier in the chapter, assign *NsgPrivateDatabaseAccess* and *NsgPrivateWebAccess* to the ADB. The first NSG defines the allowed IP range(s) that can access the database ports. The latter is for the load balancer to relay web traffic to the ADB.

The load balancer setup requires an SSL/TLS certificate for two purposes. The load balancer for supporting vanity URLs has a HTTPS listener that requires a certificate. The secondary use of the certificate is for the listener to communicate with the ADB's web endpoint, which only supports HTTPS. This channel requires a certificate chain, so self-signed certificates cannot be used.

Finally, create the load balancer on the public subnet. Define a backend set with one backend server that is located by the private IP address assigned to the ADB. You can find the IP address on the ADB's details page.

Web Application Firewall

A web application firewall is an additional layer of protection that you can place between the public network and the APEX infrastructure stack. It has the responsibility of inspecting incoming traffic and to log, warn, and, if needed, block any malicious activities. These can include the *OWASP's* top ten web application security risks (`https://owasp.org/www-project-top-ten/`), *Distributed Denial of Service* (DDoS), or simply applying access control rules, such as from which geographical locations can users access the web application.

The OCI *web application firewall* (WAF) is offered as a regional service with no software or hardware to manage. It does involve quite a bit of configuration, such as

1. Setting up the WAF policy including the origin's endpoint, access control rules, protection rules, rate limits, actions, etc.

2. Configuring security rules applied to load balancers to limit access to WAF endpoints only.

3. Create and assign SSL/TLS certificates.

Any changes to the WAF policy must then be applied and allowed to propagate between all global edge servers.

In late 2021, Oracle greatly simplified how WAFs can be deployed. Today, WAFs can attach to OCI load balancers that have a flexible shape. We will next look at the steps for creating a WAF policy and then enforcing it on a load balancer.

1. Click the navigation menu, click *Identity & Security*, and then click *Policies* under *web application firewall*.

2. Click *Create WAF Policy*.

3. Provide a name for the policy and select the compartment to place the policy. By default, three actions are predefined for you. You can use them or add a custom action now. Click *Next* to continue.

4. The next few steps require you to enable the WAF features. They are *Access Control*, *Rate Limiting*, and *Protections*. These are optional and, like actions, can be defined after a policy is created. Click *Next* to progress through the wizard.

5. After working through all the features, select the load balancers where the policies will be enforced (Figure 1-13). Again, this step is optional and can be performed later. Click *Next*.

6. Finally, review the details about the policy that you have defined and then click *Create WAF Policy*.

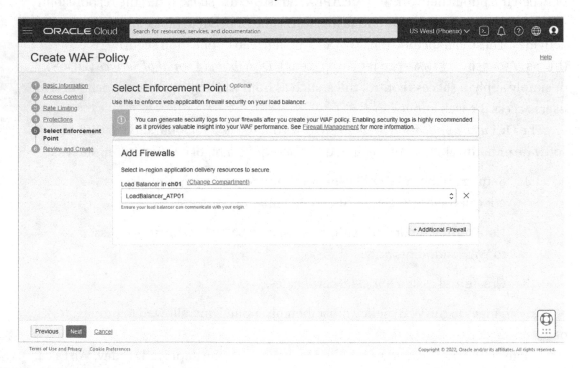

Figure 1-13.   *Create a WAF policy and enforce it on a selected load balancer*

To demonstrate WAF in action, try creating a simple access control rule that checks the client's geographical location and only permits access if the originating source is in Canada:

1. Go to the WAF policy's details page.

2. On the left side of the page and under *Policy*, click *Access Control*.

3. Under the *Request Control* tab, click *Manage Request Control*.

4. Under the *Access Rules* section, click *Add Access Rule*.

5. We will follow the "deny all and allow some" approach to security policies. This rule will list countries that are permitted to access the application (Figure 1-14). Enter a name for the access rule and set one condition using the following settings:

   a. **Condition Type**: Country/Region

   b. **Operator**: Not In List

   c. **Countries**: Canada (you may enter more than one country)

6. Select the rule action *Pre-configured 401 Response Code Action.*

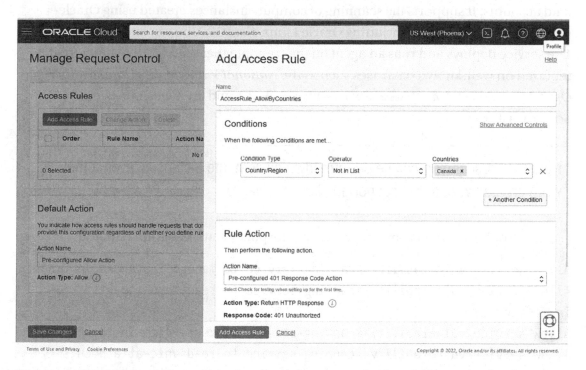

Figure 1-14. *Add an IP geolocation-based access rule that follows the "deny all and allow some" approach*

7. Click *Add Access Rule*.

8. Click *Save Changes*.

To validate the access rule, I tried to access APEX from a remote desktop located in the US region and, as expected, received the response as shown in Figure 1-15.

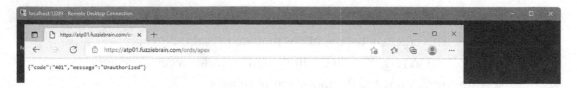

Figure 1-15. *A 401 unauthorized message when accessing the site remotely*

Vulnerability Scanning

The Vulnerability Scanning Service (VSS) is a free service offered by Oracle for all paid accounts. It supports the scanning of compute instances created using Oracle-provided platform images including Oracle Linux, CentOS, Ubuntu, and Windows. The service deploys and runs an agent on the compute that searches for vulnerabilities reported on well-known databases such as the *National Vulnerability Database* (NVD), *Open Vulnerability and Assessment Language* (OVAL), and the *Center for Internet Security* (CIS).

Note   Port scanning can be performed on all compute instances, even if they were created with a non-supported platform image.

To allow VSS to scan compute instances, the policy statements are required:

```
Allow service vulnerability-scanning-service to manage instances in tenancy
Allow service vulnerability-scanning-service to read compartments
in tenancy
Allow service vulnerability-scanning-service to read vnics in tenancy
Allow service vulnerability-scanning-service to read vnic-attachments
in tenancy
```

Replace `tenancy` with `compartment`, followed by a compartment name, to limit VSS to scan compute instances only in the specified compartment.

Next, create a *Scan Recipe* and define the level of port scanning and whether to perform agent-based scanning (Figure 1-16).

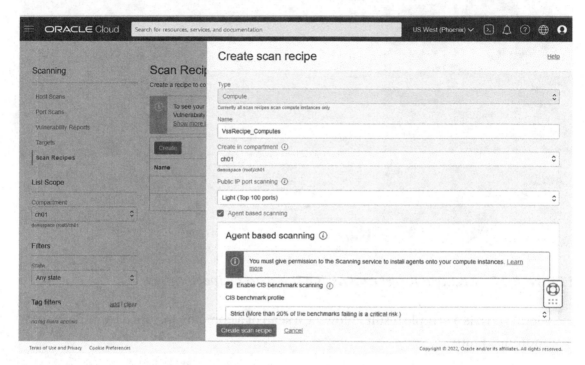

Figure 1-16. *Create a scan recipe*

If agent-based scanning is required, also indicate whether to perform CIS benchmark scanning and the threshold for flagging a critical risk. Finally, specify either a daily or weekly schedule for scanning the host targets where this recipe has been assigned to.

The final step involves creating a target, a logical grouping of compute instances that will be scanned using the selected recipe (Figure 1-17).

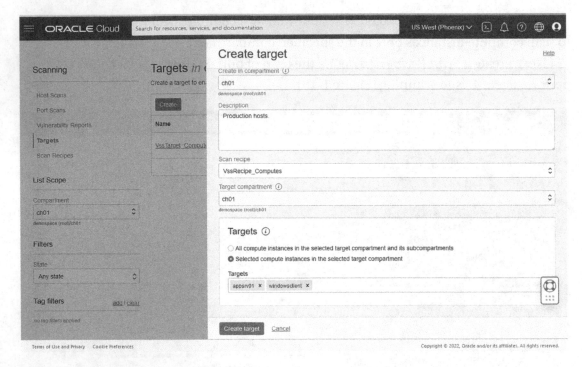

Figure 1-17. *Create a target and assign the scan recipe to apply*

Figure 1-18 is a sample result following a scan of a compute instance running Oracle Autonomous Linux.

Figure 1-18. *An example of results following a routine host scan*

Through the results, administrators can review the open ports, vulnerabilities and their risk levels, and CIS benchmarks. Remediation actions could include shutting down unneeded services, patching software vulnerabilities, and addressing system configurations to improve the CIS benchmark scores.

Logs, Metrics, and Alarms

So far, in this chapter, we have discussed issues and considerations for shoring up our APEX infrastructure's defenses against cyberattacks. We looked at isolating resources using network boundaries, reducing the attack surface with specialized and Oracle-managed services, adding a web application firewall, and routine vulnerability scanning. However, despite all our efforts to thwart attackers, it is still possible that someone may succeed in infiltrating our layers of security.

A majority of the OCI resources produces metrics and logs, both of which are often used for performance monitoring and troubleshooting issues. However, these can be used as tripwires that could indicate a server has been compromised. For example, if a compute instance that averaged under 50% CPU utilization in the past month suddenly has sustained near 100% use, then an alarm should be triggered (Figure 1-19), and notification sent to administrators for further investigation.

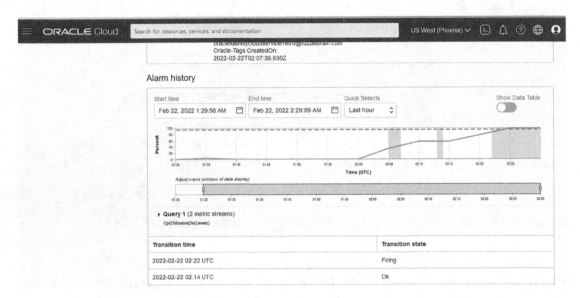

Figure 1-19. *An alarm that monitors CPU utilization triggered when usage surges*

OCI *Logging*, especially when used with *Logging Analytics*, can be a powerful tool for intrusion detection (Figure 1-20). Logging Analytics is a regional-based service that allows administrators to aggregate logs from multiple sources including the OCI *Audit* logs that report on activities related to the tenancy, logs from OCI resources, Oracle Database, and operating system events from compute instances.

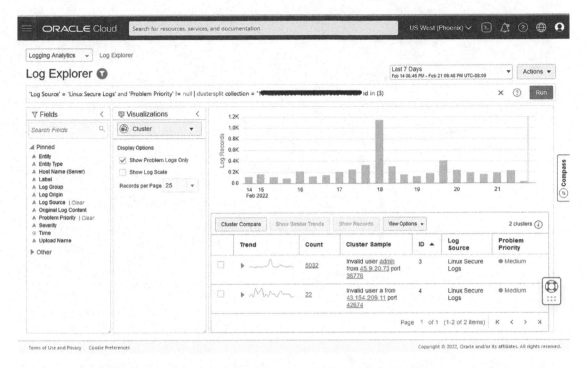

Figure 1-20. *Using reports and dashboards in Logging Analytics to isolate events of security concern*

Summary

In this chapter, we discussed issues and considerations when deploying an infrastructure on the OCI for APEX. Security is not an afterthought and needs to be factored into the architecture before a production rollout. It is such a huge topic to cover that unfortunately, a single chapter is not sufficient to cover. We have looked at the issues from a high-level perspective, but should you require more information about the various OCI services discussed, I highly recommend reading other books from the publisher that will provide the needed instructions. Some of my recommendations are

- *Getting Started with Oracle Cloud Free Tier* by Adrian Png and Luc Demanche

- *Practical Oracle Cloud Infrastructure* by Michał Tomasz Jakóbczyk

CHAPTER 2

Storing Large Objects Using Object Storage

Oracle Application Express (APEX) is an excellent software development stack that allows developers to focus on implementing crucial business logic and simply utilizing prefabricated components for core application features like authentication and interfacing with the database. Like the *Lego® Technic™* (`http://lego.com/themes/technic`) brand of products (which I am a huge fan of), these building sets include an assortment of functional parts like gears, motors, and/or pneumatic pumps. These allow budding engineers to quickly build useful vehicles or machines. However, occasionally, there may be a functional requirement where there are no existing standard blocks available that will fulfill its needs, for example, creating a fruit-sorting conveyor belt system that requires a camera and an embedded microcontroller that can recognize a fruit and channel it to a specific basket. Today, we can quite easily find embedded microcontrollers like the *ESP32* developed by *Espressif Systems* (`www.espressif.com/`) that are integrated with a small camera and has multiple GPIO (general-purpose input/output) pins that can then control Lego®-compatible motors. The GPIO pins are the key for integrating external systems within the brick ecosystem.

The *Oracle Cloud Infrastructure* (OCI) offers many interesting *Cloud Native* services that can further extend APEX applications beyond what is possible with PL/SQL alone. These services provide specialized functions, are available on demand and over the network, and often require little or no management of the underlying infrastructure. Examples of such services include *Functions*, *Event Service*, and *API Management*.

The *OCI Object Storage* is yet another useful feature that can be used to complement APEX applications for storing large files that developers otherwise store as BLOB columns in an Oracle Database. In this chapter, we will step through these concepts and learn how to extend an APEX application that uses these components available with the OCI to solve more complex requirements.

© Adrian Png and Heli Helskyaho 2022
A. Png and H. Helskyaho, *Extending Oracle Application Express with Oracle Cloud Features*,
https://doi.org/10.1007/978-1-4842-8170-3_2

Oracle Cloud Infrastructure

The Oracle Cloud Infrastructure is Oracle's second-generation cloud service that provides *Infrastructure as a Service* (IaaS) using state-of-the-art technologies, robust hardware platforms, and standards-based services. If you have not already signed up, go to the URL www.oracle.com/cloud/free/ and register for an account. It includes a 30-day trial and a standard USD 300 credits for use during this period.

After the trial, users can choose to either upgrade to a paid account or continue to use the *Always Free* resources included in the *Oracle Cloud Free Tier* offering. At the time of writing, the list of Always Free resources include

- Two *compute* instances (virtual machines) with limited OCPU and memory each.

- Two *block volume* storage with a total of 100 GB disk space allocated. Note that each compute instance requires a minimum of 47 GB for its boot volume.

- Ten GB of *OCI Object Storage* and 10 GB of *OCI Archival Storage*.

- Access to *Resource Manager* for deploying with *Terraform* (https://terraform.io).

- Two *Autonomous Databases* with four different workload types to choose from. Each database comes with 1 OCPU and 20 GB storage.

- *NoSQL Database* with 3 tables that comes with 25 GB storage each.

- One flexible and one layer-4 network load balancer.

- Management services that include limited monitoring, notifications, and service connectors.

In Chapters 3 and 4, we will cover the use of OCI Object Storage, Functions, and Events. Aside from OCI Object Storage, there is no Always Free allocation for the remaining services. You will need to either sign up for a 30-day trial or upgrade an existing Oracle Cloud Free Tier account.

Storing Files in the Oracle Database

When deciding on how to store files alongside a data record, the most common approach, and perhaps the first that comes to mind, is to store the file as a BLOB or CLOB column. The Oracle Database supports a maximum size of 8 to 128 terabytes, depending on the database configuration. Managing the large objects (LOBs) within the database record is simple and straightforward and, more importantly, enjoys the benefit of operating within a database transaction.

Over time, though, the increasing size of the tablespaces can become challenging to manage and can be expensive as data files are often situated on high-performance and thus more costly storage devices. If there are low levels of changes to these large objects, the cost gradually outweighs the benefits of storing LOBs in the tables.

There are alternatives to storing files externally and then linking the storage location within the database record. For example, the Oracle Database has a data type known as *BFILE* that stores the actual file on the OS file system and mere reference to it in the associated database record. One hidden benefit of this approach is to store the file on cheaper and lower-performance disks to save costs. The challenge, however, is obvious, and that is the ability to maintain the integrity and consistency of these links.

The OCI Object Storage Alternative

In the last decade, we have witnessed many advancements in cloud technologies. One significant development is object storage and cloud-based large storage systems. Services like Dropbox, Microsoft OneDrive, AWS S3, and many more have provided consumers and developers an alternative platform to store documents and backups. The OCI is no exception. In this section, we will explore what is involved in using the OCI Object Storage as an external LOB system and how we can integrate it with APEX applications.

The OCI Object Storage is a managed storage solution that charges based on utility, that is, the storage capacity measured in gigabyte units per month, and number of requests (GET, PUT, POST, and DELETE) in blocks of 10,000 per month, after the first 50,000. It also has auto-tiering and life cycle management policies that can be applied to move objects between three-levels of storage: standard, infrequent access, and archive. Using Oracle Cloud's cost estimator (`www.oracle.com/cloud/cost-estimator.html`),

1,000 GB would cost 25, 10, and 3 US dollars per month, respectively. In contrast, the same amount of block volume storage would cost upward of $26 at the current rates.

The storage system is highly redundant. Objects stored in the system are replicated across fault domains and, for certain regions that have multiple availability domains, across regions. Data stored in the system are actively monitored for integrity using checksums. The system is self-healing and will resolve any data corruption detected without needing any user intervention.

Objects in the storage system are organized in buckets. Access to these buckets can be managed through OCI *Identity and Access Management* (IAM) policies. Each bucket also comes with the following features:

- **Object versioning**: If enabled, OCI Object Storage will maintain older versions of an object when it is either updated or deleted.

- **Emit OCI Events**: When enabled, Object Storage will emit an Event whenever an object is created, updated, or deleted. These events can be used to trigger other OCI resources, for example, Functions to execute.

- **Auto-tiering**: If this feature is enabled, OCI monitors how the data is accessed and will automatically move larger objects (more than 1 MiB) from the Standard tier to the Infrequent Access tier. While it is cheaper to store the objects in the latter tier, note that there are fees to retrieve them when accessed.

For security, buckets are created with their visibility set to private but can be changed to public if necessary. Also, all files stored in OCI Object Storage are encrypted at rest, and users have an option to use their own encryption keys.

Once created, there are additional OCI Object Storage features to pay attention to:

- **Pre-authenticated requests**: When created, these unique URLs provide access to the bucket or object without needing to sign the HTTP request. All requests must specify an expiration date.

- **Life cycle policy rules**: Rules defined here will allow OCI Object Storage to automatically manage objects, for example, moving them to Archive storage tier, based on the specified number of days and, if necessary, object name filters.

- **Replication policy**: These policies allow the OCI Object Storage service to automatically make a copy of the object changes (create, update, and delete) to a target region.

- **Retention rules**: These specify how long objects must be retained in the bucket. No changes, updates or deletes, are permitted during the period specified by the policy. This is an extremely useful feature in situations where files uploaded to the bucket must be retained for regulatory compliance.

Note   For life cycle and replication policies, you are required to have a policy in the root compartment that allows the OCI Object Storage service in the target region to make changes to the buckets and objects. For example, a policy when the target region is in US Phoenix:

```
Allow service objectstorage-us-phoenix-1 to manage object-
family in compartment DEV
```

Using OCI Object Storage with APEX

In this section, we will walk through the steps and code necessary to demonstrate the use of OCI Object Storage for storing digital photographs through an APEX application.

Create a Compartment

OCI resources are grouped using compartments. When the tenant is freshly provisioned, it contains only two partitions of which one is called the root partition. It is a best practice to create a new compartment under the root for creating new OCI components. There are different ways and motivations to segregate your resources. They could, for example, be grouped based on the departments that they are associated with, the type of environment (DEV, TEST, PROD, etc.), or cost centers for billing.

In this chapter, we will create a compartment called *DEV* and, to do so, access the *Compartments* page from the navigation menu, under the item *Identity*. Click the *Create Compartment* button and then provide a name and description (Figure 2-1).

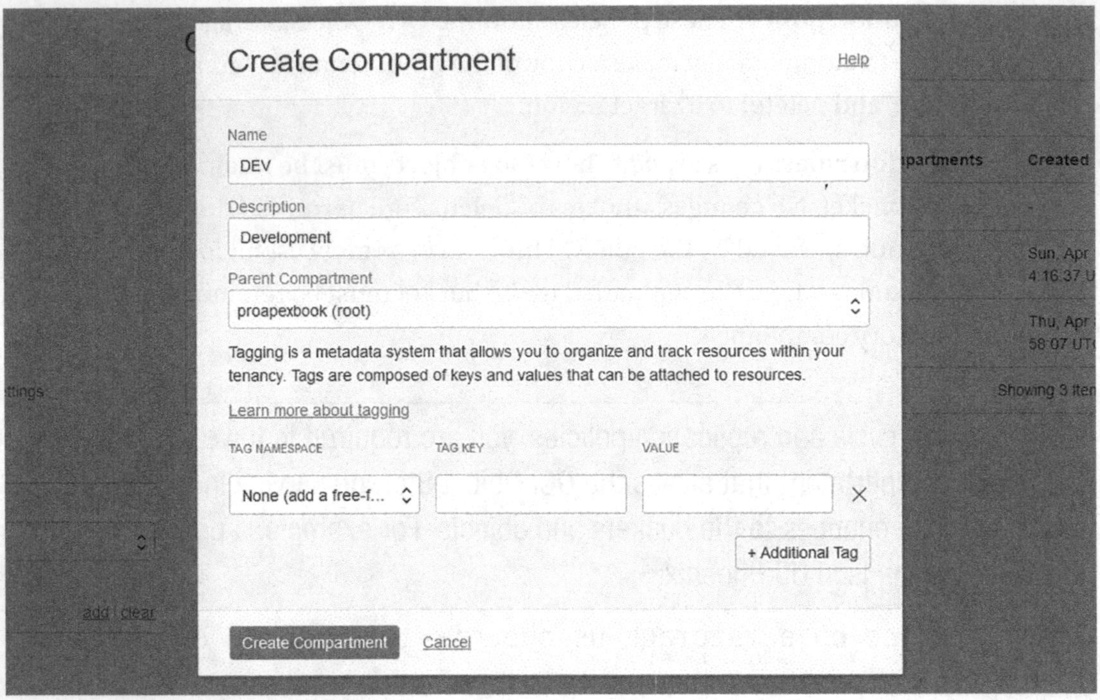

Figure 2-1. *Create a DEV compartment*

Also, ensure that you have selected the root compartment for a parent. Click the *Create Compartment* button to complete the task.

Create an OCI Object Storage Bucket

Once a compartment has been created, proceed to create a bucket in the Object Storage. Go to the *Buckets* page. The link can be found in the navigational menu, under *Storage*, and then *Object Storage*. Alternatively, enter the term "bucket" in the search box to quickly find the link.

Click the *Create Bucket* button and provide a name, for example, "photos," and select the *Standard* default storage tier. You should see the Create Bucket modal dialog as shown in Figure 2-2.

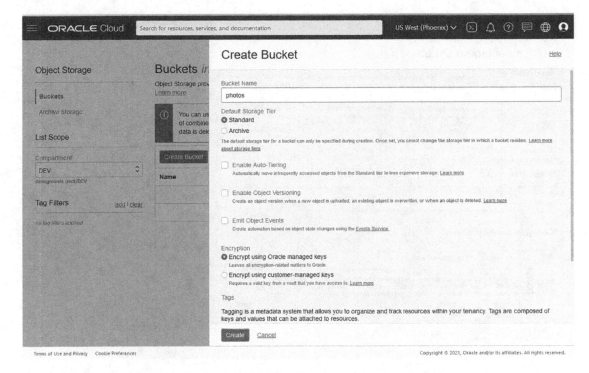

Figure 2-2. *Create an Object Storage bucket*

Create an Oracle Autonomous Database (Optional)

APEX is included with all Oracle Autonomous Databases (ADB) regardless of its workload type. This step is **optional**. Working with Object Storage *OCI REST APIs* is independent of where APEX is installed as it solely relies on the platform's ability to work with web services using its APEX_WEB_SERVICE package.

To create an ADB, click the link *Autonomous Transaction Processing* (ATP) under the navigational menu item Oracle Database. Create an Always Free ADB with the ATP workload type (Figure 2-3).

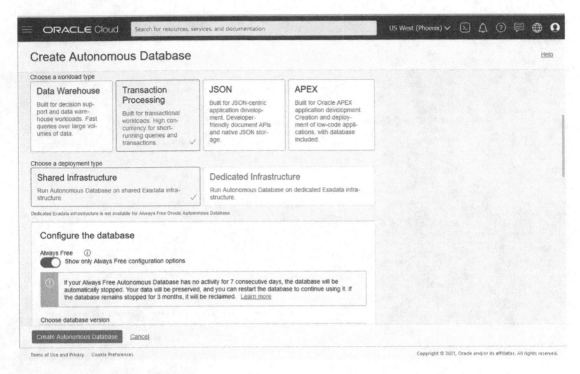

Figure 2-3. *Optionally, create an Always Free ADB with the ATP workload type*

Create Identity and Access Management Resources

What an OCI user can or cannot do is determined by the OCI Identity and Access Management (IAM). This is regardless of whether the action is performed via the OCI Console or REST API. Access is managed using OCI policies, and privileges are assigned to groups of users, instances, or resources. In this section, we will walk through the necessary IAM changes required to allow a developer to create, deploy, and manage Functions applications.

Groups

Groups are a collection of users that are then used in policy statements to define access and privileges. You can find the link to the *Groups* page through the navigation menu, under the item *Identity*. There you can view a list of existing groups and create new ones. Create a new group called *PhotosBucketManagers*.

Policies

Policies are collections of statements that determine what groups of either users or OCI resources have access to and the types of actions they may perform. You can access the tenant's policy from the navigational menu, under the *Identity* menu item. Create a policy *PhotosBucketAccessPolicy.* (Figure 2-4) with the following policy statements:

```
allow group PhotosBucketManagers to read buckets in compartment DEV
allow group PhotosBucketManagers to manage objects in compartment DEV where
any { target.bucket.name='photos' }
```

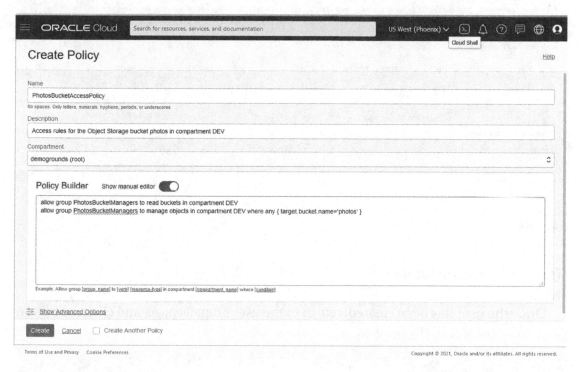

Figure 2-4. *Create a policy to manage access to a specific bucket*

These policy statements will allow members of the *PhotosBucketManager* group the ability to

1. Read all buckets in the compartment *DEV*

2. Manage objects in the *photos* bucket, created in the compartment *DEV*

IAM User

Create an IAM user for our developer using the OCI Console. Access the *Users* management page. You can find this in the OCI side navigation bar under the item *Identity*. Create the user *apexagent01* (Figure 2-5).

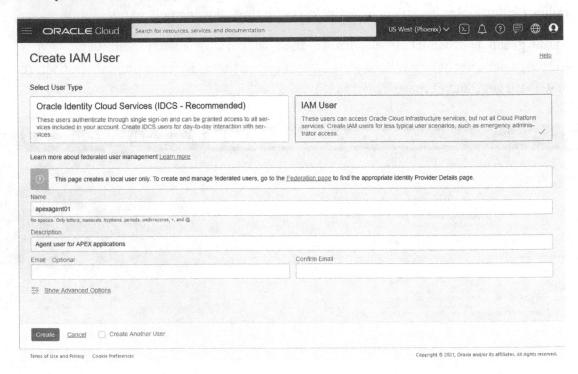

Figure 2-5. *Create the user*

Once the user has been created, return to the user's details page, and click the button *Edit User Capabilities* (Figure 2-6).

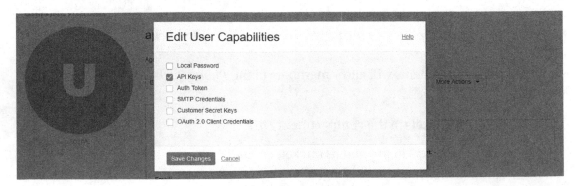

Figure 2-6. *Manage what the user can do on the OCI*

Limit the user with the ability to interact with OCI resources using API keys. These are used when working with the OCI REST APIs either directly, through an OCI *Software Development Kit* (SDK), or OCI *command-line interface* (CLI).

Also, on the user's details page, add the user to the group *PhotosBucketManager* (Figure 2-7).

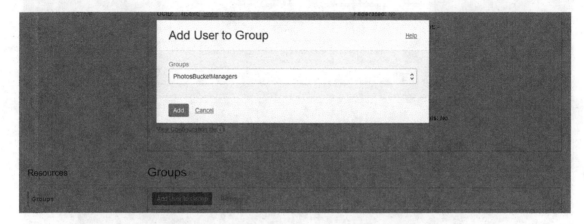

Figure 2-7. *Add the user to the PhotosBucketManager group*

API Keys

As mentioned earlier, to work with the OCI REST APIs, an API key pair is required. There are three ways to generate a key pair. Either use the OCI CLI, *OpenSSL*, or simply generate them through the OCI Console. On the user's details page, click the *API Keys* link from the list on the left, and then click the button *Add API Key* to launch the tool (Figure 2-8).

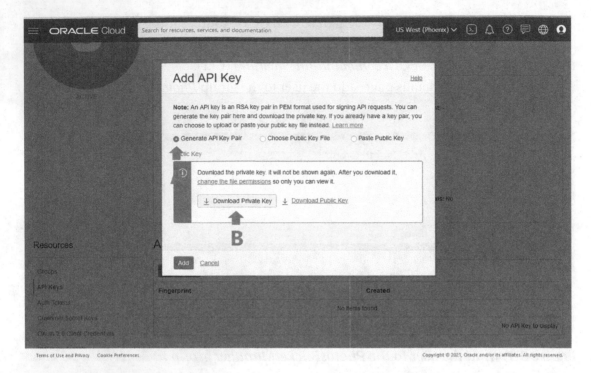

Figure 2-8. *Generate the API key pair through the OCI Console*

On the modal, select (A) *Generate API Key Pair,* click the button labeled (B) in the figure to download the private key, and then click the *Add* button to complete the process.

Gather Information for APEX Web Credentials

To work with OCI REST APIs in APEX, a Web Credential is required for authentication. Before leaving this section, take note of the following information that will be required to create it.

On the user's details page, click the link *View Configuration file* to display the information (Figure 2-9) that provides content that you would otherwise include in the configuration file to be used with the OCI CLI or SDK.

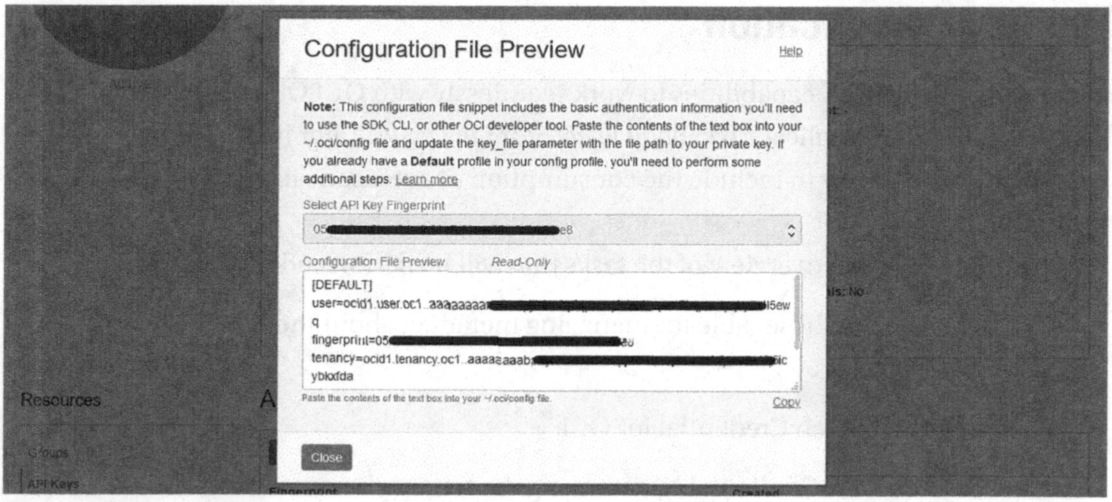

Figure 2-9. *Content for OCI CLI/SDK configuration file*

Take note of the following:

- User OCID

- Fingerprint

- Tenancy OCID

- Private key (see as follows)

The downloaded private key file is PEM-formatted text file with content that looks like this:

```
-----BEGIN PRIVATE KEY-----
MIIEvQIBADANBgkqhkiG9wOBAQEFAASCBKcwggSjAgEAAoIBAQCyX+KzKWkzrzxm
1jE/izBdIDbpcYtxHYefRRLhGabsOPOFCmcuClgWnKKk1nZb955q94LFrAidPEEP
dTjI1Tsx4ax3pcmxV7AirHYDRdccD5ymEUwE729xq/YQtALzc8NAC3AsKZnGIjyQ
...
Qsj8FQdGKhB3RvGLCUowI24ZunOmnjDuKLCQ46OoRknOxEmWlbomIQsnqcllAyfU
ff2cEC7TLdtTS7SImQOvLtw=
-----END PRIVATE KEY-----
```

Remove the header and footer, `-----BEGIN PRIVATE KEY-----` and `-----END PRIVATE KEY-----`, respectively, and all newline characters. The result is an exceptionally long string of characters. Do not save the file, but copy the contents into a safe place. This is the private key that must be entered in the Web Credential.

The APEX Application

To demonstrate APEX's capabilities to work seamlessly with OCI Object Storage, we will create an APEX application called *Object Storage Demo*. Later in the chapter, we will extend it simply to include the consumption of automatically generated thumbnail images.

The following is an overview of the tasks that will be performed in this section:

1. Create a database table for managing metadata about the digital photos.

2. Create the Web Credential for OCI.

3. Test the Web Credential by retrieving the tenancy's namespace that will be required when interacting with the Object Storage.

4. Create a REST Data Source to list the objects in the *photos* bucket.

5. Create a report and page to list, create, update, and delete the digital photo records.

Digital Photos Table

The context for the Object Storage Demo application is the storage of precious digital photos where metadata about the image is stored in the database, while the image file is stored in OCI Object Storage to take advantage of the relatively cheaper, highly redundant, and managed storage system.

Create the photo table using the following SQL statement:

```
create table photo (
  photo_id number generated always as identity
, title varchar2(500) not null
, description varchar2(2000)
, object_name varchar2(1024)
, filename varchar2(500)
, mime_type varchar2(100)
, created_by varchar2(30)
, created_on timestamp with local time zone
, updated_by varchar2(30)
, updated_on timestamp with local time zone
```

```
, constraint photo_pk primary key (photo_id)
, constraint photo_uk1 unique (object_name)
)
/
```

Create the APEX application with a form and report using the newly created table. After the application has been created, go to page 3 and make the following changes:

- Rename the page to *Photo Details*.

- Add a new page item P3_PHOTO:

  - Set the page item type *Display Image*.

  - Set the appearance template to *Optional – Above*.

  - Add the custom attribute:

    ```
    style="max-width: 100%; height: auto;"
    ```

  - Set the page item to render based on *Image URL stored in Page Item Value*.

  - Set the source type to Expression and language PL/SQL with the following code:

    ```
    apex_page.get_url(
      p_application => :APP_ID
      , p_page => 0
    , p_request =>
        'APPLICATION_PROCESS=GET_OBJECT'
    , p_items => 'APP_PHOTO_ID,APP_BUCKET_NAME'
        || ',APP_CONTENT_DISPOSITION'
    , p_values => to_char(:P3_PHOTO_ID) || ','
        || :G_PHOTOS_BUCKET_NAME || ',inline'
      , p_plain_url => true
      )
    ```

  - Set the page item to render if the page item P3_PHOTO_ID is not null.

- Add a new page item P3_FILE:

  - Set the page item type *File Browse*.

  - Display as a *Block Dropzone* if the version of APEX supports it.

  - Use the APEX_APPLICATION_TEMP_FILES and purge the files at the end of the request.

  - Limit the file types to image/*.

- Set the following items to the page item type *Display Only* and to only render when the page item P3_PHOTO_ID is not null. Also, if this is a *Form Region*, toggle the *Query Only* to enabled.

- Change the process type for the *Process form Photo* page processing process to *Execute Code*, and for now, enter the following code:

```
declare
   l_photo photo.%rowtype;
begin
  if :REQUEST = 'CREATE' then
    null; -- execute CREATE action here
  elsif :REQUEST = 'SAVE' then
    null; -- execute SAVE action here
  elsif :REQUEST = 'DELETE' then
    null; -- execute DELETE action here
  else
    null; -- do nothing
  end if;
end;
```

- Save the page.

The final page should look somewhat like in Figure 2-10.

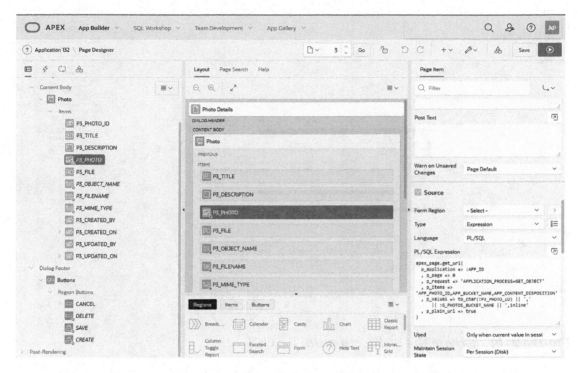

Figure 2-10. *Updated page 3 of the APEX application*

Web Credential for OCI

When working with the OCI REST APIs, all HTTP requests must be appropriately signed by an IAM user with the required API keys. Using the information collected earlier when the IAM user was created, create a new Web Credential (Figure 2-11) with the *Oracle Cloud Infrastructure (OCI)* authentication type. Fill out the fields using the values obtained earlier for the following:

- OCI User ID

- OCI Private Key

- OCI Tenancy ID

- OCI Public Key Fingerprint

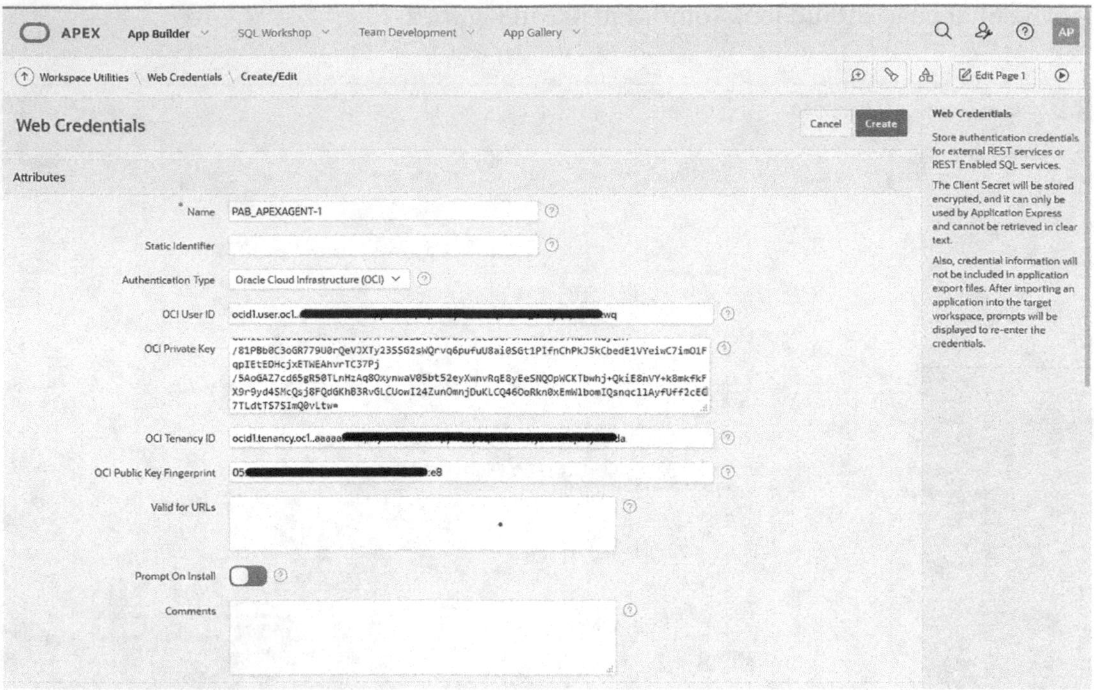

Figure 2-11. *Create the Web Credential for OCI*

Take note of the *Static Identifier* when completed. It will be required when using the `APEX_WEB_SERVICE.MAKE_REST_REQUEST` function to call the OCI REST APIs.

Retrieve Tenancy Namespace

When working the Object Storage REST API, the URL format is as follows:

```
https://objectstorage.<REGION>.oraclecloud.com/n/<NAMESPACE>/b/<BUCKET_
NAME/o/<OBJECT_NAME>
```

The appropriate value for the placeholder `<REGION>` can be obtained from the OCI documentation using this link `https://bit.ly/oci-docs-regions`, while the values for `<BUCKET_NAME>` and `<OBJECT_NAME>` are obvious. For `<NAMESPACE>`, the tenancy's namespace, its value can be obtained from the OCI Console; however, we could also obtain it using the following PL/SQL procedure:

```
declare
  c_base_url constant varchar2(59) :=
    'https://objectstorage.us-phoenix-1.oraclecloud.com';
```

```
  c_endpoint_path constant varchar2(40) := '/n/';
  c_web_credential constant varchar2(30) := 'PAB_APEXAGENT_1';

  l_response clob;
begin
  l_response := apex_web_service.make_rest_request(
    p_url => c_base_url || c_endpoint_path
      , p_http_method => 'GET'
      , p_credential_static_id => c_web_credential
    );

  dbms_output.put_line(l_response);
end;
```

You can execute the code using APEX's SQL Workshop (Figure 2-12).

Figure 2-12. *Retrieve the tenancy's namespace using the SQL Workshop*

If the OCI resources and Web Credential were created correctly, the tenancy's namespace should display in the results.

Application Attributes – Substitutions

Create and set the appropriate values for the following *Substitution Strings* (Figure 2-13):

- **G_PHOTOS_BUCKET_NAME**: The name of the Object Storage bucket where the uploaded files are stored.

- **G_THUMBNAILS_BUCKET_NAME**: The name of the bucket where generated thumbnails are stored in. This is discussed later in the chapter.

- **G_OCI_WEB_CREDENTIAL_ID**: The static identifier of the Web Credentials for access OCI REST APIs.

- **G_BASE_URL**: The base URL for accessing the OCI REST APIs that is constructed based on the OCI region and tenancy namespace.

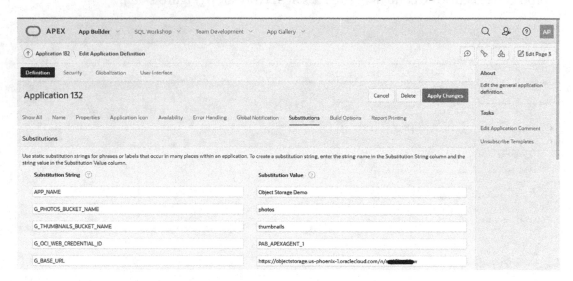

Figure 2-13. *Add substitution strings*

Complete Code to Interact with Object Storage

To facilitate working with the OCI REST APIs for Object Storage, we will create a package called pkg_oci_os_util that contains the following functions and procedures:

- f_generate_object_name

- p_upload_object

- p_delete_object

- p_get_object

The full source code can be obtained from the code repository in the directory ch02/demoapp/packages/.

It is important to realize that the Object Storage bucket structure is essentially flat, even though it is possible to create pseudo folders by separating "folders" and "files" using the "/" character. However, in the demonstration application, we opt to rely on the function pkg_oci_os_util.f_generate_object_name to generate unique filenames based on the primary key of the photo table and the name of the file as it was uploaded to the server. This will avoid a situation where files might be overwritten if the filenames of the upload files are in conflict.

When creating or updating photos with new files, both procedures rely on the package pkg_oci_os_util.p_upload_object. They depend on the apex_web_service.make_rest_request function to make a PUT HTTP request with the contents of the uploaded file embedded in the request body. The following snippet highlights the key steps of

1. Constructing the request URL using the base API address, target bucket name, and the URL-encoded form of the generated object name.

2. Write the uploaded file's MIME type to the HTTP request header.

3. Execute the REST call and retrieve the response.

4. Check that the HTTP response status code is 200 (OK), and if not, raise an error.

```
l_request_url := p_base_url || '/b/' || p_bucket_name
  || '/o/' || apex_util.url_encode(p_object_name);

apex_web_service.g_request_headers(1).name := 'Content-Type';
apex_web_service.g_request_headers(1).value := p_mime_type;

l_response := apex_web_service.make_rest_request(
  p_url => l_request_url
  , p_http_method => 'PUT'
  , p_body_blob => p_blob_content
```

```
  , p_credential_static_id => p_oci_web_credential_id
);

if apex_web_service.g_status_code != 200 then
  raise_application_error(
    -20001
    , l_response || chr(10) || 'status_code='
        || to_char(apex_web_service.g_status_code)
  );
end if;
```

Deleting the object is a little simpler. In the procedure pkg_oci_os_util.p_delete_object, after generating the request URL, submit a DELETE HTTP request instead with no additional HTTP headers or content:

```
l_response := apex_web_service.make_rest_request(
  p_url => l_request_url
  , p_http_method => 'DELETE'
  , p_credential_static_id => p_oci_web_credential_id
);

if apex_web_service.g_status_code != 204 then
  raise_application_error(
    -20003
    , l_response || chr(10) || 'status_code='
        || to_char(apex_web_service.g_status_code)
  );
end if;
```

Note   The expected HTTP response status code is **204**.

Finally, the procedure pkg_oci_os_util.p_get_object retrieves an object from the bucket, returning the file, content type, and length:

```
l_response := apex_web_service.make_rest_request_b(
  p_url => l_request_url
  , p_http_method => 'GET'
```

```
  , p_credential_static_id => p_oci_web_credential_id
);

if apex_web_service.g_status_code != 200 then
  raise_application_error(
    -20004
    , 'status_code=' || to_char(apex_web_service.g_status_code)
  );
else
  for i in 1..apex_web_service.g_headers.count
  loop
    apex_debug.info(apex_web_service.g_headers(i).name || '='
      || apex_web_service.g_headers(i).value );

    if lower(apex_web_service.g_headers(i).name) =
      'content-length'
    then
      p_content_length := to_number(
        apex_web_service.g_headers(i).value);
    end if;

    if lower(apex_web_service.g_headers(i).name) =
      'content-type'
    then
      p_content_type := apex_web_service.g_headers(i).value;
    end if;
  end loop;

  p_blob_content := l_response;
```

Unlike the earlier two procedures, this one uses the procedure apex_web_
service.make_rest_request_b to make a GET HTTP request. If successful, the
contents of the response are returned as a BLOB object. From the OCI REST API
documentation version 20160918 (https://docs.oracle.com/en-us/iaas/api/#/en/
objectstorage/20160918/), specifically the *GetObject* operation, we can extract the
content type and length from the HTTP response header.

To access the objects in Object Storage, we can opt to either (1) proxy the request
using the database, (2) generate a pre-authenticated request, or (3) make the bucket

public. The last option is generally not recommended. A pre-authenticated request generates a time-boxed unique URL that clients can use to access either a bucket and all its contents or a specific object, without needing to perform the necessary HTTP request signing. This is an acceptable practice where data security is important, but not critical. For this application, we will use the first approach to have the benefit of a fine-grained control on how the objects are retrieved and rendered.

Begin by creating three APEX application items:

- **APP_PHOTO_ID**: This is a session state–protected variable that is used to retrieve the photo record.

- **APP_BUCKET_NAME**: This is a session state–protected variable that is to specify the bucket that the object will be retrieved from.

- **APP_CONTENT_DISPOSITION**: This variable allows the client code to specify a hint for the browser to either render or download the file. The accepted values are inline and attachment, respectively.

Next, create an APEX application process named *GET_OBJECT*. Set this to execute as an *AJAX* callback. The full source code for the process' code can be found in the file ch02/demoapp/snippets/02-app-process-get_object_from_photos.sql.

The application process code utilizes the pkg_oci_os_util.p_get_object to retrieve the file specified by the record's identifier from the Object Storage and renders the HTTP response that allows the download using the file's original filename. For performance and reducing costs (for retrieval), it also allows browser caching. The page item P3_PHOTO on page 3 will call this application process using the URL securely generated with the procedure apex_page.get_url.

Also on page 3, complete the page processing process *Process from Photo* that handles page submission.

For the *CREATE* page request, replace the following line of code:

```
null; -- execute CREATE action here
```

with

```
for file in (
  select * from apex_application_temp_files
  where name = :P3_FILE
) loop
```

```
  insert into photo(
    title
    , description
    , filename
    , mime_type
  ) values (
    :P3_TITLE
    , :P3_DESCRIPTION
    , file.filename
    , file.mime_type
  ) returning photo_id into l_photo.photo_id;

  l_photo.object_name := pkg_oci_os_util.f_generate_object_name(
      p_photo_id => l_photo.photo_id
      , p_filename => file.filename);

  update photo
  set object_name = l_photo.object_name
  where photo_id = l_photo.photo_id;

  pkg_oci_os_util.p_upload_object(
    p_base_url => :G_BASE_URL
    , p_bucket_name => :G_PHOTOS_BUCKET_NAME
    , p_object_name => l_photo.object_name
    , p_blob_content => file.blob_content
    , p_mime_type => file.mime_type
    , p_oci_web_credential_id => :G_OCI_WEB_CREDENTIAL_ID
  );
end loop;
```

For the *SAVE* page request, replace the following line of code:

```
null; -- execute SAVE action here
```

with

```
select * into l_photo
from photo where photo_id = :P3_PHOTO_ID;
```

```
update photo
set
  title = :P3_TITLE
  , description = :P3_DESCRIPTION
where photo_id = l_photo.photo_id;

for file in (
  select * from apex_application_temp_files
  where name = :P3_FILE
) loop
  l_photo.object_name := pkg_oci_os_util.f_generate_object_name(
    p_photo_id => l_photo.photo_id
    , p_filename => file.filename);

  update photo
  set filename = file.filename
    , mime_type = file.mime_type
    , object_name = l_photo.object_name
  where photo_id = l_photo.photo_id;

  -- If the filename does not match what is on record, then delete
    it first.
  if l_photo.filename <> file.filename then
    pkg_oci_os_util.p_delete_object(
      p_base_url => :G_BASE_URL
      , p_bucket_name => :G_PHOTOS_BUCKET_NAME
      , p_object_name => pkg_oci_os_util.f_generate_object_name(
          p_photo_id => l_photo.photo_id
          , p_filename => l_photo.filename)
      , p_oci_web_credential_id => :G_OCI_WEB_CREDENTIAL_ID
    );
  end if;
```

```
pkg_oci_os_util.p_upload_object(
  p_base_url => :G_BASE_URL
  , p_bucket_name => :G_PHOTOS_BUCKET_NAME
  , p_object_name => l_photo.object_name
  , p_blob_content => file.blob_content
  , p_mime_type => file.mime_type
  , p_oci_web_credential_id => :G_OCI_WEB_CREDENTIAL_ID
);
end loop;
```

And finally, for the *DELETE* page request, replace the following line of code:

```
null; -- execute DELETE action here
```

with

```
select * into l_photo
from photo where photo_id = :P3_PHOTO_ID;

delete from photo where photo_id = l_photo.photo_id;

pkg_oci_os_util.p_delete_object(
  p_base_url => :G_BASE_URL
  , p_bucket_name => :G_PHOTOS_BUCKET_NAME
  , p_object_name => l_photo.object_name
  , p_oci_web_credential_id => :G_OCI_WEB_CREDENTIAL_ID
);
```

This screenshot (Figure 2-14) is what the application looks like upon completion.

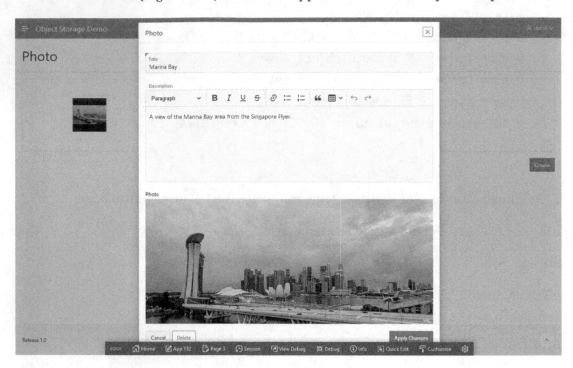

Figure 2-14. *The finished APEX application*

Considerations

As with any approach to storing files external to the database, developers must manage data integrity and consistency. In the conventional approach where files are stored as a table column, we have the luxury of using a database transaction so that the file is only saved if the database record is written successfully. When working with an external storage system, design the PL/SQL procedure such that a database transaction rollback occurs if an error occurs with the file operation.

It is also important to decide how to name files in the external storage system and link them to the associated database record. When storing the LOBs in a column, there is little or no risk in naming conflicts. With an external storage system, there is a risk of inadvertently overwriting or deleting files associated with other database records.

Summary

In this chapter, we have demonstrated how Object Storage can be used as an alternative storage medium for large files like photos, documents, and more. To manage the objects, we used OCI REST APIs that are secured using asymmetric cryptography and digital signatures. Fortunately, APEX wraps the complexity of performing the authentication process with OCI Web Credentials, making it easy to work with OCI resources to build or supplement what we otherwise have difficulty implementing in pure APEX and PL/SQL.

## CHAPTER 3

Using Oracle Cloud Functions

In the previous chapter, we created a photo album that used the OCI Object Storage to store the original images. These are large files that we do not necessarily want to render in full resolution until the user explicitly requests to view them. We can further enhance our application with image and/or data processing to create smaller preview images for rendering, thereby improving the page load performance.

One approach to create thumbnail or preview-sized images in PL/SQL is to use *Oracle Multimedia* (OMM). Unfortunately, these packages have been deprecated and desupported with version 19c of the Oracle Database. Developers who have used OMM for image processing tasks, for example, thumbnail generation, are now forced to find alternatives. With Functions, we can off-load such computationally expensive processes to a serverless platform and execute them on demand.

In this chapter, we will learn about *Oracle Cloud Functions* (Functions), a serverless computing technology, and how we can use it to perform image processing tasks.

Important   Oracle Function is not included in the Oracle Cloud *Free Tier* offerings. The usage costs will be discussed later in the chapter.

Image Processing

OMM was a no-cost Oracle Database feature for storing, accessing, and managing images, audio, video, and *Digital Imaging and Communications in Medicine* (DICOM) files in the database. It provided PL/SQL object types and packages that allowed developers to perform basic manipulation tasks like resizing images, adding watermarks, and retrieving attributes/metadata about audio and video files.

© Adrian Png and Heli Helskyaho 2022
A. Png and H. Helskyaho, *Extending Oracle Application Express with Oracle Cloud Features*,
https://doi.org/10.1007/978-1-4842-8170-3_3

For example, to create a thumbnail for a photo that is uploaded to our photo album, you can create a simple procedure that retrieves the image stored as a BLOB in the PHOTO table, performs the transformation, and then stores the output in a separate table column:

```
create or replace package body pkg_image_util as
  procedure p_generate_thumbnail(
    p_photo_id photo.photo_id%type
    , p_size number
) as
  l_image blob;
  l_thumbnail blob;
begin
  -- 1. Create a temporary BLOB for the thumbnail.
  dbms_lob.createtemporary(
    lob_loc => l_thumbnail
    , cache => true
  );

  -- 2. Retrieve the image from the table.
  select blob_content
  into l_image
  from photo
  where photo_id = p_photo_id;

  -- 3. Generate the thumbnail.
  ordsys.ordimage.processcopy(
    command => 'maxScale=' || to_char(p_size)
        || ' ' || to_char(p_size)
    , imageblob => l_image
    , dest => l_thumbnail
  );

  -- 4. Update the table with the generated image.
  update photo
  set blob_thumbnail = l_thumbnail
  where photo_id = p_photo_id;
```

```
  -- 5. Clean up.
  dbms_lob.freetemporary(l_thumbnail);
  end p_generate_thumbnail;
end pkg_image_util;
/
```

Unfortunately for us, OMM was deprecated in Oracle Database version 18c and has been desupported in version 19c. Oracle Multimedia is also not supported on any of Oracle's Autonomous Databases. How then can we continue to provide such image processing capabilities within APEX applications?

There are many approaches that we can consider, and we will examine each of them quickly before diving deep into the details on how we can quickly create an Oracle Function to handle this task using serverless technology. These are

1. Perform the image processing task in browser using JavaScript libraries.

2. Create and deploy a server-side REST API using third-party libraries from other programming languages, such as *JavaScript*, *Java*™, or *Python*.

3. Integrate a cloud-based REST API that performs the image processing task.

4. Create and deploy an application and host the application without needing to worry about managing the underlying infrastructure using Oracle Functions. The image processing tasks can be triggered either using an Oracle Event or wrapped as a REST API using *Oracle API gateway*.

5. If your database supports the *Multilingual Engine* (MLE) feature, the image processing task could be created using the supported language of choice. However, at the time of writing, MLE is only available and supported by APEX in Oracle Database version 21c.

Processing Images on the Client Browser

There is no shortage of JavaScript libraries that can be used to manipulate and transform images on the web browser, such as p5.js (`https://p5js.org/`) and Fabric.js (`http://fabricjs.com/`).

Performing the manipulation on the client-side is not hard, especially for APEX developers who are generally proficient in JavaScript. There are some concerns, however, such as browser compatibility and performance.

Custom Image Processing REST API

Thankfully, APEX has provided support for working with RESTful services through the package `APEX_WEB_SERVICE` since version 4.0. This provides APEX applications the ability to access and execute specialized tasks outside the confines of the Oracle Database.

One option for processing images server-side is to use well-known applications and programming libraries like *ImageMagick* (`https://imagemagick.org/`), Pillow (`https://python-pillow.org/`) for Python, and sharp (`https://sharp.pixelplumbing.com/`) for Node.js/JavaScript. ImageMagick is a popular cross-platform for digital image processing that has support for many image formats and transformation algorithms. Because of its popularity, many programming languages have libraries that are designed to interface with it.

Today, we may not be able to access these powerful binaries within the database, so the best alternative is to wrap them as REST APIs using frameworks such as Express (`https://expressjs.com/`) and Django (`www.djangoproject.com/`), depending on your choice of programming language.

The downside of this approach is the need to create and manage the infrastructure for supporting these web services. Developers would have to deal with issues like performance, security, and availability.

Using Third-Party REST APIs

There are services like *Filestack* (`www.filestack.com/`) that offer 100% cloud-based APIs and *APEX Media Extension* (`www.apexmediaextension.com/`) that offer a self-hosted option. However, while these services offer limited free services, they are generally for fee and can be costly depending on frequency.

The other consideration is security and data privacy. The source images are sent to the service provider's servers, and depending on their terms of services, may be retained for a predefined period.

If these issues are of high concern and matter greatly to your organization, or perhaps you require more fine-grained control of the image processing, then consider implementing a solution that involves Oracle Functions.

Oracle Cloud Functions

Oracle Cloud Functions is a cloud native, serverless offering that is built using the *Fn Project* (`https://fnproject.io/`). Serverless technology allows developers to write code to perform a specialized task and then deploy and host them on a cloud-based provider, without needing to worry about managing the infrastructure that hosts the application code. Other serverless technologies include Amazon's AWS Lambda and Microsoft's Azure Functions. Most, if not all, providers charge only when the function is called and executed, thereby reducing infrastructure costs.

Functions supports multiple programming languages. The following are currently supported:

- Go

- Java

- Node.js

- Python

- Ruby

- C#

In this chapter, we will focus on using *Node.js* as JavaScript is a language that will be familiar to most APEX developers.

Unlike the other competing serverless platforms, Functions embodies the code in a Docker (`https://docker.io`) image and is deployed on OCI as containers. This provides developers the opportunity to fully customize and deploy containers with any required dependencies, for example, ImageMagick.

The following steps outline development process for Functions:

1. Choose the programming language runtime and initialize the project using the Fn Project CLI.

2. Write the code in the language of choice.

3. Deploy the function to OCI using the Fn Project CLI.

4. Invoke the function.

We will examine each step in greater detail later, but first, let us install the required software and tools and set up the OCI environment, user, and policies to support Functions.

Required Software and Tools

Note   The following steps are for working within a Linux environment. Please refer to Oracle's official documentation and guides for other operating systems. For Windows 10 or 11, I highly recommend that you use Microsoft's *Windows Subsystem for Linux* (WSL) version 2.

OCI CLI

The OCI CLI is a tool that OCI administrators and developers can use to manage OCI components, automate tasks, and more, without needing to worry about the intricate steps needed to call OCI REST APIs. Under the hood, it uses the OCI Python SDK, and thus, a compatible version of Python is required. At the time of writing, any versions 3.6 or later is supported. You will also require administrative access in the environment that you are working in.

To install the OCI CLI, simply run the following Bash command:

```
bash -c "$(curl -L https://raw.githubusercontent.com/oracle/oci-cli/master/
scripts/install/install.sh)"
```

During the installation process, you will be prompted to specify the directory that the software artifacts will be installed to. In a Linux environment, this is typically the subdirectory `lib/oracle-cli` in the user's home directory. The installation script will also need to know where to place the binaries in. By default, this is the `bin` and `bin/oci-cli-scripts` subdirectories in the user's home directory.

For most other prompts, you may use the default responses, including the final steps of modifying your PATH environment variable.

Fn Project CLI

To deploy Functions applications, developers will require the Fn Project CLI, a command-line interface application that lets you run a local development Fn server and deploy Fn applications to either the local Fn server or the OCI.

Developers have three options of where they create and deploy Functions applications from. The first option is to use the OCI Cloud Shell that is accessible from the OCI Console's top navigation bar (Figure 3-1).

Figure 3-1. *Launching the OCI Cloud Shell*

Cloud Shell is free to use, but you will require the necessary permissions and its usage is within the tenancy's service limits. Check with your OCI tenant administrator if you are unable to launch a session. It comes with both OCI and Fn Project CLIs installed and configured.

The other two options are to install the CLI on either a local workstation or on an OCI compute instance. The latter involves setting up an instance principal to authorize access to the OCI REST API. We will focus on installing and configuring the CLI on a local workstation.

Begin by installing the CLI. Execute the following command:

```
curl -LSs \ https://raw.githubusercontent.com/fnproject/cli/master/
install \
| sh
```

Upon successful installation, you will be greeted with a banner displaying the version that has been installed:

```
fn version 0.6.11
```

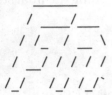

We will continue with the CLI configuration after the necessary OCI resources are created.

Virtual Cloud Network

Both the Oracle Functions and API gateways require a network subnet to deploy on, resources which we will create in the *DEV* compartment created earlier. For this chapter, we will build a simple network topology (Figure 3-2), using the *VCN Wizard*.

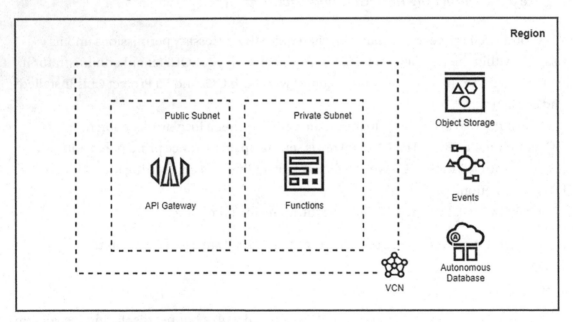

Figure 3-2. *A high-level overview showing where the various OCI components are located within the region and VCN*

1. Start by accessing the *Virtual Cloud Networks* page. You can find the link from the navigational menu, under the item *Networking*.

2. Click the *Start VCN Wizard* button.

3. Select the option *VCN with Internet Connectivity* and then click the *Start VCN Wizard* button to continue to the next step.

4. Enter the following information about the VCN that you will be creating:

    a. **VCN NAME:** VCN-Development

    b. **COMPARTMENT:** DEV

    c. **VCN CIDR BLOCK:** 10.0.0.0/16

    d. **PUBLIC SUBNET CIDR BLOCK:** 10.0.0.0/24

    e. **PRIVATE SUBNET CIDR BLOCK:** 10.0.1.0/24

    f. **USE DNS HOSTNAMES IN THIS VCN:** *Checked*

5. Review the components that will be created, and then click the *Create* button to generate them.

After the VCN components have been created, you should be redirected to the VCN details page that lists two subnets (Figure 3-3).

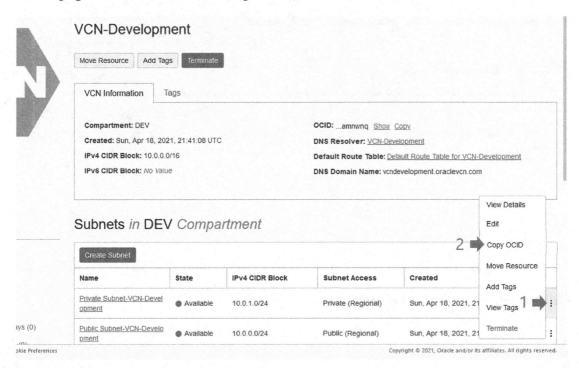

Figure 3-3. *VCN details page*

Later, when deploying an Oracle Functions application, you will need to provide the *OCID* of the subnet where it will be deployed to. To get this information, return to the VCN details page, click the three vertical dots next to the private subnet (labeled "1" in Figure 3-3) to open the context menu, and then click *Copy OCID*.

Identity and Access Management

We will create addition IAM resources for working with Oracle Functions.

User

Create an IAM user for our developer using the OCI Console. Access the *Users* management page. You can find this in the OCI side navigation bar under the item *Identity*. Create an IAM user (Figure 3-4).

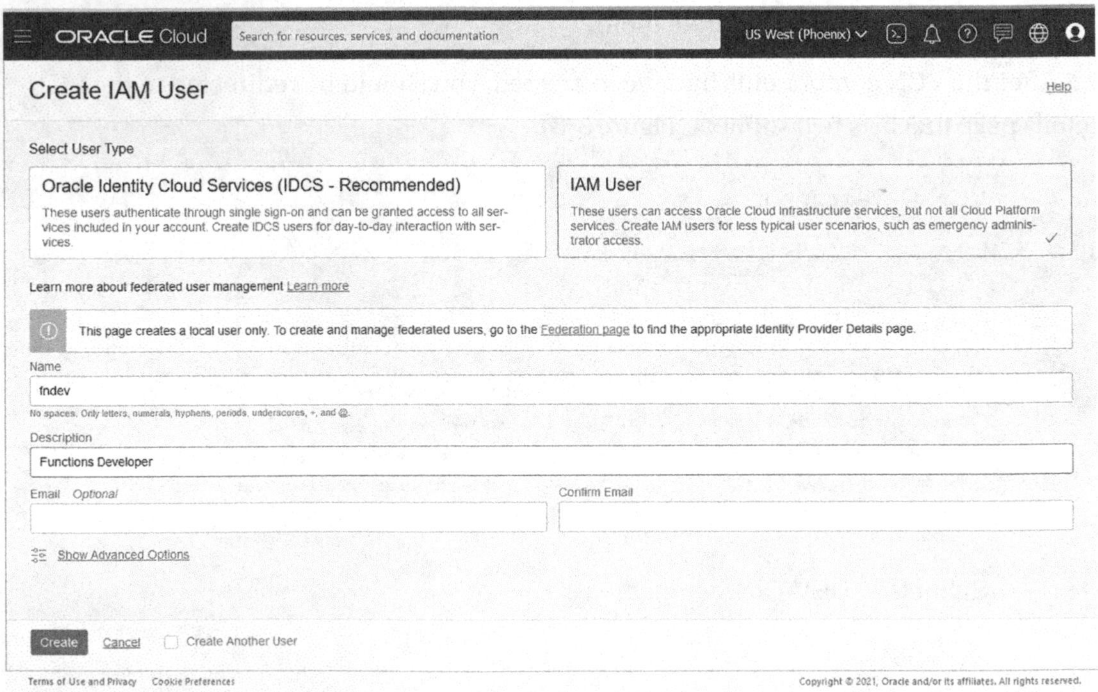

Figure 3-4. *Create an IAM user*

After the user has been successfully created, ensure that the user has the following "capabilities":

- **Local Password**: This allows the user to set a password and access the OCI Console. We can provide this to OCI developers to allow them access to visual tools to manage Oracle Functions, Events, Container Registry, and Object Storage. They will also need this to access their user profile to add their API keys.

- **API Keys**: API keys are required to access the OCI REST APIs and will be needed when working with the OCI and Fn Project CLI tools.

- **Auth Token**: The authentication tokens are required to log in to the OCI Container Registry.

You can enable these capabilities by editing the user and then clicking the *Edit User Capabilities* button. Ensure the required boxes are checked (Figure 3-5), and then click *Save Changes*.

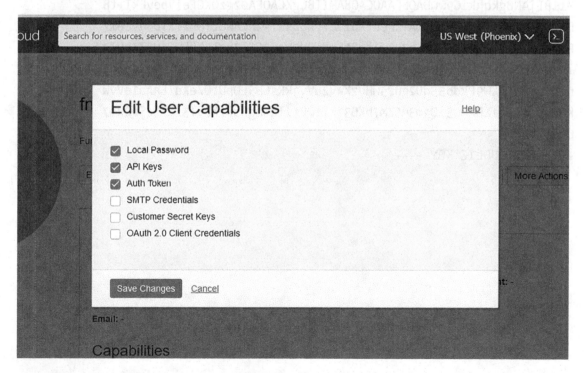

Figure 3-5. *Set the user's capabilities*

API Keys

The OCI CLI provides a convenient command that generates the API keys needed to work with the OCI and Fn Project CLI. We will use that to create the API keys by executing the command:

```
oci setup keys --key-name ociapexbook_fndev_api
```

Setting a passphrase is optional. For now, I will leave this blank (no passphrase).

The tool will generate two files in the ~/.oci directory: ociapexbook_fndev_api.pem and ociapexbook_fndev_api_public.pem. Open and read the contents of the second file and copy its contents. You may use the following Linux command:

```
cat ~/.oci/ociapexbook_fndev_api_public.pem
```

The contents of the file should look something like this:

```
-----BEGIN PUBLIC KEY-----
MIIBIjANBgkqhkiG9w0BAQEFAAOCAQ8AMIIBCgKCAQEAO2gzOKGFelJpevEkT+tB
B/U89TzDafv7EyqhEuuMmAf1PeutXoloCYyw0hxN7s2KcAWQrfMBZTXTd+NvLemz
PIz9LI9Yaw6PQunMfKRULh7p3w+tqBmFwXgQVOWq82GCJ7nzI6NzkWG1H8Z/LHZ2
+eFpEkHGcyFAptILGa5h4+5sUT31kyNMxYcZDyGBDdf+O3DIXODOEWfPsdi5pFd5
ncH7oq/W6BXW9Pkdb55dU2guP5wHUzXwV2uVvjRRsGH5LDpDLO/eKdIEhAa1eVvW
KqohdpeAEJ1XBXWo5iQgm3m5ZM7bKG3jXItQPr1TqwmgWsF+KhvT5rBFLoSoOxo7
UQIDAQCB
-----END PUBLIC KEY-----
```

Log in to the OCI Console using the IAM user you have created. Then, go to the User Settings page, accessible by clicking the top right of the page (Figure 3-6).

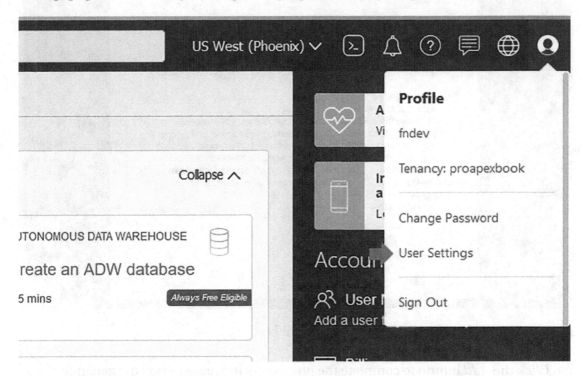

Figure 3-6. *Access the user's details*

On the left side of the page, under the *Resources* menu, click API Keys and then the *Add API Key* button. Paste the contents of the public key in the text box provided (Figure 3-7).

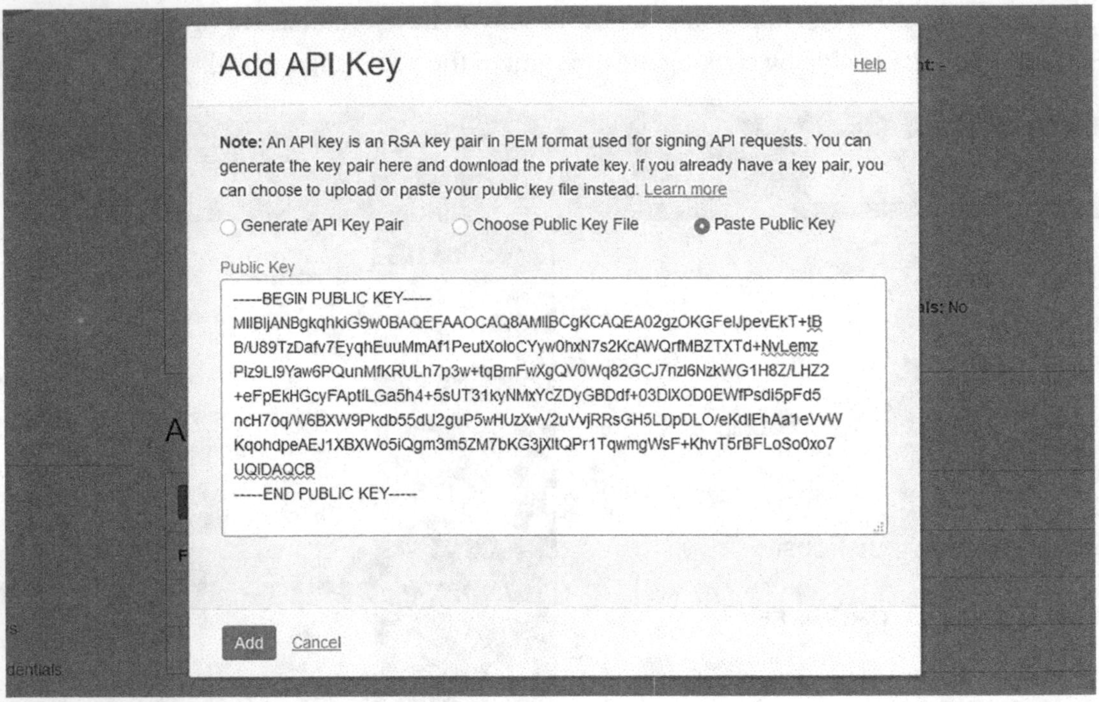

Add API Key   Help

Note: An API key is an RSA key pair in PEM format used for signing API requests. You can generate the key pair here and download the private key. If you already have a key pair, you can choose to upload or paste your public key file instead. Learn more

○ Generate API Key Pair   ○ Choose Public Key File   ● Paste Public Key

Public Key

```
-----BEGIN PUBLIC KEY-----
MIIBIjANBgkqhkiG9w0BAQEFAAOCAQ8AMIIBCgKCAQEA02gzOKGFeIJpevEkT+tB
B/U89TzDafv7EyqhEuuMmAf1PeutXoloCYyw0hxN7s2KcAWQrfMBZTXTd+NvLemz
Plz9LI9Yaw6PQunMfKRULh7p3w+tqBmFwXgQV0Wq82GCJ7nzI6NzkWG1H8Z/LHZ2
+eFpEkHGcyFAptILGa5h4+5sUT31kyNMxYcZDyGBDdf+03DlXOD0EWfPsdi5pFd5
ncH7oq/W6BXW9Pkdb55dU2guP5wHUzXwV2uVvjRRsGH5LDpDLO/eKdIEhAa1eVvW
KqohdpeAEJ1XBXWo5iQgm3m5ZM7bKG3jXItQPr1TqwmgWsF+KhvT5rBFLoSo0xo7
UQIDAQCB
-----END PUBLIC KEY-----
```

Add   Cancel

Figure 3-7. Paste the contents of the public key

Click the *Add* button to complete the process. As instructed, copy the generate configuration information and enter the content into the file ~/.oci/config.

I typically like to change the name of the profile, so I will change it from DEFAULT to something more descriptive like OCIAPEXBOOK_FNDEV_PHX:

```
[OCIAPEXBOOK_FNDEV_PHX]
user=ocid1.user.oc1..
aaaaaaaahpjocye5zqg9o6l3kkp17s7kaf4wkg3wqpxx2ghfmtysjt45lxya
fingerprint=ef:82:58:8c:ba:13:29:8a:1c:ae:71:9b:34:19:e5:9b
tenancy=ocid1.tenancy.oc1..
aaaaaaaabvron7m2kwcxrmdoqmc2cymozr5o2b3ocx63m5qttevk3fhgf32a
region=us-phoenix-1
key_file=~/.oci/ociapexbook_fndev_api.pem
```

To test that you have set up your account correctly, run the following command:

```
export OCI_CLI_PROFILE=OCIAPEXBOOK_FNDEV_PHX && \
oci os ns get
```

The command should return a JSON output with a single attribute containing the OCI namespace of your tenancy. For example:

```
{
  "data": "axtobdaknemc"
}
```

Auth Token

An authentication token is required to log in to the OCI Container Registry. Again, on the user's details page, click the *Auth Tokens* link on the left side of the page. Then click the button *Generate Token* button. Provide a useful description and then click the *Generate Token* button on the modal page. Copy the generated token and store it in a safe place. It will only be displayed once!

Groups

Navigate to the *Groups* page through the navigation menu, under the item *Identity*. Create a new group called *FunctionsDevelopers*, and assign the IAM user that we had created earlier.

Policies

Access the tenant's policy from the navigational menu, under the *Identity* menu item. The policies that you will require are as follows:

OCI Resource: Oracle Cloud Infrastructure Registry

Grantee: Functions Developers

Policy Location: Root compartment

Statements:

```
Allow group FunctionsDevelopers to manage repos in tenancy
Allow group FunctionsDevelopers to read objectstorage-namespaces
in tenancy
```

OCI Resource: Networking

Grantee: Function Developers

Policy Location: DEV compartment

Statements:

```
Allow group FunctionsDevelopers to use virtual-network-family
in compartment DEV
```

OCI Resource: Oracle Functions

Grantee: Function Developers

Policy Location: DEV compartment

Statements:

```
Allow group FunctionsDevelopers to manage functions-family
in compartment DEV
Allow group FunctionsDevelopers to read metrics in
compartment DEV
```

OCI Component: Application Performance Monitoring

Grantee: Function Developers and Functions Service

Policy Location: DEV or root compartment

Statements:

```
Allow group FunctionsDevelopers to use apm-domains in
compartment DEV
Allow service faas to use apm-domains in compartment DEV
```

OR

```
Allow group FunctionsDevelopers to use apm-domains in tenancy
Allow service faas to use apm-domains in tenancy
```

To keep it simple, we will create a single policy *Fn-Root-Policy* in the **root compartment**, using a predefined template from Oracle (Figure 3-8).

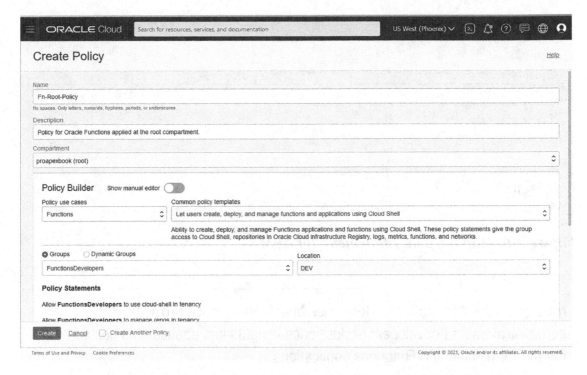

Figure 3-8. *Create a policy for Oracle Functions using a predefined template*

1. In the *Policy Builder* section, ensure that the *Show manual editor*
    is toggled off.

2. Under the *Policy* use cases, select the value "Functions."

3. For *Common policy templates*, select the option "Let users
    create, deploy, and manage functions and applications using
    Cloud Shell."

4. Select the group *FunctionsDevelopers* created earlier that will be
    the target of these policy statements.

5. Under *Location*, select the compartment *DEV*.

6. Review the policy statements that will be created and then click
    the *Create* button.

At the time of writing, *Application Performance Monitoring* (APM) was a newly
introduced feature and has not been included in the predefined template. After the
policy has been created, edit the policy, and add policy statements for APM (Figure 3-9).

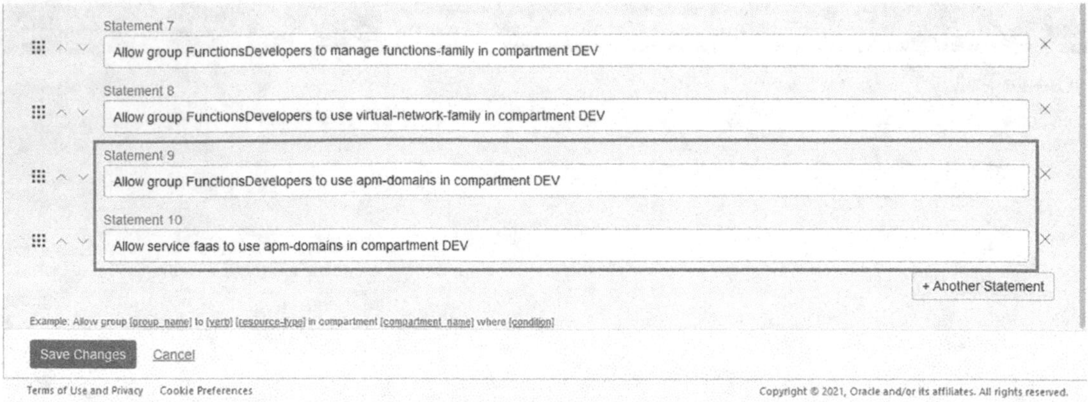

Figure 3-9. *Add the policy statements for APM*

Note (1)   The Application Performance Monitoring service provides OCI administrators and developers performance insights into applications hosted on the platform, including Functions applications.

Note (2)   The template includes a policy statement to allow users in the group *FunctionsDevelopers* to use Cloud Shell to deploy and manage Functions applications. This is not a required policy, and you can optionally remove it.

Set Up Fn Project CLI

With the necessary OCI resources created, the next step is to configure the Fn Project CLI with a context. Begin by creating a context named ociapexbook-functions using the following command:

```
fn create context ociapexbook-functions --provider oracle
```

This command creates a directory .fn in your home directory and contains a file named config.yaml and subdirectory called contexts. The YAML file contains information about your current environment for Functions, such as the CLI version number and the context used. In the contexts directory, you will find additional YAML files, each representing the context created, for example, ociapexbook-functions.yaml.

Set the profile declared in $HOME/.oci/config that you will be using with this context:

```
fn update context oracle.profile OCIAPEXBOOK_FNDEV_PHX
```

Next, change the active context by executing the command:

```
fn use context ociapexbook-functions
```

The next step requires the compartment OCID (a unique identifier that the Oracle Cloud assigns to all OCI resources) that you may obtain either through the OCI Console or issuing an OCI CLI command:

```
oci iam compartment list
```

Reminder   Set the OCI_CLI_PROFILE with the appropriate name from the $HOME/.oci/config file before you execute the OCI CLI commands.

The resulting output is in a JSON format, listing all the compartments found in your tenancy. For example:

```
{
  "data": [
    {
      "id": " ocid1.compartment.oc1..aaaaaaaa...5adq",
      "name": "DEV",

      ...

    }
  ]
}
```

Next, set the compartment OCID in the context:

```
fn update context \
  oracle.compartment-id ocid1.compartment.oc1..aaaaaaaa...5adq
```

Set the API URL based on the region that your Functions application will reside in. The template for the URL is

```
https://functions.<region-identitfier>.oci.oraclecloud.com
```

Look up the region identifier from this web page (`https://bit.ly/oci-docs-regions`) and replace the placeholder <region-identifier>. For example:

```
fn update context \
  api-url https://functions.us-phoenix-1.oci.oraclecloud.com
```

Finally, set the context's Docker container registry that has the format:

```
<region-key>.ocir.io/<tenancy-namespace>/<repo-name>
```

Three key pieces of information will be required. They are

1. **Region key**: Obtain this value based on the region where the Functions application is hosted. This value can be looked up in the same web page (`https://bit.ly/oci-docs-regions`) reference earlier.

2. **Tenancy namespace**: The tenancy's namespace can be obtained through the OCI Console either in the Tenancy Details, Object Storage Bucket Details, or Container Registry page. You may also obtain the namespace from the OCI CLI using the command earlier that was used to test the setup.

3. **Repository name**: Provide a meaningful name for the repository where the Functions application's image will be uploaded to.

Execute the command:

```
fn update context registry phx.ocir.io/axtobdaknemc/photobox
```

Verify the context information using the command:

```
fn inspect context
```

The output should contain the values that you have set:

```
Current context: ociapexbook-functions
```

```
api-url: https://functions.us-phoenix-1.oci.oraclecloud.com
oracle.compartment-id: ocid1.compartment.oc1..aaaaaaaa...5adq
oracle.profile: OCIAPEXBOOK_FNDEV_PHX
provider: oracle
registry: phx.ocir.io/axtobdaknemc/photobox
```

Oracle Cloud Infrastructure Container Registry

The *Container Registry* (OCIR) service is provided to all paid OCI accounts. It is a managed Docker container registry that allows tenants to host their Docker images that are either private or have public access. When deploying to Oracle Functions, the OCI uses this registry to host the application's images.

Before deploying application, developers will need to (1) ensure that Docker has been installed in the environment that they are working in and (2) log in to the OCIR using the authentication token generated earlier in this chapter.

Log in to the OCIR using the format:

```
docker login <region-key>.ocir.io
```

And the username format:

```
<tenancy-namespace>/<username>
```

For example:

```
$ docker login phx.ocir.io
Username: axtobdaknemc/fndev
Password:
Login Succeeded
```

Validate Setup

With all the required OCI resources created and the Fn Project CLI configured, test that you now have access to Oracle Functions and ready to deploy applications. Do this by executing a command to list Oracle Functions applications in your tenancy:

```
$ fn list apps
No apps found
NAME     ID
```

Thumbnail Generator Function

As mentioned earlier, the Fn Project supports multiple programming languages including Node.js. The CLI provides a simple operation, `init`, to create a project with the required artifacts.

```
mkdir -p ociapexbook/photobox && \
cd ociapexbook/photobox && \
fn init --runtime node thumbnail-generator
```

Note   At the time of writing, the *Function Development Kit* (FDK) for Node.js currently runs in Docker container with version 11. To run a specific version of Node.js, developers will have to deploy the application with a custom *Dockerfile*. You will also need a custom Docker container if there are required operating system binaries not found in the stock image. Unfortunately, this approach is not covered in this book.

The CLI generates the following three files:

```
$ cd thumbnail-generator && \
tree .
.
├── func.js
├── func.yaml
└── package.json
```

The YAML (https://yaml.org/) contains the required metadata from the project including the name of the function, a version number that is incremented each time it is deployed, the runtime platform, and command to execute when the serverless function is called:

```
$ cat func.yaml
schema_version: 20180708
name: thumbnail-generator
version: 0.0.1
runtime: node
entrypoint: node func.js
```

In addition to these default attributes, developers can also control certain aspects of the execution environment such as

- **Memory**: The maximum amount of memory a function can consume is set to 128 MB by default. In the OCI, we can set this to either 128, 256, 512, or 1024. Once the threshold is exceeded, the runtime will stop, and an error will be logged.

- **Timeout**: The maximum amount of time in seconds that a function can run for. By default, the threshold is set to 30 seconds and can be increased up to a value of 300.

These values can also be set through the OCI Console after the function has been created. It is important though to know that while developers do not have to worry about provisioning the required infrastructure to support the code execution, there are limits to the environment and amount of resources consumed by the function.

Note   The cost for running an Oracle Function is calculated based on the number of times it is invoked and the amount of time it runs for, measured in memory seconds. If your function is consuming a lot of time and memory to run, and/or it is invoked a lot, then it might be prudent to rethink the deployment strategy.

The next file that was created is the sole JavaScript file generated that contains basic "Helloworld" code that can be used to quickly test the setup, deployment, and execution workflow:

```
$ cat func.js
const fdk=require('@fnproject/fdk');

fdk.handle(function(input){
  let name = 'World';
  if (input.name) {
    name = input.name;
  }
  console.log('\nInside Node Hello World function')
  return {'message': 'Hello ' + name}
})
```

Finally, the Node.js FDK includes a `package.json` file for package management. It already includes the required dependency `@fnproject/fdk` to support Oracle Functions.

```json
{
  "name": "thumbnail-generator",
  "version": "1.0.0",
  "description": "A Fn serverless function for... thumbnails.",
  "main": "func.js",
  "author": "Awesome Developer <awesome.developer@example.com>",
  "license": "Apache-2.0",
  "dependencies": {
    "@fnproject/fdk": ">=0.0.20",
    "file-type": "^16.3.0",
    "image-thumbnail": "^1.0.13",
    "oci-sdk": "^1.19.1"
  }
}
```

The stock `package.json` file will require some edits. Also, in the example code provided, the following packages that I have identified (through the website `www.npmjs.com/`) for use to achieve the goals of this serverless function are

- **oci-sdk**: The *Oracle Cloud Infrastructure SDK for TypeScript and JavaScript*. This is required to facilitate access and operations on OCI resources, for example, download and uploading files from and to OCI Object Storage buckets. For more information, please see `www.npmjs.com/package/oci-sdk`.

- **image-thumbnail**: This is the core module for generating thumbnails using the supplied photos. It is easy to use. Simply provide a file path, URI (Uniform Resource Identifier), Base64 string, and, optionally, parameters for customizing the outputs to create the thumbnails. For detailed usage, please refer to `www.npmjs.com/package/image-thumbnail`.

- **file-type**: This module is used for determining the mime (content) type of the thumbnail generated. Please see `www.npmjs.com/package/file-type` for more information.

Important   If you have Node.js installed on your workstation, you may use the npm command to search, install, and save the dependency in the `package.json`. For example, to install the `oci-sdk` module, run the command npm `install --save oci-sdk`. This creates the node_modules directory that contains the downloaded code from the installed packages. If the directory is not found in the project directory, Oracle Functions runs the `npm install` command during the build process. If it exists, then it will be copied into the deployed Docker image. It is important to note that this might contain operating system (OS)–dependent binaries that may not be compatible with the target OS that the serverless function will run in. I would recommend deleting the entire node_modules directory prior to deployment.

Oracle Functions consists of an application that is made up of a collection of Functions. Both can be created either using the OCI Console or using the Fn Project CLI. We will continue to use the CLI for these operations.

Oracle Functions must be created and assigned to a subnet. They can be created on both public and private subnets, but the latter is generally preferred. You will need the target subnet's OCID (Oracle Cloud Resource Identifiers) to create the application using the CLI. You may obtain this by navigating to the target subnet's details page (see Figure 3-10).

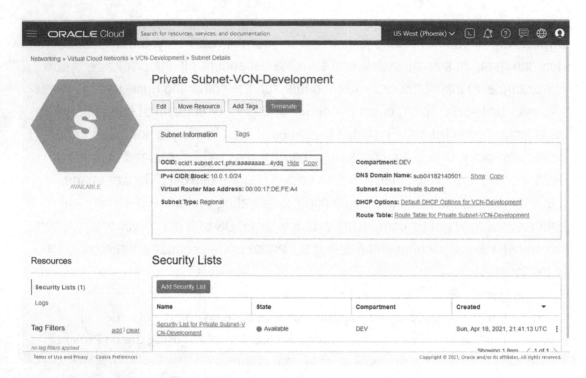

Figure 3-10. *Obtain the target subnet's OCID*

Create the application using the `fn create app` command and operation. You will need to provide the application's name, for example, *photobox*, and the target subnet's OCID using the `--annotation` argument.

```
fn create app photobox --annotation \
  oracle.com/oci/subnetIds='["ocid1.subnet.oc1.phx.aaaaaa…4ydq"]'
```

Next, create the function simply by deploying the function from the project's root directory:

```
fn deploy --app photobox
```

The process involves performing a *Docker build* in the development environment, publishing it to the Docker registry, OCIR in this case, and then associating the Oracle Function and the published image:

```
Deploying thumbnail-generator to app: photobox
Bumped to version 0.0.2
```

```
Building image phx.ocir.io/axtobdaknemc/photobox/thumbnail-generator:0.0.2
....................................................................................
....................................................................................
....................................................................................
Parts:   [phx.ocir.io axtobdaknemc photobox thumbnail-generator:0.0.2]
Pushing phx.ocir.io/axtobdaknemc/photobox/thumbnail-generator:0.0.2 to
docker registry...The push refers to repository [phx.ocir.io/axtobdaknemc/
photobox/thumbnail-generator]
1250c4163088: Pushed
e40ad43dcc99: Pushed
61e0770c3683: Pushed
a0d7b4199dce: Pushed
8aed3db29123: Pushed
9c85c117f8f6: Pushed
a464c54f93a9: Pushed
0.0.2: digest: sha256:ded9b082ea10189ed732b893634f514c5e74229e75225c34489
6e6445dce9d56 size: 1790
Updating function thumbnail-generator using image phx.ocir.io/axtobdaknemc/
photobox/thumbnail-generator:0.0.2...
Successfully created function: thumbnail-generator with phx.ocir.io/
axtobdaknemc/photobox/thumbnail-generator:0.0.2
```

Note   As you would have noticed, the deployment process relies on Docker processes and commands. Before deploying the function, Docker engine must be running!

The version number in the func.yaml file will also be incremented; however, you can prevent this behavior by adding the --no-bump parameter.

Once deployed, an Oracle Function can be invoked in several ways:

1. Using the Fn Project CLI.

2. Calling the OCI REST APIs either directly or using any of the available software development kits (SDKs).

3. Triggering execution with OCI Events.

4. Through an OCI API gateway endpoint.

We will examine the use of OCI Events later in this chapter. As for working with the OCI REST APIs, that can be challenging depending on the availability of an SDK for your preferred programming language. The simplest approach is to invoke the function using the CLI:

```
fn invoke photobox thumbnail-generator
```

This command communicates with the OCI to either launch a new or use an existing Docker container to execute the code. If a new container must be created, then there will be some delay before a response is received. Subsequent calls should take significantly less time. Invoking the stock function should return this result:

```
{"message":"Hello World"}
```

When an Oracle Function is executed, the handler `fdk.handle` will be called. This function has a parameter for a callback function and optionally an `options` parameter that will be discussed later in this chapter. The callback function takes an `input` parameter and an optional `ctx` parameter.

With the generated code, we can provide a `name` value that can be piped into the invocation command as a JSON object with the required attribute. Here is an example:

```
echo -n '{ "name": "Oracle" }' | \
  fn invoke photobox thumbnail-generator \
    --content-type application/json | jq .
```

Handling the output using the application *jq* (`https://stedolan.github.io/jq/`), we will get this beautified output:

```
{
  "message": "Hello Oracle"
}
```

With the skeletal pieces of the function created, it is now time to implement the code to perform the following:

1. Retrieve the photo/image file from the designated Object Storage bucket and save it to a temporary location.

2.   Use the *image-thumbnail* Node.js module to generate the thumbnail and replace the original.

3.   Upload the thumbnail file to a different Object Storage bucket.

Approach to Development

To deploy and invoke an Oracle Function can be expensive and time consuming. Start by decomposing the problem into portions that can be solved by running the code on your local workstation. For example, I first started writing the code that would retrieve and then upload the files from and to the buckets. This requires a few modules from the OCI SDK for TypeScript and JavaScript:

```
const common = require('oci-common');
const objectStorage = require('oci-objectstorage');
```

The process for authenticating and signing HTTP requests to the OCI REST services can be daunting. Fortunately for us, the SDK shields a lot of this complexity. To begin working with the Object Storage, we will need to create a provider and then use it to create a client for the service we wish to interact with; in this case, it is the Object Storage:

```
// Set the authentication provider.
const provider = new
  common.ConfigFileAuthenticationDetailsProvider(
    '~/.oci/config', PROFILE_NAME
  );

// Create an Object Storage client.
const client = new objectStorage.ObjectStorageClient({
  authenticationDetailsProvider: provider
});
```

To retrieve and upload objects, we generally require three key pieces of information:

1.   Namespace name

2.   Bucket name

3.   Object name

We anticipate that the bucket and object names will be obtained from function caller. For the namespace however, we will retrieve the information using OCI SDK:

```
// Create an empty request:
const request = {};

// Retrieve the namespace name using the client we had initialized earlier:
const namespaceName = (await client.getNamespace(request)).value;
```

Then, download the file from the Object Storage bucket and save it to the local file system:

```
let bucketName = PHOTOS_BUCKET_NAME;
let objectName = OBJECT_NAME;

// Prepare the request to get the object.
const getObjectRequest = {
  namespaceName: namespaceName,
  bucketName: bucketName,
  objectName: objectName
}

// Get the object.
const getObjectResponse = await client.getObject(
  getObjectRequest);

// Set the temporary file name for both the photo and thumbnail.
const tempFilepath = path.join(TEMP_DIRNAME, objectName);

// Save the file to disk.
let fileStream = fs.createWriteStream(tempFilepath);
await new Promise((resolve, reject) => {
  getObjectResponse.value.pipe(fileStream);
  fileStream.on('finish', resolve);
  fileStream.on('error', reject);
});
```

Finally, we will upload the same file and place it in a separate bucket:

```
// Set the bucket name.
bucketName = THUMBNAILS_BUCKET_NAME;

// Retrieve some file statistics.
const stats = await fs.promises.stat(tempFilepath);

// Prepare the file for upload.
const nodFsBlob = new objectStorage.NodeFSBlob(
  tempFilepath, stats.size);
const objectData = await nodFsBlob.getData();

// Create the PUT request.
const putObjectRequest = {
  namespaceName: namespaceName,
  bucketName: thumbnailBucketName,
  objectName: objectName,
  putObjectBody: objectData,
  contentLength: stats.size
}

// Perform the upload.
const putObjectResponse = await client.putObject(
  putObjectRequest);
```

The complete code is available from the book's code repository, in the file ch03/
photobox/thumbnail-generator/working-with-object-storage.js. To run the code

1. Upload an image file named my-photo.jpg to the bucket photos.

2. If you have not already done so, run the following command to
    have *npm* install the required dependencies:

    ```
    npm install
    ```

3. Run the code:

    ```
    node working-with-object-storage.js
    ```

> **Note**   Many of these functions are asynchronous calls that need to be executed sequentially. The code relies heavily on the `await` keyword and, thus, executes within an asynchronous function that is executed immediately: `(async() => {` `... })();`

The next step involves creating the thumbnail from the source image (the full source code can be found in ch03/photobox/thumbnail-generator/generate-thumbnail.js). For this, we will create a function that takes in the source and target file paths and an options object to set the parameters for the thumbnail generation.

```
async function generateThumbnail(sourceFilepath, targetFilepath,
  options)
{
  console.log('Processing', sourceFilepath);
  try {
    const thumbnail = await imageThumbnail(
      sourceFilepath, options);
    await fs.promises.writeFile(targetFilepath, thumbnail);
    console.log('Thumbnail created successfully.');
  } catch(errorMessage) {
    console.error(errorMessage);
  }
}
```

Then call this function after the file has been downloaded from the Object Storage:

```
// Generate the thumbnail, override the original.
await generateThumbnail(
  tempFilepath,
  tempFilepath,
  { width: THUMBNAIL_SIZE_PIXEL, height: THUMBNAIL_SIZE_PIXEL }
);
```

Notice in the code that we set the thumbnail pixel size using an environment variable:

```
const THUMBNAIL_SIZE_PIXEL =
  parseInt(process.env.THUMBNAIL_SIZE_PIXEL);
```

Before executing the code, be sure to set the environment variable:

```
export THUMBAIL_SIZE_PIXEL = 80 && \
node generate-thumbnail.js
```

To understand why we are using environment variables, read on.

Configuration Parameters

The OCI provides Oracle Functions developers the ability to set and manage configuration parameters once the serverless functions are deployed. We can do this either using the OCI Console or using the CLI as demonstrated as follows:

```
fn config app photobox THUMBNAIL_BUCKET_NAME thumbnails
```

Configuration parameters can be applied to either the application or function. When set at the application level, all functions within the application have access to the same configuration.

To set the function-specific parameters, use the following command instead:

```
fn config function photobox thumbnail-generator \
  THUMBNAIL_BUCKET_NAME thumbnails
```

Triggering Functions with Oracle Events

Earlier in the chapter, we had set up the photos bucket in Object Storage to store the photos uploaded through our APEX application. To process these files automatically and generate their thumbnails, we will need to turn on the bucket's ability to emit events each time an object is created, updated, or deleted. The event will then be used to trigger the serverless function.

To do so, navigate to the bucket's detail page and click the Edit link next to field *Emit Object Events* (Figure 3-11).

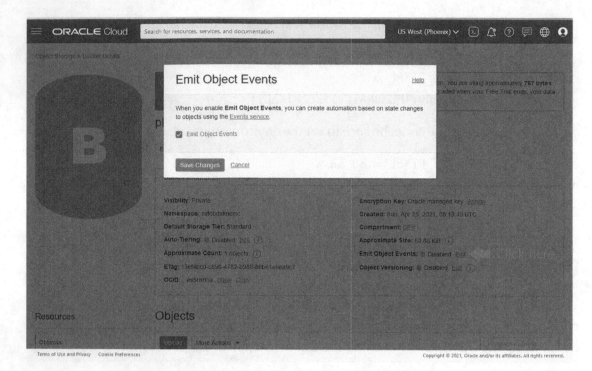

Figure 3-11. *Enable the bucket to emit object events*

Check the only box in the modal and then click *Save Changes*.

Next, create a rule in the OCI Events Services. You can find this by using the navigation menu and clicking *Observability & Management*. Click *Rules* under the *Events Service* header. There you will find a button to create a new rule.

A rule consists of a set of conditions and actions that are trigger when those conditions are met. A condition can be of the following:

- Event Type

- Attribute

- Filter Tag

Many services on the OCI can emit events. Select the Object Storage service, and then under the field *Event Type*, choose the following:

- Object: Create

- Object: Delete

- Object: Update

Any bucket can be emitting object events if we allowed it to do so. For this rule, we would like it to be triggered only when the source is the photos bucket. Add a new condition and this time, choose *Attribute*. The list of available attribute names is scoped based on the select service. Choose the value bucketName and then enter the text "photos" in the *Attribute Values* field. Figure 3-12 shows what the final rule conditions should look like.

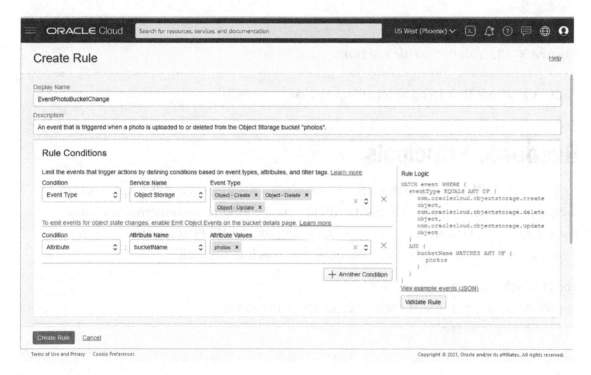

Figure 3-12. *Enter the rule's conditions*

Scroll down to the rule's list of actions. The following action types are available to choose from:

- Streaming

- Notifications

- Functions

Choose *Functions* to display the relevant drop-down menus. These select lists cascade, so begin by selecting the compartment that the serverless function resides in, and then choose the target application and function (Figure 3-13).

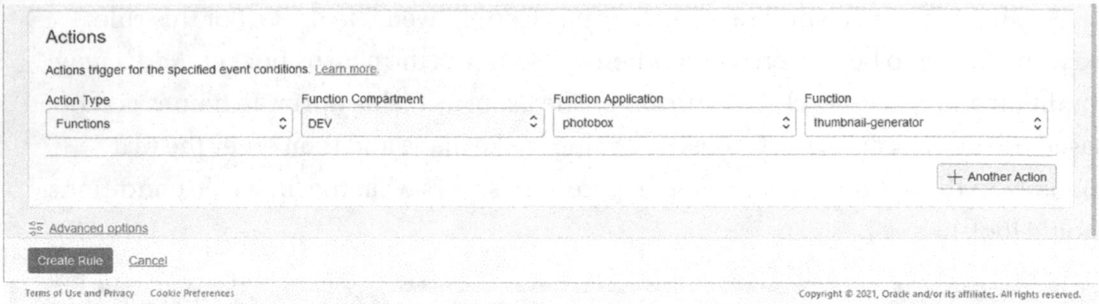

Figure 3-13. *Enter the rule's actions*

Click *Create Rule* to complete the process.

Resource Principals

As mentioned earlier in the chapter, accessing OCI resources via REST APIs requires developers to generate the necessary API key pair, configure the environment, and then sign all HTTP requests. The OCI SDKs simplify the HTTP request signing. In the demonstration code, you might have observed this function call:

```
const authenticationProvider =
  common.ConfigFileAuthenticationDetailsProvider(
    '~/.oci/config',
    PROFILE_NAME
);
```

This creates an authentication provider that is subsequently used to create resource-based clients for performing the required operations. The `ConfigFileAuthenticationDetailsProvider` is a file-based authentication provider that uses the API key pairs and configuration on the local machine. To use this authentication provider, a custom Docker image would have to be created with the required API key pairs and configuration files embedded. This is not ideal.

Fortunately, the OCI has alternative methods for authenticating that relies on *Dynamic Groups* and IAM Policies. Developers can either use *Instance Principal Authentication* or *Resource Principal Authentication*, depending on the environment the code runs on. For serverless, we would use the latter.

First, create a dynamic group for Oracle Functions (Figure 3-14). You will find the dynamic groups in the navigation menu, under *Identity & Security*.

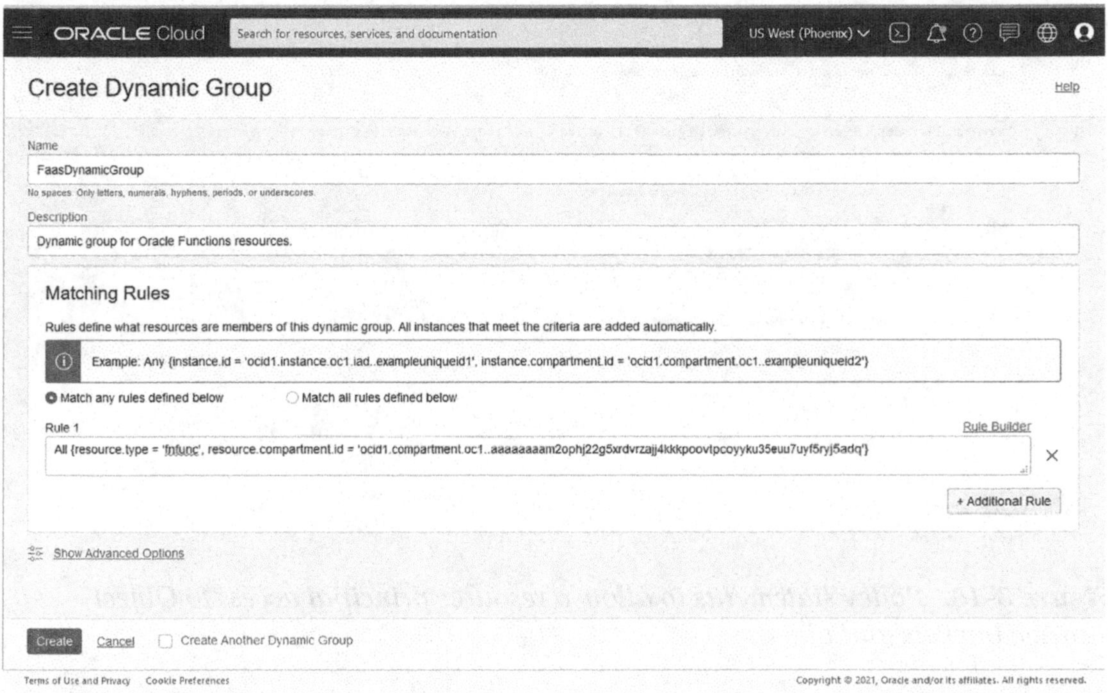

Figure 3-14. *Create a dynamic group using resource type and compartment OCID*

Add a single rule that includes all Oracle Functions (`resource.type = 'fnfunc'`) created in the compartment using its OCID:

```
All { resource.type = 'fnfunc', resource.compartment.id = 'ocid1.
compartment.oc1..aaaaaaaa...' }
```

Next, create or update any existing policies that govern the Object Storage bucket access, to include the dynamic group. For example, in this policy (Figure 3-15), the following rules were added.

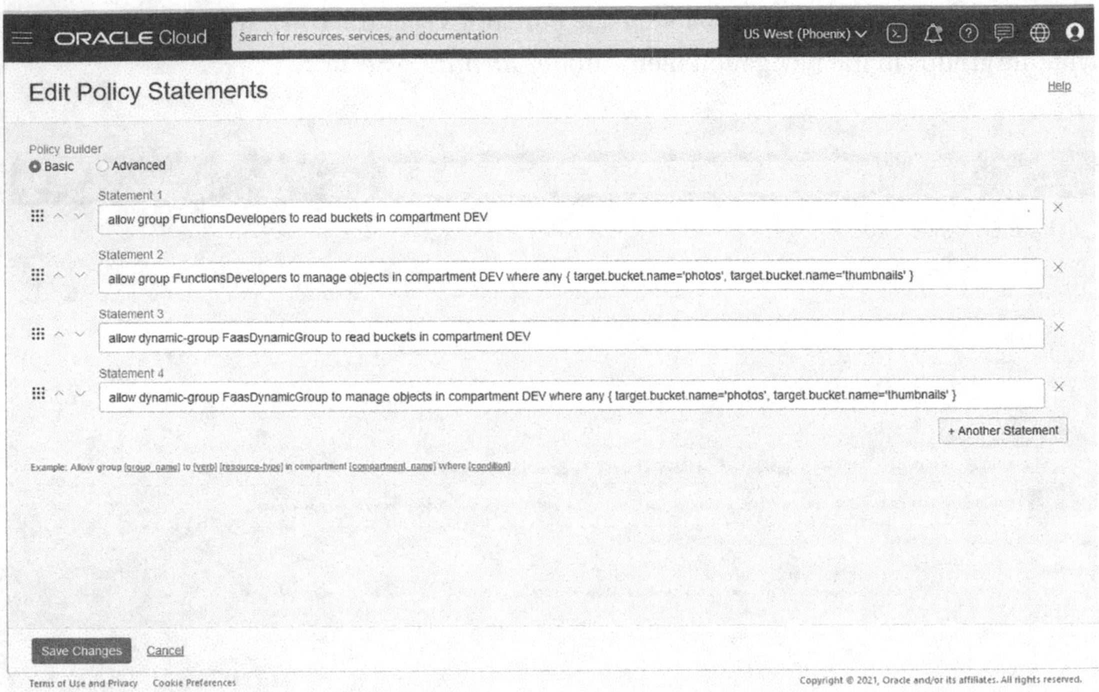

Figure 3-15. *Policy statements to allow a resource principal access to Object Storage buckets and objects*

To allow the dynamic group to read all buckets in a specific compartment:

```
allow dynamic-group FaasDynamicGroup to read buckets in compartment DEV
```

To allow the dynamic group to manage objects in specific buckets and compartment:

```
allow dynamic-group FaasDynamicGroup to manage objects in compartment DEV
where any { target.bucket.name='photos', target.bucket.name='thumbnails' }
```

Then, in the func.js code, adjust the authenticator provider code to use resource principals instead:

```
// Set the authentication provider using resource principals.
const authenticationProvider =
  await common
    .ResourcePrincipalAuthenticationDetailsProvider
    .builder();
```

We will then no longer be required to include the OCI CLI configuration files and API key pairs in the Docker image.

Complete Function and Deploy

As many of the operations used are asynchronous, for example, working with objects and file system, we will need to ensure that the FDK's function handle calls an asynchronous handler, or it will exit before the tasks are completed.

```
async function functionHandler(input, ctx) {
  // 1. Create a resource principal authentication provider.

  ...

  // 2. Get the thumbnails bucket name and pixel size settings
  //    from the environment.
  const THUMBNAIL_BUCKET_NAME =
    process.env.THUMBNAIL_BUCKET_NAME
    || DEFAULT_THUMBNAIL_BUCKET_NAME;
  const THUMBNAIL_SIZE_PIXEL =
    parseInt(process.env.THUMBNAIL_SIZE_PIXEL)
    || DEFAULT_THUMBNAIL_SIZE_PIXEL;

  // 3. Read event information.
  const eventType = input.eventType;
  const bucketName = input.data.additionalDetails.bucketName;
  const objectName = input.data.resourceName;

  // 4. Create an Object Storage client.
  const client = new objectStorage.ObjectStorageClient({
    authenticationDetailsProvider: authenticationProvider
  });

  if (eventType === OBJECT_CREATE_EVENT
    || eventType === OBJECT_UPDATE_EVENT)
  {
    /**
```

```
    * 5. Code to download the object that triggered the event.
    * 6. Generate the thumbnail.
    * 7. Upload the thumbnail to the thumbnail bucket.
    */
  ...
}

  return '{ "status": "success" }';
}

// Specify the callback function that the FDK should call when
// when the serverless function is executed.
fdk.handle(functionHandler);
```

The preceding code snippet provides an overview of the tasks involved:

1. Creating a resource principal authentication provider.

2. Get the configuration parameters from the environment variables in the running container.

3. Retrieve the information about the event and associated object received by Oracle Functions.

4. As we did in the code that was executed locally, create the OCI Object Storage client, and then perform the rest of the workflow for downloading the source photo, generating the thumbnail, and uploading the output.

The final code for the Oracle Function can be found in the file ch03/photobox/ thumbnail-generator/func.js. It includes code to delete thumbnails when their source photos are deleted from the bucket.

To deploy the function, remember to first delete the node_modules directory if it exists, and then run the CLI command to deploy

```
rm -rf ./node_modules && \
fn deploy -app photobox
```

The next time a file is dropped in the photos bucket, the thumbnail-generator function should be triggered, and the thumbnail uploaded to the thumbnails bucket.

Troubleshooting and Logging

And what happens if you do not see the thumbnail image show up in the target bucket?

Firstly, remember that if this is the first time that the serverless function is called, it might take a while for the service to create and start a new container, so please wait a while. If it still does not show up, then let us look at how we can troubleshoot and debug issues.

Included in every developer's toolbox should be a tool for logging what happens when the code executes. The OCI provides an extensive logging support for its resources, including Oracle Functions. To enable logging, return to the application's details page. On the left side of the page, click the link *Logs* and then toggle the switch to enable the *Function Invocation Logs*. A modal will pop out from the right (Figure 3-16) with the defaults set.

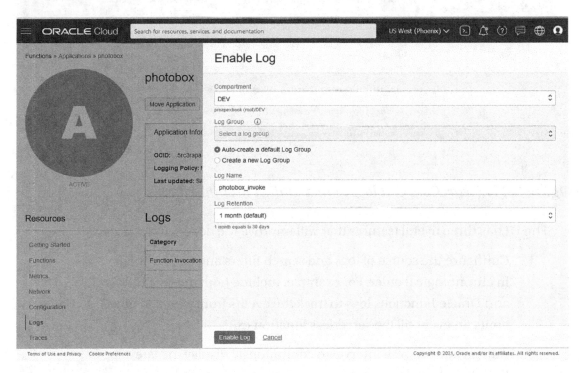

Figure 3-16. *Enable the Function Invocation Logs*

Accept the default values and click the *Enable Log* button. Once the log has been created, click the log name to view the logs. Alternatively, use the *Log Search* (Figure 3-17) that you can find the link to in the navigational menu, under *Observability & Management.*

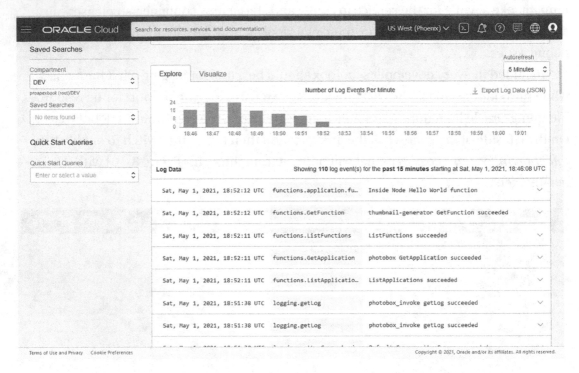

Figure 3-17. *Searching OCI logs with a unified user interface*

The UI has three useful features that will improve the debugging process:

1. Configure the source of logs and search filters and display them in chronological order. For example, include both the OCI Events and Oracle Functions logs to track the events from when an object emits an event till the serverless function exits.

2. Add an auto-refresh interval to continuously display the latest logs based on the search filters.

3. Download the logs in JSON format for external analysis.

In the Node.js runtime, any outputs to console, that is, `console.log()`, will be sent to the Function invocation logs.

Thumbnails Applied

Returning to the APEX application that we were working on earlier in the chapter, when the application was created, it had generated both a report and form page, pages 2 and 3, respectively. Most of the work we did center around page 3 and the mechanisms for uploading, retrieving, and deleting objects from the Object Storage using APEX PL/SQL APIs.

The next goal is to have a page to browse all the uploaded photos using a Cards Region. Each card would render the thumbnails that were automatically generated by the Oracle Functions application we had just deployed. Loading only thumbnails and not the original photo would greatly improve the performance and loading time on this page.

Before beginning to work on the APEX application, we need to update the *PhotosBucketAccessPolicy* policy to allow the IAM user, whose credentials are used in APEX, to have access to the bucket for thumbnails as well:

```
allow group PhotosBucketManagers to manage objects in compartment DEV where
any { target.bucket.name='photos', target.bucket.name='thumbnails' }
```

On page 2, we will replace the *Interactive Report* with a *Cards Region* to display our photo collection (Figure 3-18).

Figure 3-18. *Display the photo collection using the Cards Region*

Make the following changes to page 2:

- Rename the page and title to *Photo Collection*.

- Change the Interactive Reports to a Cards Region.

- The cards will display each photo's title, description, and a thumbnail preview. The URL for the image will use the apex_page.get_url function, like how we rendered the uploaded image in the photo details page. The difference is the bucket name that will be submitted to the application process. Update region's source to the following SQL query:

```
select
  photo_id
  , title
  , description
  , apex_page.get_url(
      p_application => :APP_ID
```

```
      , p_page => 0
      , p_request => 'APPLICATION_PROCESS=GET_OBJECT'
      , p_items => 'APP_PHOTO_ID,APP_BUCKET_NAME'
          || ',APP_CONTENT_DISPOSITION'
      , p_values => to_char(photo_id) || ','
          || :G_THUMBNAILS_BUCKET_NAME || ',inline'
    ) as image_url
from photo
```

- Change the following Cards Region attributes:

  - Set the layout to *Horizontal (Row)*.

  - Set the card's *Primary Key Column 1* to the column photo_id.

  - Map the card's title *Column* to the column title returned by the SQL query.

  - For the card's *Body*, toggle the *Advanced Formatting* and set the *HTML Expression* to

    &DESCRIPTION!RAW.

  - Set the card's *Media Source* to *Image URL* and then select to use the image_url column returned by the SQL query. Set the *Position* to *Body*, *Appearance* to *Auto*, and *Sizing* to *Fit*. Finally, set the *Image Description* to the title column returned by the SQL query.

  - Toggle the *Lazy Loading* for performance.

- Under the Cards Region's actions, add a button, and set the label to *View Details*. Set the link to open page 3 and set the primary key page item P3_PHOTO_ID with the record's primary key (column photo_id) value as returned in the source's SQL query. It should also clear the cache on page 3.

- Adjust the *CREATE* button so that it renders in the *Bottom of Region* position, and then save the changes.

When you are done with the changes, page 2 would somewhat like in Figure 3-19.

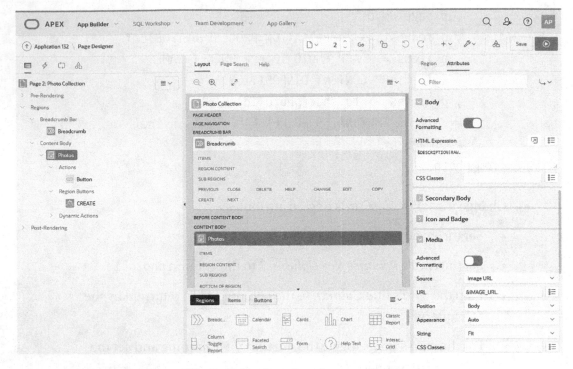

Figure 3-19. *Page 2 modified to display the photo collection*

Note   For the card's body, note that we are displaying the `description` column value without any filtering (`&DESCRIPTION!RAW.`). Ensure that the data entry fields are properly sanitized before saving the data as this is potential security risk. To allow HTML editing of the content, the page item type for `P3_DESCRIPTION` was changed from *Textarea* to *Rich Text Editor*.

Summary

The Oracle Cloud Infrastructure offers a wide variety of managed resources like the Object Storage, Events, Functions, and, more recently, *AI Services*, which can easily be integrated with APEX applications through the OCI REST APIs. For security, this Oracle requires these API requests to be digitally signed. Fortunately, APEX wraps the complexity of performing the authentication process with OCI Web Credentials, making it easy to work with OCI resources to build supplement what we otherwise have difficulty implementing in pure APEX and PL/SQL.

CHAPTER 4

Exposing Functionality with API Gateway

In the previous chapter, we learned about *Oracle Functions*, Oracle's serverless computing product offering on the *Oracle Cloud Infrastructure* (OCI), and how we can extend an *Oracle Application Express* (APEX) application's functionality, outside of the Oracle Database. With Oracle Functions, developers have a choice of several programming languages to implement a function without needing to manage the infrastructure that supports and hosts the application.

Note In future, the Oracle Database will support other scripting language such as *JavaScript* through its *Multilingual Engine* (MLE) feature.

To recap, Oracle Functions can be invoked by the following:

- Fn Project CLI

- OCI SDK and REST APIs

- A signed HTTP request to the function's invoke endpoint

- An Oracle Cloud service, for example, Events and API gateway

In Chapter 3, we focused on using events that were triggered by the OCI *Events* service when files are created, updated, or deleted from the OCI *Object Storage*. However, not every use case will involve files and events raised by the object storage.

Invoking functions using a CLI is not practical when integrating external services in APEX applications. And while Oracle offers a PL/SQL SDK to work with the OCI REST APIs, it is not readily available in all database installations. At the time of writing, packages that work with the web services are only available with the Oracle Autonomous Database.

© Adrian Png and Heli Helskyaho 2022
A. Png and H. Helskyaho, *Extending Oracle Application Express with Oracle Cloud Features*,
https://doi.org/10.1007/978-1-4842-8170-3_4

One possible option for APEX developers is to use the `APEX_WEB_SERVICE` package to call either the OCI REST API directly or the function's invoke endpoint. However, the latter involves signing the HTTP request, and again, this may not be possible to do in all database versions due to the public-key encryption algorithms required to sign these requests.

Fortunately, there is one approach that will make it relatively easier to invoke Oracle Functions, and that involves an intermediary OCI service. Using the *API gateway* service, developers can shield web service consumers from the backend implementation, for example, using Oracle Functions or running a *Node.js*® application on an *Oracle Kubernetes Engine* (OKE) cluster. Should the implementation change, there will be little or no impact to the client applications.

The API gateway is a virtual network appliance that is deployed within a *Virtual Cloud Network* (VCN) subnet that can either be public or private. As a regional service, it is fault-tolerant across availability domains and fault domains. And for that reason, API gateways can only be deployed on regional subnets.

An API gateway has an endpoint that receives HTTP requests and, based on the path and HTTP method, routes them to the assigned back end. A back end can be a HTTP service, an Oracle Functions, or a stock response. This mapping between a request path and a back end is defined as a route within a *Deployment*. Each API gateway contains one or more deployments, and each deployment may have one or more routes.

Deployments also allow developers to define policies for handling requests and responses, such as rate limits, Cross-Origin Resource Sharing (CORS) support, security, and manipulating HTTP header and query parameters.

Use Case Definition

For this chapter, we will create a simple APEX application to perform language translations from English to either Japanese or Spanish (see Figure 4-1). This application will demonstrate how an API gateway can be used together with Oracle Functions to add functionality to an APEX application.

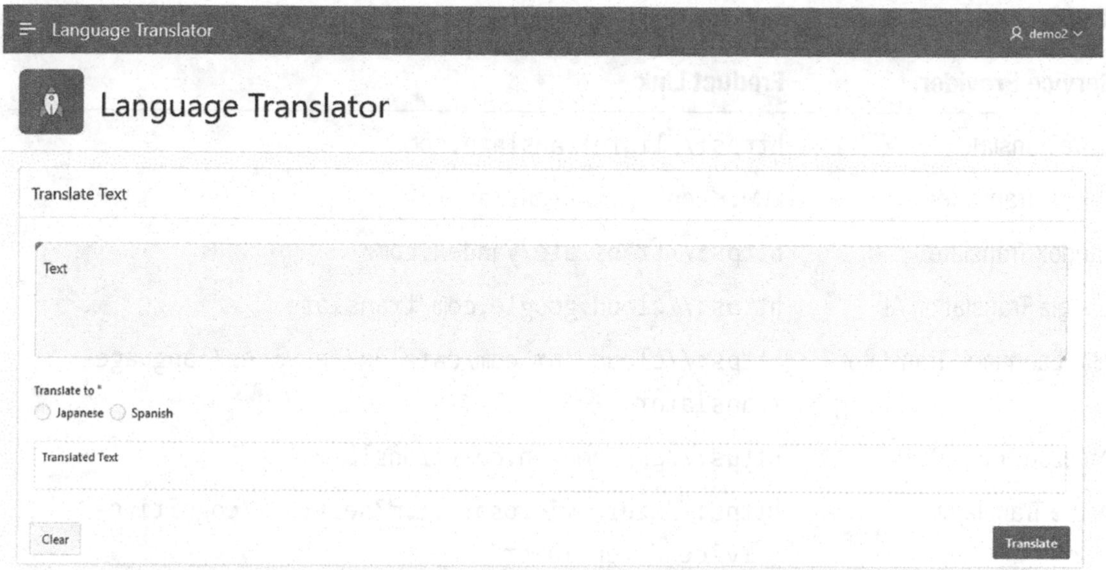

Figure 4-1. *An APEX application for translating languages*

Creating an application to perform language translations can be challenging. It often involves a combination of creating/collecting a sizable dictionary that maps the vocabulary of different language pairs and a large corpus of text written in these languages for training a machine learning model to perform *Natural Language Processing* (NLP).

There are several off -the-shelf solutions that are available today, and many are accessed using RESTful APIs. Some are free, but most are for free. Several major cloud vendors also provide these services as part of their services portfolio. Examples of these service providers are listed in Table 4-1.

Table 4-1. *Examples of vendors providing language translation services*

Service Provider	Product Link
LibreTranslate	https://libretranslate.com/
DeepL Translator	www.deepl.com/translator
Yandex Translate	https://translate.yandex.com/
Google Translation AI	https://cloud.google.com/translate
IBM Language Translator	https://cloud.ibm.com/catalog/services/language-translator
Amazon Translate	https://aws.amazon.com/translate/
Azure Translator	https://azure.microsoft.com/services/cognitive-services/translator/
iTranslate	https://itranslate.com/

APEX provides a comprehensive API to work with REST services, and it would be easy to subscribe and use any of the listed translation services. However, the client that we are building the proof of concept (PoC) for has a few other business requirements, and it will not be possible to use a publicly accessible service.

1. User-submitted text may contain confidential and/or personal identifiable information.

2. The company eventually wants to develop its own machine learning models and has hired a team of experts to implement an in-house service that will eventually be made available to business partners for a fee.

3. The APIs for accessing the language translation services must be well defined and resilient to the back-end implementation.

LibreTranslate is an open source machine translation software that provides options for self-hosting its web services and, thus, is a suitable candidate for our PoC. There is also an open source Node.js package called *Translate* (https://github.com/franciscop/translate) that works with its API.

Throughout this chapter, we will be deploying and using the following OCI services:

- API gateway

- APEX on an Autonomous Database

- Bastion

- Compute

- Networking

- Oracle Functions

The diagram in Figure 4-2 illustrates how these OCI resources will interact with each other in a secure environment.

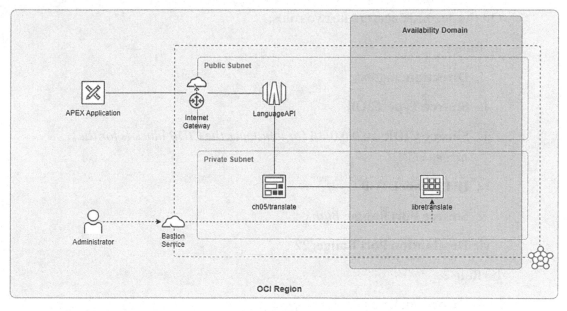

Figure 4-2. *Architecture of the desired environment*

Deploy the Language Translation Engine

To host the LibreTranslate services, we will deploy an OCI compute on a private subnet, install Docker (www.docker.com), and then deploy the software using a pre-build Docker image.

Note   The procedure for creating a VCN is provided in the previous chapter.

Before creating the new compute instance, in the VCN, create a Network Security Group (NSG) each for allowing TCP traffic over ports 22 (for SSH) and 8080 (for LibreTranslate web services).

1. Click the navigation menu, and then click *Networking*, followed by *Virtual Cloud Networks*.

2. Click the target VCN.

3. Scroll down, and then on the left, click *Network Security Groups*.

4. In the first step, provide the name for the NSG, for example, *NsgSshAccess*.

5. On the second page, create two rules:

    a. Rule 1:

        i.   **Direction**: Ingress

        ii. **Source Type**: CIDR

        iii. **Source CIDR**: 10.0.0.0/16 *(or whatever the CIDR block is for the target VCN)*

        iv. **IP Protocol**: TCP

        v.   **Source Port Range**: *Blank*

        vi. **Destination Port Range**: 22

    b. Rule 2:

        i.   **Direction**: Egress

        ii. **Source Type**: CIDR

        iii. **Source CIDR**: 0.0.0.0/0

        iv. **IP Protocol**: All Protocols

6. Click *Create*.

7. Repeat the procedure from step 3 for allowing access to the LibreTranslate web service. Create a NSG named *NsgWebApplications* and configure the first rule to allow ingress TCP traffic from port 8080.

Next, create the compute instance:

1. Begin by navigating to the Instances page. Click the navigation menu, click *Compute*, and then click *Instances*.

2. Click *Create Instance*.

   a. Choose the desired placement and shape, but select *Oracle Linux 7.9* for its image.

   b. Expand the network settings and ensure a private subnet is selected.

   c. Check the option *Use network security groups to control traffic*, and then assign the NSGs *NsgSshAccess* and *NsgPublicWebServices* (Figure 4-3).

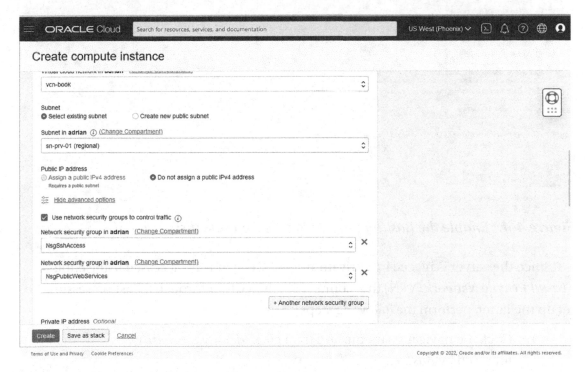

Figure 4-3. *Assign the required Network Security Groups to the new compute instance*

   d. For the boot volume, the minimum size is more than sufficient.

   e. Generate a SSH key pair and upload the public key.

    f. Click *Show advanced options*, and then under the *Oracle Cloud Agent* tab, ensure that the *Bastion* plug-in is checked (Figure 4-4).

3. Click *Create*.

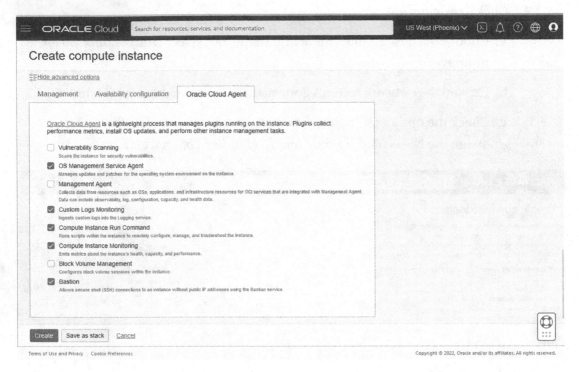

Figure 4-4. *Enable the Bastion plug-in for the compute instance*

Since the server is placed in a private subnet, it can only be accessed using either a *Virtual Private Network* (VPN) that connects to the VCN or through a Bastion session. To set up the latter, perform the following steps:

1. Click the navigation menu, and then click *Identity & Security*, followed by *Bastion*.

2. Click *Create bastion*.

3. Give the bastion a name and then select the target VCN and subnet. This should be a public subnet (Figure 4-5). For the *CIDR block allowlist*, specify a subnet or enter 0.0.0.0/0 to allow connections from anywhere on the Internet.

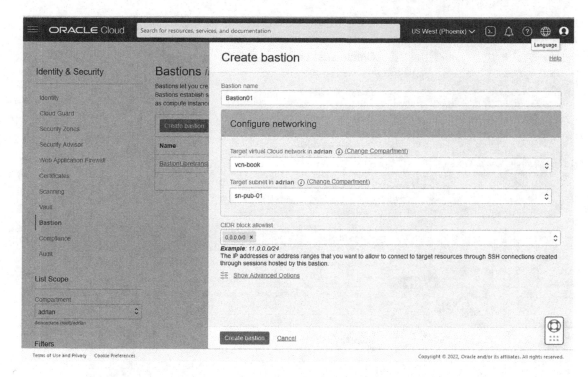

Figure 4-5. *Create a bastion and place it in a public subnet within the target VCN*

4. Click *Create bastion*.

5. After the bastion has been provisioned successfully, click the bastion to go to its details page.

6. Click *Create session*.

7. Enter session details (Figure 4-6) using the following:

    a. **Session type**: Managed SSH session

    b. **Session name**: Any name

    c. **Username**: opc

    d. **Compute instance in compartment**: *The target instance*

    e. Upload the SSH public key that will be used to connect to the host.

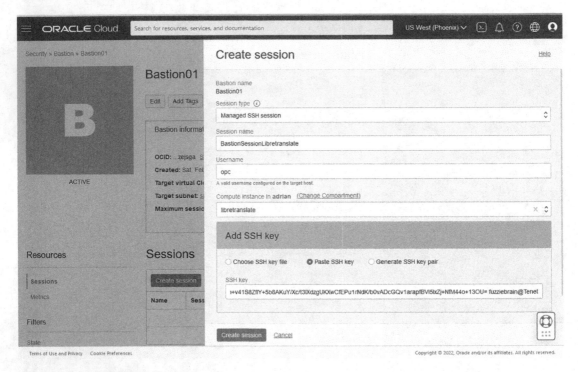

Figure 4-6. *Create a session to access the compute instance for deploying LibreTranslate*

8. Once the session has been created, click the button with three vertical dots indicated by the red-colored box in Figure 4-7, and then click *Copy SSH command*.

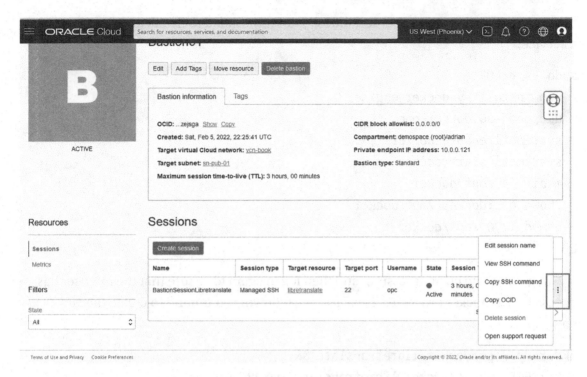

Figure 4-7. *Access options to get the required SSH command to connect to the compute instance*

The SSH command provided is in the following format:

```
ssh -i <privateKey> -o ProxyCommand="ssh -i <privateKey>
-W %h:%p -p 22 ocid1.bastionsession.oc1.phx.
amaaaaaafy4s5yqazggb6krqvlzh2v3atyblc5f4xexwyseqpsqs5uda3bya@host.bastion.
us-phoenix-1.oci.oraclecloud.com" -p 22 opc@10.0.1.133
```

Replace `<privateKey>` with the path to the SSH private key, for example:

```
ssh -i ~/.ssh/id_rsa -o ProxyCommand="ssh -i ~/.ssh/
id_rsa -W %h:%p -p 22 ocid1.bastionsession.oc1.phx.
amaaaaaafy4s5yqazggb6krqvlzh2v3atyblc5f4xexwyseqpsqs5uda3bya@host.bastion.
us-phoenix-1.oci.oraclecloud.com" -p 22 opc@10.0.1.133
```

Once logged in as user *opc*, run the following command to install and run Docker as a service:

```
sudo -s <<EOF
  yum install -y docker-engine
  usermod -aG docker opc
  systemctl enable docker
  systemctl start docker
  mkdir -p /opt/docker
  chown opc:docker /opt/docker
  chmod 2770 /opt/docker
EOF
```

Log out of the current session, and then log in again to ensure that the *opc* user has access to the Docker processes. Next, run the following command to create the run.sh script:

```
mkdir -p /opt/docker/libretranslate && \
cat <<EOF > /opt/docker/libretranslate/run.sh
#!/usr/bin/env bash

docker run -d -p 8080:5000 --name libretranslate \\
  --restart unless-stopped \\
  libretranslate/libretranslate
EOF
chmod a+x /opt/docker/libretranslate/run.sh
```

Finally, run the container using the created script:

```
/opt/docker/libretranslate/run.sh
```

Docker will pull the image, and then create and run the container. Once the script has executed successfully, run the following to check its status:

```
docker ps
```

Docker will display all the running containers and the container named *libretranslate* should be running and a port mapping from 8080 to 5000 exists.

Oracle Functions for Language Translation

The next step in setting up the language translation system is to deploy a serverless function that will process the HTTP request payload and return the translated text. Both the HTTP request and response payloads will be in JSON.

Sample request body:

```
{ "text": "Good morning" }
```

Sample response body:

```
{ "translatedText": "おはようございます" }
```

Details about setting up the OCI tenancy for Oracle Functions were discussed in Chapter 4. Make sure that your tenancy and developer's workstation have been configured correctly before continuing with deploying the *translate* function. The following is a quick checklist:

- On the OCI tenancy:

  - Required *Identity and Access Management* (IAM) user, group, and policies created or defined

  - VCN and target subnet created

- On the developer's workstation:

  - Docker, OCI CLI, and Fn Project CLI installed

  - API keys generated and registered on the OCI

  - OCI profile and Fn context configured

The serverless function will be deployed using the following files:

```
translate
├── func.js
├── func.yaml
├── package.json
└── package-lock.json
```

To recap, the func.js file contains the Node.js code that implements the *Function Development Kit* (FDK) handler code that is called each time the function is invoked.

The func.yaml file contains the metadata about the function, and the package.json file contains the Node.js application's metadata, including its dependencies.

Set the environment variable SUBNET_OCID using the target subnet's OCID that you can get through the OCI Console. Then, create the Oracle Functions application using the Fn Project CLI command:

```
fn create app ch05 --annotation \
  oracle.com/oci/subnetIds=[\"$SUBNET_OCID\"]
```

From the project's root directory, deploy the function:

```
fn deploy -v --app ch05
```

The Fn Project CLI will build the Docker image, deploy it to the OCI *Container Registry* (OCIR), and then register the functions. Once that's completed, run the following command to set the LIBRE_SERVER_URL parameter. Substitute the placeholder COMPUTE_INSTANCE_ID with the IP address of the compute instance where LibreTranslate has been deployed to.

```
fn config function ch05 translate \
  LIBRE_SERVER_URL http://<COMPUTE_INSTANCE_IP>:8080/translate
```

API Gateway for Language Translation

The last OCI resource to create and configure is the API gateway. To recap, the API gateway requires a VCN subnet to be assigned to. If the resource is to be accessed *via* the Internet, then it must be attached to a public subnet. This must be decided before it is created and cannot be changed thereafter.

There are also security-related tasks to be performed before creating the resource and will be discussed next.

IAM Policy

For the API gateway to be able to invoke Oracle Functions, the service must be granted the necessary permissions using an IAM policy statement. Either create a new policy or add the required statement to an existing policy.

The following statement is required:

```
Allow any-user to use functions-family in compartment <COMPARTMENT_NAME>
where all {request.principal.type= 'ApiGateway', request.resource.
compartment.id = '<COMPARTMENT_OCID>'}
```

Replace the placeholder COMPARTMENT_NAME with the name of the compartment where the Oracle Functions has been deployed to. And for COMPARTMENT_OCID, replace it with the OCID of the compartment where the API gateway is located.

Network Security Group

The API gateway is always associated with a VCN subnet, and the subnet can be either private or public. Regardless, the resource will require network security rules that permit TCP traffic on port 443, a standard port used for secure web traffic.

Create a NSG with the following rules:

1. Rule 1:

    a. **Direction**: Ingress

    b. **Source Type**: CIDR

    c. **Source CIDR**: 0.0.0.0/0

    d. **IP Protocol**: TCP

    e. **Source Port Range**: *Blank*

    f. **Destination Port Range**: 443

2. Rule 2:

    a. **Direction**: Egress

    b. **Source Type**: CIDR

    c. **Source CIDR**: 0.0.0.0/0

    d. **IP Protocol**: All Protocols

API Gateway

With the dependent OCI resources created and configured, we are now ready to create an API gateway to expose the Oracle Functions as a REST endpoint.

1. Click the navigation menu and then click *Developer Services*,
   followed by *Gateways* under the section *API Management*.

2. On the *Gateways* page, click *Create Gateway*.

3. Provide the following information (see Figure 4-8) for the new
   gateway:

   a. **Name**: LanguageAPI

   b. **Type**: Public

   c. **Compartment**: *The compartment name where the gateway will be
      deployed to.*

   d. **Virtual Cloud Network**: *Select the compartment and then choose
      the VCN that the gateway will belong to.*

   e. **Subnet**: *Select the compartment and then the subnet within the
      VCN that the gateway will attach to.*

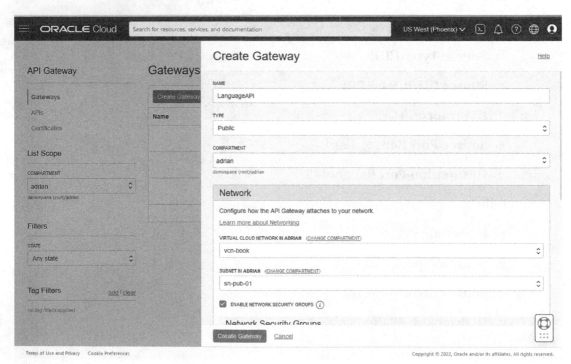

Figure 4-8. *Provide the required information for creating a gateway*

4. The endpoint will be exposed over a certain network port, and the necessary security rules will need to be applied to the gateway before it can communicate with client applications. Specify these rules using the network security group that was created earlier. Check the option *Enable Network Security Groups* and then choose the NSG to assign (Figure 4-9).

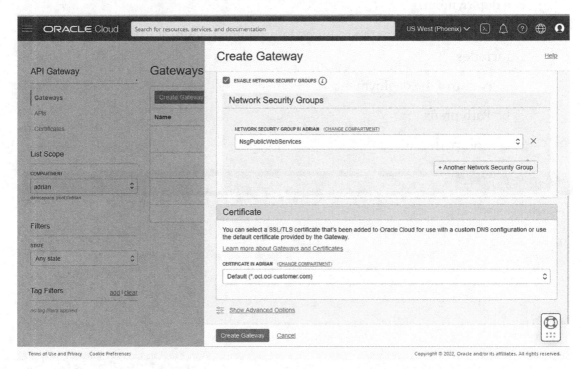

Figure 4-9. *Assign a network security group so that the API gateway endpoint can be accessed by client applications over the network*

Note   API gateways can be accessed using custom domains. However, a compatible and valid SSL/TLS certificate must be assigned to the API gateway. After the resource has been created, add a DNS "A" record for the custom domain and point it to the IP address that has been assigned to the API gateway.

---

5. Click *Create Gateway*.

6. Once the API gateway has been created successfully, on its details page, scroll down and click the *Deployments* link that you can find on the left side of the page, under the section *Resources*.

7. Click *Create Deployment* to launch the multipage wizard to create a deployment.

8. In the first step, enter the required information (Figure 4-10) that includes

   a. Name of the deployment

   b. Path prefix

   c. Compartment

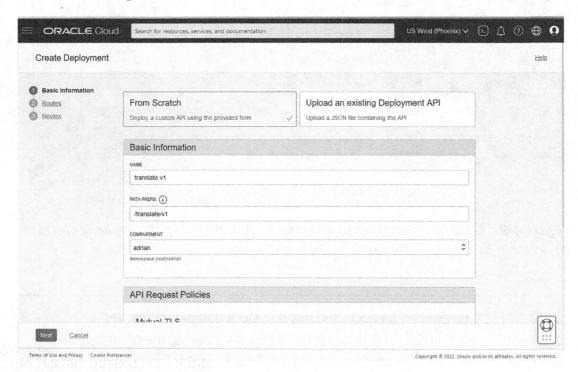

Figure 4-10. *Basic information required to create a deployment*

Tip   There are no strict rules on how the deployment should be named. However, I would recommend giving it a name that describes plainly what its intent is and consider even including a version number. I would also do the same with the path prefix. This approach will allow us to create and deploy a new version/implementation while continuing to support older ones till they are no longer used by clients.

9. Click *Next* to move on to the next step.

10. Enter the following information for *Route 1* (see Figure 4-11):

    a. **Path**: /japanese

    b. **Methods**: POST

    c. **Type**: Oracle Functions

    d. **Application**: *Select the compartment that the function is in and then the application.*

    e. **Function Name**: *Select the function we had deployed earlier.*

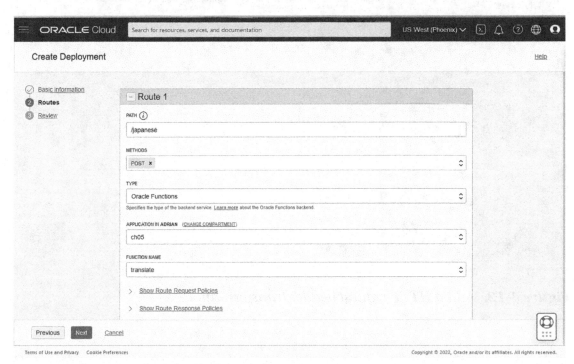

Figure 4-11. *Define the routes for the deployment*

11. Click the link *Show Route Request Policies* to expand the options for manipulating or validating the HTTP request properties. These include the CORS policy, header variables, query parameters, and request body.

12. For each route, specify a header transform to set the variable X-TO_LANG that will be passed on to the serverless function. Click the *Add* button, and then provide the following details (see Figure 4-12):

    a. **Action**: Set

    b. **Behavior**: Overwrite

    c. **Header Name**: X-TO_LANG

    d. **Values**: ja

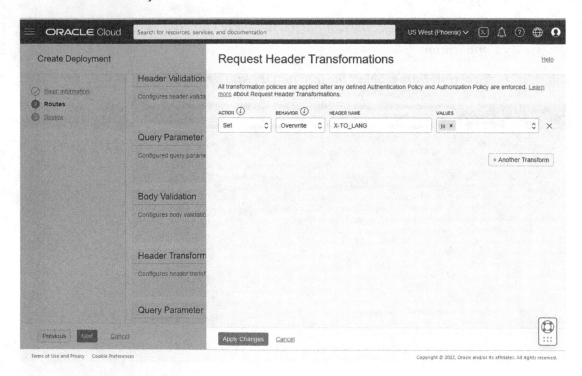

Figure 4-12. *Add a HTTP request header transformation*

13. Click *Apply Changes*.

14. Repeat steps 10 to 13 to create *Route 2*. Set the route's path to `/spanish` and `es` for the `X-TO_LANG` header value.

15. Once all the routes have been defined, click *Next* to proceed to the final step.

16. Review all values entered and then click *Create*.

Once the deployment is completed, return to the API gateway deployment's details page, and click *Show* to reveal the endpoint's URL (Figure 4-13). To call the serverless function through the API gateway, concatenate the relevant route's path. For example, to translate text from English to Japanese, the complete URL to send a `POST` request to is in the following format:

```
https://<API_GATEWAY_HOSTNAME>/<DEPLOYMENT_PATH_PREFIX>/<ROUTE_PATH>
```

Figure 4-13. *Obtain the endpoint URL from the deployment's details page*

For example, given the following details:

- **API_GATEWAY_HOSTNAME**: gnz7v3tbeywrr4xdbxaasa7cim.apigateway.us-phoenix-1.oci.customer-oci.com

- **DEPLOYMENT_PATH_PREFIX**: /translate/v1

- **ROUTE_PATH**: /japanese

The URL to call would be

```
https://gnz7v3tbeywrr4xdbxaasa7cim.apigateway.us-phoenix-1.oci.customer-oci.com/translate/v1/japanese
```

Note   As mentioned earlier, the API_GATEWAY_HOSTNAME could be a custom domain; however, please ensure that a valid SSL/TLS certificate is assigned to the API gateway and a DNS "A" record added to map the domain to the IP address that has been provisioned for the API gateway.

Calling the API Gateway from APEX

Once deployed, the API gateway endpoint is simply a REST endpoint that APEX developers can call in PL/SQL, using the package APEX_WEB_SERVICE. The API gateway shields APEX from needing to implement code to authenticate and invoke the Oracle Functions endpoints. The IAM policy introduced earlier authorizes the API gateway to invoke the function on the REST client's behalf.

The Oracle Functions function that we have deployed expects the following:

- A request payload that contains a JSON object with one attribute, text, with the value containing the text in English to be translated

- A HTTP header variable, X_TO-LANG, with a two-letter value that defines the target language that LibreTranslate will translate the text to

The API gateway relays the payload sent by APEX and injects any HTTP header variables and query parameters, required by the function. The default Oracle Functions function handler then makes this available through the `input` and `ctx` parameters.

```
async function functionHandler(input, ctx) {
  ...
}
```

Though it is documented (https://github.com/fnproject/docs/tree/master/fdks/fdk-node) that the HTTP header variables can be accessed by using the code `ctx.protocol.header(key)`, the API gateway appears to populate the `ctx` object differently. By enabling OCI Logging for the function and some debugging code, it is possible to identify the location of the injected HTTP header variable. Here, we find `X-TO_LANG` can be referenced by accessing the `ctx._headers` array and using the key `Fn-Http-H-X-To_Lang`.

```
if (ctx._headers["Fn-Http-H-X-To-Lang"]) {
  toLanguage = ctx._headers["Fn-Http-H-X-To-Lang"].toString();
}
```

With that understanding of how API gateway and Oracle Functions work together, we are now ready to create the APEX application and components to consume its services:

1. Create a page (Figure 4-14) and add three page items:

   - **P1_TEXT**: A text field for entering the text in English that needs to be translated.

   - **P1_TO_LANG**: A radio button group for setting the target language that is set to values "ja" and "es" when Japanese and Spanish are selected, respectively.

   - **P1_TRANSLATED_TEXT**: A display-only page item that renders the translated text in the selected language.

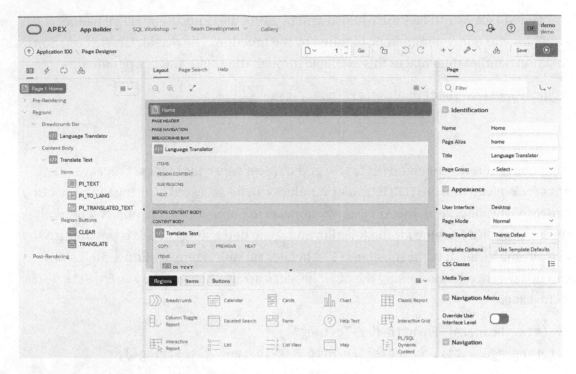

Figure 4-14. *Create an APEX page for the Language Translator application*

2. Create two buttons, one for submitting the page and another for resetting the page.

3. Create a page process (Figure 4-15) that only executes when the *TRANSLATE* button is clicked. Configure it to execute the following PL/SQL code:

```
declare
  c_rest_url constant varchar2(200) :=
    'https://**.apigateway.**.oci.customer-oci.com/translate/v1';

  l_response clob;
begin
  l_response := apex_web_service.make_rest_request(
    p_http_method => 'POST'
  , p_url => c_rest_url || '/'
      || case :P1_TO_LANG
           when 'es' then 'spanish'
```

```
              else 'japanese'
          end
  , p_body => json_object('text' value :P1_TEXT)
);

if apex_web_service.g_status_code = 200 then
  :P1_TRANSLATED_TEXT := json_value(l_response
    ,'$.translatedText');
else
  raise_application_error(-20001
    , 'Error invoking service. HTTP status code: '
        || apex_web_service.g_status_code);
  apex_debug.error(l_response);
end if;
end;
```

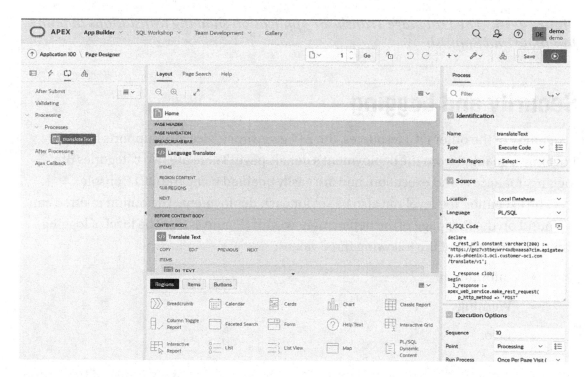

Figure 4-15. *Create a page process to invoke the language translation REST service and process its response*

Save the page and run it. Enter some text in English, select the desired language to translate to, and then click *Translate*. Figure 4-16 shows text translated in both languages.

Figure 4-16. *The Language Translator application showing translations in both Japanese and Spanish*

Security and Logging

Like many of the other OCI resources, the API gateway service also supports logging. Logging is enabled from the deployment's details page. There are two categories of logging, for access and execution, and are easily enabled using the OCI Console.

The execution log level can also be set for each deployment. The option to do so can be found on the first page of the deployment wizard (Figure 4-17). The level of logging can be set to either of the following three values:

- Information
- Warning
- Error

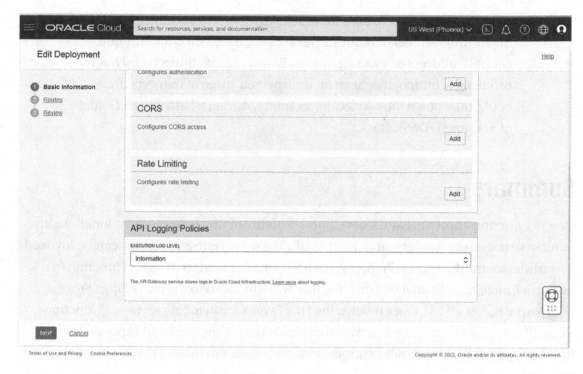

Figure 4-17. *Set the execution log level from the deployment wizard*

On the same page, there are options to set the following security features:

- **Mutual-TLS (mTLS)**: When enabled, REST clients must present an SSL/TLS that the API gateway will validate. Deployments may optionally restrict access to specific *Subject Alternative Names* (SANs) or *Common Name* (CN). When enabled, a custom Certificate Authority (CA) bundle that contains the CA certificates that signed the client's certificate must be added to the API gateway.

- **Authentication**: The API gateway service supports using a separate Oracle Functions function, or JSON Web Tokens (JWTs), to manage access to the endpoint.

- **CORS**: Cross-Origin Resource Sharing policies are commonly used to prevent code from a different origin to make requests. The deployment can specify the allowed origins, methods, and headers.

137

- **Rate Limiting**: This feature allows deployments to specify the maximum number of requests per second, based on either unique client IP address or as an aggregate. Enforcing rate limits could help protect the endpoint against an unexpected surge of requests that could take down the service, for example, during a Distributed Denial of Service (DDoS) attack.

Summary

Oracle Functions provides APEX developers with the ability to implement functionality otherwise not easily implemented in PL/SQL. These serverless functions can be invoked by various methods, and in Chapter 3, we used Oracle Events to trigger a function to perform image transformations on a file that was uploaded to the OCI Object Storage.

However, not all use cases involve the OCI Events for invoking serverless functions. The API gateway is a managed service that wraps these functions and exposes them as a REST endpoint. It also provides various security features to protect these services against malicious attacks.

Oracle Machine Learning in Autonomous Database

Oracle Machine Learning (OML) harnesses the massive power of a database to process data for the machine learning process, without the hassle of moving the data outside the database, or risking the data security. OML supports three programming languages: SQL (OML4SQL), R (OML4R), and Python (OML4Py). SQL and Python are automatically available in an Oracle Autonomous Database via their APIs. Soon, also R will most likely be available. Currently R is only available on Oracle Database, not on Autonomous Database.

To use the Oracle Machine Learning in OCI, you need an Oracle Cloud Infrastructure (OCI) account and an Oracle Autonomous Database. You also need a user with Oracle Machine Learning privileges.

Setting Up the Oracle Machine Learning Environment

To be able to use the OML, you need an *OCI Account*, an *Autonomous Database*, and an *OCI User*. OML does not require a separate license, so an Oracle Cloud Free Tier account is enough for testing the service. If you do not have an OCI account, go to `www.oracle.com/cloud/free/` and create a Free Tier account following the instructions. Log in to the account.

Creating an Autonomous Database

If you do not have an Autonomous Database yet, you need to create it. If you already have an Autonomous Database created, you can skip this.

© Adrian Png and Heli Helskyaho 2022
A. Png and H. Helskyaho, *Extending Oracle Application Express with Oracle Cloud Features*,
https://doi.org/10.1007/978-1-4842-8170-3_5

If you want to have a separate Compartment for the Autonomous Database, go to the navigation menu in OCI Console, select *Identity & Security* and *Compartment*. Click *Create Compartment*. Define a *Name* for the Compartment, and a *Description*, as shown in Figure 5-1. Select the parent compartment from the *Parent Compartment* list. Click *Create Compartment*.

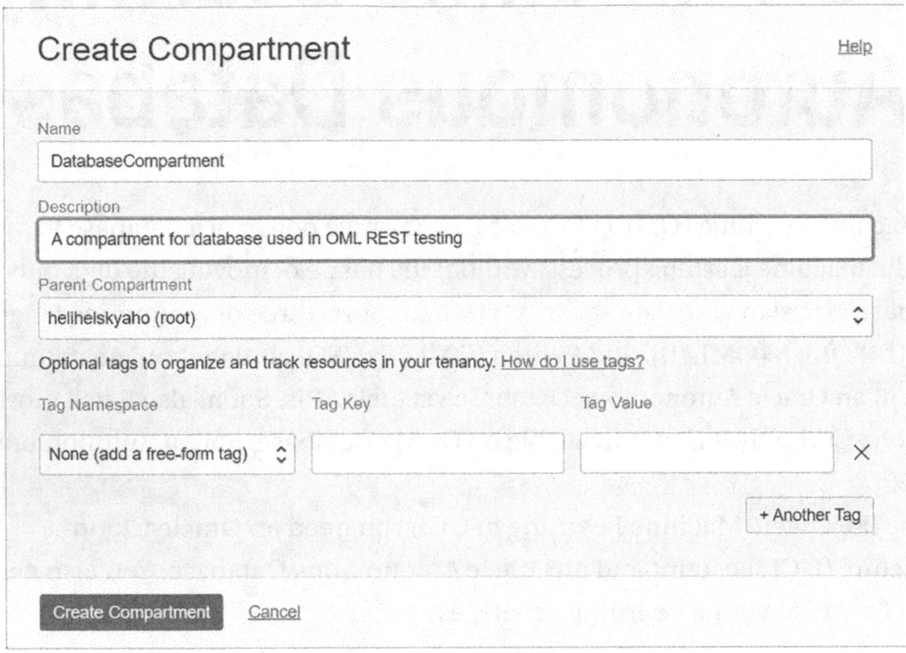

Figure 5-1. *Creating a compartment*

Then create the database. Select *Oracle Database* from the OCI navigation menu, and then select *Autonomous Database*. Select the *Compartment* you want to use for this Autonomous Database, as shown in Figure 5-2. Then, click *Create Autonomous Database*.

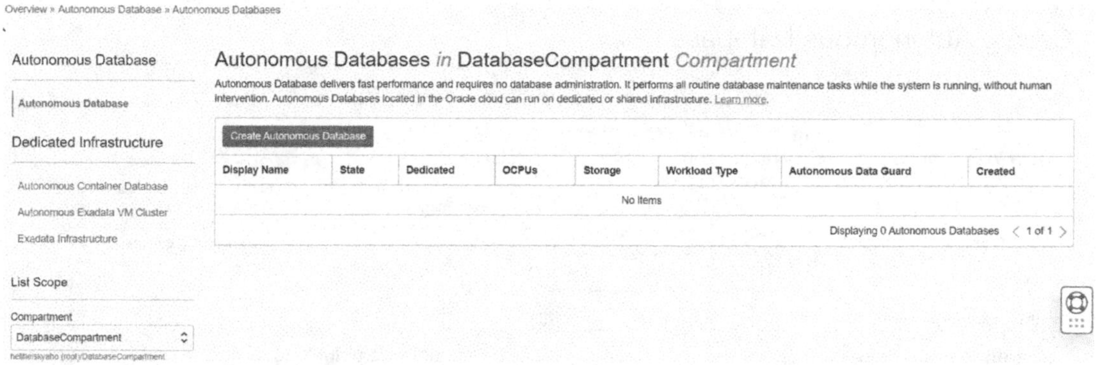

Figure 5-2. *Selecting a compartment and creating an autonomous database*

First, you need to provide the basic information for the Autonomous Database as seen in Figure 5-3. Verify that the *Compartment* is correct. If it is not, change it by selecting the correct Compartment from the list. Oracle suggests a *Display name* and a *Database name* automatically, but you can change one or both of them as you prefer.

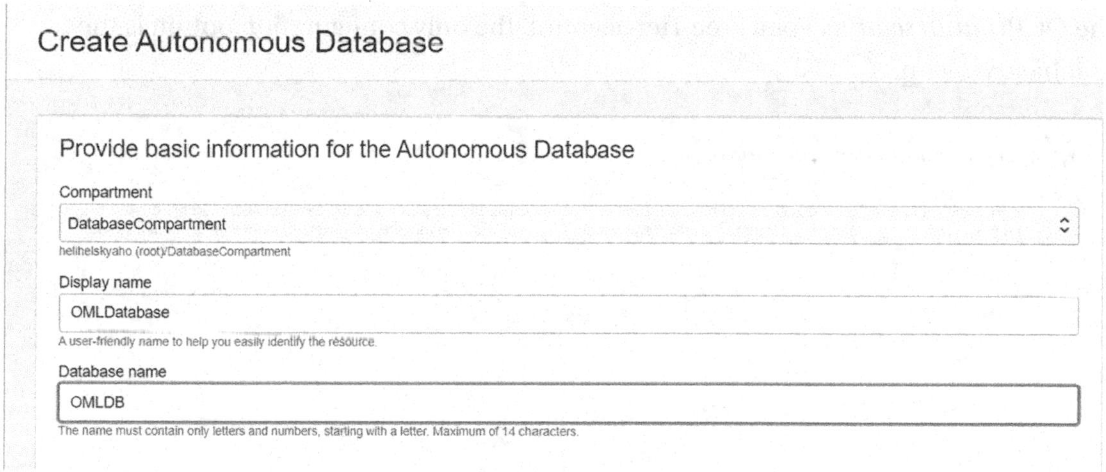

Figure 5-3. *Basic information for creating an autonomous database*

Then, choose the *workload type* (Figure 5-4) and the *deployment type*. Select *Transaction Processing* and *Shared Infrastructure*. If you prefer creating an autonomous database for data warehousing, select *Data Warehouse* as the workload type.

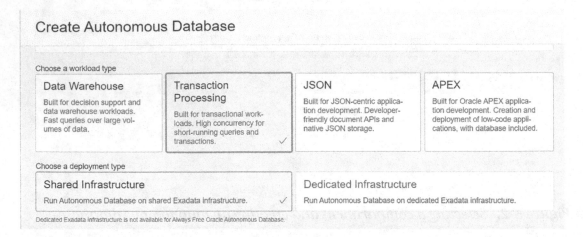

Figure 5-4. *Choosing the workload type and the deployment type for an autonomous database*

Then, configure the database as shown in Figure 5-5. Select the *database version*. If you are using a paid account, define the *OCPU count*, the *Storage* size, and maybe enable the *OCPU auto scaling*. For a Free Tier account, the only configuration option is the database version.

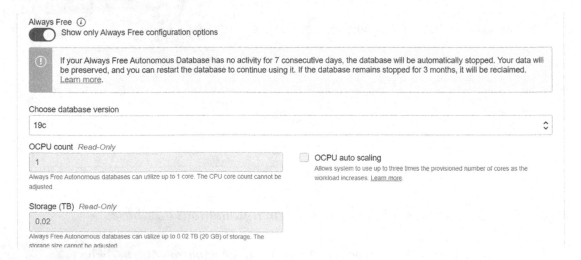

Figure 5-5. *Choosing the database version, OCPU count and storage size of an autonomous database*

Then, define the password for the admin user (Admin) of the database as seen in Figure 5-6.

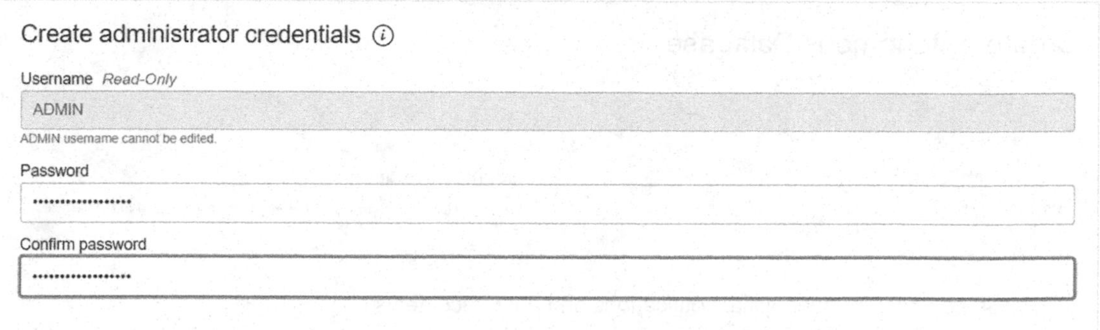

Create administrator credentials ⓘ

Username *Read-Only*

ADMIN

ADMIN username cannot be edited.

Password

••••••••••••••••••

Confirm password

••••••••••••••••••

Figure 5-6. *Define the password for the admin user of the autonomous database*

Choose the network access as shown in Figure 5-7.

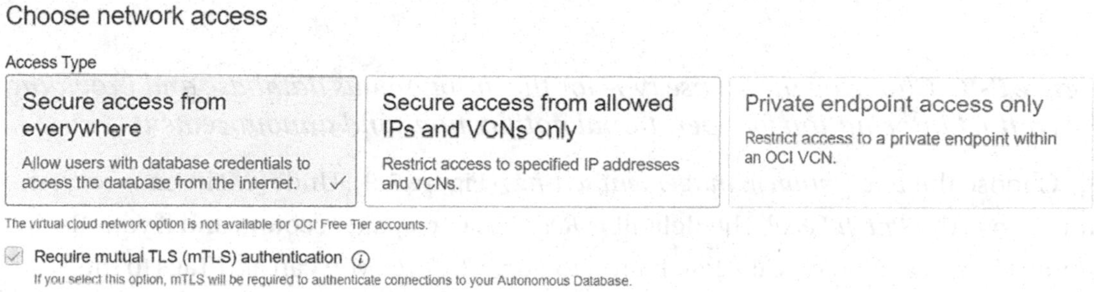

Choose network access

Access Type

Secure access from everywhere

Allow users with database credentials to access the database from the internet. ✓

Secure access from allowed IPs and VCNs only

Restrict access to specified IP addresses and VCNs.

Private endpoint access only

Restrict access to a private endpoint within an OCI VCN.

The virtual cloud network option is not available for OCI Free Tier accounts.

☑ Require mutual TLS (mTLS) authentication ⓘ
If you select this option, mTLS will be required to authenticate connections to your Autonomous Database.

Figure 5-7. *Defining the network access for the autonomous database*

Choose the *license type* and define a *contact email address* for notifications or announcements as shown in Figure 5-8. Click *Show Advanced Options*.

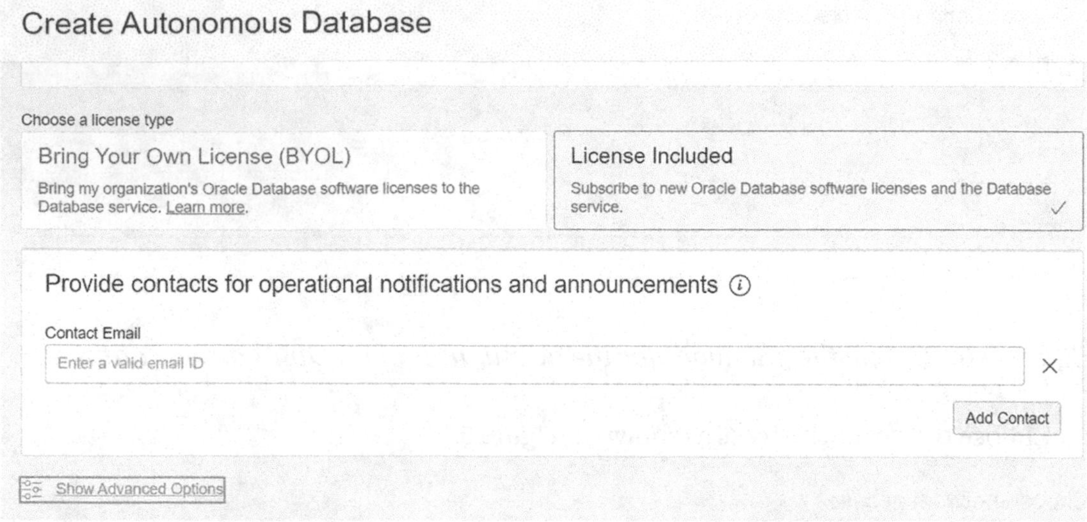

Create Autonomous Database

Choose a license type

Bring Your Own License (BYOL)

Bring my organization's Oracle Database software licenses to the Database service. Learn more.

License Included

Subscribe to new Oracle Database software licenses and the Database service. ✓

Provide contacts for operational notifications and announcements ⓘ

Contact Email

Enter a valid email ID   ✕

Add Contact

⊞ Show Advanced Options

Figure 5-8. *Choosing the license type for the autonomous database and providing the contact information for operational notifications and announcement*

Choose the *Encryption management settings* (Figure 5-9). Under Maintenance, you can choose the *Patch Level*. The default is *Regular*. For a paid account, and if your Region support it, you can change the Patch level to *Early*. In *Tags*, you can add Tags to the database. Click *Create Autonomous Database*.

Create Autonomous Database

Contact Email

Enter a valid email ID   ✕

Add Contact

⊞ Hide Advanced Options

| Encryption Key | Maintenance | Tags |

Choose encryption management settings
◉ Encrypt using Oracle-managed keys
    Oracle manages encryption.
◯ Encrypt using customer-managed keys
    You must have access to a valid encryption key. Learn more.

Create Autonomous Database   Cancel

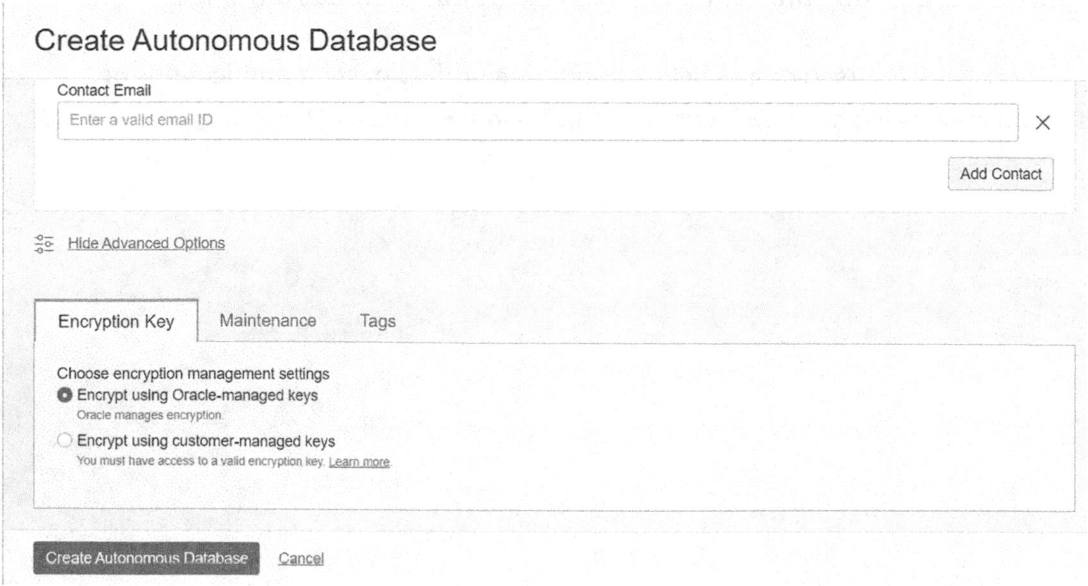

Figure 5-9. *Defining the encryption management settings, maintenance preferences, and adding tags if needed for the autonomous database*

The database has now been provisioned. The *Lifecycle status* is Provisioning and the color of the ATP logo is yellow until the database has been fully provisioned. Then the color changes to green and the Lifecycle status to Available (Figure 5-10).

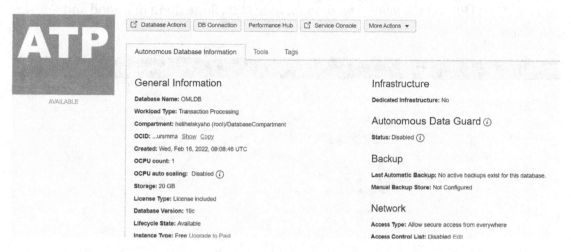

Figure 5-10. *Details page for an autonomous database*

Obtaining the URLs Needed for Using the OML Service

To be able to use the Oracle Machine Learning Services, you need the correct URL. Click *Service Console*. Log in using Admin as the user and the password you created earlier as the password. Navigate to *Development* as shown in Figure 5-11.

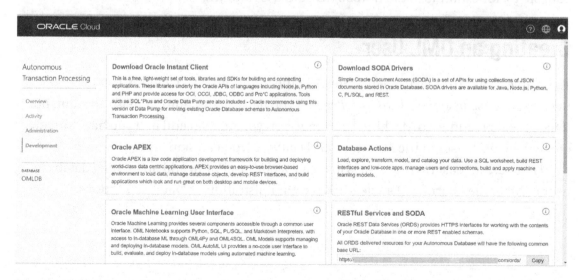

Figure 5-11. *Development section of an autonomous database*

Scroll down to *Oracle Machine Learning RESTful services* (Figure 5-12). Copy the URLs of *Use this URL to obtain a REST authentication token for OML-provided REST APIs*, *All OML Services REST APIs use the following common base URL*, and *All embedded Python REST APIs use the following common base URL*. Store them in a good and safe place.

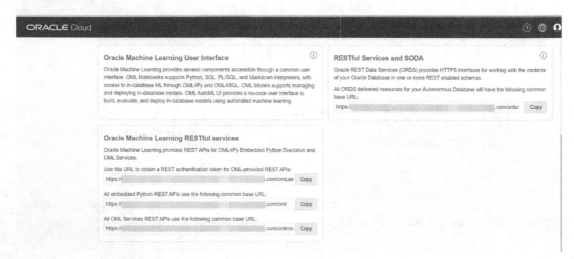

Figure 5-12. *Obtaining URLs needed for using Oracle Machine Learning*

To get the URL for the OML user interface, click *Oracle Machine Learning User Interface* (Figure 5-12) and save the URL. You will need this, if you want to use the OML console to, for example, build notebooks or to use AutoML.

Creating an OML User

To be able to use the OML functionalities in the Autonomous Database, you need to have a database user with *OML privileges*. If you have an existing database account, but it has not been added to Machine Learning, then you need to add it. If you have already created an OML user in the Autonomous Database, you can skip this.

There are at least two easy ways to create a new user or to add an existing database user to Machine Learning: Oracle ML User Administration or Database Actions.

Creating a User Using Oracle ML User Administration

In the *Autonomous Database Details* page (Figure 5-10), select the *Tools* tab
(Figure 5-13).

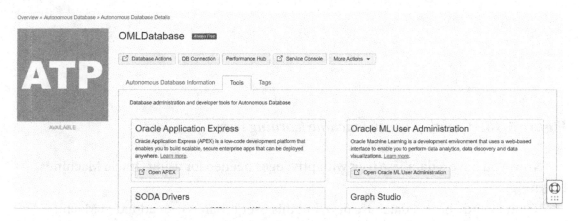

Figure 5-13. *Tools tab on Autonomous Details page*

Navigate to *Oracle ML User Administration* and click *Open Oracle ML
Administration*.

Sign in using your Admin credentials. Click *Create* (Figure 5-14).

Figure 5-14. *The Oracle Machine Learning User Administration page*

Define (Figure 5-15) the *Username*, optionally the *First* and *Last Name*, and *Email
Address*. If you want to define the password now, disable the *Generate password and
email account details to user. User will be required to reset the password on first sign in.*
Click *Create*.

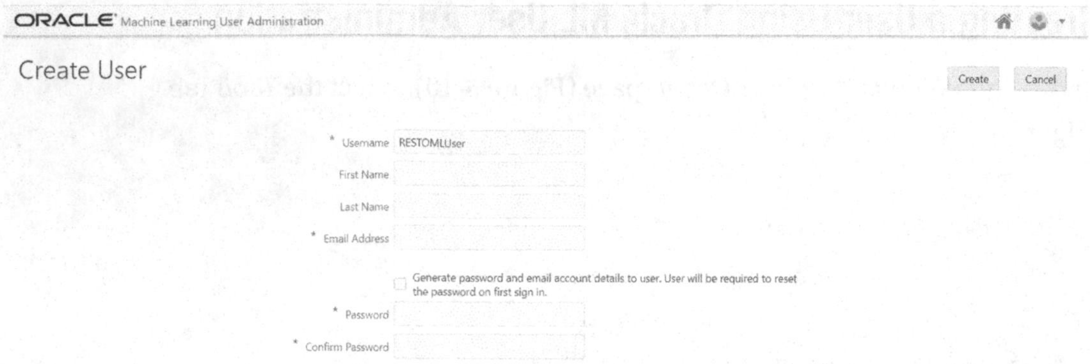

Figure 5-15. *Creating a new machine learning user*

Now, you have a database user with privileges needed for using Oracle Machine Learning.

If you already have a database user, but this user has not been added to Machine Learning, enable *Show All Users* on the *Users* page (Figure 5-14). The *Role* for this user is *None*. Select the user from the list by clicking the Username. Then edit the user data on the *Edit User* page seen in Figure 5-16 and click *Save*. Now the database user is able to use machine learning. The role of this user is now *Developer* in the list of users.

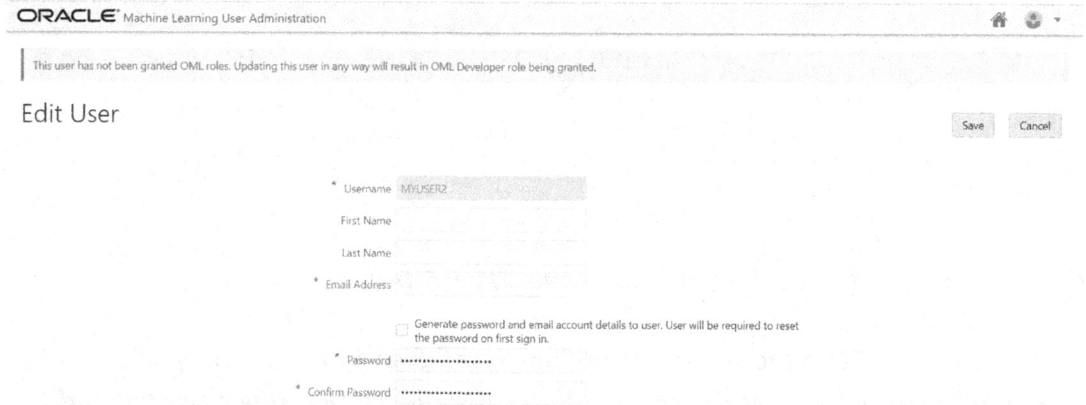

Figure 5-16. *Adding privileges for an existing user to use Oracle Machine Learning*

Creating a User Using Database Actions

Another way to create a user or add the user to machine learning is to use the Database Actions. On the *Autonomous Database Details* page (Figure 5-13), select *Database Actions*. Log in using the Admin credentials. Select *Database Users*. If you do not have a database user created yet, click *Create User*. Insert the data needed for creating a user (Figure 5-17).

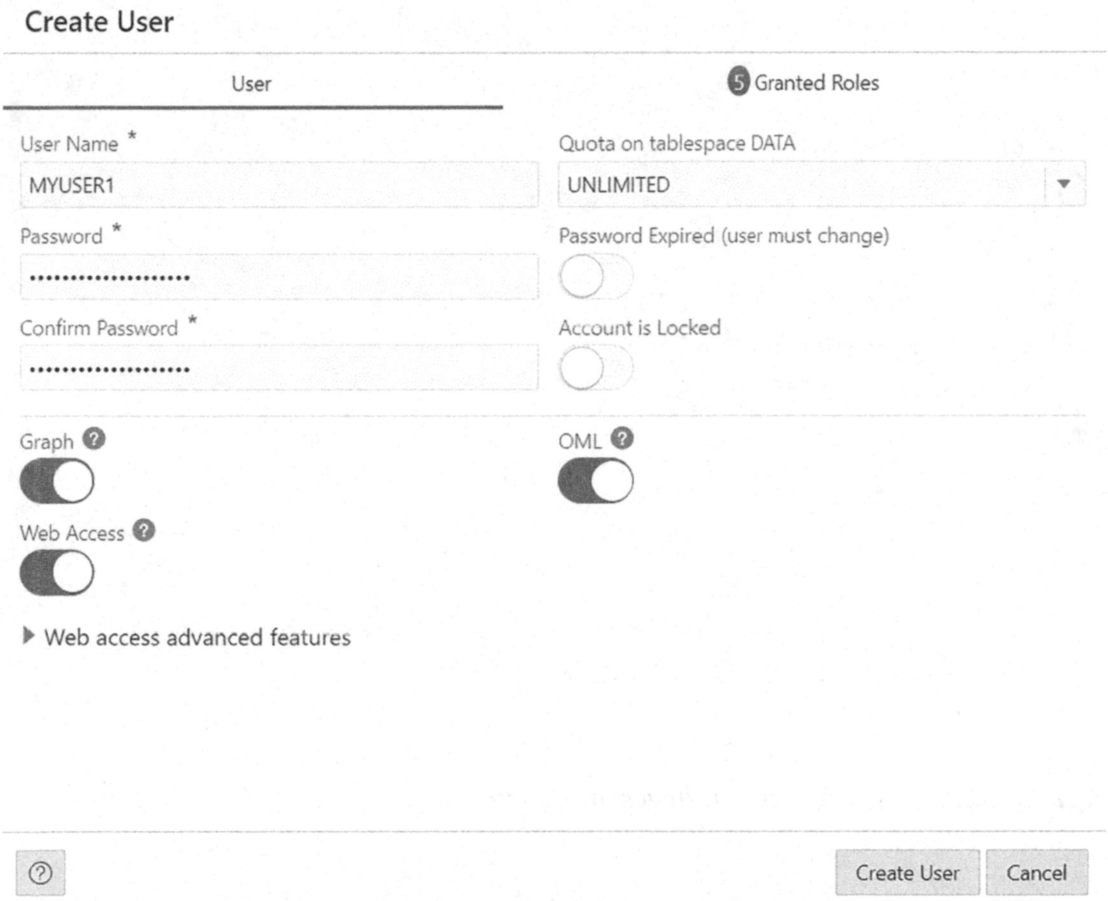

Figure 5-17. *Creating a user in Database Actions*

Then define the privileges needed by enabling the privileges as seen in Figure 5-18. You will need to enable *OML* to get the user added to machine learning. You can enable the other privileges if needed. *Graph* gives the user privileges to use the Graph service. This is not mandatory for our example, but is needed if you want to build machine learning models on graph data. Enabling Web Access is needed if you want to enable the user access to Database Actions. Enabling *Web Access* automatically fills in the information in the *Web access advanced features* section.

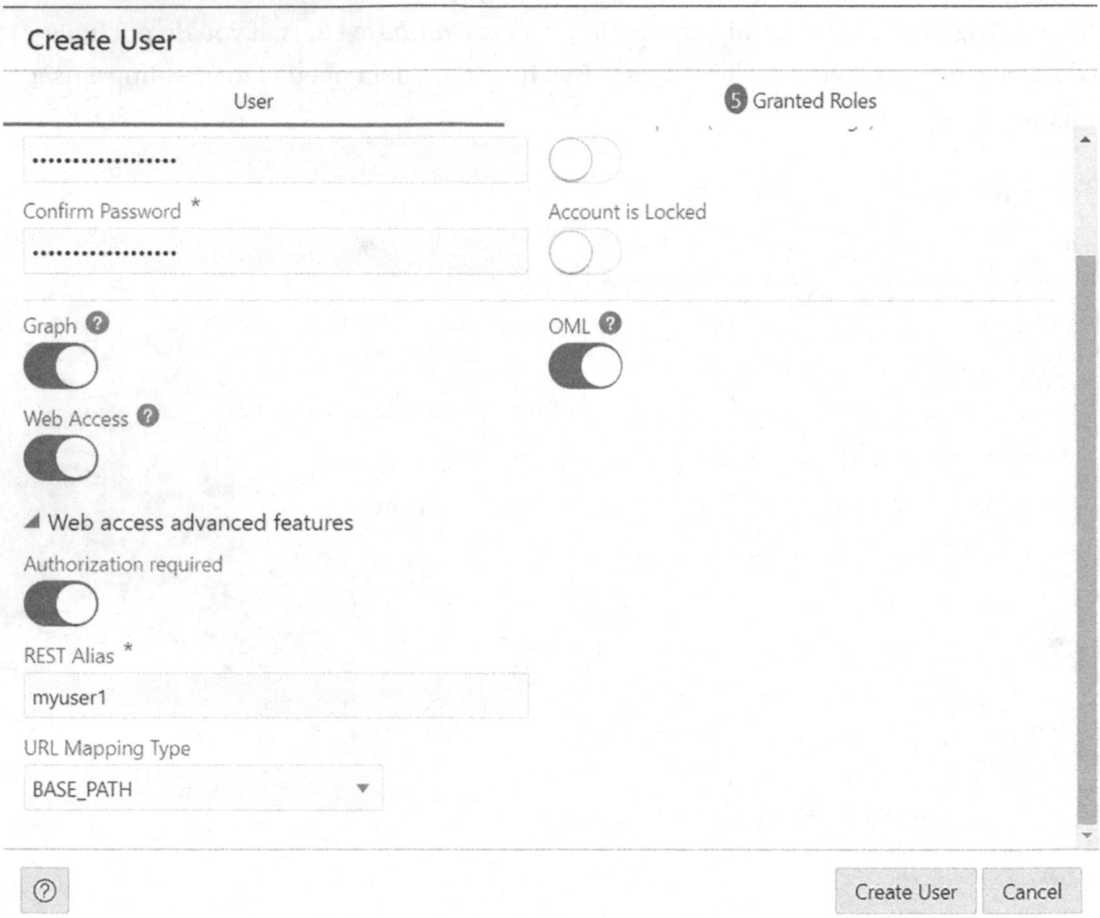

Create User

User			5 Granted Roles

Confirm Password *

Account is Locked

Graph ❓

OML ❓

Web Access ❓

◢ Web access advanced features

Authorization required

REST Alias *

myuser1

URL Mapping Type

BASE_PATH ▼

⑦   Create User   Cancel

Figure 5-18. *Defining the privileges for a new user*

Oracle Machine Learning

OML4SQL is a set of PL/SQL packages for machine learning implemented in the Oracle database. OML4SQL consists of three PL/SQL packages:

- DBMS_PREDICTIVE_ANALYTICS, which has routines for performing semi-automized machine learning using predictive analytics

- DBMS_DATA_MINING_TRANSFORMING, which has routines for transforming the data for OML4SQL algorithms

- DBMS_DATA_MINING, which has routines, for instance, for creating and managing the machine learning models and evaluating them

All of them have several subprograms.

Oracle Machine Learning for Python (*OML4Py*) enables you to run Python commands for data transformations, statistical, machine learning, and graphical analysis on data stored in or accessible through an Oracle database using a Python API. OML4Py is included with the Oracle Autonomous Database. It is a Python module that enables users to manipulate data in database tables and views using Python syntax without the need to move the data outside of the database. OML4Py functions and methods transparently translate a select set of Python functions into SQL for in-database execution. OML4Py consists of typical Python machine learning libraries. But, the specialty of OMP4Py is that it also includes Oracle-specific libraries. AutoML functionality is built on Python. To use AutoML functionalities in a notebook, you import library oml and, from oml, the automl. If you want to use OML4Py on your on-premises database, you must install Python, the required Python libraries, and the OML4Py server components in the database, and you must install the OML4Py client.

OML4R is a set of R libraries inside the Oracle Database. OML4R is not yet available in the cloud, but it is available on premises. *OML4Spark* is a component of Oracle Big Data Connectors software suite for on-premise Big Data solutions and is included with Oracle Big Data Service.

An Introduction to Oracle Machine Learning User Interface

Navigate to the *Development* section of your Autonomous Database Service Console as seen in Figure 5-11, and select *Oracle Machine Learning User Interface*. Log in as the machine learning user we created earlier in this chapter (Figure 5-19).

Tip   To find the login page easier in the future, save the URL to your favorites.

Figure 5-19.   *Signing in to Oracle Machine Learning*

The Oracle Machine Learning (OML) console opens as seen in Figure 5-20. This console has a section *How Do I?* which has a lot of content on how to get started with Oracle Machine Learning (OML). On the top-right corner of the console, you can see the username you used to log in to Oracle Machine Learning. If you select the drop-down menu, you are able to change the *Preferences* and the *password* of the user. One of the Preferences is, for example, your time zone. You can also see the *Help* and *About* information, as well as *Sign Out* from the service. When working on Oracle Machine Learning, you are always working inside a Workspace that consists of one or more Projects. Next to the User information, you can find the information about the *Workspace* and the *Project*. Depending on your privileges, you can *Manage Workspaces* (Figure 5-21) and *Workspace Permissions*, create a *New Project, Select Project*, or see the *Recent Projects*. If you choose to Manage Workspaces, you can *Edit, Delete*, or grant *Permissions* to the workspace selected as seen on Figure 5-21. You are able to grant permissions to your own workspace.

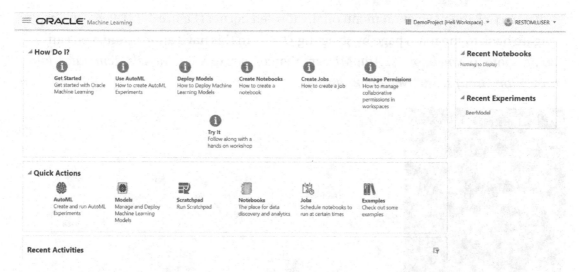

Figure 5-20. *Oracle Machine Learning console*

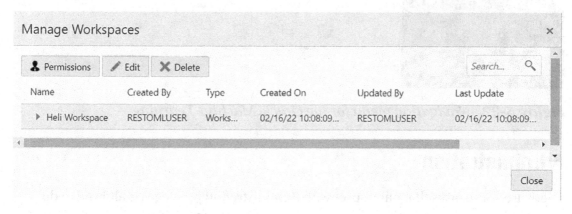

Figure 5-21. *Managing workspaces*

In the *Quick Actions* section (Figure 5-20), you can use the *AutoML* functionality, manage and deploy the machine learning *Models*, use the *Scratchpad*, work with *Notebooks* and *Jobs*, and see prebuild *Examples*.

On the left, you can also see a list for *Recent Notebooks* and *Recent Experiments*. An Experiment is the result of AutoML process.

On the bottom of the screen, you can also see the *Recent Activities* section that shows the log of actions taken in Oracle Machine Learning.

If you click the navigation menu on the top-left corner (Figure 5-22), you can always navigate back to the main page by selecting *Home*. In this navigation menu, you can also navigate to *Notebooks* or *AutoML* experiences; see existing *Models*, *Templates*, *Jobs*, *Connection Groups*, and *Notebook Sessions*.

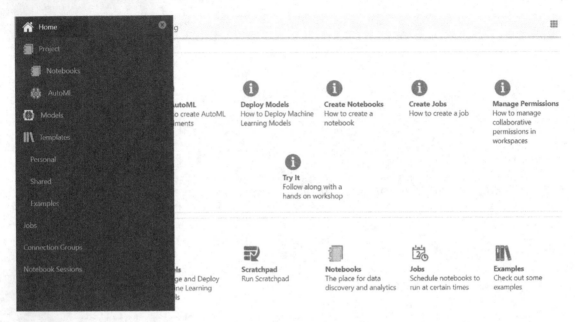

Figure 5-22. *Navigation menu for the Oracle Machine Learning*

Administration

There are some tasks that only a user with Administration privileges is allowed to do. An Admin user creates, edits, and deletes Oracle Machine Learning user accounts and reassigns user workspaces.

To administer the machine learning service, log in using the *Admin* credentials. You will get a warning: "Administrator is restricted from creating notebooks and jobs, please create a new OML user or use an existing OML user for notebook and job creations." This means that an administration user is only allowed to do the administrative work, not anything to do with the machine learning process itself. The Oracle Machine Learning console does show the *How do I?* and *Quick Actions*, but if you select, for example, Notebooks, the list of notebooks is empty and you are not able to create a new notebook. If you select the drop-down menu from the upper-right corner (Figure 5-23), you can *Select Project*, create a *New Project*, or *Manage Workspaces*.

Figure 5-23. *Oracle Machine Learning console when logged in as the Admin user*

If you select the *ADMIN* drop-down menu on the top-right corner, you can edit the user *Preferences*, *Manage OML Users*, see the *Help* and *About*, and *Sign Out*.

You can also select the navigation menu on the top-left corner. The menu (Figure 5-24) includes a separate section for Administration tasks. You can *Manage OML Users*, manage *User Data*, or check *Compute Resources*. If you choose Manage OML Users, you will be able to *Create* a new user, *Delete* a user, see all users in the database by selecting *Show All Users*, or *Search* a use from a list. You can also edit a user by selecting the user from the list.

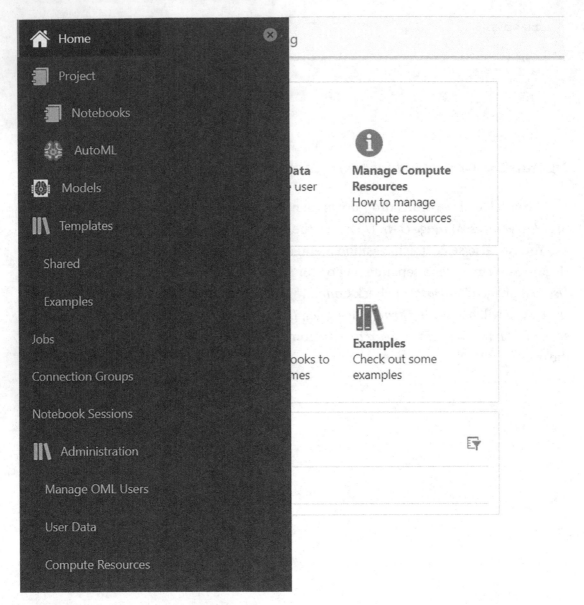

Figure 5-24.   *The Oracle Machine Learning navigation menu for the Admin user*

By selecting *User Data*, the Admin user can delete users and all user-related objects such as the workspace, projects, and notebooks. Or, the Admin can perform workspace reassignments for users.

A *Compute Resource* refers to a back-end service to which an interpreter connects, for example, the database. You can see an example of Compute Resources in Figure 5-25. The Compute Resources page lists each resource, its type, comments, and last updated details.

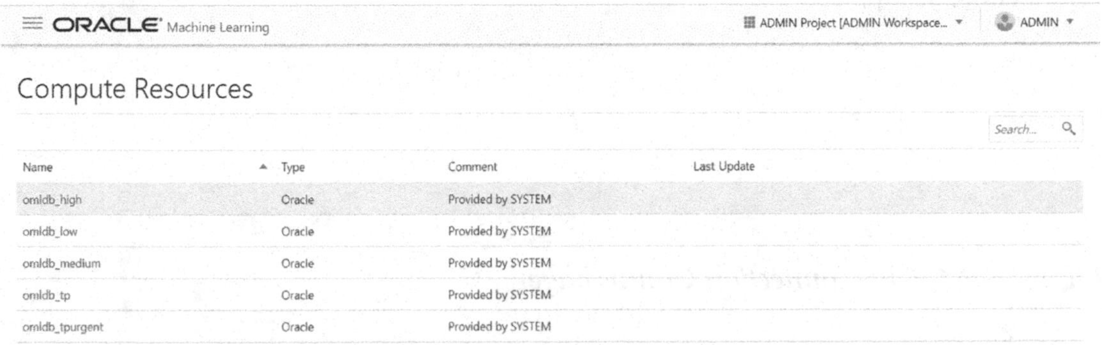

Figure 5-25. *Compute Resources*

If you select a Compute Resource of a database from the list, you can see the resource details (Figure 5-26). The data is read only except the memory setting which can be changed. For the resource *databasename_high*, the memory settings must be between 8 and 16, for *databasename_medium* between 4 and 8, and for the resource *databasename_low* between 2 and 4. The memory setting is applicable only for the Python interpreter. Click *Back to Compute Resources* to go back to the list and to save possible changes on the memory reservation. You can read more about the limitations of numbers of OCPU and concurrent notebooks from the Oracle documentation.

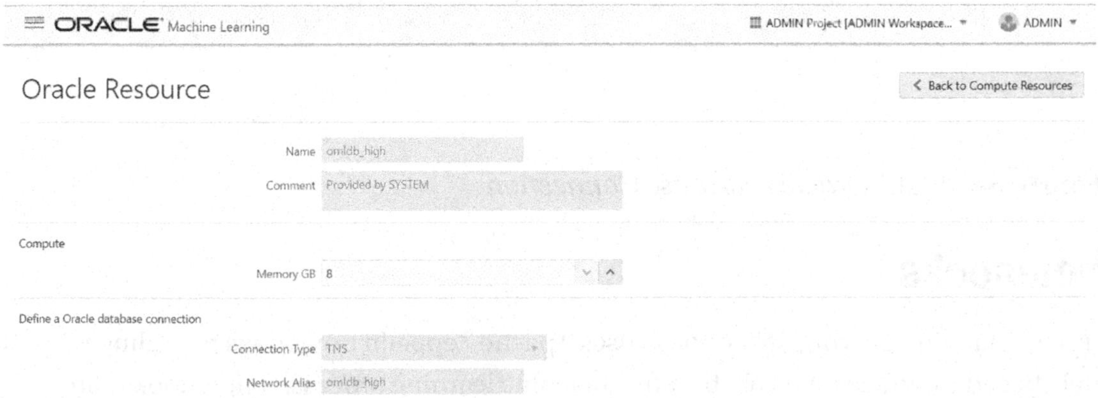

Figure 5-26. *Oracle Resources page*

If you select *Connection Groups* from the navigation menu, a user with Administrator role can manage a Zeppelin interpreter set, a collection of database connections, which form the Connection Group (Figure 5-27). The *Global* Connection Group is created automatically when a new database is provisioned. You can *Edit*, *Stop*, or *Refresh* a Connection Group.

Figure 5-27. *The Connection Groups page*

You can select an individual connection from the Connection Group and edit that. For example, in Figure 5-28, you can see the details of an Oracle Database Connection.

Figure 5-28. *An Oracle Database Connection*

Notebooks

Oracle Machine Learning Notebooks uses Apache Zeppelin notebooks providing a web-based interface for a collaborative machine learning process. A notebook is an interface to perform and document the machine learning process: data exploration, data visualizations, data preparation, training and testing machine learning models, evaluating the models, and deploying them.

If you select the *Examples* from the OML console, you can find several examples of predefined notebooks as seen in Figure 5-29.

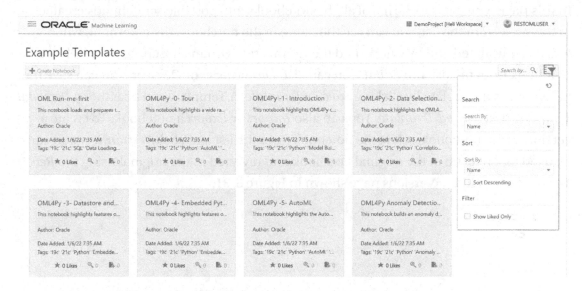

Figure 5-29. *Example Templates on Oracle Machine Learning*

You can select any of these example notebooks to investigate it and to learn about notebooks in general. You are not able to edit the example notebooks, but you can export a notebook and import it as a base for your own notebook.

You can use the *Search* functionality to find a suitable example for your needs. You can use *Search By* to search a notebook by its name or the *Sort By* to sort the notebooks by their names. You can also mark example notebooks as liked notebooks by clicking the star symbol in the notebook. Then by selecting the *Show Liked Only* in the Search, you can narrow down the list of examples to your favorites.

A *Scratchpad* (Figure 5-20) can be used to quickly test SQL statements, PL/SQL scripts, or Python scripts. The Scratchpad is a regular notebook prepopulated with three paragraphs: %sql, %script, and %python. After you run your scripts, the Scratchpad is automatically saved as a notebook by the default name Scratchpad. You can access it in the Notebooks page and, for example, rename it. Note that if using Python, you still need to import *oml* and other Python libraries you will be using. Scratchpad is not a full notebook, since you are not able to document the whole process using it. It is just a platform for simple tests.

To create a notebook, click *Notebooks* in *Quick Actions* (Figure 5-20), or select Notebooks from the navigation menu. The Notebooks page opens as seen in Figure 5-30. In this page, you can see the list of all the notebooks and possible scratchpads created in the project. In the list, you can see the name of the notebook, the comment, when was it last updated and by whom, and the Connection Group chosen. You can select a notebook from the list and *Edit* it. You can also *Duplicate* it, or *Delete* it. You can save the notebook as a template by clicking *Save as Template*. A Template can be either a *Personal Template* or a *Shared Template*. You can also *Import* or *Export* a notebook. To create a version of the notebook, select the notebook from the list and click *Version*. Version can be used as a backup of the original notebook and reverted as the original using the *Revert Version* button in the Versions page shown in Figure 5-31.

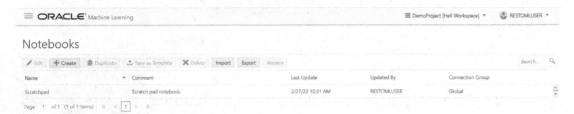

Figure 5-30. *Notebooks page in Oracle Machine Learning*

Figure 5-31. *The Versions page for Notebooks*

If you want to create a new notebook, click *Create*. Insert the *Name* for the notebook, optionally a *Comment*, and choose the *Connection* as shown in Figure 5-32. Click *OK*.

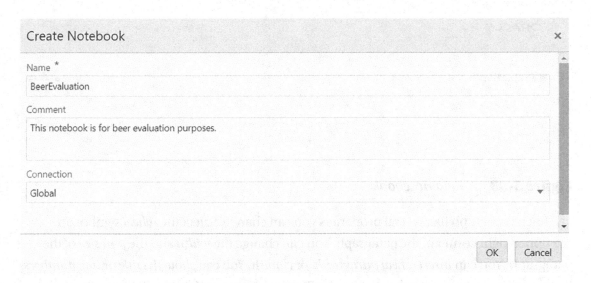

Figure 5-32. *Creating a new Notebook*

The notebook server starts and the notebook opens. The notebook has a name you just specified and one paragraph ready to be used (Figure 5-33). A notebook consists of one or more paragraphs. The paragraphs can be of four different kinds:

- %md

- %sql

- %script

- %python

Each of these paragraphs includes a certain kind of data. *%md* includes description of the process, or the analysis done during the process. *%sql* includes SQL queries, and *%script* has PL/SQL scripts. A *%python* paragraph has Python code. A notebook can consist of all of these types of paragraphs: in one notebook, you can call SQL, PL/SQL, and Python and also document it all.

Figure 5-33. *A new notebook*

Each paragraph has several properties you can change. Select the *wheel* symbol on the upper-right corner of the paragraph. You can change the *width* and the *font size* of the paragraph. You can *insert a new paragraph,* or *clone* it. You can *show the title* or *line numbers.* You can *disable the run,* or *clear the output.* These settings are shown in Figure 5-34.

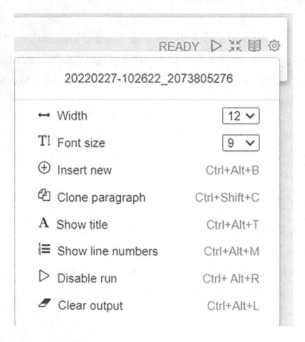

Figure 5-34. *Settings for a paragraph in a notebook*

If you want to use the notebook to show the process and the outcome to a business user, you can click the symbol of *four arrows* (Figure 5-34) to hide the editor, or press Ctrl+Alt+E combination. If you want to display just the code without the output, you can click the symbol of a *book* (Figure 5-34) or press Ctrl+Alt+O combination to hide the output. If you want to run the code in the paragraph, click the *Play* symbol (Figure 5-34).

Beside the name of the notebook (Figure 5-35), you can find the actions possible for a notebook. The *Play* symbol runs all the paragraphs in the notebook. The *four-arrow* symbol shows or hides the code, whereas the *book* symbol shows or hides the output in all paragraphs of the notebook. The *eraser* symbol clears output from all paragraphs, and the *rubber bin* symbol clears the notebook. The *download* symbol lets you export the notebook either as it is or without the output. Clicking the *magnifier* symbol, you can *search* the code and *replace* strings with other strings if needed.

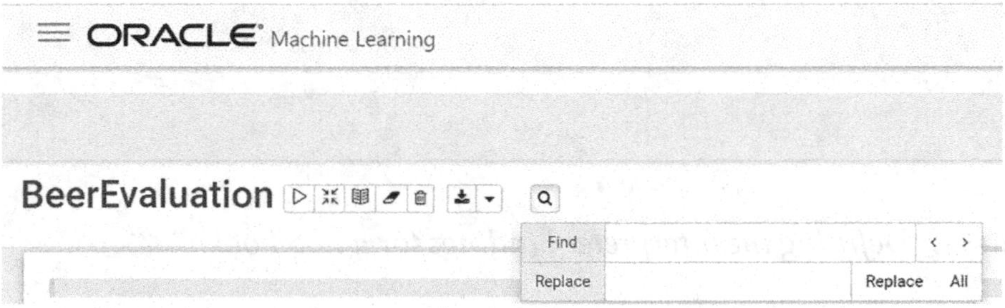

Figure 5-35. *Action icons for a notebook*

An *interpreter* is a plug-in that allows you to use a specific data processing language back end. Notebooks have an internal list of bindings that define the order of the interpreter bindings in an interpreter group. If you select the wheel symbol on the notebook level (Figure 5-36), you can see the list of interpreters (Figure 5-36). When creating a notebook, either from scratch or from a template, the notebook inherits the default interpreter binding order: low, medium, and high (Figure 5-37). When importing or exporting a notebook, the notebook inherits the interpreter bindings defined for the original notebook. You can bind or unbind interpreters by selecting the interpreter from the list. Or you can reorder them by dragging and dropping them in the list. When you change the list, it affects the whole notebook. The first interpreter on the list becomes default.

Figure 5-36. *The interpreter bindings for a notebook*

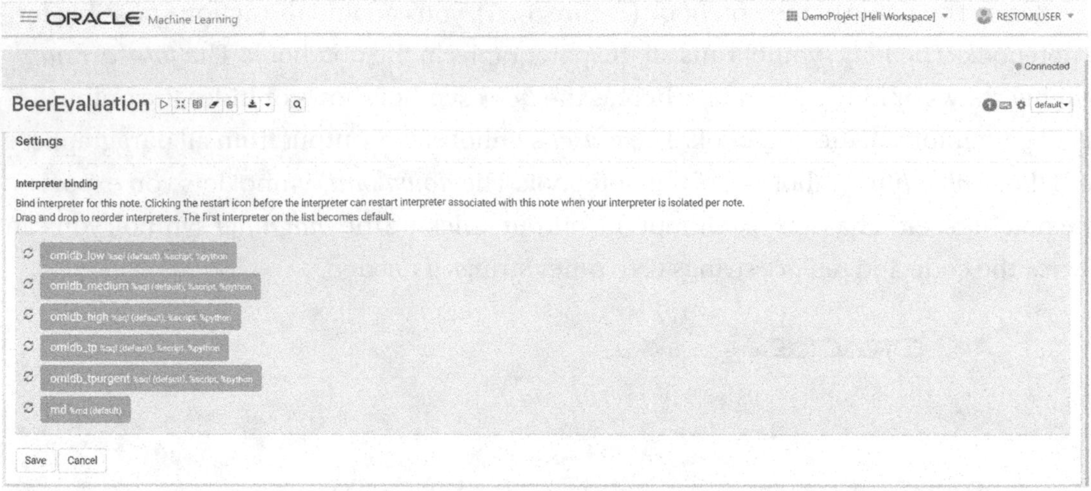

Figure 5-37. Defining the interpreter bindings for a notebook

You can check the interpreter binding of a paragraph with this SQL clause:

```
%sql
SELECT SYS_CONTEXT ('USERENV', 'SERVICE_NAME') FROM DUAL;

QXNTYWWDCCYSDET_OMLDB_low.adb.oraclecloud.com
```

The result is *tenantname_databasename_servicename.domain*.

You can change the interpreter binding for a specific paragraph in a notebook by binding an interpreter for it. To change the binding, start the paragraph with

%databasename_servicename

For example:

```
%omldb_medium
SELECT SYS_CONTEXT ('USERENV', 'SERVICE_NAME') FROM DUAL;

QXNTYWWDCCYSDET_OMLDB_medium.adb.oraclecloud.com
```

Note   Do not override the interpreter binding at the paragraph level, when working with a Python Notebook.

You can set the output format of a paragraph using *SET SQLFORMAT* in a paragraph of type %script. You can define the output as the format_option parameter:

- CSV, comma-separated variable output, with string values enclosed in double quotes.

- HTML, HTML format.

- XML, a tag-based XML document; data is presented as CDATA tags.

- JSON, a JSON document containing the definitions of the columns and the data it contains.

- ANSICONSOLE, resizes the columns to the width of the data and underlines the columns.

- INSERT, produces the INSERT statements that to be used to insert the rows in a table.

- LOADER, produces pipe delimited output with string values enclosed in double quotes, not including the column names.

- FIXED, produces fixed width columns with all data enclosed in double quotes.

- DEFAULT, clears all previous SQLFORMAT settings and returns to the default output.

- DELIMITED, allows you to define the delimiter string and the characters that are enclosed in the string values. For example:

```
%script
SET SQLFORMAT DELIMITED -d- " "
select bedrooms, floors, price from HOUSEDATA_TRAIN where
id=100123;

"BEDROOMS"-d-"FLOORS"-d-"PRICE"4-d-2-d-480000
```

It first shows the column names using the enclosed character define (" ") and then lists the values of those columns using the delimiter defined (-d-). In this example, the value for bedrooms is 4, the value for floors is 2, and the price is 480000.

A Notebook can be created based on a *Template*. Select either *Personal* or *Shared* under *Template* on the navigation menu. Then select the Template from the list of templates and click *Create Notebook*. You can also *Edit* the Template, *Delete* it, or *Share* it, if it is a Personal Template. Shared Templates are similar to *Examples*. They both can be found under Templates on the navigation menu.

Notebooks can be scheduled to be run at certain time automatically using a *Job*. Select *Jobs* from the navigation menu. You can *Create, Duplicate,* and *Delete* Jobs. And you can *Start* or *Stop* a Job. To create a job, click the *Create* button seen in Figure 5-38. Insert a *Name* for the job, select a *notebook* from the list, and define the *parameters* for running the job. You can define the *Start Date* and optionally either define the *Repeat Frequency* or a *Custom* rule for the job. In *Advanced Settings*, you can define the *Maximum Number of Runs, Timeout in minutes,* and the *Failure Handling*. For the failure handling, you can define either the *Maximum Failures Allowed*, or you can define it to use an *Automatic Retry*.

Figure 5-38. *Creating a Job to run a Notebook*

If you want to manage your Notebook Sessions, you can do that by selecting *Notebook Sessions* from the navigation menu. The Notebook Sessions page allows you to get an overview of your notebooks and manage Notebook Sessions that are either running on your workspace or in workspaces that you have collaboration rights. On the page, you can unload or stop a Notebook Session. *Unload* removes the selected notebook from memory on the server, and *Stop* stops the selected notebook in the server.

Using the notebooks, you can build and document the whole machine learning process starting from data visualization and preparation to deploying the model. Usually, a machine learning process is done in a team of different kinds of experts. For example, one team member might be specialized in machine learning and would build the model for a developer to use in an application.

AutoML

Automated Machine Learning (AutoML) provides an automatic machine learning environment for a user who is not very familiar with the data scientist work. AutoML creates *Experiments* that consist of several machine learning models, built using different algorithms, to choose the best for the purpose. The only tasks for you are to prepare the data, start the AutoML, and choose the best model.

Select *AutoML* from the Oracle Machine Learning console (Figure 5-20). The AutoML Experiments page opens as seen in Figure 5-39. On this page, you can *Create, Edit, Delete, Duplicate, Start,* or *Stop* AutoML Experiments.

Figure 5-39. *An AutoML Experiments page on Oracle Machine Learning*

To create an experiment, click *Create*. There are several sections on the Create Experiment page. On top of the page (Figure 5-40), you specify the *Name, Comment, Data Source, Predict,* and *Case ID* for the experiment. These are the basic information for machine learning model creation. The Name is the name for the model. The Data Source is the table where the training data is stored. Predict is the target column, the column that will be predicted with the model. Case ID is the unique identifier in the table of the training data. The Prediction Type is automatically defined based on the data type of the Predict column. If the data type is number, the Prediction Type will be regression. If it is varchar, the Prediction Type is classification. The Case ID is optional; all other information is mandatory for the model creation.

The *Features* section (Figure 5-40) contains a lot of useful information about the features, for example, the columns of the training data table. For each column is shown

- The name of the column

- The data type

- The percent of null values in that column

- The number of distinct values in the column

- Minimum value in the column

- Maximum value in the column

- The mean of the values in the column

- The standard deviation of the values in the column

You can use this information to understand the data better, and you can deselect those features/columns that are not useful in model creation. The more features there are, the longer the model creation lasts. Also, some columns might be not just useless but also harmful in model creation due to missing data or several outliers.

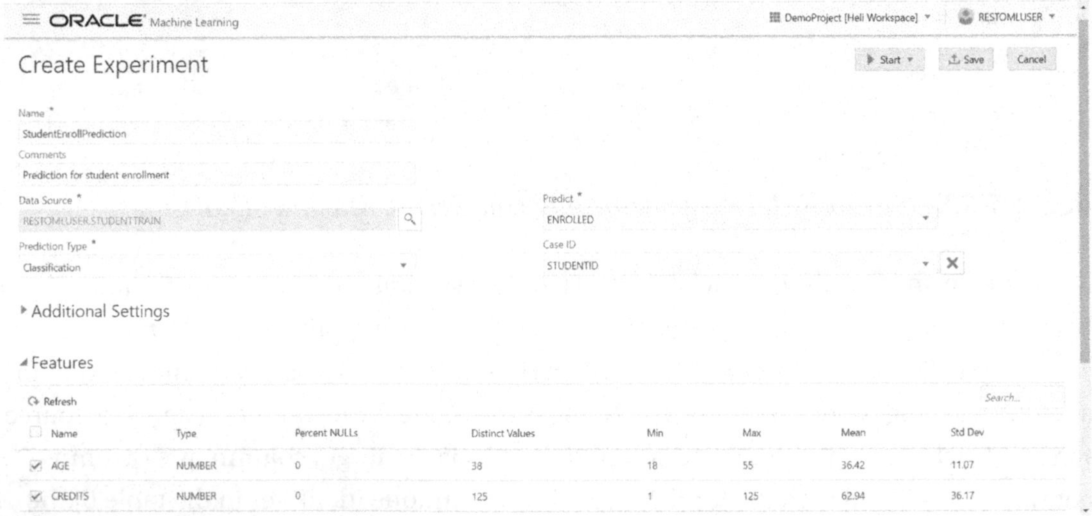

Figure 5-40. *Creating an AutoML Experiment*

Additional Settings section (Figure 5-41) defines the model creation process. There are several algorithms available in Oracle Database for both regression and classification models. The *Algorithms* section lists all algorithms available for the machine learning

CHAPTER 5   ORACLE MACHINE LEARNING IN AUTONOMOUS DATABASE

function chosen: classification or regression. You can select or deselect algorithms from that list. A model is created for each algorithm you selected. After the models have been created, you can compare the models to choose the best. You can define the number of *Maximum Top Models* and the *Maximum Run Duration* to limit the result set of models to the best n of all the models and to define the maximum time the training can take. *Database Service Level* has three values: high, medium, and low. You can choose which of these will be used in model creation. The *Model Metric* defines the metric used to compare the models and to define which of them is the best. For example, for classification, you can use Accuracy, Balanced Accuracy, ROC AUC, F1, Precision, or Recall. The metric selection depends on the use case.

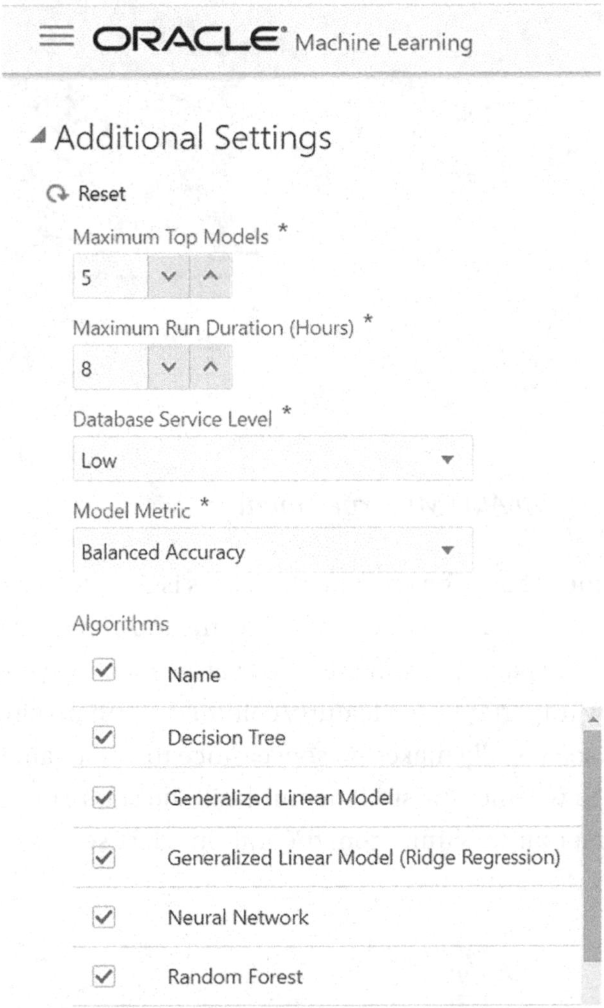

Figure 5-41. *An example of Additional Settings for an AutoML Experiment*

When you have defined all settings for the Experiment creation, click the *Start* button on the top-right corner of the page (Figure 5-40). There are two options for Experiment creation: *Faster Result* or *Better Accuracy*. Choose Faster Result to get the Experiment created faster, or Better Accuracy to let the model creation take the time needed to create as accurate a model as possible. You can follow the Experiment creation as seen in Figure 5-42. If you want to stop it for some reason, click the *Stop* button on the top-right corner. The creation of an Experiment takes some time. During that time, it performs several tasks automatically as seen in the box with a title Running in Figure 5-42.

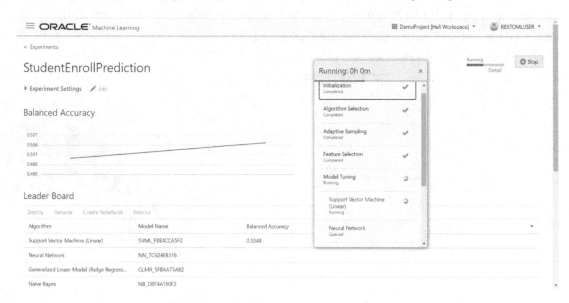

Figure 5-42. *Running an AutoML Experiment*

When the Experiment has been created, the status is updated from *Running* to *Completed*. Close the status bar by clicking the x on the top-right corner.

If you scroll down the page, you will find the Features section (Figure 5-43). This section describes how important each feature/column was on making the prediction. In our example, we can see it really makes no sense, since the first name definitely has no impact on the decision whether the student enrolls in the class or not. This might give an idea to remove the first name column from the training data set.

◢ Features

↻ Refresh   Search...

Name	Importance	Type	Percent NULLs	Distinct Values	Min	Max	Mean	Std Dev
FIRSTNAME	▮▮▮▮	VARCHAR2	0	13501				
AGE	▮▮▮	NUMBER	0	38	18	55	36.42	11.07
CREDITS	▮▮	NUMBER	0	125	1	125	62.94	36.17
GENDER		VARCHAR2	0	2				
LASTNAME		VARCHAR2	0	45				
⊚ ENROLLED		VARCHAR2	0	2				
STUDENTID		NUMBER	0	13596	1024	14825	0	0

Figure 5-43. *Features section in an AutoML Experiment*

The Leader Board section (Figure 5-44) shows the best n models created using the algorithms chosen. n is the number you chose as Maximum Top Models.

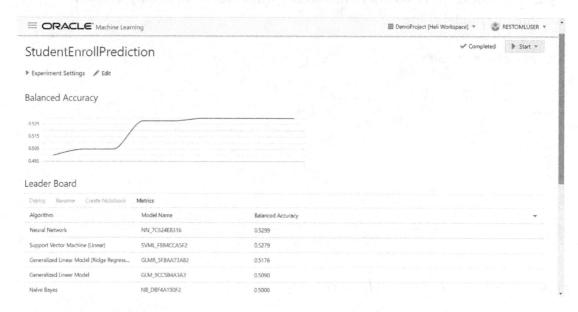

Figure 5-44. *The Leader Board section of an AutoML Experiment*

If you want to add additional Metrics to compare the models better, click *Metrics* on the *Leader Board*. Select the additional metrics you want to use from the list. Then close the list from the x.

We chose F1 as an additional metric as seen in Figure 5-45.

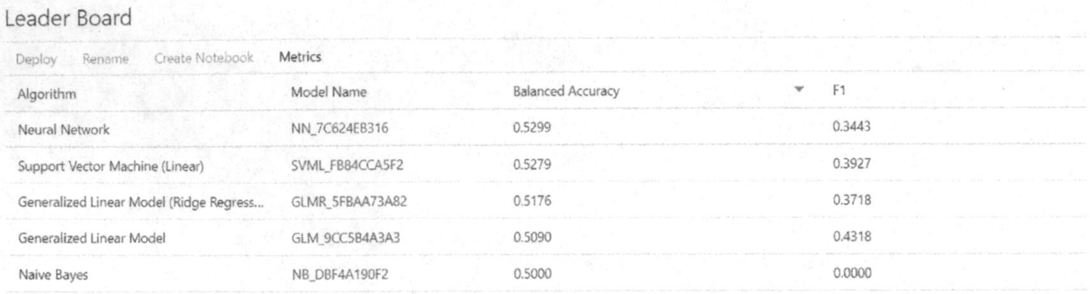

Leader Board

Deploy   Rename   Create Notebook   **Metrics**

Algorithm	Model Name	Balanced Accuracy ▼	F1
Neural Network	NN_7C624EB316	0.5299	0.3443
Support Vector Machine (Linear)	SVML_FB84CCA5F2	0.5279	0.3927
Generalized Linear Model (Ridge Regress...	GLMR_5FBAA73A82	0.5176	0.3718
Generalized Linear Model	GLM_9CC5B4A3A3	0.5090	0.4318
Naive Bayes	NB_DBF4A190F2	0.5000	0.0000

Figure 5-45. The Metrics tab of an AutoML Experiment with an additional metric

You can select one row from the Leader Board list. The *Prediction Impact* (Figure 5-46) describes the importance of each feature/column to the prediction outcome this model made.

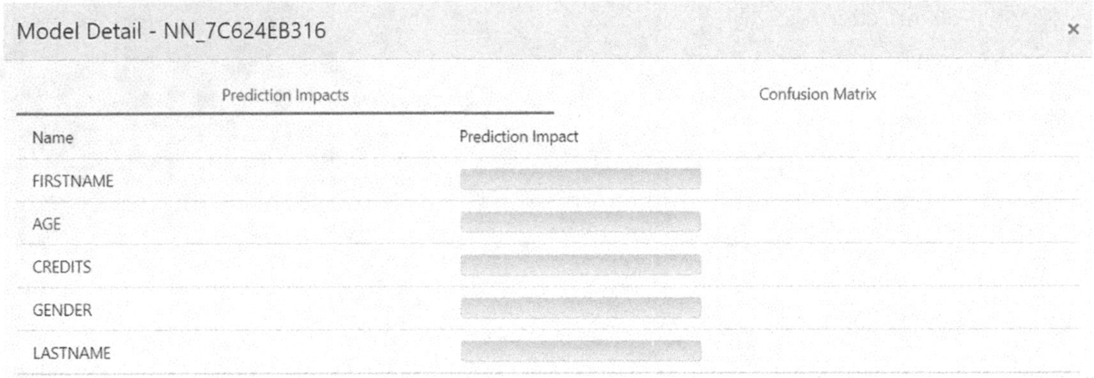

Figure 5-46. The Prediction Impact tab of a model

The *Confusion Matrix* (Figure 5-47) describes how well the model predicted each value of the target column. All this information is important for you to know to be able to select the best model.

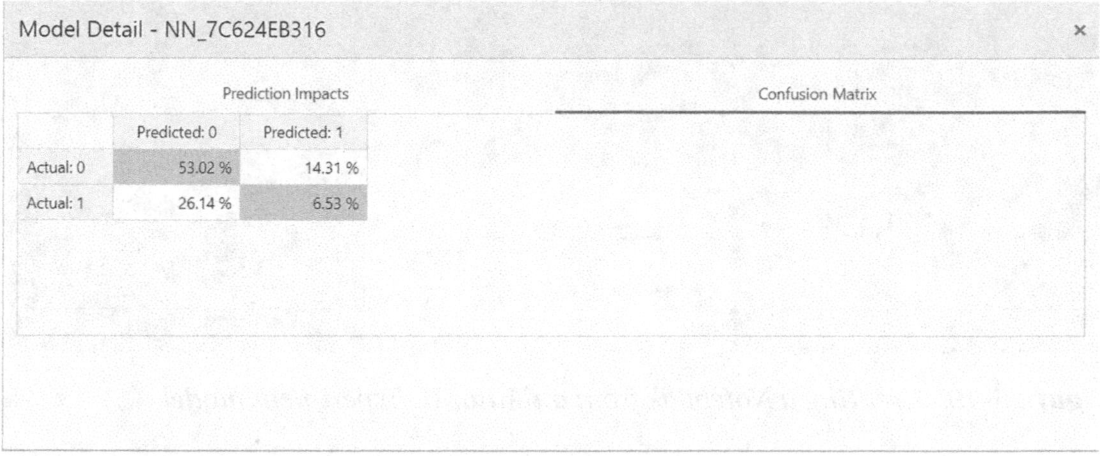

Model Detail - NN_7C624EB316			✕

Prediction Impacts			Confusion Matrix
	Predicted: 0	Predicted: 1	
Actual: 0	53.02 %	14.31 %	
Actual: 1	26.14 %	6.53 %	

Figure 5-47. *The Confusion Matrix of a model*

When the model is selected, you can click *Rename* and give the model a better name as seen in Figure 5-48.

Figure 5-48. *Renaming a model*

You can also create a notebook from the model created by clicking *Create Notebook* and defining it a name as shown in Figure 5-49.

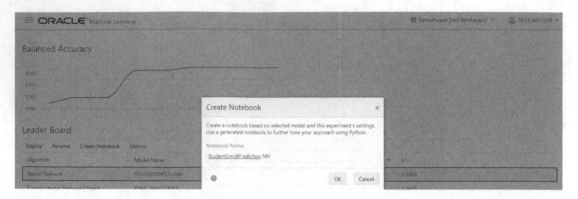

Figure 5-49. *Creating a Notebook from an AutoML Experiment model*

You can open this notebook, as any other notebook, and start editing it. The notebook is written in Python as seen in Figure 5-50.

Figure 5-50. *An example of a notebook created based on an AutoML Experiment model*

Also, after you are happy with the model, you can deploy it as seen in Figure 5-51. Click *Deploy*. Then, define the *Name, URI, Version,* and the *Namespace*. And decide whether you want to share the notebook to other users or not. Then click *OK*.

Figure 5-51. *Deploying a model*

If you are not happy with the model, you can click *Edit* on the top-left corner of the page (Figure 5-44) and start editing the definition to create a better model. Maybe you will add more and better data or prepare the data better. Maybe you will deselect some of the columns from the data set. Or, you change some of the other settings, for example, the metrics. Oftentimes, the dataset is just not enough for making predictions, like it was in our example. Then you need to find more or better data that has the answer to the question and the capability to make a good enough prediction.

Let's see another example. In this example, we should build a model to predict the house price. In Figure 5-52, we define the basic setup for the prediction. This time, the Predict is of type number and therefore the AutoML chooses Regression as the Prediction Type.

Figure 5-52. *A regression example of an AutoML Experiment*

And in Figure 5-53, we define Maximum Top Models, Maximum Run Duration, Database Service Level, Model Metric, and the Algorithms used for building the models. As you can see, the metrics and algorithms are different from the previous example. Both metrics and algorithms available depend on the machine learning function chosen.

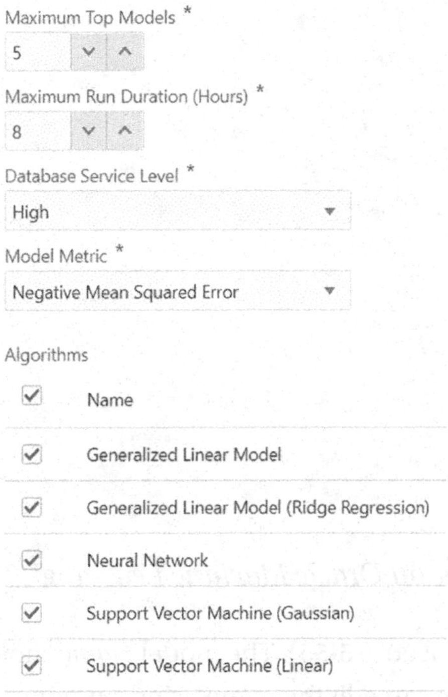

Maximum Top Models *

5   ∨ ∧

Maximum Run Duration (Hours) *

8   ∨ ∧

Database Service Level *

High   ▼

Model Metric *

Negative Mean Squared Error   ▼

Algorithms

☑   Name

☑   Generalized Linear Model

☑   Generalized Linear Model (Ridge Regression)

☑   Neural Network

☑   Support Vector Machine (Gaussian)

☑   Support Vector Machine (Linear)

Figure 5-53. *Defining the settings for creating a regression type of experiment*

The AutoML Experiment automatically saves the models created in a database using the name shown in the Leaders Board (Figure 5-45). If you want to delete the AutoML Experiment, select the experiment from the list and click *Delete* on the AutoML Experiments page (Figure 5-39). You are then able to define that also all the models are deleted by enabling *Drop Models*. If you do not enable it, only the experiment is deleted and the models remain in the database.

Models

If you choose *Models* (Figure 5-22) from the navigation menu, you can maintain and deploy machine learning models, and see the deployments. On the User Models tab, you can *Deploy* or *Delete* models as seen in Figure 5-54. When you deploy a model, you create an Oracle Machine Learning Services endpoint for scoring using this model. To deploy a model, select it from the list and click *Deploy*.

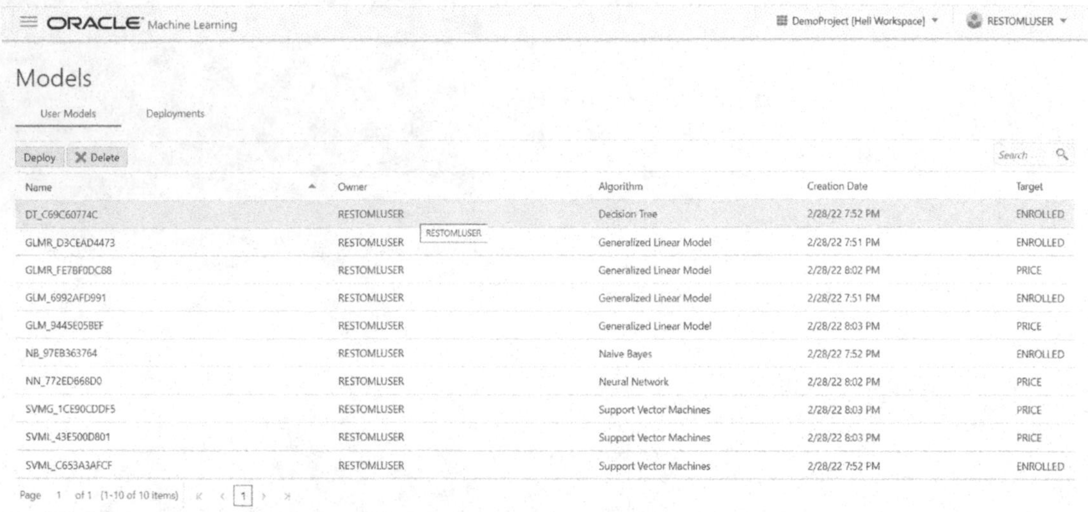

Figure 5-54. *Models page on Oracle Machine Learning*

Insert the data needed (Figure 5-55). The model *Name* shows the system-generated model name by default. You can edit the name using a unique alphanumeric name with a maximum of 50 characters. The model *URI* must be an alphanumeric string with a maximum length of 200 characters. Enter the *Version*. The version must be in the format xx.xx where each x is a number. Enter the model *Namespace*. And select *Shared* to allow other privileged users to view and deploy the model.

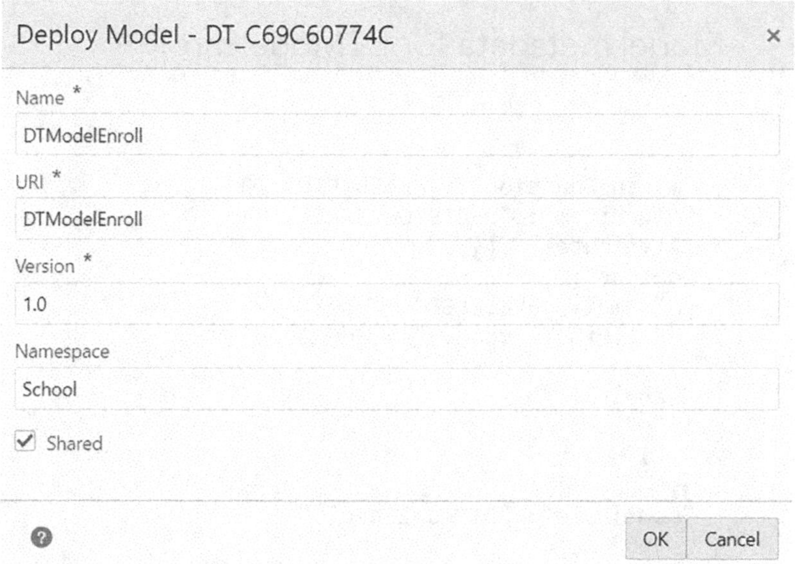

Deploy Model - DT_C69C60774C
Name *
DTModelEnroll
URI *
DTModelEnroll
Version *
1.0
Namespace
School
Shared
OK
Cancel

Figure 5-55. *Deploying a model*

When a model has been deployed, it can be seen on the Deployments tab (Figure 5-56) on the Models page (Figure 5-45). In the Deployments tab, you can *Delete* a model deployment or investigate it.

ORACLE Machine Learning
DemoProject [Heli Workspace]
RESTOMLUSER
Models
User Models
Deployments
Delete
Search
Name
Shared
Version
Namespace
Owner
Deployed Date
URI
DTModelEnroll
1.0
School
RESTOMLUSER
3/9/22 4:07 PM
DTModelEnroll

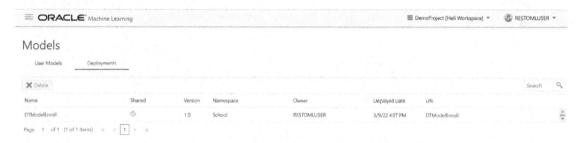

Figure 5-56. *Deployments tab of the Models page*

If you click the model's name on the Deployments tab, you can see the model details, the metadata. An example of those details is on Figure 5-57.

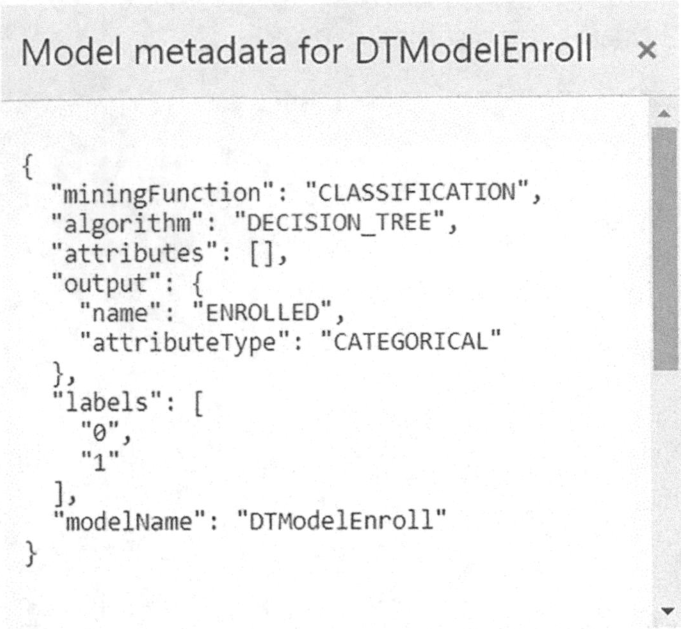

Model metadata for DTModelEnroll   ✕

```
{
  "miningFunction": "CLASSIFICATION",
  "algorithm": "DECISION_TREE",
  "attributes": [],
  "output": {
    "name": "ENROLLED",
    "attributeType": "CATEGORICAL"
  },
  "labels": [
    "0",
    "1"
  ],
  "modelName": "DTModelEnroll"
}
```

Figure 5-57. *An example of a model metadata*

If you click the URI of the model (Figure 5-56), you can see the API specification for the model as seen in Figure 5-58.

Figure 5-58. *An example of an Open API Specification for a model*

Oracle Machine Learning for SQL (OML4SQL)

OML4SQL is implemented in the Oracle Database kernel. Models are database objects, and the access to them is controlled by database privileges. There are several database views (ALL_/DBA_/USER_) for investigating their data: ALL_MINING_MODELS, ALL_MINING_MODEL_ATTRIBUTES, ALL_MINING_MODEL_PARTITIONS, ALL_MINING_MODEL_SETTINGS, ALL_MINING_MODEL_VIEWS, and ALL_MINING_MODEL_XFORMS. You will find more information on these from the Oracle documentation.

OML4SQL supports *SQL functions* for performing prediction, clustering, and feature extraction. These SQL functions include *SQL scoring functions*, such as PREDICTION, PREDICTION_COST, FEATURE_COMPARE, or CLUSTER_PROBABILITY, and *SQL statistical functions*, for example, CORR, STATS_F_TEST, STATS_T_TEST_ONE, STDDEV, or SUM.

Note   Do not confuse a SQL function with a machine learning function. A machine learning function specifies a class of problems that can be modeled and solved, for example, classification or regression.

In short, the machine learning process consists of data preparation, model creation, model evaluation, and deployment. OML4SQL offers tools for all of these. For example, *Automatic Data Preparation* (ADP) transforms data automatically so that it is usable by the algorithms on model creation. You can also supplement the automatic transformations with additional transformations. All these transformations are automatically performed to a new data set.

The OML application programming interfaces (APIs) for SQL (OML4SQL) consist of PL/SQL packages, SQL functions, and data dictionary views. OML4SQL consists of three PL/SQL packages:

- DBMS_PREDICTIVE_ANALYTICS, routines for performing semi-automized machine learning using predictive analytics

- DBMS_DATA_MINING_TRANSFORMING, routines for transforming the data for OML4SQL algorithms

- DBMS_DATA_MINING, routines, for instance, for creating and managing the machine learning models and evaluating them

Creating a machine learning user as described earlier in this chapter makes sure the user has all privileges needed to use these packages.

The DBMS_PREDICTIVE_ANALYTICS package is for faster machine learning using predictive analytics. The package can be used for simple machine learning predictions with or without a predefined model. The procedure does not create a model that can be stored in the database for further exploration, but it does automatically perform data preparation for the data using Automatic Data Preparation (ADP). It consists of three procedures: EXPLAIN, PREDICT, and PROFILE. EXPLAIN ranks attributes in order of their influence on explaining the target column. PREDICT makes a prediction. PROFILE generates rules that describe the cases from the input data.

The DBMS_DATA_MINING_TRANSFORMING package includes functionalities for transforming and preparing the data so that it makes sense to the algorithms for building the machine learning models. These operations include transformations such as binning, normalization, and outlier treatment.

DBMS_DATA_MINING package contains routines for machine learning model creation, operations on the models, and for querying them.

Machine learning activities require the data to be available on a single table or a view, containing one record in each row. First, you define the task for the machine learning activity, then you choose the data containing the information for solving the task, and define the machine learning function, the method used to solve the problem. When creating the model using CREATE_MODEL or CREATE_MODEL2 procedures, you define the machine learning function used. OML4SQL support these machine learning functions: ASSOCIATION, ATTRIBUTE_IMPORTANCE, CLASSIFICATION, CLUSTERING, FEATURE_EXTRACTION, REGRESSION, and TIME_SERIES. Then, you use the *Settings* table to define the rest of the settings for model creation. Create a separate settings table for each model you want to create. The table consists of two columns:

setting_name VARCHAR2(30)

setting_value VARCHAR2(4000).

This table includes rows to specify the model creation: the algorithms used for model creation, will ADP be used or not, etc. There are some machine learning functions and algorithm-specific settings as well that you can define using the settings table. You can specify the cost matrix used, prior probabilities, class weights, and much more using these setting tables. You can, for example, define a solver for a neural network algorithm via the settings table.

You are also able to *partition* a model. Partitioned models make it possible to build a model for each data partition. A data set can be divided into subsets based on their content, and each subset can have its own submodel. The submodels are automatically managed and used as a single model.

Model detail views provide information about the models created. The views used depend on the algorithm chosen when creating the models.

After the models have been created, you evaluate them. The DBMS_DATA_MINING package has subprograms for that. When a model is evaluated and found working, you deploy it to the target environment. Since the models are database objects, they can be exported from the source database and imported to the target database. When the model has been deployed, it can be used in the database using the OML4SQL API or using the OML REST API. Applying a machine learning model to the data of interest is referred to as *scoring*. That can be done directly using the OML4SQL scoring functions or with the APPLY procedure of DBMS_DATA_MINING package.

Note   The data preparation and transformations defined when creating the model are automatically performed to the new data set when using the model.

OML4SQL packages are in the Oracle Database and therefore available with any tool used for writing SQL.: the OML Notebooks, Oracle SQL Developer, APEX, and many more. OML4SQL is easy to learn for somebody using SQL and PL/SQL in everyday work. OML4SQL comes with the database without any extra costs.

Oracle Machine Learning for Python (OML4Py)

Oracle Machine Learning for Python (OML4Py) is automatically installed in an Oracle Autonomous Database and can be used without extra costs. Oracle Autonomous Database includes Oracle Autonomous Data Warehouse (ADW), Oracle Autonomous Transaction Processing (ATP), and Oracle Autonomous JSON Database (AJD). OML4Py is available through the Python interpreter in Oracle Machine Learning Notebooks (OML Notebooks) or via the REST API. To use OML4Py in OML Notebooks, simply import the package oml. AutoML is using the same package. Python can be used in the Oracle Autonomous Database also using user-defined functions and the Python API for Embedded Python Execution.

Note   Python can be installed to Oracle Database manually. Install Python, the required Python libraries, and the OML4Py server components in the database. Instructions can be found from the Oracle documentation.

OML4Py enables machine learning with Python using the data inside the database without moving it to a local storage and worrying about synchronization or security of the local data. The latest data is always available and can be processed using all the powerful data processing capabilities of a database. The Python functions are transparently translated to standard SQL, and OML4Py can automatically optimize the SQL by using the database query optimization. Even the backup and recovery of the data are taken care of.

OML4Py integrates Python with the database using a transparency layer. The OML4Py transparency layer converts Python objects to database objects or vice versa. And it invokes overloaded Python functions to invoke the corresponding SQL.

The oml package is the core for using Python in the Oracle Autonomous Database. The `oml.cursor` function creates a `cx_Oracle` cursor object for the current database connection. This cursor can be used to run queries against the database. The oml library creates a proxy object for a Python session to represent a database object. This enables you to move data between your local Python session and an Oracle database schema and, for example, to store the Python proxy object to the database. For example, `oml.push` creates a temporary database table in the user's schema and the corresponding proxy `oml.DataFrame` object to be used in Python code from a Python object in a local Python session. On the other hand, `oml.pull` creates a local Python object as a **copy** of the corresponding database object. `Oml.push` pushes data from a Python session into an object in a database schema, `oml.pull` pulls the data from the database to a Python `pandas.DataFrame` object. You can pull data to a local `pandas.DataFrame` only if the data can fit into the local Python session memory. You can use `oml.sync` to create a Python object as a proxy for a database table, view, or SQL statement. Being a proxy for a table, view, or SQL statement means that when you run Python code that uses data from the database, it returns the **current** data from the database object.

Note   If the metadata of the database object was changed, for example, a column was added, the `oml.DataFrame` proxy object does not reflect that change unless you invoke `oml.sync` for the database object again.

`Oml.dir` lists all the `oml.DataFrame` proxy objects in the environment for a schema.

When the OML Notebook or OML4Py client connection to the database ends, the temporary table is automatically deleted and the Python objects do not remain in the memory. Save the data to a database as a table or a proxy object into an OMP4Py datastore before disconnecting, if you want to keep them in persistent memory for future use. `Oml.create` creates a persistent database table and a corresponding `oml.DataFrame` proxy object from a Python data set. The proxy `oml.DataFrame` object has the same name as the table. Using **uppercase** letters for the table and column names makes using the data easier. If you use lowercase or mixed case for the name of the table or column, you must use the same lowercase or mixed case name in double quotation marks when using the table/column name in a SQL query or function. For uppercase names, you can use uppercase, lowercase, or mixed case, without using double quotation marks, when referring to the table/column. You can delete the persistent table in a database schema using `oml.drop`. An oml.DataFrame proxy object and its associated temporary table can be removed using `del` statement.

You can store Python objects, including `oml` proxy objects, to a named OML4Py *datastore* to be used in subsequent Python sessions or by other users or programs. OML4Py creates this datastore in the user's database schema. A datastore and the objects it contains persist in the database until you delete them. You can grant (`oml.grant`) or revoke (`oml.revoke`) read privilege permission to another user to that datastore or to objects in it. To save objects to an OML4Py datastore, use `oml.ds.save`; to load objects from the datastore into the user's Python session, use `oml.ds.load`; to list the datastores available for you, use `oml.ds.dir`; and to delete a datastore or objects from the datastore, use `oml.ds.delete`. To get information about the objects in an OML4Py datastore, use `oml.ds.describe`.

OML4Py lets you prepare data for machine learning analysis and perform exploratory data analysis using the overloaded versions of the most common Python libraries. OML4Py also provides functions for rendering graphical displays of data. You can, for example, use `oml.boxplot` to generate box and whisker plots, `oml.hist` to compute and draw histograms, or `oml.matplotlib` to render the output.

You can use the in-database algorithms, also used by OML4SQL, with OML4Py. For example, to get the understanding whether the data has the answer to the question, who of the students will enroll the course, you could use attribute importance algorithm (ai) to see what attributes affect most to the ENROLLED attribute. In this example, we do not see very good results: none of the attributes have the knowledge. Using this data, we will not be able to predict who will and will not enroll for the course.

```
%python
# import the libraries needed
import oml
from oml import ai
# get handle to an existing table
ENROLL = oml.sync(table = "STUDENTTRAIN")
# drop the ENROLLED attribute from the data set
ENROLL_x = ENROLL.drop('ENROLLED')
# define ENROLLED as the attribute for the ai algorithm
ENROLL_y = ENROLL ['ENROLLED']
```

```
# create attribute importance object
ai_obj = ai()
# fit the model
ai_obj = ai_obj.fit(ENROLL_x, ENROLL_y)
# print out the content
ai_obj
```

Algorithm Name: Attribute Importance

Mining Function: ATTRIBUTE_IMPORTANCE

Settings:

	setting name	setting value
0	ALGO_NAME	ALGO_AI_MDL
1	ODMS_DETAILS	ODMS_ENABLE
2	ODMS_MISSING_VALUE_TREATMENT	ODMS_MISSING_VALUE_AUTO
3	ODMS_SAMPLING	ODMS_SAMPLING_DISABLE
4	PREP_AUTO	ON

Global Statistics:

	attribute name	attribute value
0	NUM_ROWS	13596

Attributes:
AGE
CREDITS
FIRSTNAME
GENDER
LASTNAME
STUDENTID

Partition: NO

Importance:

	variable	importance	rank
0	AGE	0.0	1
1	CREDITS	0.0	1
2	FIRSTNAME	0.0	1

3	GENDER	0.0	1
4	LASTNAME	0.0	1
5	STUDENTID	0.0	1

You can specify settings for these models created using the in-database algorithms just like we did in the OML4SQL section. The default settings are used if you do not define any. Some of the settings are shared settings, for example, will the Automatic Data Preparation (ADP) be used, and some are algorithm specific.

You can also create an OML4Py model as a proxy object for an existing in-database machine learning model created using OML4Py, OML4SQL, or OML4R. You can use the `predict` and `predict_proba` methods of the model object to score new data or use the `PREDICTION` SQL function on the model proxy objects, which scores directly in the database. You can export a model from Python using the `export_sermodel` function, save it into a database table, and then import it to another Oracle Database using the `DBMS_DATA_MINING.IMPORT_SERMODEL` procedure. You can use the REST API for Oracle Machine Learning Services to, for example, store OML models and to create scoring endpoints for the models.

Automated Machine Learning (AutoML) is also part of the OML4Py implementation. AutoML performs common modeling tasks such as algorithm selection (`oml.automl.AlgorithmSelection`), feature selection (`oml.automl.FeatureSelection`), model selection (`oml.automl.ModelSelection`), or hyperparameter tuning (`oml.automl.ModelTuning`) automatically. AutoML currently manages only classification and regression use cases of machine learning.

Embedded Python Execution allows you to invoke user-defined Python functions directly in an Oracle database instance and to store and manage them as scripts in the database, using the Python script repository. The user-defined Python function can be defined either private or global. User-defined Python functions can produce results in structured or PNG image formats.

You can, for example, build native Python models. Then, you can store and manage them in a *Python script repository*.

This is a mockup example of creating a user-defined function my_own_function:

```
def my_own_function(data):
    import oml
...
    return something
```

You can save the function to the Python script repository by first defining a string for it and then saving it to the repository. Let's see a mockup example on how to do it. Define the string:

```
my_own_function_str = """ def my_own_function(data):
    import oml
...
    return something
"""
```

Then, save the string as a script to the Python script repository:

```
oml.script.create("my_own_function", func=my_own_function_str,
overwrite = True)
```

To check the scripts in the repository:

```
oml.script.dir()
```

You can load the scripts from the repository into a Python session using `oml.script.load` and remove them from the repository using `oml.script.drop`. You can grant and revoke privileges to the scripts using the same commands as granting and revoking privileges to datastores and datastore objects: `oml.grant` and `oml.revoke`.

User-defined Python functions can be run in a single Python engine or in a *data-parallel* or *task-parallel* manner using multiple Python engines. In data-parallel processing, you *partition the data* and invoke the Python function of each data subset using one or more Python engines. In task-parallel processing, you *invoke the function multiple times* in one or more Python engines with a unique index passed in as an argument.

To invoke the user-defined Python function, you can use the Embedded Python Execution functions. They are part of the Python API for Embedded Python Execution.

- `oml.do_eval`, runs a user-defined Python function

- `oml.group_apply`, partitions a database table by the *values* in one or more columns and runs the function on each partition

- `oml.index_apply`, runs a Python function multiple times, passing in a unique index of the invocation to the user-defined function. This can be used to perform parallel simulations such as Monte Carlo analysis.

- `oml.row_apply`, partitions a database table into chunks, sets of rows, and runs the user-defined function on the data in each chunk

- `oml.table_apply`, runs a Python function on data in the database as a single pandas.DataFrame

You can invoke our example user-defined function with new data set (newdata) using, for example, `table_apply`:

```
something = oml.table_apply(data=NEWDATA, func = my_own_function)
```

OM4Py and the embedded Python execution have *data dictionary views* (ALL_, DBA_, USER_):

- ALL_PYQ_DATASTORES, information about the OML4Py datastores

- ALL_PYQ_DATASTORE_CONTENTS, information about the objects in the OML4Py datastores

- ALL_PYQ_SCRIPTS, the user-defined Python functions in the script repository

Sometimes you need to monitor and manage resources used by OML4Py. The Python library `psutil` can be used for system monitoring, profiling, limiting Python process resources, and managing running processes. You can read more about it from the psutil documentation (`https://psutil.readthedocs.io/en/latest/#`).

In-Database Machine Learning and APEX

Since the in-database machine learning is in the database, it is very easy to use OML from APEX. You can, for example, create a new table (or view) based on the predictions by a machine learning model and use it in APEX. For example, we have customers that are either households or companies. We build one model for households (Household_model) and another for companies (Company_model) to predict how likely they will buy our product1. Then, we create a table (Household_contacts) that includes data about the household customers, the prediction on buying product1 (0=not buying, 1=buying), and the probability for the prediction. In this example, we only take those customers who have not yet bought product1 (product1 = 0). We use a model (Household_model) to give us the prediction data.

```
Create table Household_contacts as
select cust_id, PREDICTION (Household_model using *) prediction,
PREDICTION_PROBABILITY(Household_model using *) pred_probability
from household_customers where product1 = 0;
```

The sky is the limit for what you can do with OML and APEX if they are in the same database. If they are in different databases, you can either export/import the model to the same database with APEX, or you can use the Oracle Machine Learning REST services.

Summary

Oracle Machine Learning can be used with three languages: SQL, Python, and R. To use those languages in the Oracle Database, you call their OML APIs: OML4SQL, OML4Py, and OML4R. The OML4SQL consists of database packages for machine learning. OML4Py can be used for the machine learning process with the Python syntax and libraries, the Embedded Python Execution with user-defined functions, or by using the AutoML functionality. You can store Python objects and data into Python datastore and user-defined functions in Python script repository. At the OML4Py datastore and Python script repository, you can manage and use them. OML4R is not yet available in the Oracle Autonomous Database.

The Oracle Machine Learning console in the Oracle Autonomous Database offers, for example, Notebooks and AutoML functionalities.

## CHAPTER 6

Oracle Machine Learning REST Services

REST APIs give one more option to use machine learning functionalities in an Oracle Database, both Oracle Machine Learning and Embedded Python Execution.

A Short Introduction to REST APIs

API comes from the words Application Programming Interface. API is a set of rules that define how applications or devices can connect to and communicate with each other. *REST* is an acronym for REpresentational State Transfer. REST is a set of architectural constraints first presented by Roy Fielding in his dissertation in 2000: `www.ics.uci.edu/~fielding/pubs/dissertation/rest_arch_style.htm`

REST is not a protocol; it is not a standard. It is a style of architecting and designing web applications. Developers can implement REST in a variety of ways. REST APIs are commonly served over Hypertext Transfer Protocol (*HTTP*). In other words, in the context of a REST API, HTTP is a *contract*, a communication protocol, and REST is a *concept*.

HTTP is an application-layer protocol. It is a stateless protocol and it follows a client-server model: clients and servers communicate by exchanging messages. A client opens a connection to make a *request* and waits until it receives a *response* from the server. These requests and responses are called *HTTP messages*.

A request consists of a *request line*, optional *header lines* followed by CRLF (Carriage Return and Line Feed), an *empty line* (followed by CRLF) that indicates the end of the header fields, and optionally a *message body*. The request line consists of the basic information about the request: HTTP request method, the path of the resource to fetch (request URI), and the version of the HTTP protocol used. For example:

```
GET /<oml-cloud-service-location-url>/omlmod/v1/api/ HTTP/1.1
```

© Adrian Png and Heli Helskyaho 2022
A. Png and H. Helskyaho, *Extending Oracle Application Express with Oracle Cloud Features*,
https://doi.org/10.1007/978-1-4842-8170-3_6

There are nine HTTP request methods that can be used for REST API calls: GET, HEAD, POST, PUT, DELETE, CONNECT, OPTIONS, TRACE, and PATCH. The Request URI (Uniform Resource Identifier) identifies the resource to apply the request.

HTTP headers represent the metadata associated with an API request or a response. An *HTTP header* consists of name-value pairs with a colon (:) between them. For example:

```
Accept-Language: en-us
Accept-Encoding: gzip, deflate
Content-Type: application/json
Accept: application/json
```

Whitespaces before the value are ignored.

A media type (Multipurpose Internet Mail Extensions or MIME type), used in a header, is a two-part identifier for file formats used on the Internet. The two parts, a type and a subtype, are separated by a slash (/). For example:

```
application/json
audio/mpeg
image/png
```

Multipart types represent composite documents: separate files which are all part of the same transaction. There are two multipart types: message and multipart. *Message* encapsulates other messages and *multipart* consists of multiple components which may individually have different media types. For example:

```
message/rfc822
multipart/form-data
```

You can see all defined media types from `www.iana.org/assignments/media-types/media-types.xhtml`.

The cookie data is also transmitted inside an HTTP header. HTTP protocol is stateless, but *HTTP cookies* makes it possible to use stateful sessions by allowing session creation on each HTTP request to share the same context or the same state.

An empty line indicates that the header section ends and the optional message body starts. The message body carries actual HTTP request data you want to fetch. The content of the message data depends on the service that will be called. For example, if the service needs a customer id as a parameter to be able to return the response, the customer id is given in the message part of the request message.

A response consists of the version of the HTTP protocol, a status code, a status message, HTTP headers, and optionally a body containing the fetched resource.

A *HTTP response status code* indicates whether a specific HTTP request has been successfully completed or has there been an error. Responses are grouped in five classes:

- Informational responses (100–199)

- Successful responses (200–299)

- Redirection messages (300–399)

- Client error responses (400–499)

- Server error responses (500–599)

You can read more about HTTP from `https://developer.mozilla.org/en-US/docs/Web/HTTP/Resources_and_specifications`.

The REST API request might need verifying the authorization to the resource in the server side. One option is to use *OAuth 2.0*. OAuth 2.0 is an open-standard authorization protocol using access tokens for authorization. The idea of the token is that you will get access to the service without giving your credentials to it. You authenticate first to get the token, and then using that token, you call the service. Access tokens can be either bearer or sender-constrained tokens. A *bearer token* means that anybody who bears the token can use it. If you lose it, anybody can use it. A *sender-constrained token* can only be used by a person who is *entitled* to use it. It is like an airline boarding pass: it allows the flight from A to B but only for the person it is valid for. The name on the boarding pass must match the name on the passport, and the picture on the passport and the face of a customer must match. In OAuth 2.0, this is usually implemented through cryptographic key solutions.

To get the token, you must first authenticate. There are several OAuth *Grant types* for authenticating. For example:

- authorization_code (Authorization Code Grant)

- client_credentials (Client Credentials Grant)

- password (Resource Owner Password Grant)

- urn:ietf:params:oauth:grant-type:device_code (Device Authorization Grant)

The grant type refers to the authentication method. For example, Client Credentials Grant uses the client id and the client secret to receive the token outside of the context of a user. The Password Grant exchanges a user's credentials (username, password) for an access token to access the recourse with that user's credentials. Password Grant has been deprecated, but it is still in use with OML REST APIs.

After you have authenticated using one of the Grant types, you get the authorization token and are ready to use the service. The authorization usually has an expiration time, and you need to obtain a new token after it expires.

Introduction to OML REST Services

The REST API for Oracle Machine Learning Services provides REST API endpoints hosted on Oracle Autonomous Database for using the Oracle Machine Learning functionalities, for example, to create and store machine learning models and create scoring endpoints for the model. The REST API for OML Services supports both OML models and Open Neural Networks Exchange (ONNX) format models. ONNX is an open standard for machine learning interoperability. The REST API for Embedded Python Execution enables you to execute user-defined Python functions stored in an Autonomous Database in the Python script repository or to use Python objects stored in an OML4Py datastore.

To be able to use the REST services, you need an authentication token. You retrieve the token from the autonomous database from /omlusers endpoint and then, using this user token and an operation in a REST API endpoint, call machine learning functionalities in an Oracle Database.

REST API for Oracle Machine Learning Services

The REST API for Oracle Machine Learning Services provides access to in-database machine learning using the /omlmod/ REST API endpoints hosted on Oracle Autonomous Database. The REST API for Oracle Machine Learning Services supports Oracle Machine Learning models and Open Neural Networks Exchange (ONNX) format models. ONNX is an open standard for machine learning interoperability. You can read more about it from https://onnx.ai/.

Supported machine learning model types (machine learning functions) for Oracle Machine Learning are, for example, classification, regression, clustering, and feature extraction. For ONNX format models, the supported machine learning model functions are classification, regression, and clustering. The ONNX classification also includes image models.

The key benefits of OML (on top of improved security and many more) are that all the hard work with the data is done inside the database and that all database features are available for it. Oracle Machine Learning even supports partitioned models. You can split the data in the most useful way and build different models for different data splits of the dataset.

The *OML REST services* consist of four types of APIs: generic, repository, deployment, and cognitive text. *Generic* endpoints return metadata about all available versions of the OML Service APIs, Open API Specification for the OML Services in JSON format, and metadata of version 1 of the OML Services API. *Repository* endpoints handle data related to machine learning models. You can use those endpoints, for example, to get model details or to delete a model. *Deployment* endpoints allow you, for example, to create or delete model endpoints, get details of a model endpoint, or to score model using endpoint. *Cognitive text* endpoints include features like finding most relevant keywords, topics, or sentiment analysis from a text.

Using the Oracle Machine Learning Services REST API, you can perform several functions on both Oracle Machine Learning and ONNX format models. You can

- Get metadata about all available versions of the OML Service APIs

- Get Open API Specification for the OML Services in JSON format

- Get metadata of version 1 of the OML Services API

- Store, delete, and list deployed models

- Retrieve metadata, information, or content of a model

- Organize models under namespace

- Create, delete, and list model endpoints

- Get the details of an endpoint, or score with model endpoints

- Get the Open API 3.0 (Swagger) documentation for the model endpoint

- Get all cognitive text endpoints provided by OML Services

- Get the most relevant keywords or topics

- Get numeric features, semantic similarities, sentiments, or summaries for the provided list of text strings

You can find all these REST endpoints here: `https://docs.oracle.com/en/database/oracle/machine-learning/omlss/omlss/rest-endpoints.html`.

The supported request methods are GET, POST, and DELETE, and the URL structure for the HTTP request line is of form

`https://<oml-cloud-service-location-url>.oraclecloudapps.com`

where the oml-cloud-service-location-url consists of tenancy ID, database name, and region.

The OML Services REST API supports the following headers to be passed in the header section of the HTTP request or response:

- Authorization

- Location

- Content-Type.

In REST APIs, a media type is a format of a request or response message body data. The media types supported by OML Services REST APIs are

- application/json

- multipart/form-data

- application/octet-stream.

REST API for Embedded Python Execution

The REST API for Embedded Python Execution can be used to execute Python code in the Oracle Autonomous Database using a REST client. It calls user-defined functions (UDFs) stored as named scripts in the Python script repository or Python objects stored in the OML4Py datastore in an Oracle Autonomous Database. You can find all the endpoints from here: `https://docs.oracle.com/en/database/oracle/machine-learning/oml4py/1/mlepe/rest-endpoints.html`.

To get started with it, you need to obtain a token using the `.../omlusers/` and then call the REST API on `.../api/py-scripts/` using that token. These REST APIs are located in the Autonomous Database, and they use tokens to authenticate an Oracle Machine Learning *user*. The token is obtained by providing the username and the password of the user. The token is valid only for a limited time.

When executing a REST API Embedded Python Execution function, you can specify the Autonomous Database service level to be used with the optional `service` argument. The service names provide different levels of performance and concurrency for an Oracle Autonomous Database. The service names available are LOW, MEDIUM, and HIGH.

Standard HTTP method requests are used to perform operations on REST API for Embedded Python Execution endpoints. The supported HTTP method requests are GET, HEAD, and POST. The REST API for Embedded Python Execution supports the `application/json` media type and the following headers that may be passed in the header section of the HTTP request or response:

- Accept-Encoding

- Content-Encoding

- Content-Type

The response message always includes a status code to express whether the request was successful or not. Status codes returned by the response message are:

- 200 OK

- 201 Created

- 202 Accepted

- 302 Found

- 400 Bad Request

- 401 Unauthorized

- 500 Internal Server

The default mode for REST API for Embedded Python Execution function endpoint calls is synchronous, but you can use it in an asynchronous manner using these status codes. Call the script execution function with the `async Flag` parameter set to `true`. Then, get the status code of the job using the job id returned by the function. Status code

202 indicates that the job is pending, and 302 indicates it has finished. When the job has finished, the return also includes a `Content-Location` header. Use that to fetch the results of the script.

The REST APIs consist of three types of tasks: *Get Version Metadata*, *List Scripts*, and *Execute Scripts*. Get Version Metadata REST endpoints return metadata about the API versions. The List Scripts REST endpoint returns a list of scripts available in the Python script repository. Execute Scripts REST endpoints execute scripts from the Python script repository in a similar way as explained in this chapter, in in-database Oracle Machine Learning in OCI in the OML4Py section. The `/api/py-scripts/v1/` endpoint has several operations for executing user-defined functions:

- `do-eval`, to execute a Python function; optionally, you can specify the owner of the script.

- `table-apply`, to execute a Python function on specified data; optionally, you can specify the owner of the script.

- `group-apply`, to execute a Python function on grouped data; optionally, you can specify the owner of the script.

- `index-apply`, to execute a function multiple; optionally, you can specify the owner of the script.

- `row-apply`, to execute a Python function on chunks of rows; optionally, you can specify the owner of the script.

- `jobs`, to retrieve the status or the result of an asynchronous job.

Using OML REST Services

To be able to use the OML REST services, you need a REST client, a token, and the endpoint to send the requests.

Installing and Setting Up a REST Client (cURL)

You need a REST client to use the REST APIs. Any REST client can be used, but in this example, we will use cURL. To connect securely to the server, you must have a version of cURL that supports SSL and provide an SSL certificate authority (CA) certificate file or bundle to authenticate against the Verisign CA certificate.

If you do not have it installed, follow these steps:

1. Navigate to the cURL home page at `http://curl.haxx.se` using your browser, and click Download on the header menu of the page.

2. Select the correct version of cURL.

3. Click the link to download the ZIP file, and install the software.

4. Navigate to the cURL CA Certs page at `http://curl.haxx.se/docs/caextract.html`.

5. Download the ca-bundle.crt SSL CA certificate bundle (*cacert.pem*).

6. Save it in the same folder where you installed cURL.

7. Open a command window (Command Prompt).

8. Navigate to the directory where you installed cURL.

9. Set the cURL environment variable, CURL_CA_BUNDLE, to the location of an SSL certificate authority (CA) certificate bundle. For example:

    ```
    C:\Curl> set CURL_CA_BUNDLE=ca-bundle.crt
    ```

Creating an Access Token

To access OML Services using the REST API, you must provide an access *token*. Obtain the URL for REST authentication token as shown in Figure 5-12. To authenticate and obtain an access token, use cURL.

The -d option is used for passing the username and password. The username is the username for the Autonomous Database OML user we created earlier in this chapter. The token is obtained using the OML REST URL (the one we called: "Use this URL to obtain a REST authentication token for OML-provided REST APIs") added with *api/oauth2/v1/token*.

The syntax looks like this:

```
curl -X POST --header "Content-Type: application/json" --header "Accept:
application/json" -d "{"grant_type":"password", "username":"'MyUser'",
"password":"'MyPassword'"}" "<oml-cloud-service-location-url> /omluser/api/
oauth2/v1/token"
```

Edit the username, password, and the URL to the script. Go to Command Prompt and navigate to the folder you installed cURL. Execute the script. Copy the token and save it in a safe place. Note that the token is only valid for the defined time. The response message includes the expiration time.

Then, using the token, send a request. For example, to obtain the existing deployed models, edit the *<oml-cloud-service-location-url>* and copy/paste the Token to *addTokenHere* and run this code:

```
curl --location --request GET "https://<oml-cloud-service-location-url>/
omlmod/v1/models" --header "Authorization: Bearer addTokenHere"
```

Or, you can request for the Open API Specification (Swagger) documentation for an endpoint:

```
curl --location --request GET "https://<oml-cloud-service-location-url>/
omlmod/v1/api" --header "Authorization: Bearer addTokenHere"
```

You can call any endpoint by adding a `deployment` and a `uri` to the path and editing the value of the uri: `/omlmod/v1/`*deployment*`/{`*uri*`}/api`. This will return the Open API Specification (Swagger documentation) of that endpoint.

To query the existing registered Python scripts from the database

```
curl -i -X GET --header "Authorization: Bearer eyJhbGciOiJSUz...=" --header
"Accept: application/json" https://<oml-cloud-service-location-url>/oml/
api/py-scripts/v1/scripts
```

It returns the header and after the empty line the message body with the data:

```
HTTP/1.1 200 OK
Date: Thu, 28 Apr 2022 12:50:41 GMT
Content-Type: application/json
Content-Length: 1129
Connection: keep-alive
```

```
Cache-Control: no-cache, no-store, must-revalidate
Pragma: no-cache
X-Frame-Options: SAMEORIGIN
X-XSS-Protection: 1;mode=block
Strict-Transport-Security: max-age=31536000; includeSubDomains
X-Content-Type-Options: nosniff
Content-Security-Policy: frame-ancestors 'none'
Set-Cookie: JSESSIONID=node01itqttned1z86151jt3ijn0mge4.node0; Path=/oml;
Secure; HttpOnly
Expires: Thu, 01 Jan 1970 00:00:00 GMT
```

```
{"result":[{"owner":"RESTMLUSER","date":"2022-04-27T07:23:12.000Z",
"name":"nb_predict","description":"A UDF built based on an AutoML notebook
to predict Beer OVERALL rating using data from a table Beer_data_
autoML.","script":"def nb_predict(): \n  import pandas as pd ...
return(json_result)"}]}
```

When using cURL, you can also use cURL environment variables, for example, $token to represent the token. To assign the token to a variable use, export and insert the value inside the single quotes:

```
export token='eyJhbG...='
```

Examples of Using OML REST Services

To call the REST API for OML Services, you first need to obtain the token as explained earlier. Then, using that token, you can call the operations in the REST endpoints. The REST endpoint path for token is /omusers/; for OML, it is /omlmod/ and for Python /oml/.

Let's see the cognitive text REST endpoints as an example. This is a REST API that requires also a message body to pass the data. We take the description of the book *Getting Started with Oracle Cloud Free Tier: Create Modern Web Applications Using Always Free Resources* by Adrian Png and Luc Demanche and ask the Get Most Relevant Topics endpoint to find the top ten topics from the description.

```
curl -X POST --header "Authorization: Bearer eyJhbGciOiJSUzI1NiJ9....="
"https://<oml-cloud-service-location-url>/omlmod/v1/cognitive-text/topics"
```

```
--header 'Content-Type: application/json'
-d '{"textList":["Use this comprehensive guide to get started with the
Oracle Cloud Free Tier. Reading this book and creating your own application
in the Free Tier is an excellent way to build familiarity with, and
expertise in, Oracle Cloud Infrastructure. Even better is that the Free
Tier by itself is capable enough and provides all the ingredients needed
for you to create secure and robust, multi-tiered web applications of
modest size. Examples in this book introduce the broad suite of Always Free
options that are available from Oracle Cloud Infrastructure. You will learn
how to provision autonomous databases and autonomous Linux compute nodes.
And you will see how to use Terraform to manage infrastructure as code. You
also will learn about the virtual cloud network and application deployment,
including how to create and deploy public-facing Oracle Application Express
solutions and three-tier web applications on a foundation of Oracle REST
Data Services. The book also includes a brief introduction to using and
managing access to Oracle Machine Learning Notebooks. Cloud computing is a
strong industry trend. Mastering the content in this book leaves you well-
positioned to make the transition into providing and supporting cloud-based
applications and databases. You will have the knowledge and skills that
you need to deploy modest applications along with a growing understanding
of Oracle's Cloud platform that will serve you well as you go beyond the
limits of the Always Free options and take full advantage of all that
Oracle Cloud Infrastructure can offer."], "topN":10}'
```

The response message body returns the topicResults:

```
..."topicResults": [{
    "topic": "Cloud computing",
    "weight": 0.21997470116809562
}, {
    "topic": "Google Cloud Platform",
    "weight": 0.213551581196215733
}, {
    "topic": "Oracle Corporation",
    "weight": 0.18296549446070967
}, {
```

```
        "topic": "IT infrastructure",
        "weight": 0.1509873670535844
    }, {
        "topic": "Cloud storage",
        "weight": 0.14193632625983807
    }, {
        "topic": "Platform as a service",
        "weight": 0.12096843030927087
    }, {
        "topic": "Web application",
        "weight": 0.1108704736442413
    }, {
        "topic": "Linux Foundation",
        "weight": 0.09169194469729022
    }, {
        "topic": "Google App Engine",
        "weight": 0.09149938274982759
    }, {
        "topic": "Virtual learning environment",
        "weight": 0.08927694707494302
    }]
}]
```

What kind of sentiments does this text include? Let's call the sentiment on the cognitive-text REST endpoint with the same text and find out. The text is the same; for the sake of space, some of it has been replaced with three dots.

```
curl -X POST --header "Authorization: Bearer eyJhbGciOiJSUzI1NiJ9...="
"https://<oml-cloud-service-location-url>/omlmod/v1/cognitive-text/
sentiment"
--header 'Content-Type: application/json'
-d '{"textList":["Use this comprehensive guide to get started with the
Oracle Cloud Free Tier. ...that Oracle Cloud Infrastructure can offer."]}'
```

The result message body looks like this:

```
...     "sentimentResults": [{
          "sentiment": "positive",
          "confidence": 0.7928020390465644
      }, {
          "sentiment": "neutral",
          "confidence": 0.11748919864179037
      }, {
          "sentiment": "negative",
          "confidence": 0.08970876231164532
      }]
}]
```

To get a summary of the text, we can call the cognitive-text REST endpoint using `summary`:

```
curl -X POST --header "Authorization: Bearer ...=" "https://<oml-cloud-
service-location-url>/omlmod/v1/cognitive-text/summary"
--header 'Content-Type: application/json'
-d '{"textList":["Use this comprehensive guide to get started with the
Oracle Cloud Free Tier. ...that Oracle Cloud Infrastructure can offer."],
"topN":5}'
```

The response message body:

```
... [{
     "text": "Use this comprehensive guide to get started with the Oracle
     Cloud Free Tier. ...that Oracle Cloud Infrastructure can offer.",
     "summaryResults": [{
         "sentence": "Reading this book and creating your own application in
         the Free Tier is an excellent way to build familiarity with, and
         expertise in, Oracle Cloud Infrastructure. ",
         "weight": 0.6736350343541044
     }, {
         "sentence": "Examples in this book introduce the broad suite
         of Always Free options that are available from Oracle Cloud
         Infrastructure. ",
```

```
        "weight": 0.596030953896922
    }, {
        "sentence": "You also will learn about the virtual cloud network
        and application deployment, including how to create and deploy
        public-facing Oracle Application Express solutions and three-tier
        web applications on a foundation of Oracle REST Data Services. ",
        "weight": 0.8162674885046073
    }, {
        "sentence": "Mastering the content in this book leaves you well-
        positioned to make the transition into providing and supporting
        cloud-based applications and databases. ",
        "weight": 0.6206552547451695
    }, {
        "sentence": "You will have the knowledge and skills that you need
        to deploy modest applications along with a growing understanding of
        Oracle's Cloud platform that will serve you well as you go beyond
        the limits of the Always Free options and take full advantage of
        all that Oracle Cloud Infrastructure can offer.",
        "weight": 0.7240305647558988
    }]
}]
```

The request in this example would look like this as an HTTP request message:

```
POST /omlmod/v1/cognitive-text/summary HTTP/1.1
Host: <oml-cloud-service-location-url>
Authorization: Bearer eyJ...ik=
Content-Type: application/json
Content-Length: 1590

{"textList":["Use this comprehensive guide to get started with the Oracle
Cloud Free Tier. ...that Oracle Cloud Infrastructure can offer."],
"topN":5}
```

The first row is the request line, then header data, and, after the empty line, the message body.

And the response message would look like this:

```
HTTP/1.1 200 OK
Date: Fri, 22 Apr 2022 07:58:43 GMT
Content-Type: application/json
Content-Length: 2803
Connection: keep-alive
```

[{"text":"Use this comprehensive guide to get started with the Oracle
Cloud Free Tier. ...that Oracle Cloud Infrastructure can offer.",
"summaryResults":[{"sentence":"Reading this book and creating your own
application in the Free Tier is an excellent way to build familiarity
with, and expertise in, Oracle Cloud Infrastructure. ","weight":0.6
736350343541044},{"sentence":"Examples in this book introduce the broad
suite of Always Free options that are available from Oracle Cloud
Infrastructure. ","weight":0.596030953896922},{"sentence":"You also
will learn about the virtual cloud network and application deployment,
including how to create and deploy public-facing Oracle Application
Express solutions and three-tier web applications on a foundation of
Oracle REST Data Services. ","weight":0.8162674885046073},{"sentence":
"Mastering the content in this book leaves you well-positioned to make
the transition into providing and supporting cloud-based applications and
databases. ","weight":0.6206552547451695},{"sentence":"You will have the
knowledge and skills that you need to deploy modest applications along with
a growing understanding of Oracle's Cloud platform that will serve you
well as you go beyond the limits of the Always Free options and take full
advantage of all that Oracle Cloud Infrastructure can offer.",
"weight":0.7240305647558988}]}]

The response message starts with the HTTP version and the HTTP response status code. Then, it includes some header data and the message body.

To be able to use the Python REST API for embedded Python code execution, you need to have UDF Python functions registered in a Python script repository or Python objects registered in an OML4Py datastore located in the database. The Python objects only exist during the Python session if they are not stored in the Python script repository or OML4Py datastore.

To see the UDF scripts in the Python script repository, call the endpoint `scripts`:

```
curl -i -X GET --header "Authorization: Bearer ...PTik="oml/api/py-scripts/
v1/scripts
```

It returns, as explained earlier in this chapter, the header with the status code and the body (`results`) (some of the data has been replaced with three dots):

```
HTTP/1.1 200 OK
Date: Mon, 25 Apr 2022 07:09:45 GMT
Content-Type: application/json
Content-Length: 3132
Connection: keep-alive
Cache-Control: no-cache, no-store, must-revalidate
Pragma: no-cache
X-Frame-Options: SAMEORIGIN
X-XSS-Protection: 1;mode=block
Strict-Transport-Security: max-age=31536000; includeSubDomains
X-Content-Type-Options: nosniff
Content-Security-Policy: frame-ancestors 'none'
Set-Cookie: JSESSIONID=node0au1vdygtmknu10sn1bbxkbukb6.node0; Path=/oml;
Secure; HttpOnly
Expires: Thu, 01 Jan 1970 00:00:00 GMT
```

```
{"result":[
{"owner":"PYQSYS","date":"2022-04-23T12:36:14.000Z","name":"nn_pred",
"description":"A UDF built based on an AutoML notebook to predict ENROLLED
using a tablename as an input parameter","script":"def nn_pred...)\n
return (pred)"},
{"owner":"PYQSYS","date":"2022-04-23T12:37:44.000Z","name":"nn_predi",
"description":"A UDF built based on an AutoML ...\n  return (pred)"},
{"owner":"PYQSYS","date":"2022-04-23T09:09:20.000Z","name":"nn_predict",
"description":"A UDF built based on an AutoML..."},
{"owner":"PYQSYS","date":"2022-04-23T12:15:23.000Z","name":"nn_
prediction..."}
]}
```

Let's use a notebook we created in Chapter 5 based on the AutoML Experiment. The model created is a Python proxy object, and it will be gone after the session is closed. Therefore, we need to run all the steps on the notebook to get the proxy objects in the Python session. To store the model in the OML4Py datastore, we add a step in the notebook to register the model created (nn_mod) to the OML4Py datastore (ds_pymodel):

```
%python
oml.ds.save(objs={'nn_mod':nn_mod}, name="ds_pymodel", grantable=True,
overwrite=True)
```

In this example, the model nn_mod is stored in the OML4Py datastore called ds_pymodel and privileges are granted to all users. Now that it has been stored in the OML4Py datastore, we can call it whenever needed.

A Python object is always registered in the OML4Py datastore on the *user's schema*. You can add privileges using `oml.grant` and remove them using `oml.revoke`. In this example, there are two OML4Py datastores for the user: ds_pymodel and ds_pymodel_test. We grant privileges to ds_pymodel_test for only one user (MYUSER1) and privileges for all users (None) to datastore ds_pymodel:

```
%python
oml.grant(name="ds_pymodel_test", typ="datastore", user="MYUSER1")
```

```
%python
oml.grant(name="ds_pymodel", typ="datastore", user=None)
```

You can check that the model is in the OML4Py datastore using `oml.ds.dir`. It can be defined with parameters: user, grant, granted, grantable, all, and private.

```
%python
oml.ds.dir(dstype='grant')
    datastore_name  grantee
0        ds_pymodel   PUBLIC
1   ds_pymodel_test   MYUSER1
```

To find out what the OML4Py datastore includes, use `oml.ds.describe`:

```
%python
oml.ds.describe(name='ds_pymodel', owner=None)
  object_name   class  size  length  row_count  col_count
0      nn_mod  oml.nn  3198       1          1          1
```

You can delete an object from the OML4Py datastore using `oml.ds.delete`.

There are two database view for OML4Py datastores: `ALL_PYQ_DATASTORES` and `ALL_PYQ_DATASTORE_CONTENTS`. You can query those, using SQL, to get information about existing OML4Py datastores.

Let's create a UDF called `nn_predict`. The UDF will create predictions for the ENROLLED base on the data in a table called STUDENTTRAIN using the `nn_mod` model stored in the OML4Py datastore `ds_pymodel`. The result also includes the STUDENTID so that we will be able to join the data to the data from a database when building the APEX application. In the UDF, we import libraries needed, get the content of the table to a data frame, load the model from the OML4Py datastore, predict using the model, and finally return the result in JSON format.

```
nn_predict = """def nn_predict():
  import pandas as pd
  import oml
  import json
  data = oml.sync(table = ' STUDENTTRAIN ')
  obj_dict = oml.ds.load(name="ds_pymodel", to_globals=False)
  nn_mod = obj_dict["nn_mod"]
  mod_predict = nn_mod.predict(data ,supplemental_cols = data
  [:, ['STUDENTID']]).pull()
  json_result = mod_predict.to_json(orient='records')
  return(json_result)"""
```

And then, store the UDF in the Python script repository:

```
oml.script.create("nn_predict",
  func=nn_predict,
  is_global=True,
  overwrite=True,
  description= 'A UDF built based on an AutoML notebook to predict ENROLLED
  using data from a table STUDENTTRAIN.')
```

A UDF is registered to *PYQSYS* schema.

To call it from a notebook on another Python session, you import oml and load the UDF from the Python script repository. Then, call it with one of the functions of executing Python code. In this example do_eval:

```
%python
import oml
nn_predict =oml.script.load(name="nn_predict")
oml.do_eval(nn_predict)
```

To get a list of available scripts registered for the user, use oml.script.dir:

```
%python
oml.script.dir(sctype='user')
             name   ...                date
0       nn_predict  ... 2022-04-25 08:04:45
1  nn_predict_test  ... 2022-04-25 11:55:38

[2 rows x 4 columns]
```

Or, to list scripts that have been defined as Global:

```
%python
oml.script.dir(sctype='global')
             name   ...                date
0         nn_pred  ... 2022-04-23 12:36:14
1        nn_predi  ... 2022-04-23 12:37:44
2      nn_predict  ... 2022-04-25 08:05:32
3   nn_prediction  ... 2022-04-23 12:15:23

[4 rows x 4 columns]
```

You can grant and revoke privileges using the same `oml.grant` and `oml.revoke` as for Python objects in an OML4Py datastore, but for scripts, define `typ="pyqscript"`.

Another way to call the UDF is using the REST API:

```
curl -i -X POST --header "Authorization: Bearer ...="
--header "Content-Type: application/json"
--header "Accept: application/json"
-d '{"service":"MEDIUM"}'
"https://<oml-cloud-service-location-url>/oml/tenants/MyTenancy/
databases/MyDatabase/api/py-scripts/v1/do-eval/nn_predict"
```

Note that you can obtain the URL needed from the OCI Database Service Console.

If you want to drop the UDF from the Python script repository, use the `oml.script.drop` and add the function name in `" "`:

```
%python
import oml
oml.script.drop("nn_predict")
```

If you want to see the UDFs in the database, you can query the database view ALL_PYQ_SCRIPTS using SQL.

Using OML REST Services from APEX

In APEX, you can use OML4SQL through its PL/SQL packages and OML4Py using the OML4Py Embedded Python Execution (EPE) SQL API. To invoke Python UDFs from SQL, you can include OML4Py EPE functions in SQL queries. These functions include similar functions as Embedded Python REST API: pyqEval, pyqTableEval, pyqRowEval, pyqGroupEval, and pyqIndexEval.

You can also use REST APIs. This works even though APEX would be located in a different database than the machine learning objects.

The first step is to authenticate to get the authorization token. The OML REST services use OAuth 2.0 Password Grant flow, while only the Client Credentials flow is supported in APEX. Password Grant flow means that an access token is given with a username and a password and attached to a user's privileges. It might be useful to create a dedicated user for OML REST API, having only the limited privileges needed for using the service. Client Credentials flow instead uses server-to-server authentication.

Web Credentials are the best way to handle credentials in APEX. Because APEX Web Credentials only allow Client Credential OAuth 2.0 tokens, not Password tokens, you cannot just create a Web Credential for getting the token. There are several technical solutions for it. Let's see one possible solution.

In this solution, we create a Web Credential for the token, but we use a REST Data Service to obtain the token for it. Let's create the Web Credential for the token. Go to App Builder, Workspace Utilities, and select Web Credentials. This Web Credential does not call the service and get the token; it only stores it while it has been fetched to it using another mechanism explained later. The simple Web Credential needed is shown in Figure 6-1. Just give a name for the Credential and select HTTP Header as Authentication Type.

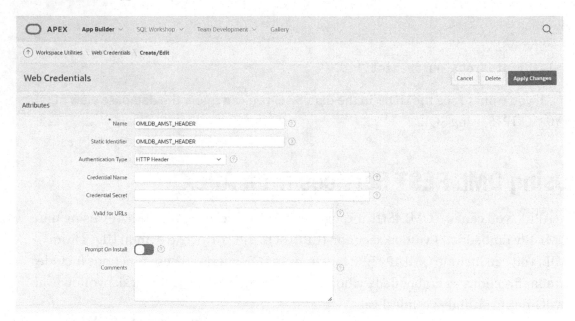

Figure 6-1. *Creating a Web Credential*

Then, we create a Data Source for obtaining the OAuth2 token. Select the application and then select *Shared Components*. Navigate to the bottom left corner and click *REST Data Sources*. Click *Create*. Select *From scratch* and click *Next*. Select *Simple HTTP* as REST Data Source Type, define a *name*, and insert the *<oml-cloud-service-location-url>/omluser/* as the *URL Endpoint*. Click *Next*. Now, you have the Remote Server defined including the Remote Server, Base URL, and Service URL Path. Click *Next*. For the Pagination type, keep the default: *No Pagination*, and click *Next*. Do **not** enable *Authentication Required*. Click *Advanced*. Add all the parameters needed as seen in Figure 6-2.

First, add the HTTP Header parameters for the request message: Content-Type = application/json, and Accept = application/json. Then, select POST as the HTTP method. In the request body, insert the information needed for the Password Flow.

```
{

     "grant_type" : "password",
     "username" : "YourUsername",
     "password" : "YourPassword"

}
```

Insert your username and password to YourUsername and YourPassword. Then, define the response message by selecting Choose File in a Response Sample field in the page and inserting the file. You can find that from the Oracle documentation under REST API endpoints.

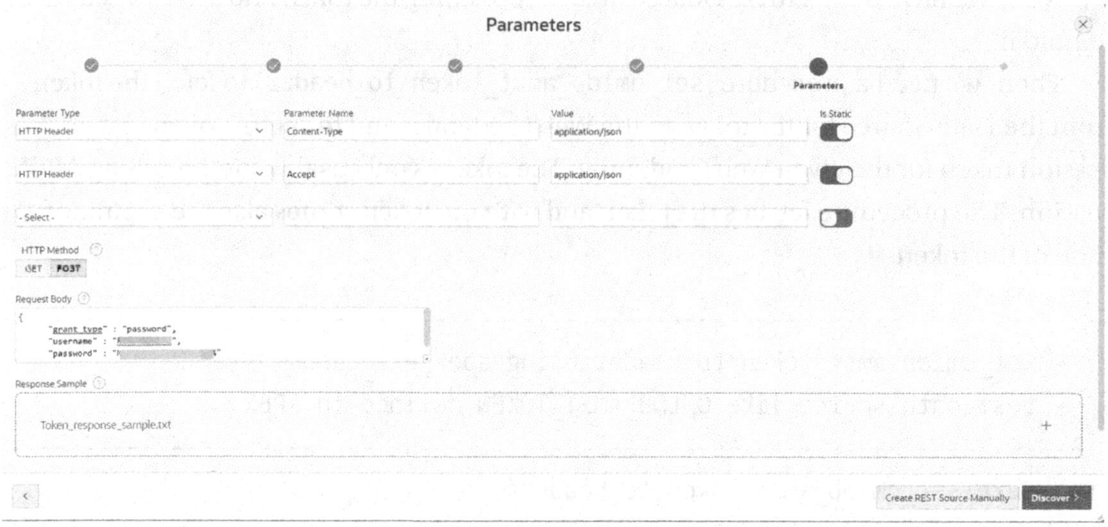

Figure 6-2. *Parameters for a REST Data Service*

Then click *Discover*. If the token is successfully obtained, as seen in Figure 6-3, click *Create REST Data Source*.

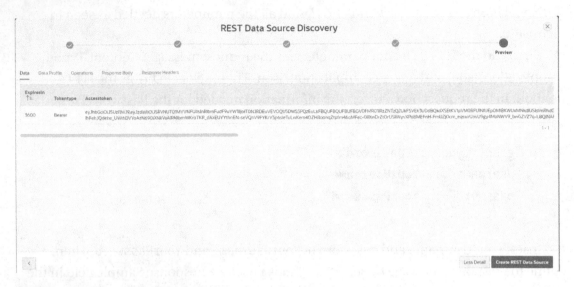

Figure 6-3. *The REST Data Service returns a token*

Now, we have built a REST Data Source for obtaining the token and a Web Credential to hold it.

Then, we need a procedure (`set_omldb_amst_token_to_header`) to fetch the token from the Data Source for the token to the Web Credential and to set the token as a session token for the given Web Credential. The token is only usable for the calling APEX session. The procedure fetches the token and with the token comes also the expiration time of the token.

```
-------------------------------------------------------------------------
  -- set_omldb_amst_token_to_header using apex_exec and
  -- rest data source like OMLDB_AMST_TOKEN defined in APEX
-------------------------------------------------------------------------
procedure set_omldb_amst_token_to_header(
p_token_source in  varchar2,
p_credential in  varchar2,
p_token_expiry_epoch out number) is
    --
    l_columns apex_exec.t_columns;
    l_context apex_exec.t_context;
```

```
  type t_column_position is table of pls_integer index by
  varchar2(32767);
  l_column_position t_column_position;
begin
  --
  -- specify columns to select from the web source module
  apex_exec.add_column(p_columns => l_columns, p_column_name =>
  'ACCESSTOKEN');
  apex_exec.add_column(p_columns => l_columns, p_column_name =>
  'EXPIRESIN');
  apex_exec.add_column(p_columns => l_columns, p_column_name =>
  'TOKENTYPE');
  --
  -- invoke Web Source Module and select data
  l_context := apex_exec.open_rest_source_query(
      p_static_id  => p_token_source,
      p_columns    => l_columns );
  --
  -- now get result set positions for the selected columns
  l_column_position('ACCESSTOKEN') := apex_exec.get_column_position
  (l_context, 'ACCESSTOKEN');
  l_column_position('EXPIRESIN')   := apex_exec.get_column_position
  (l_context, 'EXPIRESIN');
  l_column_position('TOKENTYPE')   := apex_exec.get_column_position
  (l_context, 'TOKENTYPE');
  --
  -- loop through result set (this case only one row) and set token to
    session credential and set token expiration as epoch
  while apex_exec.next_row( l_context ) loop
    apex_credential.set_session_credentials (
      p_credential_static_id => p_credential,
      p_key                  => 'Authorization',
      p_value                => 'Bearer ' ||apex_exec.get_varchar2
                                (l_context, l_column_position
                                ('ACCESSTOKEN')));
```

```
      p_token_expiry_epoch := convert_to_epoch(sysdate) + apex_exec.get_
      number( l_context, l_column_position('EXPIRESIN'));
    end loop;
    --
    -- finally: release all resources
    apex_exec.close( l_context );
  exception
    when others then
        -- IMPORTANT: also release all resources, when an exception occurs!
        apex_exec.close( l_context );
        raise;
end set_omldb_amst_token_to_header;
```

A function convert_to_epoch converts the given day to epoch. Epoch is used to handle the token expiration. A token is valid for an hour.

```
-------------------------------------------------------------------------
-- convert_to_epoch converts a given date to epoch, which is seconds from
-- the date 1.1.1970
-------------------------------------------------------------------------
function convert_to_epoch(p_date in date) return number is
  l_epoch number(38);
begin
  select (p_date - to_date('1-1-1970 00:00:00','MM-DD-YYYY
  HH24:Mi:SS'))*24*3600 into l_epoch from dual;
  return l_epoch;
end convert_to_epoch;
```

For the expiration, we need an Application Item. In APEX, go to the application, select *Shared Components*, *Application Items*, and add the application item as shown in Figure 6-4.

Figure 6-4. *Adding an Application Item*

Now, we are now ready to call an OML REST API. We will call the same `cognitive-text/summary` we used earlier in this chapter. To be able to call it, we define a *REST Data Source*. Select the application, and then select *Shared Components*. Navigate to the bottom left corner and click *REST Data Sources*. Create a new REST Data Source as seen in Figure 6-5. Define a name, and select *Simple HTTP* for REST Data Source Type. Define the path to the service endpoint and select the Web Credential defined earlier as Credentials in the Authentication section.

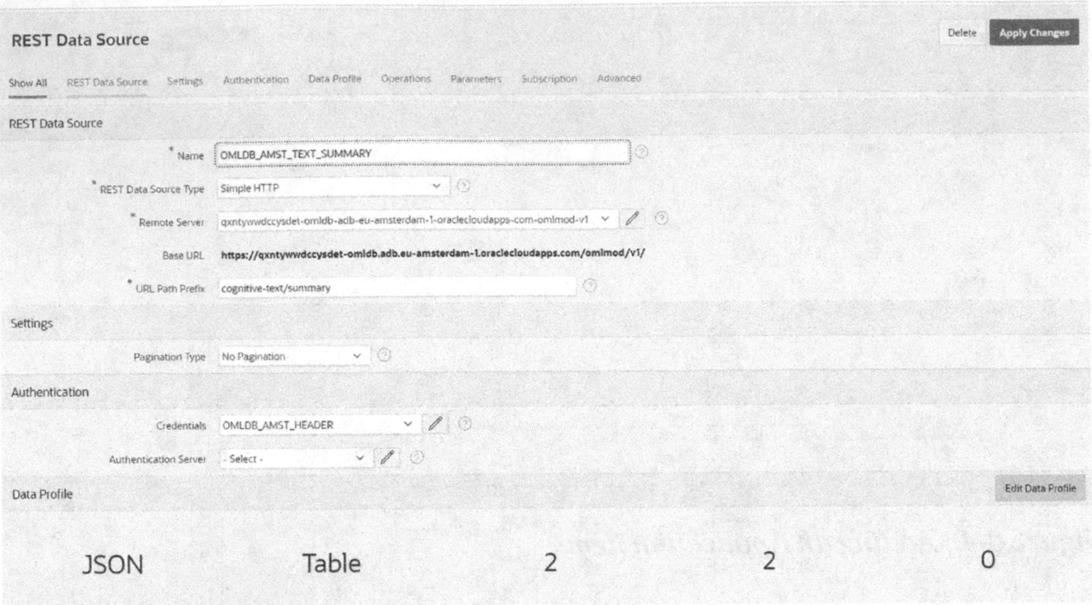

Figure 6-5. *Creating a REST Data Source for the Summary API endpoint*

The request operation type for Summary endpoint is POST. You can remove all other operations as seen in Figure 6-6.

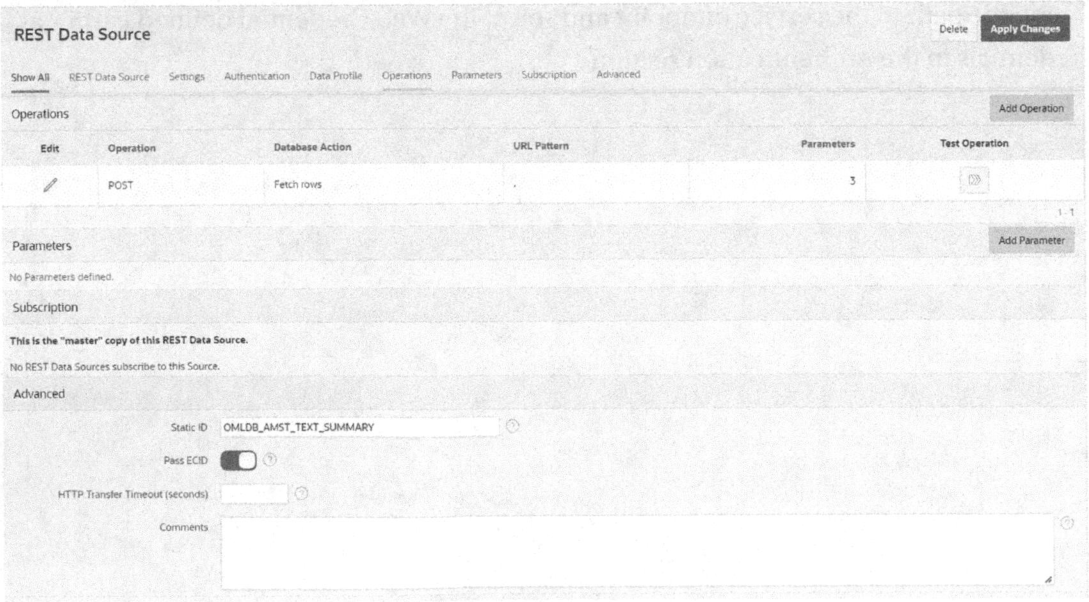

Figure 6-6. *REST Data Source Operations*

Select *Fetch Rows* as the Database Operation, and insert the request body template (Figure 6-7).

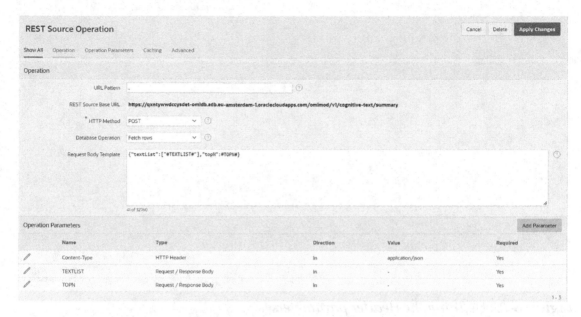

Figure 6-7. *Operation Parameters for the POST operation*

Define the parameters. Insert a Content-Type: application/json parameter for the HTTP Header as shown in Figure 6-8.

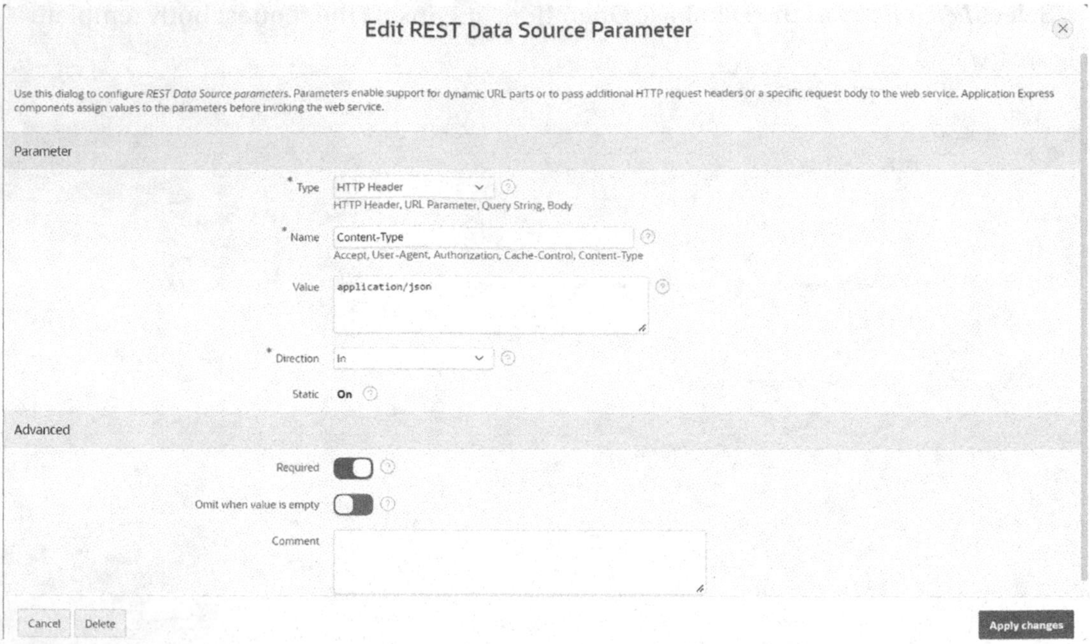

Figure 6-8. *Defining the Header parameters*

Then, insert the Request Body parameters: Textlist (Figure 6-9) and TopN (Figure 6-10).

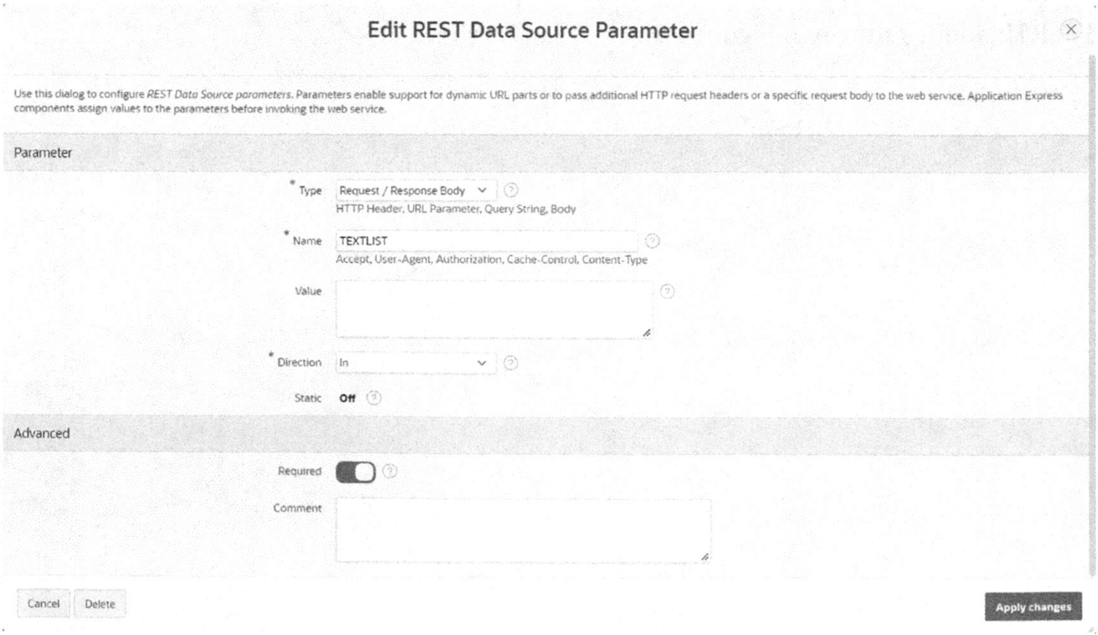

Figure 6-9. *Defining the message body parameter TextList*

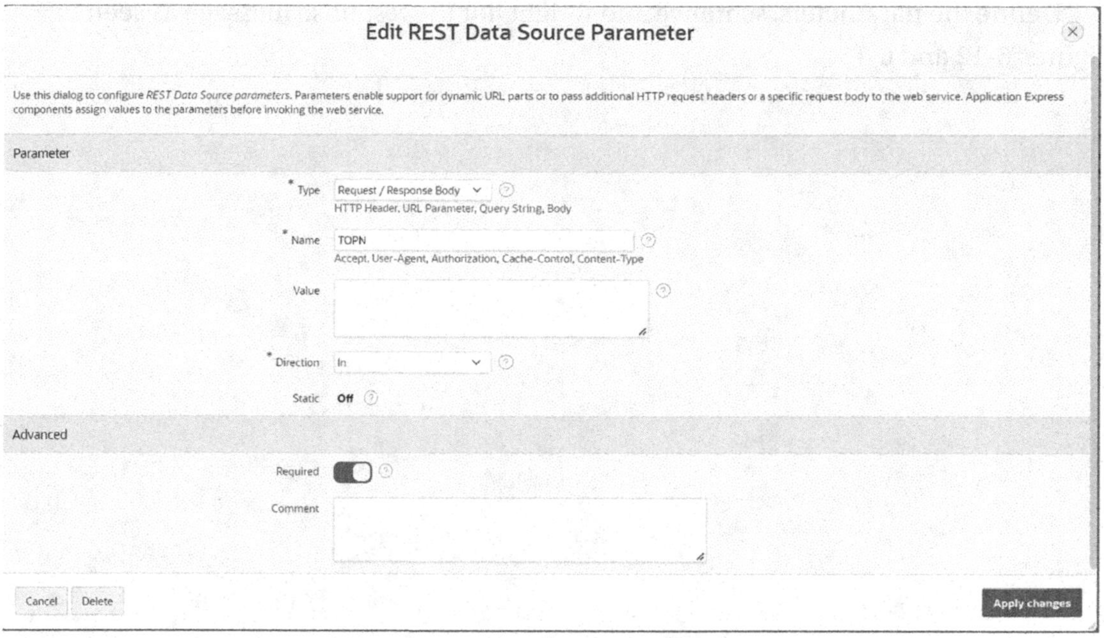

Figure 6-10. *Defining a message body parameter TopN*

Define the response message as seen in Figure 6-11.

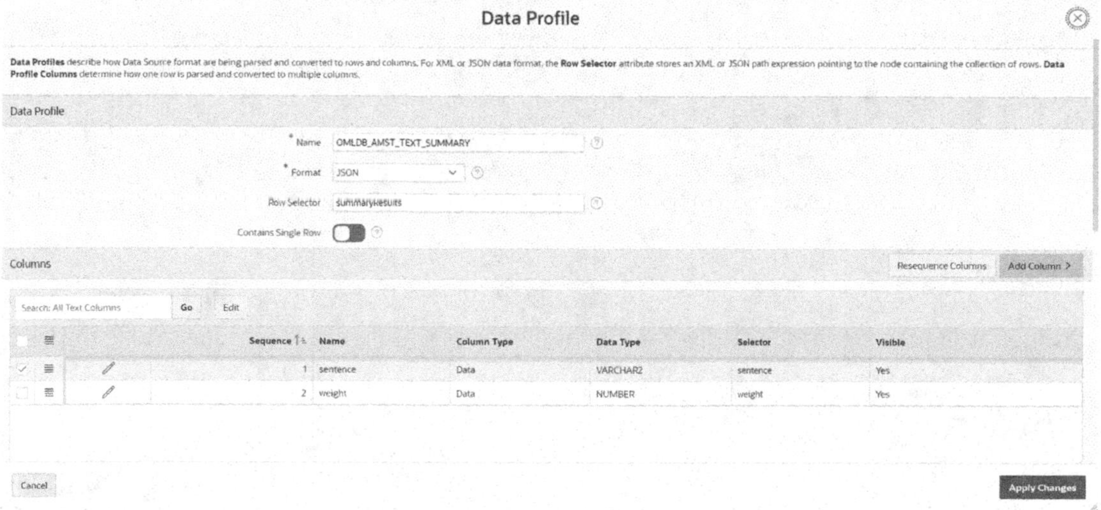

Figure 6-11. *Defining the response message*

Define the parameters, sentence and weight, for the response message as seen in Figures 6-12 and 6-13.

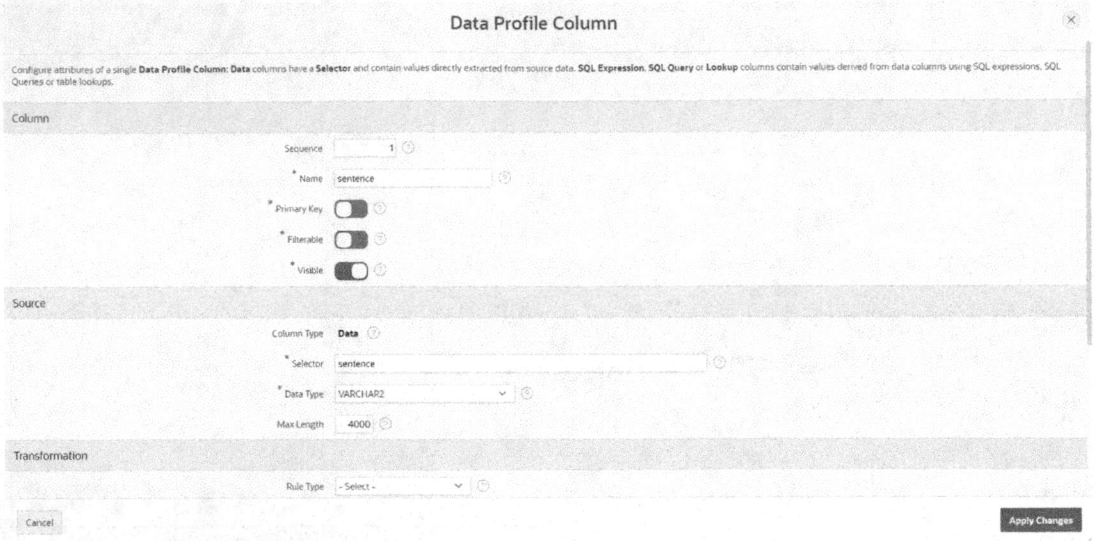

Figure 6-12. *Defining the sentence parameter*

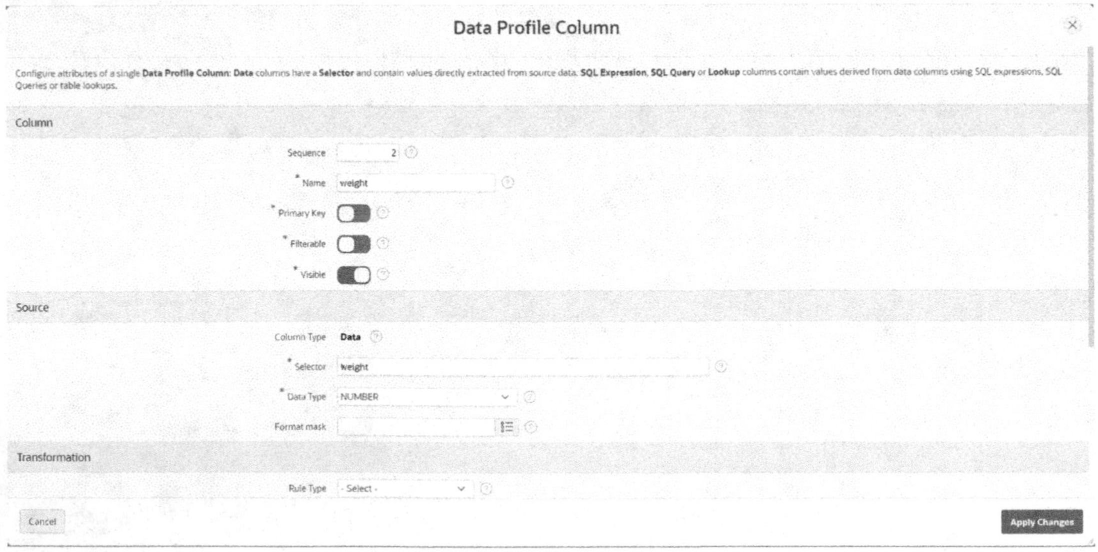

Figure 6-13. *Defining the weight parameter*

Now, you are able to use the Web Data Source to get summaries for the provided list of text strings using the OML REST API.

Create a page, for example, an interactive report, using the wizard. Select REST Data Source and then the REST Data Source you created earlier for REST Data Source, as seen in Figure 6-14.

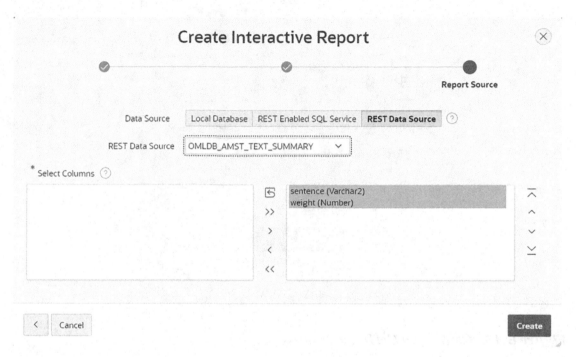

Figure 6-14. *Creating an Interactive Report*

Open the page for editing. First, create a GetToken Process as shown in Figures 6-15 and 6-16.

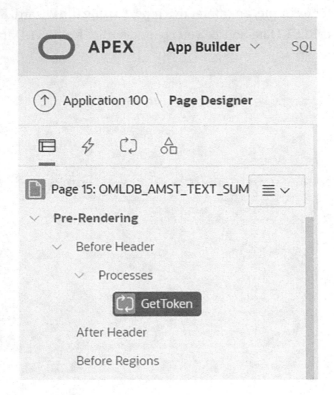

Figure 6-15. *Creating a GetToken Process*

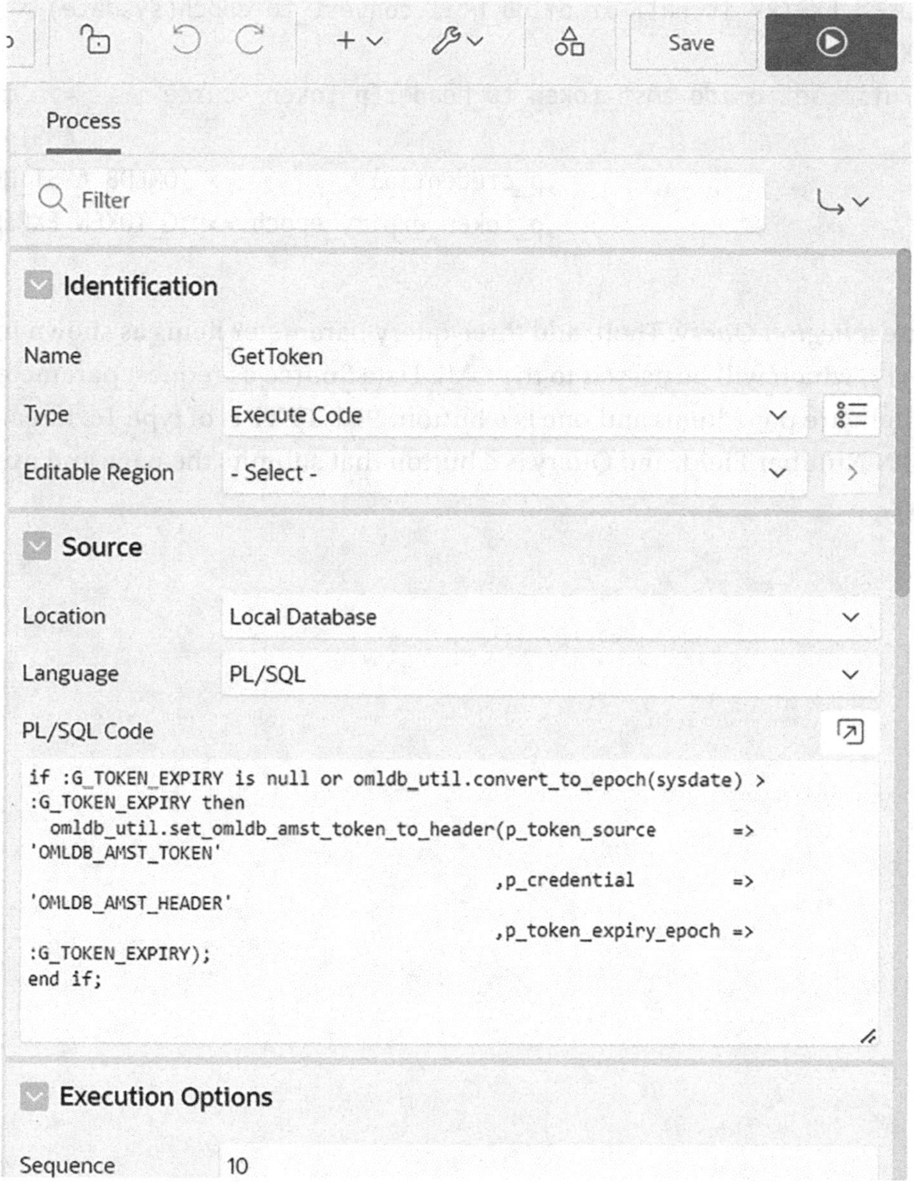

Figure 6-16. *PL/SQL code for the GetToken Process*

```
if :G_TOKEN_EXPIRY is null or omldb_util.convert_to_epoch(sysdate) > :G_
TOKEN_EXPIRY then
  omldb_util.set_omldb_amst_token_to_header(p_token_source      => 'OMLDB_
                                                              AMST_TOKEN'
                            ,p_credential         => 'OMLDB_AMST_HEADER'
                            ,p_token_expiry_epoch => :G_TOKEN_EXPIRY);
end if;
```

Create a *Region Query*. Then, add three query parameter items as shown in Figure 6-17, which will be passed to the OML Data Source as request parameters. Two of them are page items and one is a button. P15_TEXT is of type Textarea, P15_TOPN Number Field, and Query is a button that submits the page and executes the query.

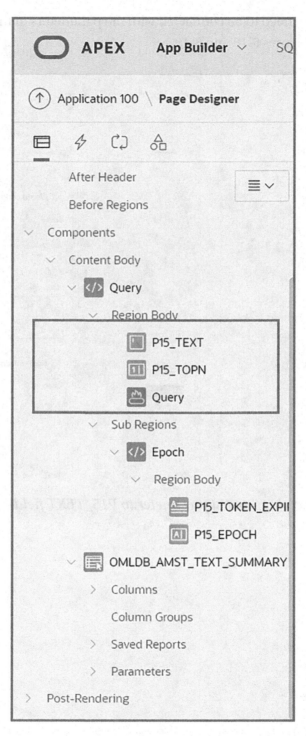

Figure 6-17. *Adding items to the APEX page*

These parameters need to be connected with the parameters in the REST Data Source as shown in Figures 6-18 and 6-19.

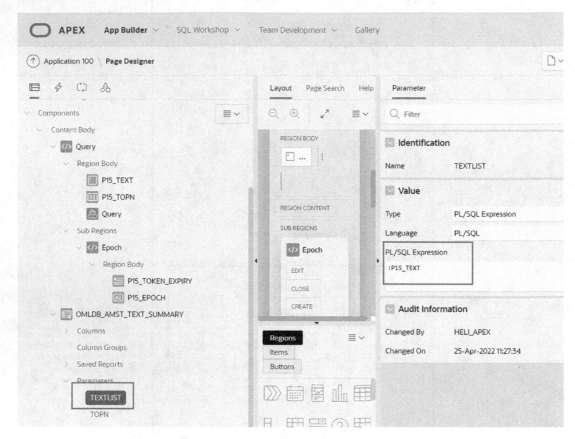

Figure 6-18. *Connecting Textlist parameter to P15_TEXT field*

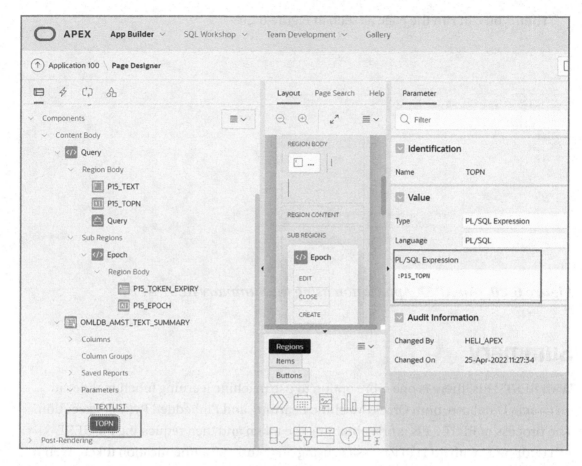

Figure 6-19. *Connecting TopN parameter to P15_TOPN field*

Also, create *Subregion* epoch (Figure 6-17) and the two page items: F15_TOKEN_
EXPIRY as Display Only and F15_TOKEN as Text Field.

Then, you can run the page as seen in Figure 6-20.

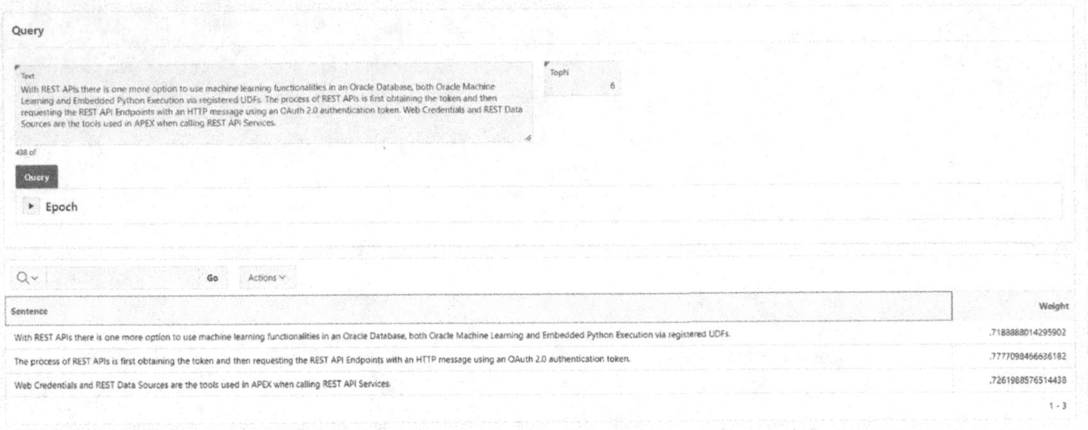

Figure 6-20. *An APEX Application using the Summary REST API*

Summary

With REST APIs, there is one more option to use machine learning functionalities in an Oracle Database, both Oracle Machine Learning and Embedded Python Execution. The process of REST APIs is first obtaining the token and then requesting the REST API endpoints with an HTTP message using an OAuth 2.0 authentication token. Web Credentials and REST Data Sources are the tools used in APEX when calling REST API Services.

CHAPTER 7

Data Labeling

Supervised learning is a subcategory of machine learning where the process is supervised with labeled data. The model is trained and tested with known input and known output data. For known output data, that means the data has to be labeled. Data Labeling changes a dataset not usable by supervised learning into dataset usable by it.

The Data Labeling service provides a process for identifying features of complex objects such as documents, text, and images and to annotate, or label, them based on those features. Data Labeling process consists of creating datasets of data records and applying labels to those records. Datasets can be exported as line-delimited JSON (JSONL) for further use in a supervised machine learning process.

Using this service, you can label documents in PDF, TIF, and TIFF format, text files in TXT format, and images in JPG, JPEG, and PNG format.

Setting Up the Service

To start with the Data Labeling service, you need an Oracle Cloud Infrastructure (OCI) account with Service Administrator role privileges or somebody who can set up the service and grant you the privileges needed. You also need a supported browser. Please check the supported browsers from the OCI documentation.

To start, create a compartment for the Data Labeling resources. This is not a mandatory step, but recommended for better security and easier management of privileges. Select *Identity & Security* from the navigation menu and select *Compartments*. Select the compartment where you want to create the subcompartment to, and click *Create Compartment* as seen in Figure 7-1.

© Adrian Png and Heli Helskyaho 2022
A. Png and H. Helskyaho, *Extending Oracle Application Express with Oracle Cloud Features*,
https://doi.org/10.1007/978-1-4842-8170-3_7

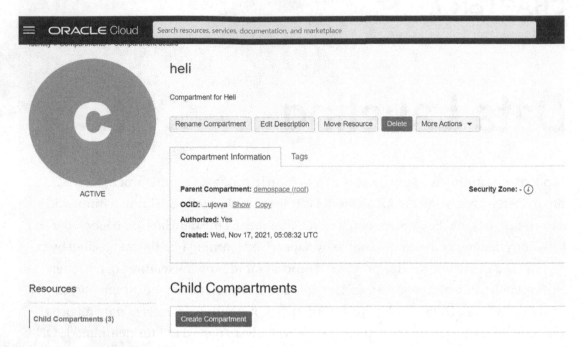

Figure 7-1. *The Child Compartments section of the Compartment page*

Insert the data needed as seen in Figure 7-2: the name, a description, and possibly some tags. Then, click *Create Compartment*.

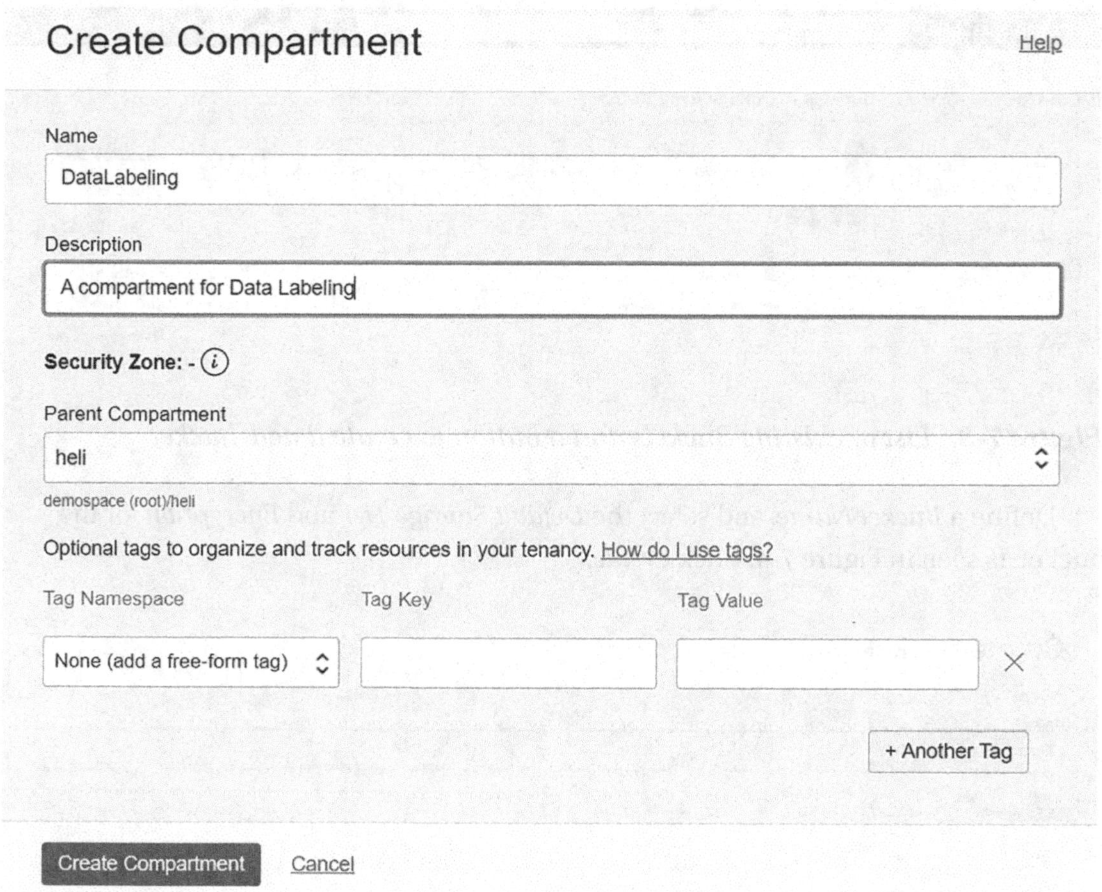

Create Compartment

Help

Name

DataLabeling

Description

A compartment for Data Labeling

Security Zone: - (i)

Parent Compartment

heli

demospace (root)/heli

Optional tags to organize and track resources in your tenancy. How do I use tags?

Tag Namespace   Tag Key   Tag Value

None (add a free-form tag)   ✕

+ Another Tag

Create Compartment   Cancel

Figure 7-2. *Creating a compartment*

Then, create the *buckets* needed for storing the data. Even if you use data from a local computer, you need an object storage and a bucket to store the datasets and records created by the Data Labeling process. To create a bucket, select *Storage* from the navigation menu. Then, select *Buckets*. Select the correct Compartment from the list and click *Create Bucket* (Figure 7-3).

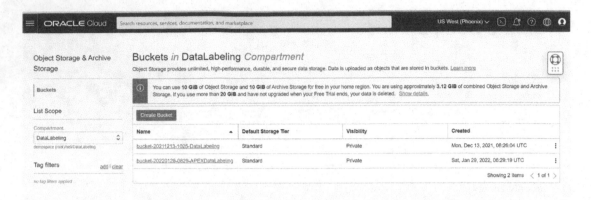

Figure 7-3. *List of existing Buckets and a button to create a new bucket*

Define a *Bucket Name,* and select the *Default Storage Tier* and *Encryption* for the bucket as seen in Figure 7-4. Click *Create.*

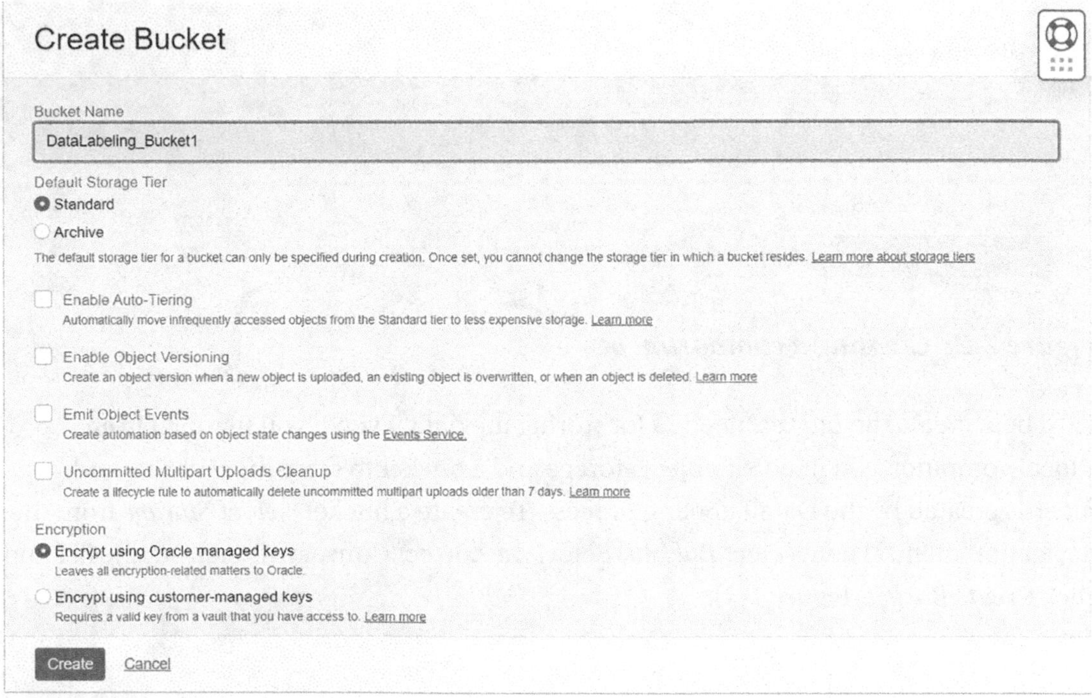

Create Bucket

Bucket Name

DataLabeling_Bucket1

Default Storage Tier
- ● Standard
- ○ Archive

The default storage tier for a bucket can only be specified during creation. Once set, you cannot change the storage tier in which a bucket resides. Learn more about storage tiers

☐ Enable Auto-Tiering
Automatically move infrequently accessed objects from the Standard tier to less expensive storage. Learn more

☐ Enable Object Versioning
Create an object version when a new object is uploaded, an existing object is overwritten, or when an object is deleted. Learn more

☐ Emit Object Events
Create automation based on object state changes using the Events Service.

☐ Uncommitted Multipart Uploads Cleanup
Create a lifecycle rule to automatically delete uncommitted multipart uploads older than 7 days. Learn more

Encryption
- ● Encrypt using Oracle managed keys
  Leaves all encryption-related matters to Oracle.
- ○ Encrypt using customer-managed keys
  Requires a valid key from a vault that you have access to. Learn more

Create   Cancel

Figure 7-4. *Creating a new bucket*

The access to Data Labeling service, and the type of access a user has, is controlled with *policies*. By default, only the users in the Administrators group have access to all Data Labeling resources. All other user group privileges must be managed with policies. The policies can be defined for an individual user, but the best practice is to create a user group, define the policies for that group, and then add users to that group. Using this method makes maintaining the privileges easier.

Start by creating a user group for Data Labeling users. Then, add the users to this group. In this example, we will create an IAM user group and an IAM user.

Note If you are using an Identity Cloud Service Provider (IDCS Provider), for example, Oracle Identity Cloud Service (OICS), create the group and assign the users under *Federation.*

Create a user group for Data Labeling by selecting *Identity & Security* from the navigation menu. Then, select *Groups* to see the Groups page as seen in Figure 7-5.

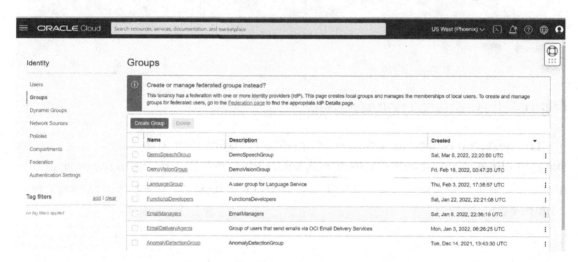

Figure 7-5. *A list of user groups and a button to create a new*

Click *Create Group*. Define the *Name* and the *Description* (Figure 7-6). Then, click *Create*.

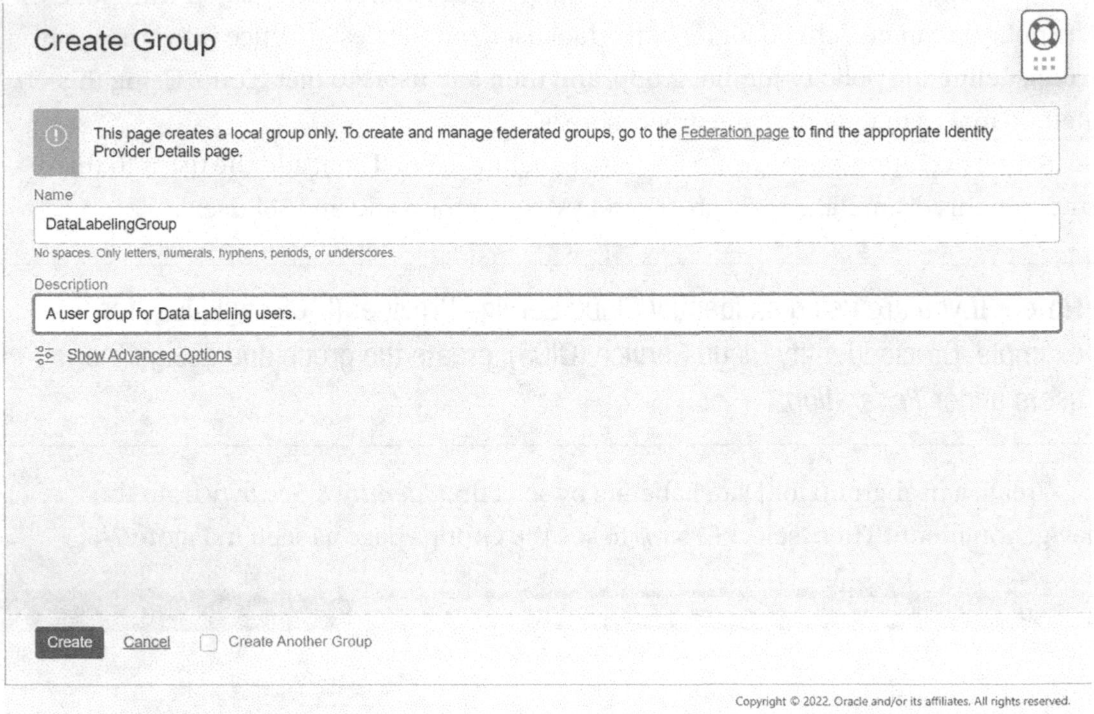
Create Group
This page creates a local group only. To create and manage federated groups, go to the Federation page to find the appropriate Identity Provider Details page.
Name
DataLabelingGroup
No spaces. Only letters, numerals, hyphens, periods, or underscores.
Description
A user group for Data Labeling users.
Show Advanced Options
Create
Cancel
Create Another Group
Copyright © 2022, Oracle and/or its affiliates. All rights reserved.

Figure 7-6. *Creating a new user group*

The next step is to create a new user or add an existing user to this DataLabelingGroup. To create a new user, select *Identity & Security* from the navigation menu. Then, select *Users*. A new user is added by clicking *Create User* in the Users page (Figure 7-7).

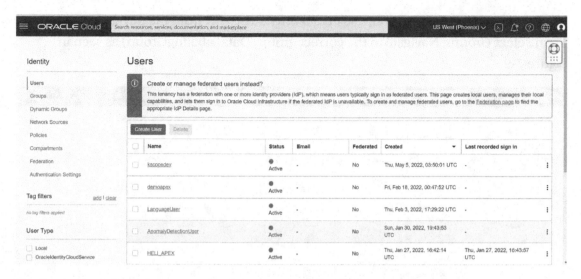

Figure 7-7. *A list of users and a button to add a new user*

Insert the *Name* and the *Description* for the user (Figure 7-8). You can also add the *email address.* Click *Create.*

Note   If you are creating an Oracle Identity Cloud Services user, you can add the user to a user group while creating a user.

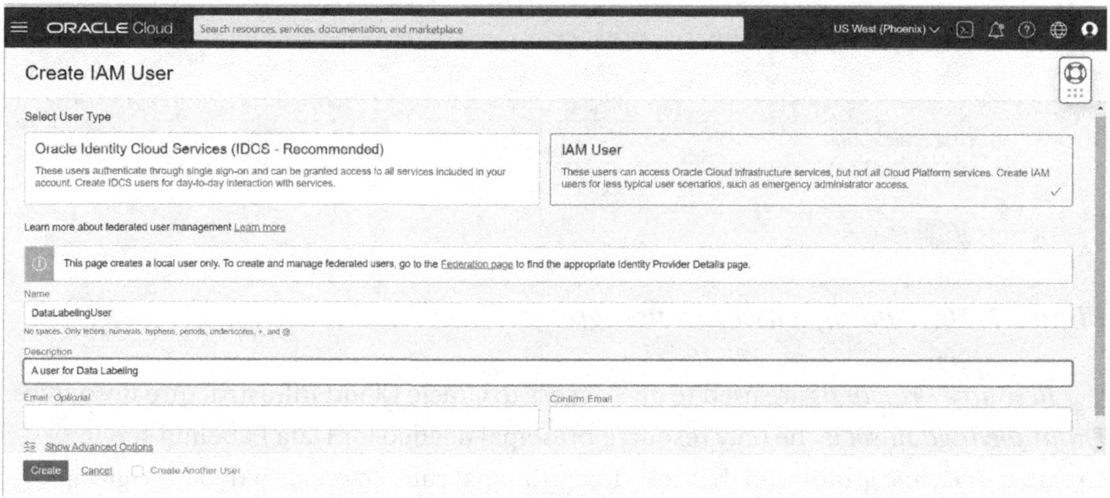

Figure 7-8. *Creating a new user*

To add a user to a user group, select *Identity & Security* from the navigation menu. Then select *Groups*. Navigate to the correct group (DataLabelingGroup) as seen in Figure 7-9.

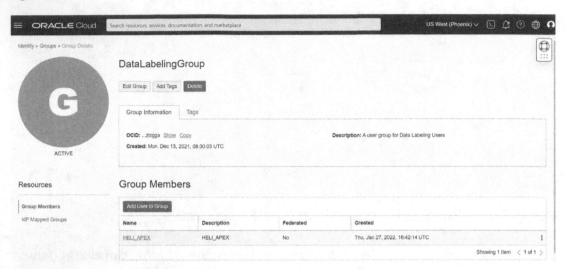

Figure 7-9. *A list of group members and a button to add new members to the group*

Click *Add User to Group*. Select the user from the list of users and click *Add* (Figure 7-10).

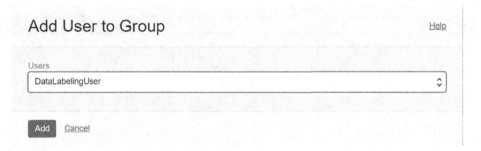

Figure 7-10. *Adding a user to a user group*

Resource Principals are used to give access to Oracle Cloud Infrastructure Resources. *Datalabelingdataset* is the only resource principal needed for Data Labeling service. Create a *dynamic group* with that resource principal rule. To create a dynamic group, select *Identity & Security* from the navigation menu and then select *Dynamic Groups*. The Dynamic Groups page is shown in Figure 7-11.

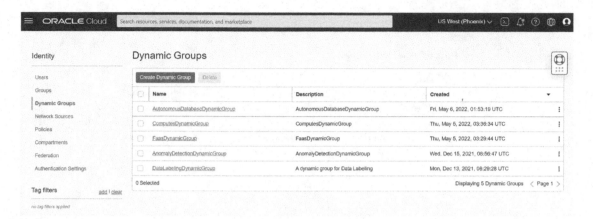

Figure 7-11. *A list of dynamic groups and a button for creating a new dynamic group*

Click *Create Dynamic Group*. Insert the *Name* and a *description* for the dynamic group. For the rule, define ALL {resource.type = 'datalabelingdataset'} as shown in Figure 7-12.

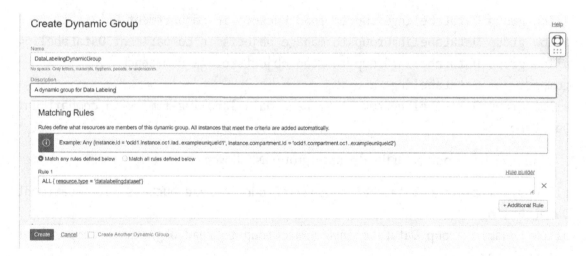

Figure 7-12. *Creating a new dynamic group with rules defined*

The next step is to create two *policies* in the parent compartment. Select *Identity & Security* from the navigation menu and then select *Policies*. Navigate to the parent compartment (in our example compartment Heli). The policies we are creating for the demo are DataLabeling-non-tech-user-policy and DataLabeling-dynamic-group-policy shown in Figure 7-13.

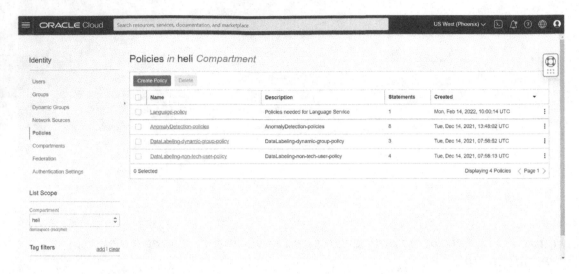

Figure 7-13. *A list of policies and a button for creating new policies*

To create a policy, click *Create Policy*.

First, create a policy for the user group (non-administrator users) as follows:

```
allow group DataLabelingGroup to read buckets in compartment DataLabeling
allow group DataLabelingGroup to manage objects in compartment DataLabeling
allow group DataLabelingGroup to read objectstorage-namespaces in
compartment DataLabeling
allow group DataLabelingGroup to manage data-labeling-family in compartment
DataLabeling
```

Then, create a policy for the dynamic group as follows:

```
allow dynamic-group DataLabelingDynamicGroup to read buckets in compartment
DataLabeling
allow dynamic-group DataLabelingDynamicGroup to read objects in compartment
DataLabeling
allow dynamic-group DataLabelingDynamicGroup to manage objects in
compartment DataLabeling where any {request.permission='OBJECT_CREATE'}
```

Remember to click the *Show manual editor* in the Policy Builder to be able to add these policies.

In our example, we have created a compartment DataLabeling, a user group DataLabelingGroup, and a dynamic user group DataLabelingDynamicGroup. Then we created two policy sets, DataLabeling-non-tech-user-policy and DataLabeling-dynamic-group-policy.

To learn more about the best practices, setting up the OCI environment and the policies, see the Oracle manual. For example, to learn more about the policies, go to `https://docs.oracle.com/en-us/iaas/Content/Identity/Concepts/policies.htm`.

To start with the Data Labeling service, click *Analytics & AI* on the navigation menu. Select *Data Labeling* under Machine Learning (Figure 7-14).

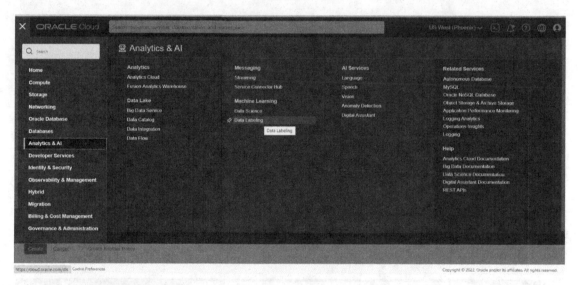

Figure 7-14. *Data Labeling in the OCI Console*

Datasets, Records, and Labeling

The Data Labeling process labels records in a dataset. The first step in the process is to create a dataset. A dataset consists of one or more data records. Select files that include the data to be labeled. The process of creating a dataset converts those files to records. Then, you manually label the record in a dataset. Labeling means you give each record in a dataset a label or an annotation.

Creating a Dataset and Records

In Data Labeling (Figure 7-15), select *Datasets*. Select the correct Compartment. This is the compartment you set the policies to. Click *Create dataset* button.

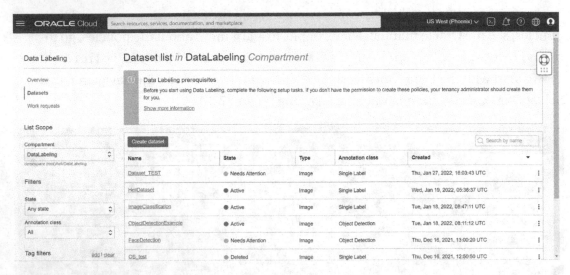

Figure 7-15. *A list of datasets and a button for creating a new dataset*

Define a *name* for the dataset, and optionally define a *description*. Then, choose the type of the data, the *Dataset Format*: Images, Text, or Documents. In Figure 7-16, the Image option has been selected.

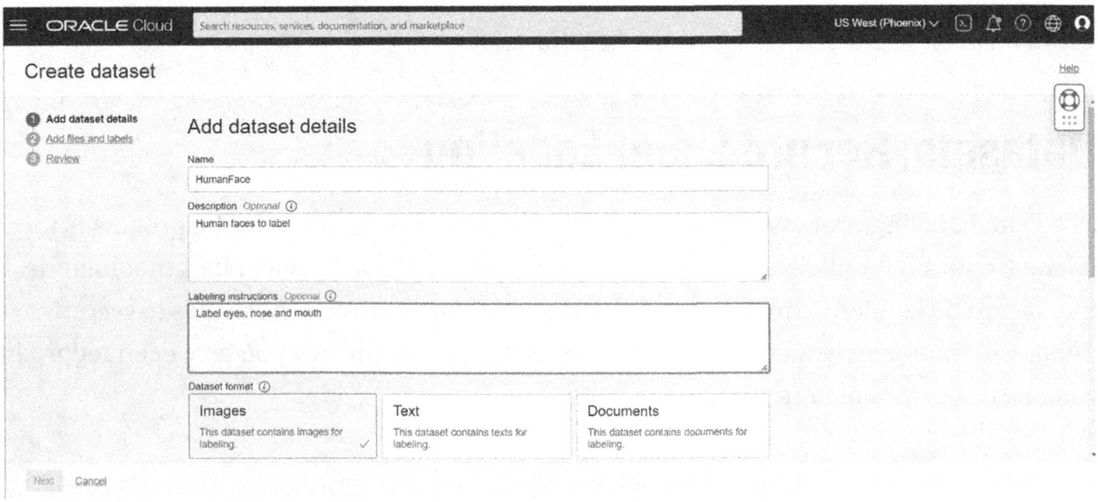

Figure 7-16. *Adding the details for a new dataset*

The *Annotation class* options depend on the chosen dataset format. For *Images*, the annotation class options are single label, multiple labels, or object detection. For *Text*, the options are single label, multiple labels, or entity extraction. For *Documents*, the options are single label or multiple labels. Choose the preferred annotation class. In Figure 7-17, you can see the annotation class options for image data. If you want, you can also add *Tags* for the dataset. When you are ready, click *Next*.

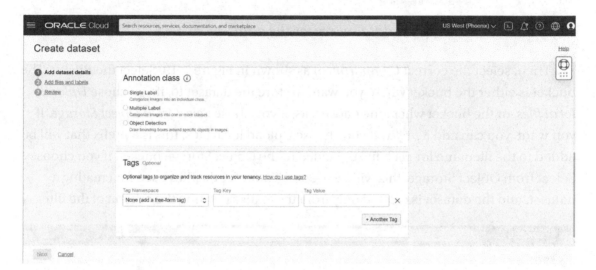

Figure 7-17. *Available annotation classes for images*

There are two options for adding the files that will be used for creating the dataset (Figure 7-18): *Upload local files* or *Select from Object Storage*. Choose the option based on the data you are going to label.

Note   If you want to load more than 100 files at a time from a local folder, either load them into an Object Storage bucket before creating the dataset, or use the CLI or SDK.

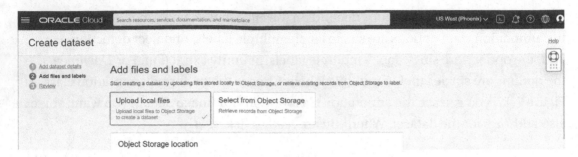

Figure 7-18. *Selecting the data source for the dataset*

Then, select the correct *Compartment* as shown in Figure 7-19. Select the *Bucket*. The bucket is either the bucket where you want to store the dataset to, if you chose *Upload local files*, or the bucket where the data exists, if you chose *Select from Object Storage*. If you want, you can add a *prefix*. If you choose Upload local files, this is a prefix that will be added to the filename for each file uploaded to the Object Storage bucket. If you choose Select from Object Storage, this will be used as a filter for the files used for creating a dataset, and the dataset is created only from those files meeting the criteria of the filter.

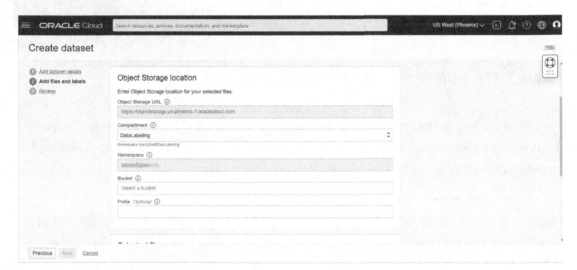

Figure 7-19. *Defining the Object Storage details for a dataset*

Then, select the files that will be added to the dataset. If you choose Upload local files as the data source (Figure 7-18), you will select files from your local computer (Figure 7-20). If you choose Select from Object Storage, the files from that Object Storage are shown to be selected.

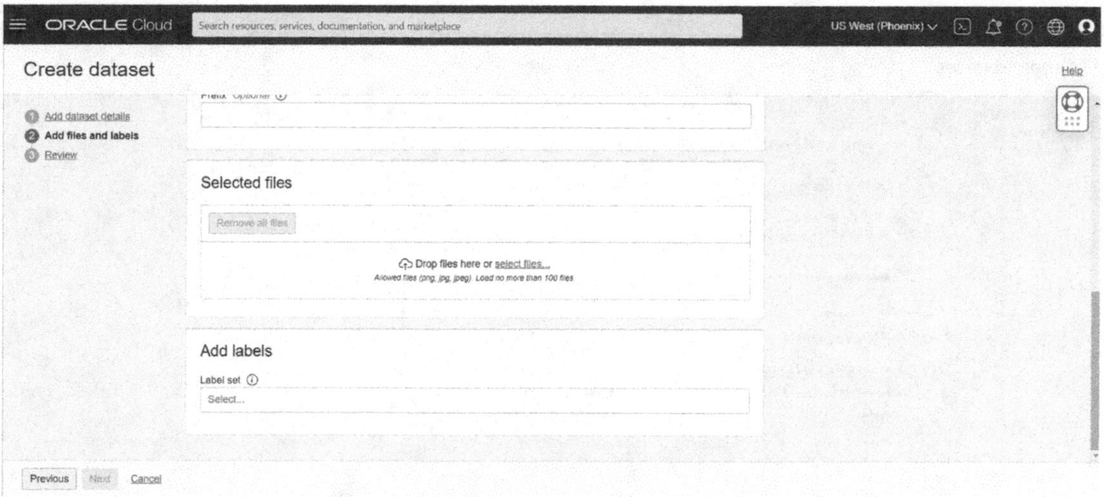

Figure 7-20. *Selecting files for a dataset*

The last step is to add labels that will be used when labeling the records in the dataset (Figure 7-21). You must add at least one label, but it is better to add all labels needed. You can add more labels later, if you realize they are missing. Click *Next*.

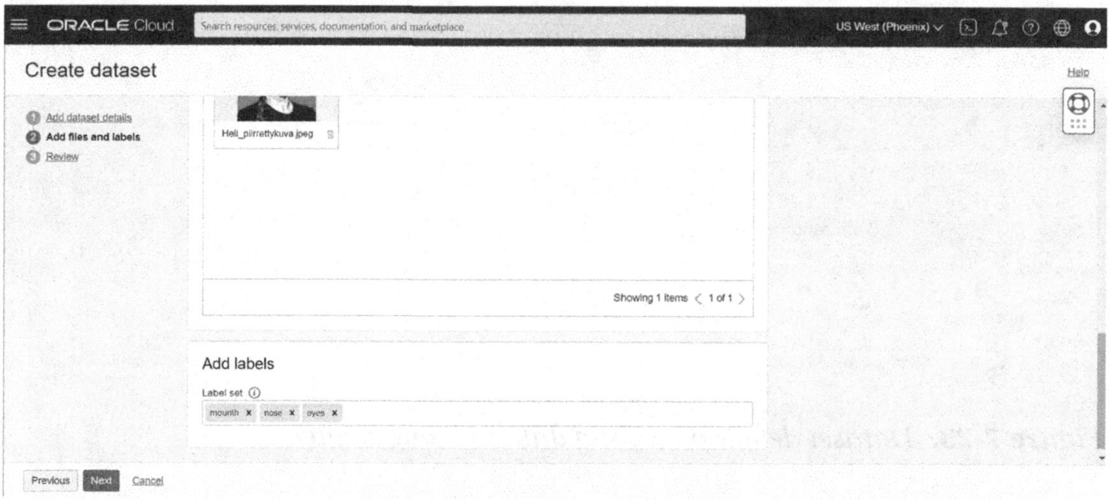

Figure 7-21. *Defining the labels for a dataset*

Now on the *Review page* (Figure 7-22), check that all is as you wanted. If you notice anything wrong, click either *Edit dataset details* or *Edit files and labels* to correct the mistake. If all is ok, click *Create*. The dataset creation process starts and can be seen on the Dataset details page showing the status as *Creating* (Figure 7-23).

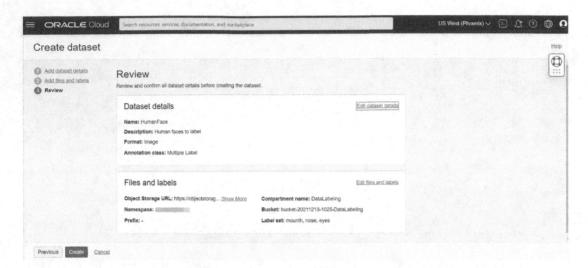

Figure 7-22. *The review page to check the details before creating a dataset*

Figure 7-23. *Dataset details page for a dataset being created*

Each file selected for the dataset will be transformed to one record in the dataset. When the dataset has been successfully created, you can see the records in the *Dataset details* page of the chosen dataset showing its status as *Active*. This is shown in Figure 7-24. When the dataset has been created the first time, all the records are marked as unlabeled.

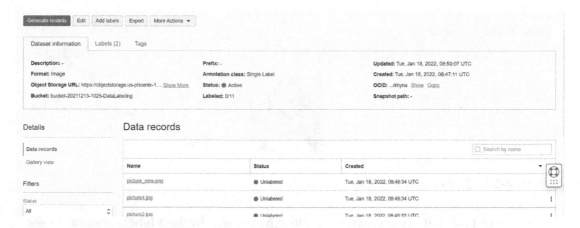

Figure 7-24. *Dataset details*

You can follow the progress of the dataset creation process on the *Work request* (Figure 7-26) tab found from the Data Labeling main page. You can see in detail how the Work request is progressing by selecting *Log messages* (Figure 7-29). If there are any errors during the dataset creation, you can find information about that in the *Error messages* tab (Figure 7-30).

Labeling Records in a Dataset

The next step is to label the records. If you did not add all labels needed while creating the dataset, you can click the *Add Label* button (Figure 7-24) on Dataset details page to add more labels. The maximum number of labels is 255. You can find a list of tags of a dataset under Labels tab shown in Figure 7-24.

To label a record, you can either click the name of the record on the list or select the three-dot menu and select *Label*. Select the correct label/labels from the label list. Then, click *Save* if you do not want to label more records, or click *Save & Next* if you want to label the next record. If you do not want to label the record, click *Skip* and the next record will be opened. In Figure 7-25, there is an example of object detection. The labels are used to mark the nose, the mouth, and the eyes of the person in the picture. To label, select the *Bounding box*, the *label* wanted, and then *mark the area* for that label in the picture. You can use the *Remove box* to remove any boxes that were drawn in the wrong place. The toolbar has tools for moving the picture in the canvas, zooming in and out, resetting the zoom, and adjusting the image.

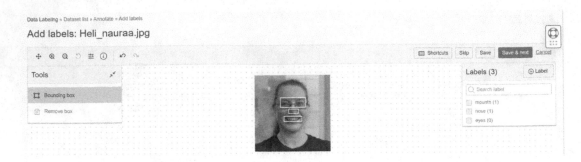

Figure 7-25. *Labeling records*

On the Dataset details page, you can filter the records by their labeling status to see only labeled record or unlabeled records. You can also choose to see the records as *Data records* or as *Gallery View*. The Gallery View shows the content of the record, not just the name. In Gallery View, you can search the records by the labels to list those records that have the label wanted. In the Data records view, you can sort the records by the record name or by the creation time by clicking the header.

If you want to edit the dataset information, you can click *Edit* (Figure 7-24). You are allowed to edit the name of the dataset and its description, but you are not allowed to change the object storage information.

If you want to add more files from your local drive, you can add them from the same Edit dataset form. Simply drag and drop files, or select them using the select files functionality. The record for the file is automatically generated.

If you select *More Actions* on Dataset details (Figure 7-24), you are able to Move Resource, Add Tags, View work request, or Delete the dataset. *Move Resource* lets you move the dataset from one compartment to another. *Add Tags* allows you to add new tags to the dataset. The system automatically generates two tags, CreatedBy and CreatedOn, when you create the dataset. *View work request* shows all work requests on the compartment as seen in Figure 7-26. The three-dot menu lets you open a support request if there is a problem with the work request that you are not able to solve by yourself. *Delete* deletes the dataset.

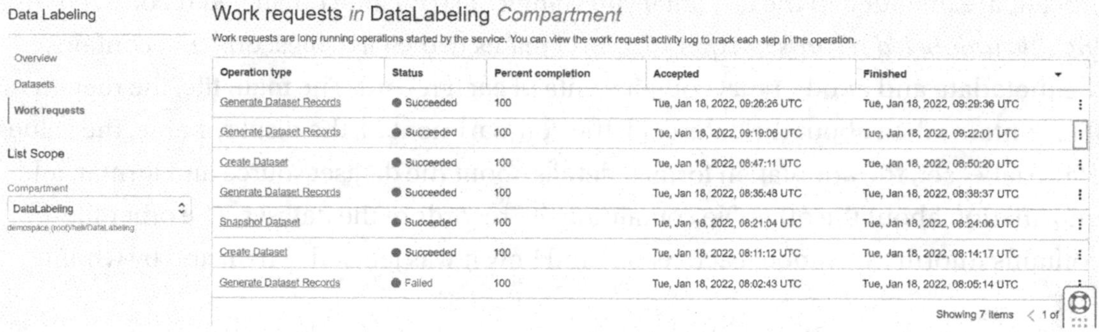

Figure 7-26. *Work requests*

When the dataset has been created, it can be found from the dataset list (shown in Figure 7-27). If the dataset was created successfully, the state is *Active*. Other possible states for a dataset are *Creating, Updating, Deleting, Deleted, Failed,* and *Needs Attention*. Both Failed and Needs Attention mean that the creation was not successful. As the list gets longer, you might appreciate the *Filters* on the left-hand side of the dataset list. Using the filters, you can filter by the *State of the dataset* or by its *Annotation class*.

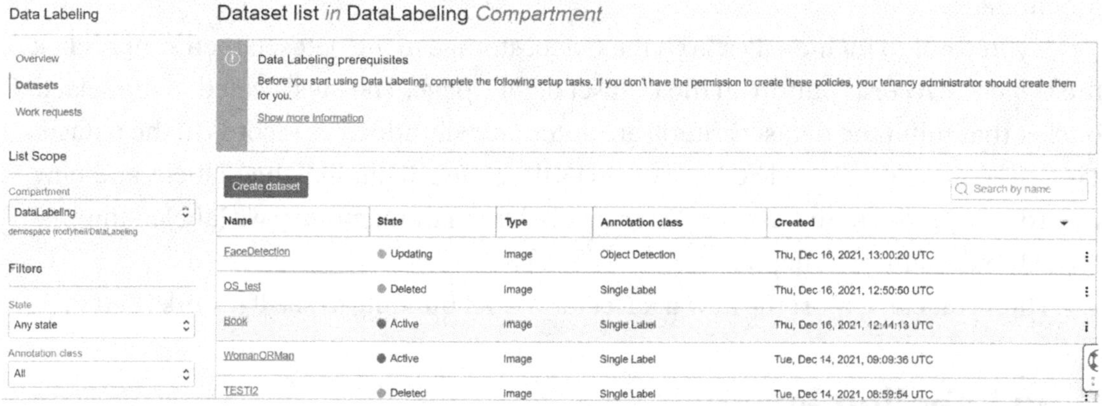

Figure 7-27. *Dataset list*

To see the dataset details, select the dataset either by clicking its name or selecting Details from the three-dot menu, the menu on the right-hand side marked by three dots (Figure 7-27).

To be able to use the labeled data in any machine learning process, export it using the *Export* button in the Dataset details page (Figure 7-24). The outcome of this export is stored in JSONL (JSON Lines format) files. You can choose the bucket where the files will be stored and optionally define a prefix for them. By default, only records that have been labeled are included in the file, but if you want to also include unlabeled records, choose *Include unlabeled records to export*. Export creates two JSONL files: one that contains the metadata and another that contains data of each record. The main file, the metadata file, contains data about the dataset id, the compartment id, the display name, the values of the label set, the annotation format, details about the dataset source and format, and information about the other file containing the records of the dataset. The other file contains information about each record and how it was labeled, when, and by whom.

Adding New Records to the Dataset

In many cases, the amount of labeled data is not enough, does not have enough variation, or for some reason, you are not able to train the model well enough and need more/better data to train the model. After you have created the dataset and its records, it is possible to add new records to the dataset.

As mentioned earlier in this chapter, if you want to add new records to the dataset from a local directory, you can do it by selecting *Edit* on the Dataset details page (Figure 7-24) and either drag and drop the files or select them using the select files functionality.

If you want to include files from the object storage to the dataset, then simply click the *Generate records* button on the Dataset details page. The files located in the selected bucket that fulfill the dataset criteria are automatically added as records to the dataset. Those records that existed before remain as they were, including their labels, and new records are added to the dataset. You can label them the same way we labeled the records earlier in this chapter.

Then you can export the new dataset for model building to see if it works better.

Data Labeling Errors

When you start the creation of a dataset, a *Work request* is created. You can find all work requests under Data Labeling and Work request as shown in Figure 7-28.

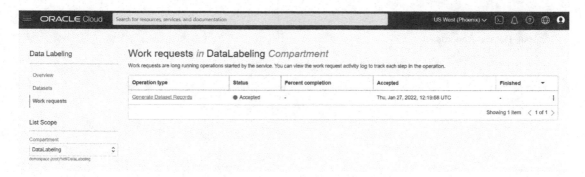

Figure 7-28. *The list of Work requests*

If you select one Work request from the list, you can see all the actions done during that Work request from the *Log messages* page shown in Figure 7-29.

Generate Dataset Records

Work request information	
Operation type: Generate Dataset Records	**Accepted:** Thu, Jan 27, 2022, 12:19:58 UTC
OCID: ...3h7xtg7l3q Show Copy	**Started:** Thu, Jan 27, 2022, 12:20:19 UTC
	Finished: -

Details

Log messages
Error messages

Log messages

Timestamp	Message
Thu, Jan 27, 2022, 12:20:51 UTC	Polling for record generation to complete
Thu, Jan 27, 2022, 12:20:22 UTC	Polling for instance to be ready
Thu, Jan 27, 2022, 12:20:20 UTC	Launching compute instance
Thu, Jan 27, 2022, 12:20:19 UTC	Validating customer bucket /n/axcew3ppxexo/b/bucket-20211213-1025-DataLabeling

Figure 7-29. *The Log messages of a Work request*

If the Work request fails for some reason and the dataset is in Needs Attention State, you can see the details in the *Error messages* page shown in Figure 7-30. If you select the three-dot menu on the right of the Message field, you can select *View full message* to see the full error message.

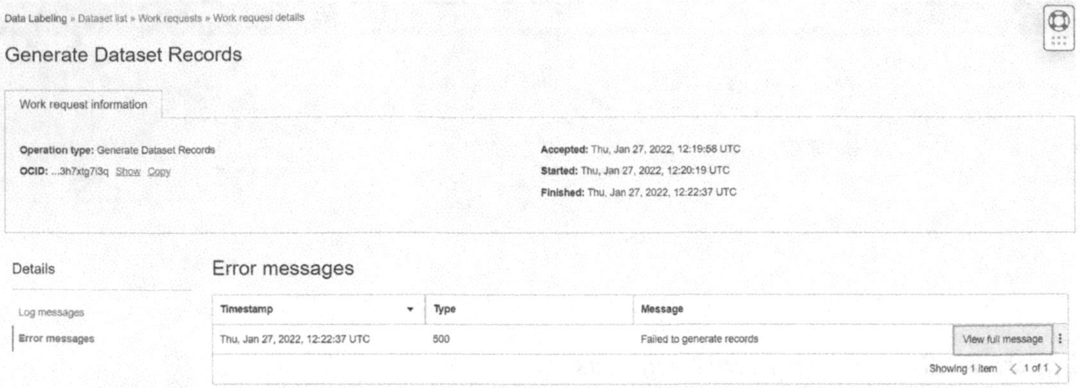

Data Labeling » Dataset list » Work requests » Work request details

Generate Dataset Records

Work request information		
Operation type: Generate Dataset Records		**Accepted:** Thu, Jan 27, 2022, 12:19:56 UTC
OCID: ...3h7xtg7I3q Show Copy		**Started:** Thu, Jan 27, 2022, 12:20:19 UTC
		Finished: Thu, Jan 27, 2022, 12:22:37 UTC

Details

Log messages

Error messages

Error messages

Timestamp ▾	Type	Message	
Thu, Jan 27, 2022, 12:22:37 UTC	500	Failed to generate records	View full message ⋮

Showing 1 item 〈 1 of 1 〉

Figure 7-30. *An error message of a Work request*

Sometimes this message is useful, and you are able to fix the issue. But sometimes you simply need to raise a support ticket with Oracle support.

A very typical problem is that you have selected the wrong compartment, or you simply do not have enough privileges to all of the resources needed. Or, maybe the bucket is missing, or you do not have permission to use it.

It might also be that you have hit one of the *limitations*. The supported file formats for documents are PDF, TIF, and TIFF, and for text, the supported file format is TXT. For images, the supported file formats are JPEG, JPG, and PNG. Also, note that images bigger than 6 MB in size are not saved when creating a dataset. It is also possible that you have exhausted resources or quota limits. In Figure 7-31, you can see the *Limits, Quotas and Usage* for the Data Labeling service. If you select the three-dot menu for any of the limitations, you are able to select *Create Quota Policy Stub* to get the stub for changing the quota policy, or you can open a support request.

Figure 7-31. *Limits, Quotas and Usage*

Data Labeling with APEX Using OCI APIs

If you prefer using the Data Labeling Service from APEX, that can be done using the OCI Data Labeling APIs.

Data Labeling APIs

There are two APIs for Data Labeling: Data Labeling API and Data Labeling Management API. *Data Labeling API* is used to create annotations (labels) on images, texts, or documents and to generate snapshots. *Data Labeling Management API* can be used to create, list, edit, and delete datasets. The version of these APIs is /20211001, while writing this book. The documentation for Data Labeling API can be found from `https://docs.oracle.com/en-us/iaas/api/#/en/datalabeling-dp/20211001/` and the documentation for Data Labeling Management API from `https://docs.oracle.com/en-us/iaas/api/#/en/datalabeling/20211001/`.

Setting Up APEX for Data Labeling APIs

To start, create an IAM user in the OCI Console, if you have not done so yet, and add the user to the group for Data Labeling, in our example DataLabelingGroup. Then, go back to the user's detail page to make sure the user has API keys selected. Select *Identity & Security* from the navigation menu. Then, select *Users*. Select the user from the list of users to get to the user details page (Figure 7-32).

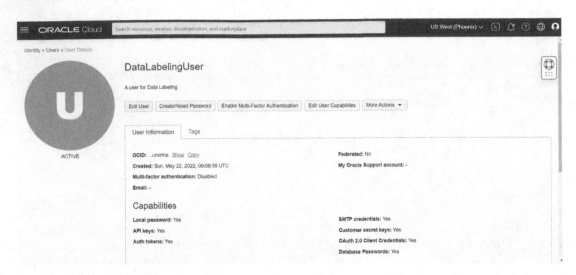

Figure 7-32. *The user details page*

Click *Edit User Capabilities* and check that *API Keys* is selected (Figure 7-33). To limit the user to interact with OCI resources using API keys only, deselect all the other options.

Note   If you want the user to be able to use other methods, do not limit the access to API Keys.

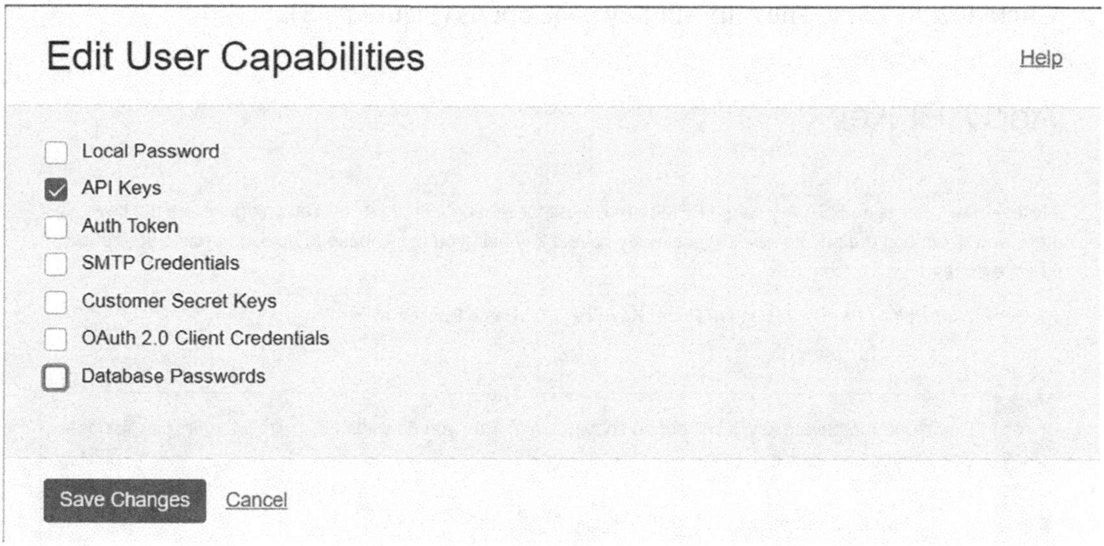

Edit User Capabilities

Help

- ☐ Local Password
- ☑ API Keys
- ☐ Auth Token
- ☐ SMTP Credentials
- ☐ Customer Secret Keys
- ☐ OAuth 2.0 Client Credentials
- ☐ Database Passwords

Save Changes   Cancel

Figure 7-33. *Defining User Capabilities*

An API key pair is required to be able to work with the OCI REST APIs. To get the API key pair, select *API Keys* from the left-hand side of the user details page (Figure 7-34).

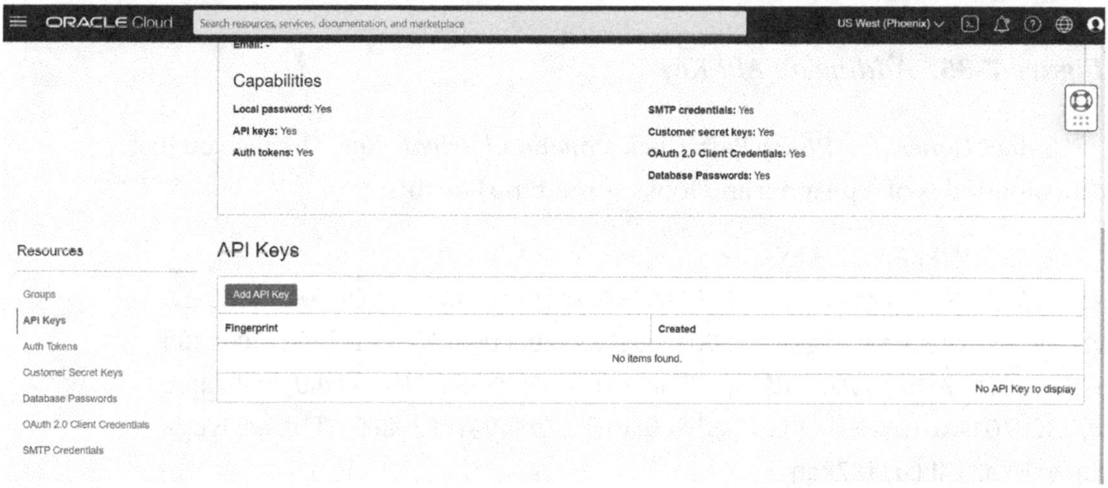

Figure 7-34. *The API Key resource page*

Click *Add API Key*. The Add API Key page opens (Figure 7-35).

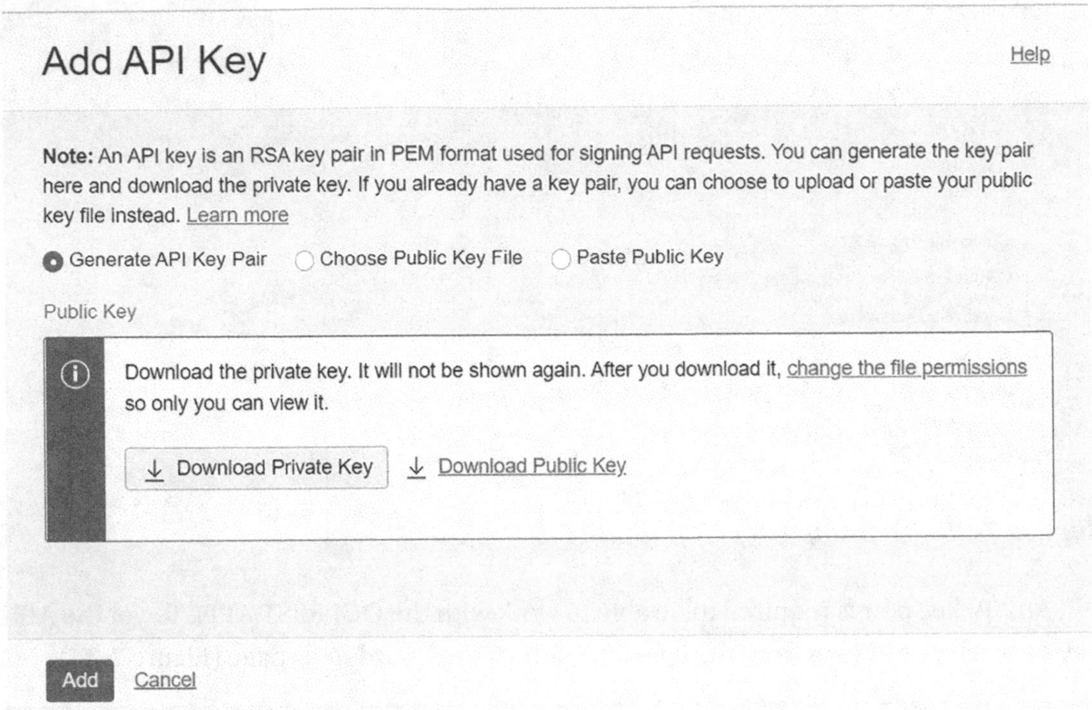

Add API Key

Help

Note: An API key is an RSA key pair in PEM format used for signing API requests. You can generate the key pair here and download the private key. If you already have a key pair, you can choose to upload or paste your public key file instead. Learn more

● Generate API Key Pair   ○ Choose Public Key File   ○ Paste Public Key

Public Key

ⓘ   Download the private key. It will not be shown again. After you download it, change the file permissions so only you can view it.

↓ Download Private Key   ↓ Download Public Key

Add   Cancel

Figure 7-35. *Adding an API Key*

Select *Generate API Key Pair*. Click *Download Private Key*. The file you just downloaded is of type .pem and looks something like this:

```
-----BEGIN PRIVATE KEY-----
MIIEvAIBADANBgkqhkiG9w0BAQEFAASCBKYwggSiAgEAAoIBAQCv2FWr73tHBsrA
VhqKE/Wf0rzE6WzaYDzgAycr2SGOa3bQrkXx31uoOO9Rk2GHy71Zl+SzwFOQz3Bh
+HTDlaSC1FZSHZ/9DAUMidAjSpvMBnPAcIKGmmECgYASx9EM7tdWvhD3kpN9uBuc
r7ZBCU/O1mxeIm7eNlbCbLCfGsVhP4Q8v1HKQZz54y9YMRZW8eO3YEHtwwRJVegz
8n+yYWYa/IMLLq1i8ZRqhg==
-----END PRIVATE KEY-----
```

Remove the first (-----BEGIN PRIVATE KEY-----) and last line (-----END PRIVATE KEY-----), and then copy the content to a safe place. This is the private key used in Web Credentials. Then click *Add*. Check the *Configuration File Preview* (Figure 7-36) for the other details needed for Web Credentials in APEX.

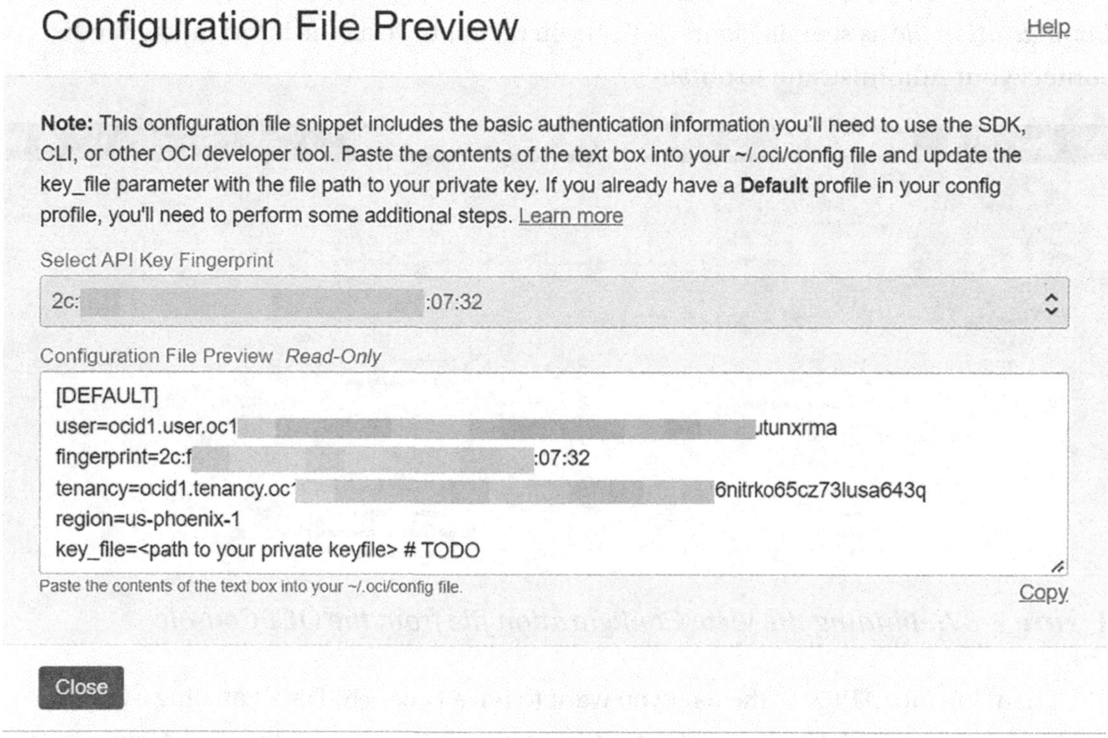

Configuration File Preview

Note: This configuration file snippet includes the basic authentication information you'll need to use the SDK, CLI, or other OCI developer tool. Paste the contents of the text box into your ~/.oci/config file and update the key_file parameter with the file path to your private key. If you already have a **Default** profile in your config profile, you'll need to perform some additional steps. Learn more

Select API Key Fingerprint

2c: :07:32

Configuration File Preview *Read-Only*

```
[DEFAULT]
user=ocid1.user.oc1                                         utunxrma
fingerprint=2c:f                            :07:32
tenancy=ocid1.tenancy.oc1                          6nitrko65cz73lusa643q
region=us-phoenix-1
key_file=<path to your private keyfile> # TODO
```

Paste the contents of the text box into your ~/.oci/config file.   Copy

Close

Figure 7-36. *The Configuration File Preview*

The information you will need for the Web Credentials and REST Data Source we will create later is

- User OCID

- Fingerprint

- OCI Private key

- Tenancy OCID

- Compartment OCID

- Region of the tenancy

- Namespace

You can always find the information from the User page by selecting the *View Configuration file* as seen in Figure 7-37. If you do not have all the information needed, contact your Administrator to obtain it.

Figure 7-37. *Finding the View Configuration file from the OCI Console*

Then, log into APEX as the user you want to have access to Data Labeling APIs.

Create a new *Web Credential*. Go to *Workspace Utilities*, and select *Web Credentials*. Click *Create*. Give the Web Credential a *Name*, and select OCI as the *Authentication Type*. Then, paste the OCI userid (User OCID), OCI Private key, OCI Tenancy ID (Tenancy OCID), and OCI Public Key Fingerprint to correct fields as shown in Figure 7-38. Click *Create*.

Note   If you do not have all the information, you can go back to the OCI Console and check it from Identity & Security. Select Users and the correct APEX user from the user list. From User Details, select View Configuration file.

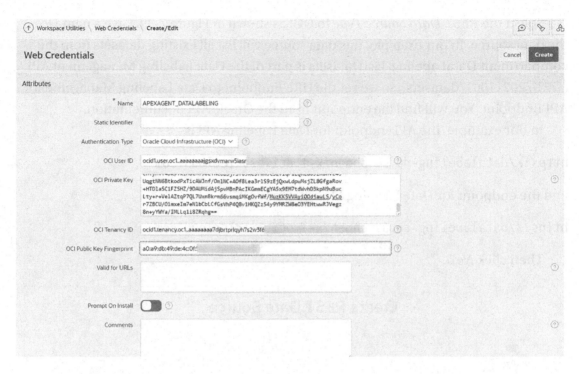

Figure 7-38. *Creating Web Credentials*

Using Data Labeling APIs with APEX

When you have created the Web Credentials, you are able to use the OCI API services. For Data Labeling, there are two APIs: Data Labeling API and Data Labeling Management API. The OCI API references and endpoints can be found from Oracle documentation:

`https://docs.oracle.com/en-us/iaas/api/#/`

To see the request details of an API request, navigate to that API reference.

To be able to use a particular API request, you need to create a *REST Data Source* for it. In APEX *App builder*, select the application in which you want to create this REST Data Source. Select *Shared Components*. Navigate to *Data Sources* and select *REST Data Source*. Click *Create*. Select *From scratch* and click *Next*.

Select the *REST Data Source Type* to OCI as shown in Figure 7-39. Give a name to the data source. In our example, this data source will list all existing datasets from the compartment DataLabeling. ListDatasets is part of the Data Labeling Management API (GET /20211001/datasets), so we set the URL Endpoint to Data Labeling Management API Endpoint. You will find the endpoint from the Oracle API documentation.

In our example, the API endpoint for Data Labeling API is

```
https://datalabeling-dp.us-phoenix-1.oci.oraclecloud.com
```

and the endpoint for Data Labeling Management API is

```
https://datalabeling-cp.us-phoenix-1.oci.oraclecloud.com
```

Then click *Next*.

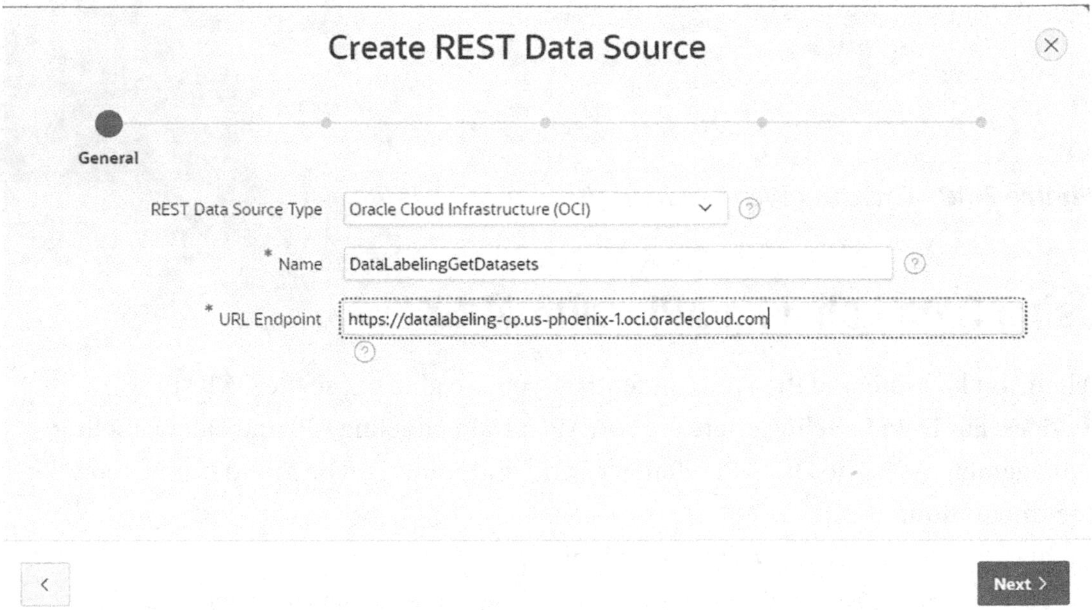

Create REST Data Source

General

REST Data Source Type	Oracle Cloud Infrastructure (OCI)
* Name	DataLabelingGetDatasets
* URL Endpoint	https://datalabeling-cp.us-phoenix-1.oci.oraclecloud.com

< Next >

Figure 7-39. *Defining an OCI REST Data Source for Data Labeling Management API service*

The next step is to specify the *Request* to be used. In our example, it is Datasets. Insert the information in the Service URL Path field as shown in Figure 7-40. You can find the Service URL Path from the Oracle manual under the API documentation. Then click *Next*.

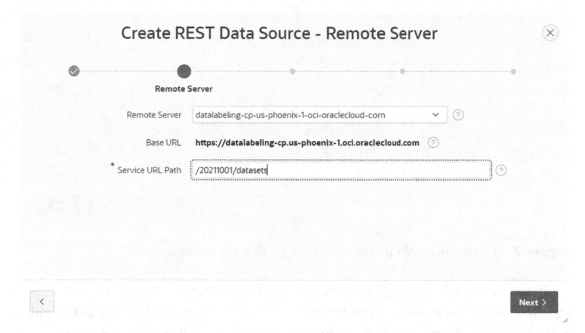

Figure 7-40. *Defining a remote server for Dataset request in Data Labeling Management API*

Select *Authentication Required,* and then select the Web Credential from the list as shown in Figure 7-41. The Credentials are listed using their Static Identifier. Then click *Advanced*.

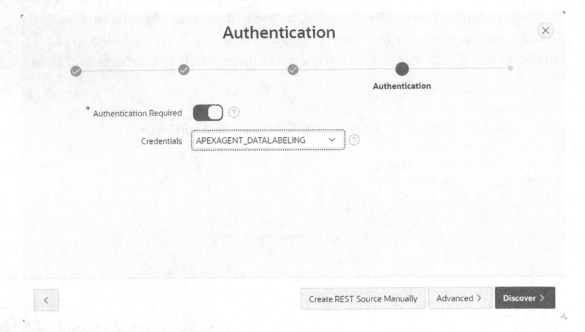

Figure 7-41. *Defining the authentication for the API request*

In the Advanced section (Figure 7-42), define the compartment used for Data Labeling. Select *Query String variable* from the Parameter Type list, type compartmentId as the Parameter Name, and copy/paste the compartment id of the Data Labeling compartment into the Value field. Select *Is Static*. Then click *Discover*.

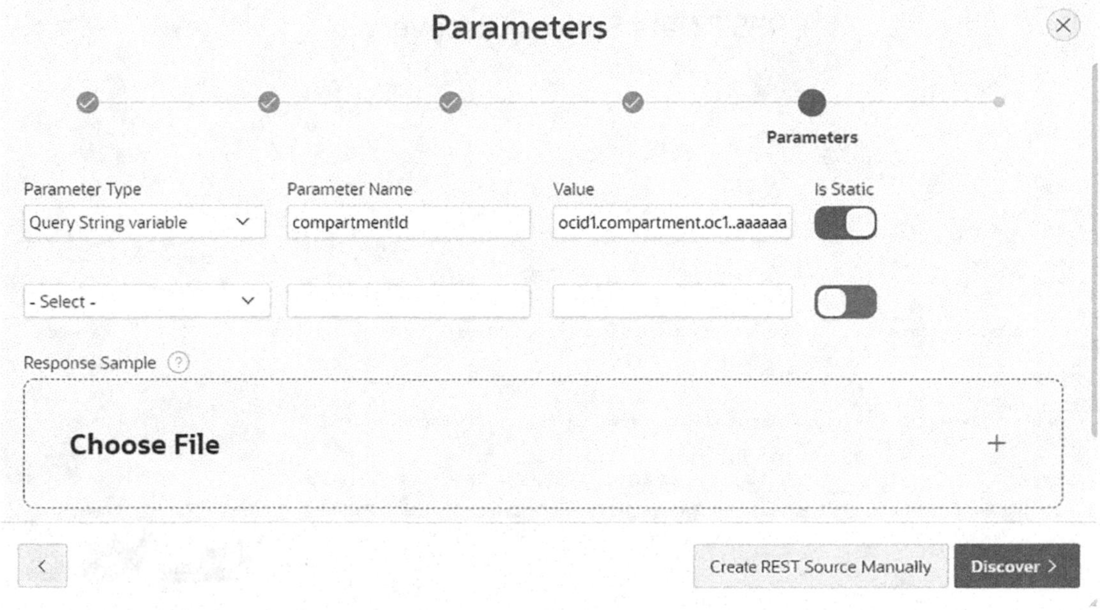

Parameters

Parameter Type	Parameter Name	Value	Is Static
Query String variable ⌄	compartmentId	ocid1.compartment.oc1..aaaaaa	⬤◯
- Select - ⌄			◯⬤

Response Sample ⓘ

Choose File   +

‹   Create REST Source Manually   Discover ›

Figure 7-42. *Defining advanced parameters for the REST Data Source*

If all the settings for the REST Data Source are correct and the privileges are in place, the discovery will list the datasets in the Data Labeling compartment as shown in Figure 7-43. Then click *Create REST Data Source*.

Figure 7-43. *Preview of the REST Data Source: list of Data Labeling datasets in selected compartment*

Now that you have a REST Data Source created, you can use it in APEX as a data source and build an APEX application. In the similar way, you can create REST Data Sources for all Data Labeling or Data Labeling Management API requests needed.

Using REST Data Sources in APEX is very simple. You can, for example, create a page from the API request we just created to list all datasets in a selected compartment. In your APEX application, select *Create Page*. Select *Report and Interactive Grid*. Fill in the information needed. Click *Next*. Then, as shown in Figure 7-44, select *REST Data Source* as a Data Source. Then select the REST Data Source created from the REST Data Source list. Select the columns you want for the interactive grid. Then click *Create*.

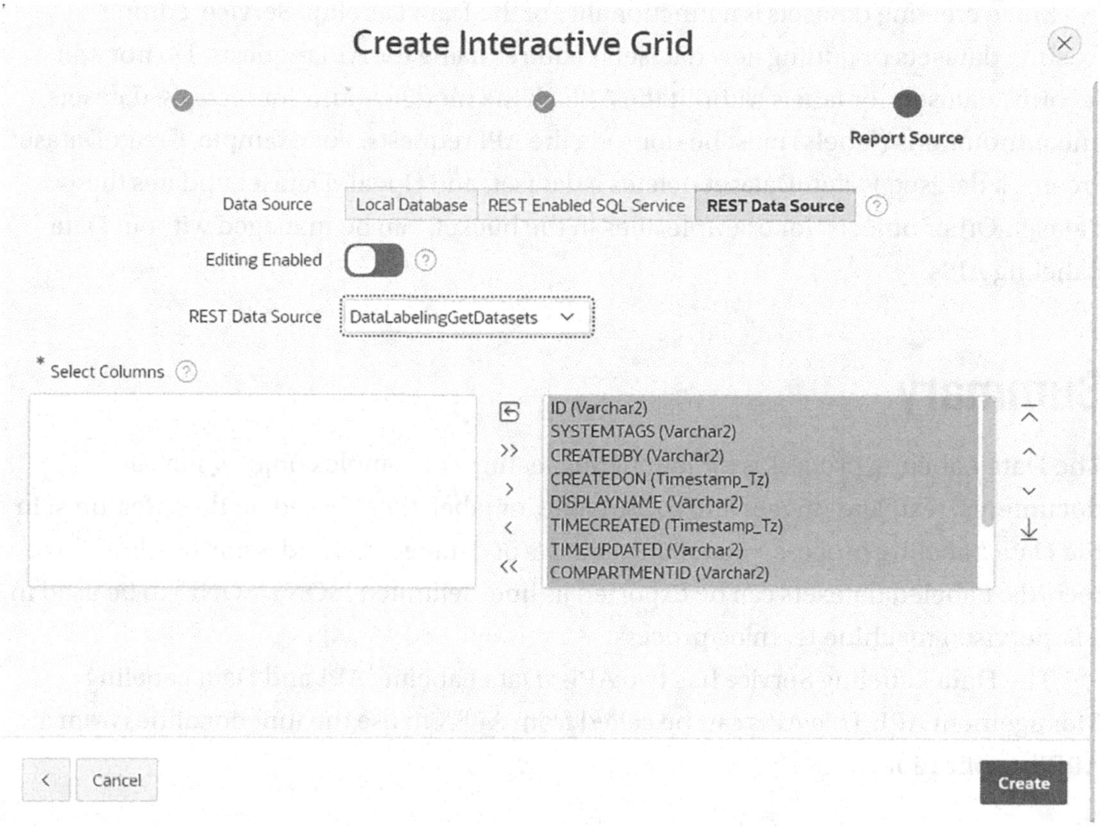

Figure 7-44. *Creating an interactive grid based on a REST Data Source*

In Figure 7-45, you can see this simple APEX application.

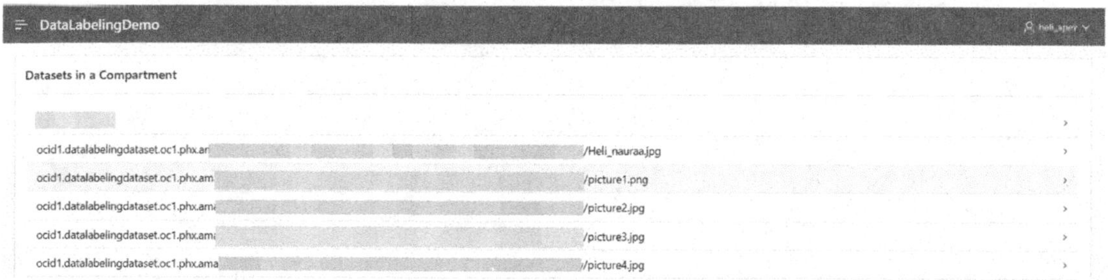

Figure 7-45. *A simple APEX application showing the datasets in the selected compartment*

Since creating datasets is a functionality of the Data Labeling Service, editing existing datasets or adding new datasets requires using the API requests. Do **not** edit records, datasets, or labels without the API: all the modifications for records, datasets, and annotations (labels) must be done via the API requests. For example, CreateDataset creates a dataset, DeleteDataset deletes a dataset, and UpdateDataset updates the dataset. Other objects, for example, files in the bucket, can be managed without Data Labeling APIs.

Summary

The Data Labeling process is for identifying features of complex objects such as documents, text, and images and to annotate, or label, them based on those features. In the Data Labeling process, you create datasets of data records and apply labels to those records. Labeled datasets can be exported as line-delimited JSON (JSONL) to be used in a supervised machine learning process.

The Data Labeling Service has two APIs: Data Labeling API and Data Labeling Management API. This APIs can be called from APEX to use the functionalities from an APEX application.

CHAPTER 8

Anomaly Detection

Anomaly detection identifies unexpected events, observations, or items that differ significantly from the norm. To detect anomalies, first, a model is trained to learn what normal behavior is. Then, a statistical technique is applied to determine, if a specific data point is an anomaly.

OCI Anomaly Detection Service is a managed service to use anomaly detection without deep machine learning knowledge. You can easily build a machine learning model using your own data and then use it to detect anomalies from another set of data. The Anomaly Detection Service uses a Multivariate State Estimation Technique (MSET) and then incorporates the Sequential Probability Ratio Test (SPRT) to monitor the residuals between the actual observations and the estimates MSET predicts on the basis of the correlated variables. The service can detect different kinds of anomalies, including the ones never seen before, as long as the model has been trained to determine what is considered normal for a given time series.

Anomaly Detection identifies events/observations that are very different from the majority of the data. The model is created and trained using typical, normal data. Then a new dataset is given to the model. The actual values of the dataset are compared to the predictions of the model. If the actual value is far from the value the model predicts, it might be an anomaly. The training data should not include outliers because the data should be teaching the model what normal looks like. The dataset should include normal data for all possible business use cases to be able to teach the correct "normal."

There are many reasons for the anomaly. The reasons for an anomaly could be caused by a human error, a sampling error, a data processing error, an experimental error, or many other reasons, but it could also be a true anomaly that has a severe meaning for the business. An outlier could indicate something has gone wrong in the process, and it should be fixed to avoid disturbance for the business. For example, an anomaly on the temperature can cause a machinery breakdown causing system disruptions. To avoid the errors in the process, the temperature changes should be

© Adrian Png and Heli Helskyaho 2022
A. Png and H. Helskyaho, *Extending Oracle Application Express with Oracle Cloud Features*,
https://doi.org/10.1007/978-1-4842-8170-3_8

avoided. Or, it could be an instrument error identifying that this particular instrument is faulty. It is also possible the anomaly is not an anomaly but a perfectly normal data that was not originally included in the training dataset to teach the model what normal is. Then it would be smart to add more examples to the training dataset and train the model again.

This is the first version of Anomaly Detection Service, and Oracle has a lot of plans to improve it with functionalities like streaming support for real-time detection or user feedback inclusion for the learning process.

To use Anomaly Detection Service, select *Analytics & AI* from the OCI Console navigation menu. Then select *Anomaly Detection* under *AI Services*.

Setting Up the Anomaly Detection Service

To start with the Anomaly Detection Service, you need an Oracle Cloud Infrastructure (OCI) account with Service Administrator role privileges or somebody who can set up the service and grant you the privileges needed. You also need a supported browser. Please check the supported browsers from the OCI documentation.

Next, we will see how to set up the OCI environment so that you will be able to use the Anomaly Detection Service.

Compartment, Policies, User Groups, and a User

Create a *compartment* for resources used by Anomaly Detection service. This is not a mandatory step but might be a good idea since it allows you to grant privileges to resources on that compartment. To create a compartment

1. Select *Identity & Security* from the OCI Console navigation menu.

2. Select *Compartments*.

3. Navigate to the compartment under which you want to create the new compartment as a child compartment.

4. In the *Child Compartments* section (Figure 8-1), click *Create Compartment*.

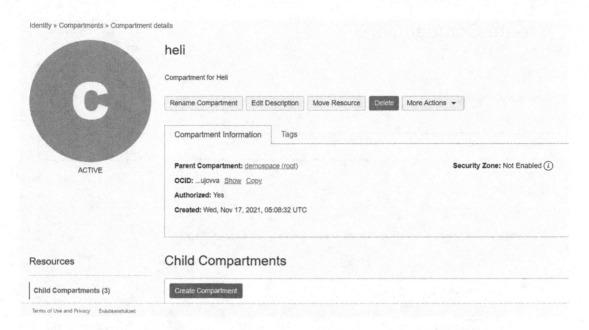

Figure 8-1. Compartment Details and the Child Compartment section for creating new Compartment under the Parent Compartment

5. Fill in the information needed as shown in Figure 8-2.

6. Click *Create Compartment*.

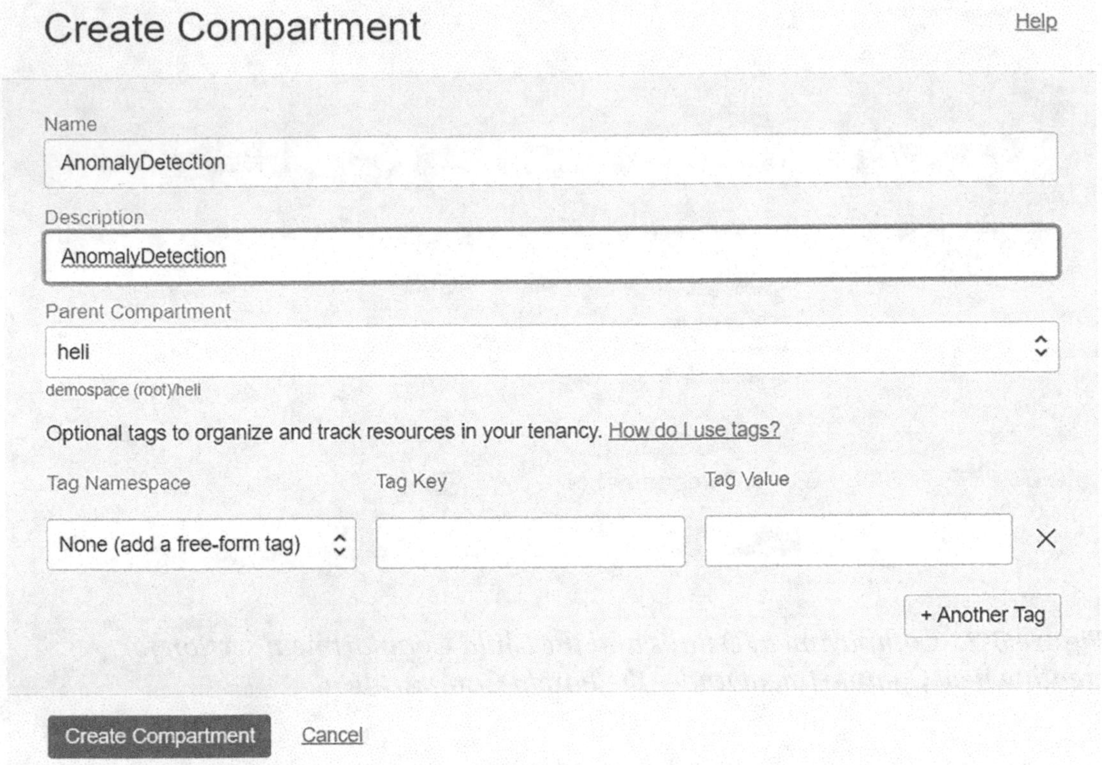

Create Compartment

Name

AnomalyDetection

Description

AnomalyDetection

Parent Compartment

heli

demospace (root)/heli

Optional tags to organize and track resources in your tenancy. How do I use tags?

Tag Namespace   Tag Key   Tag Value

None (add a free-form tag)   ✕

+ Another Tag

Create Compartment   Cancel

Figure 8-2. *Filling the information needed for creating a new compartment*

In our example, we created a compartment AnomalyDetection.

Then, we need a *user* with correct *privileges* to use the services in that compartment. Those privileges are granted using *policies*.

There are two kinds of users: IAM users and federated users that are using an identity provider service to log in. One example of those identity providers is Oracle Identity Cloud Server. An IAM user uses the *Oracle Cloud Infrastructure Direct Sign-In* login shown in Figure 8-3, while the Oracle Identity Cloud Server user uses the *Single Sign-On (SSO)* login shown in the same figure.

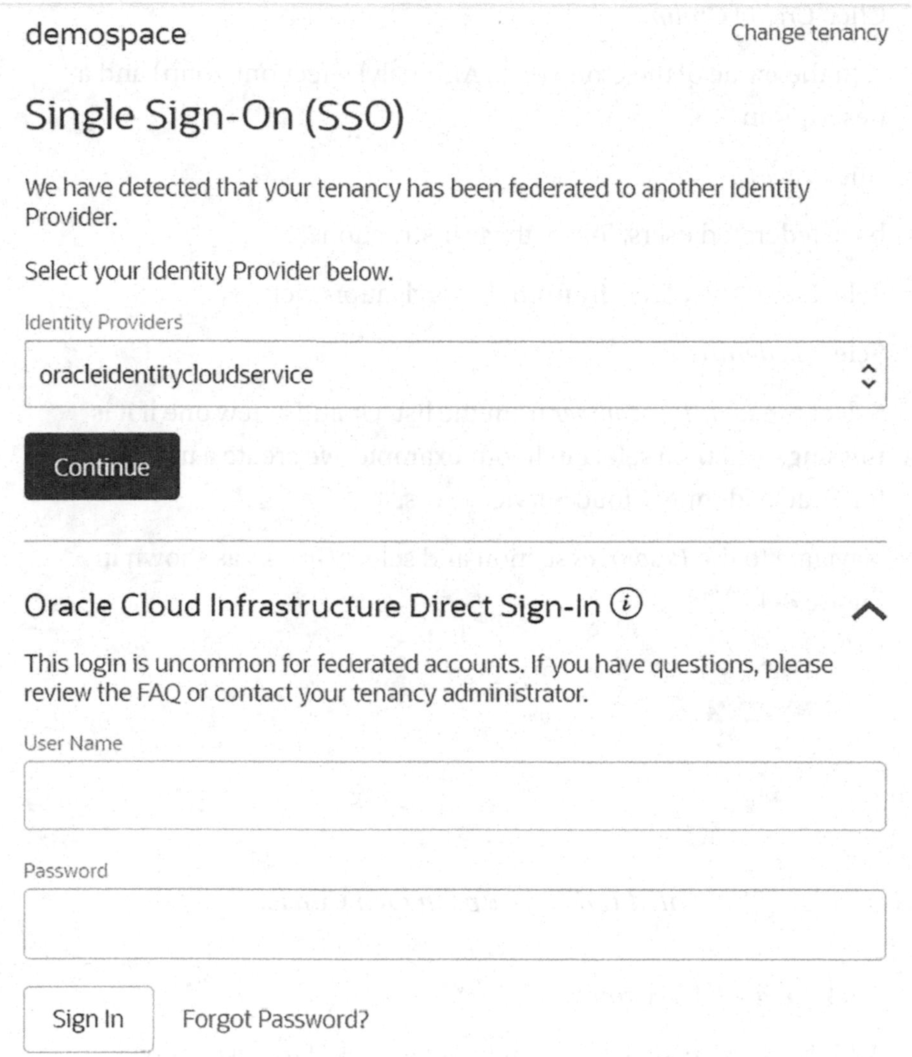

demospace   Change tenancy

Single Sign-On (SSO)

We have detected that your tenancy has been federated to another Identity Provider.

Select your Identity Provider below.

Identity Providers

| oracleidentitycloudservice | ⌄ |

Continue

Oracle Cloud Infrastructure Direct Sign-In ⓘ   ⌃

This login is uncommon for federated accounts. If you have questions, please review the FAQ or contact your tenancy administrator.

User Name

| |

Password

| |

Sign In   Forgot Password?

Figure 8-3. *Login options for Oracle Infrastructure Cloud (OCI)*

It is possible to grant all policies directly to a user, but the best practice is to create a user group, assign the policies to that, and then add the user to the user group.

To follow that practice, create a user group. The way a user group is created depends on the user type.

If you have IAM users, follow these instructions:

1. Select *Identity & Security* from the navigation menu.

2. Select *Groups* from the Identity & Security.

3. Click *Create Group.*

4. Add the name of the group (e.g., AnomalyDetectionGroup) and a description.

5. Click *Create.*

If you have federated users, follow these instructions:

1. Select *Identity & Security* from the navigation menu.

2. Select *Federation.*

3. Select the *identity provider* from the list. Or add a new one if it is missing. And then select it. In our example, we create a user group for Oracle Identity Cloud Service users.

4. Navigate to the *Resources* section and select *Groups* as shown in Figure 8-4.

Figure 8-4. *List of federated IDCS groups in OCI Console*

5. Click *Create IDCS Group.*

6. Add the data needed as shown in Figure 8-5. If the user already exists, you can add it to the group by selecting the user from the *Users* list.

7. Click *Create.*

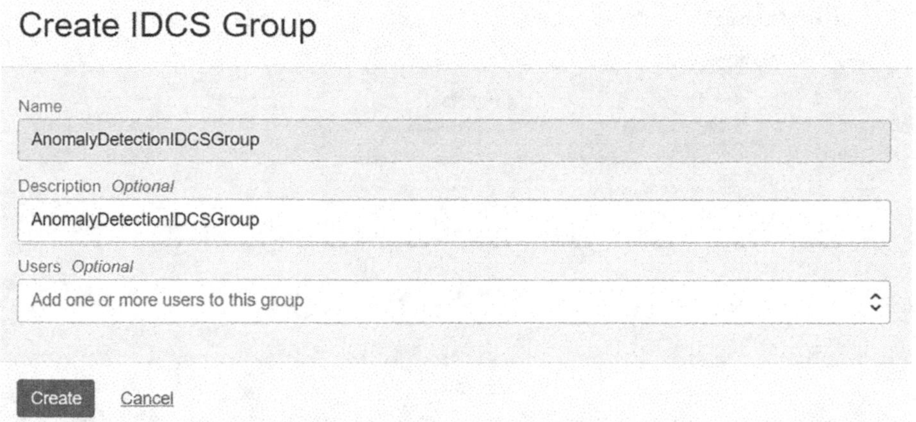

Create IDCS Group

Name

AnomalyDetectionIDCSGroup

Description *Optional*

AnomalyDetectionIDCSGroup

Users *Optional*

Add one or more users to this group

Create   Cancel

Figure 8-5. *Creating a new IDCS Group*

Then, create *policies* for using Anomaly Detection Service. The needed policy is

```
allow <subject> to manage ai-service-anomaly-detection-family in
compartment
```

where subject can be

```
group <group_name> | group id <group_ocid> | dynamic-group <dynamic-group_
name> | dynamic-group id <dynamic-group_ocid> | any-user
```

In our example, we will create a policy like this:

```
allow group AnomalyDetectionGroup to manage ai-service-anomaly-detection-
family in compartment AnomalyDetection
```

To add the policies needed, follow these instructions:

1. Select *Identity & Security* from the navigation menu.

2. Select *Policies.*

3. Select the Parent Compartment of the anomaly detection compartment.

4. Click *Create Policies* button seen in Figure 8-6.

Figure 8-6. *Policies section for Compartments for creating a new policy*

    5.   Fill in the name and description for the policy as shown in Figure 8-7. Check that the compartment is correct.

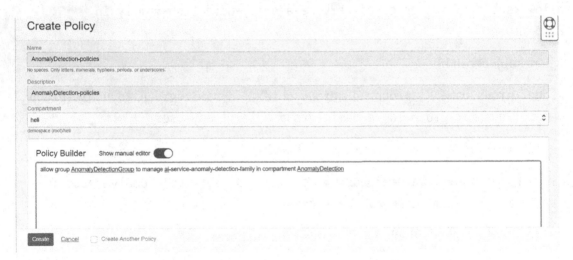

Figure 8-7. *Creating a new policy*

    6.   In *Policy Builder*, enable *Show manual editor*.

    7.   Paste the policy text to the editor.

    8.   Click *Create*.

Now you have a user group with the privileges needed for the Anomaly Detection Service.

If you have not created a user, then create a *user* (either IAM user or Oracle Identity Cloud Server user). To create an IAM user

1. Select *Identity & Security* from the OCI Console navigation menu.

2. Select *Users*.

3. Click *Create User* and fill in the data needed. In this example, we create an IAM user called Anomalydetectionuser.

4. Click *Create*.

To create an Oracle Identity Cloud Server user (or another identity provider federated user)

1. Select *Identity & Security* from the OCI Console navigation menu.

2. Select *Federation*.

3. If you do not have the identity provider defined, click Add Identity Provider and a new Federation.

4. Then, select the federation you want. In our example, it is OracleIdentityCloudService.

5. Navigate to *Users* section shown in Figure 8-8.

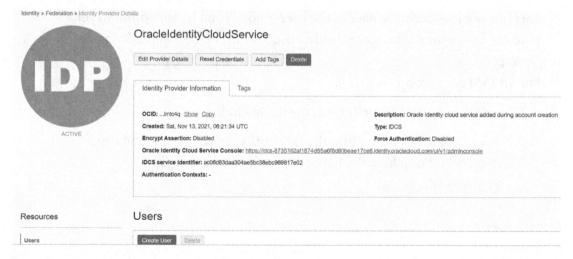

Figure 8-8. *Oracle Identity Cloud Service users*

6. Click *Create User*.

7. Fill in the username, the email address, and optionally the first
    and last names of the user as shown in Figure 8-9.

Figure 8-9. *Creating an IDCS user*

8. If you want, you can add the user to the user group created earlier
    by selecting the user group name from the list.

9. Click *Create*.

Last but not least, add the user to the user group, if you haven't done so yet.
Find the user group you created, either the IAM user group or the federated
user group.

For an IAM user group

1. Select *Identity & Security* from the navigation menu.

2. Select *Groups* from the Identity & Security. Select the anomaly
    detection group from the list of user groups as shown in
    Figure 8-10.

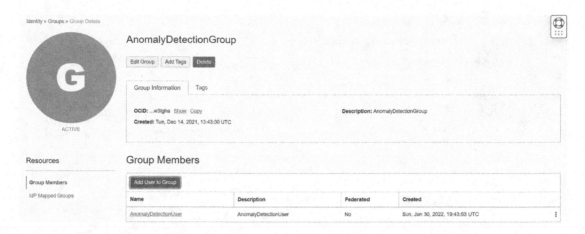

Figure 8-10. *Group Details page and adding a member to a user group*

3. Click *Add User to Group.*

4. Select the user from the *Users* list.

5. Click *Add.*

In our example, we added the user AnomalyDetectionUser to the user group AnomalyDetectionGroup.

For a federated user group, you can either select a user and add the user to a user group, or you can select a user group and add users to it.

1. Select *Identity & Security* from the navigation menu.

2. Select *Federation* from the Identity & Security.

3. Select the Federation wanted (the Identity Provider) from the list.

4. Then, either select the user from the users list, or select Groups from Resources.

5. If you selected the user, then click *Add to IDCS Group* and select the group from the *Groups* menu.

6. If you selected *Groups,* then select the anomaly detection group from the list of user groups as shown in Figure 8-11. Click *Add User to Group.* Click *Add to IDCS Group,* and select the user from the *Users* list. Click *Add.*

Figure 8-11. *Group Details page for IDCS user groups and adding a member to a group*

Now you have created a *compartment* for the Anomaly Detection Service, a *user group* with the *privileges* needed for using the service, and you have created a *user* and *added* the user to a user group. You are ready to use the service.

Vault, Keys, and Secrets

If you want to use a table in the Autonomous Database as a data source for the machine model creation, you should have Vault, Keys, and Secrets set up as well. If you are only using Object Storage buckets and local files as a data source, you can skip this. To be able to do all this, you either need to have permissions to manage vaults and keys, or you should ask an Administrator to do this for you.

A *Vault* is a place to store all kinds of secret information about authentication details to access any resource in OCI. You do not need to show any authentication details in your configuration files or code, you can simply use it from the Vault, safely. Vault is a managed cloud service in OCI. It provides a secure store for *secrets*. You can store passwords, wallets, certificates, SSH keys, or authentication token, which you use in configuration files, as secrets in OCI Vault. You can retrieve these secrets from the Vault, when you need to access resources or other services. A *Master Encryption Key* is used to encrypt the Secret information.

To create a *Vault*

1. Select *Identity & Security* from the OCI Console navigation menu, and select *Vault*.

2. Select the Compartment wanted, and click *Create Vault*.

3. Check that the compartment is correct, and insert the *name* for the Vault.

4. Click *Create Vault*.

Then, you need to create a *key*. To do that

1. Select the Vault you just created to get to *Vault Details* page.

2. Navigate to *Master Encryption Keys* in the *Resources*.

3. In Master Encryption Keys, click *Create Key*.

4. Define the *Protection Mode*: HSM or software. Choose HSM.

5. Define a *Name for the Key*.

6. Select the *Key Shape: Algorithm.* This is the mathematical mechanism by which a key encrypts, decrypts, signs, or verifies data. Different algorithms are used for different purposes. Supported algorithms are Advanced Encryption Standard (AES), Rivest–Shamir–Adleman (RSA), and elliptic curve cryptography digital signature algorithm (ECDSA). AES is the default. Select that.

7. Select the value for *Key Shape: Length*. The default is 256 bits. Select that.

8. Click *Create Key*.

Then, we need to create all Secrets needed. To create a Secret

1. In the *Vault Details* page, navigate to *Secrets* in the *Resources*.

2. Click *Create Secret*.

3. Provide the following details as seen in Figure 8-12:

    a. *Compartment*: Check that the compartment selected is correct. The Secret does not have to be in the same compartment as the Vault.

    b. *Name*: Unique name to the secret.

    c. *Description*: Description for the secret.

d. *Encryption Key*: Select the encryption key you just created from the list. This key will be used to encrypt the secret. If you cannot find it, check that the compartment is correct. If not, click *Change Compartment* and choose the correct compartment from the list.

e. *Secret Type Template*: Plain-Text or Base64. Select Plain-Text.

f. *Secret Contents*: Type the password for the anomaly detection user.

g. Click *Create Secret*.

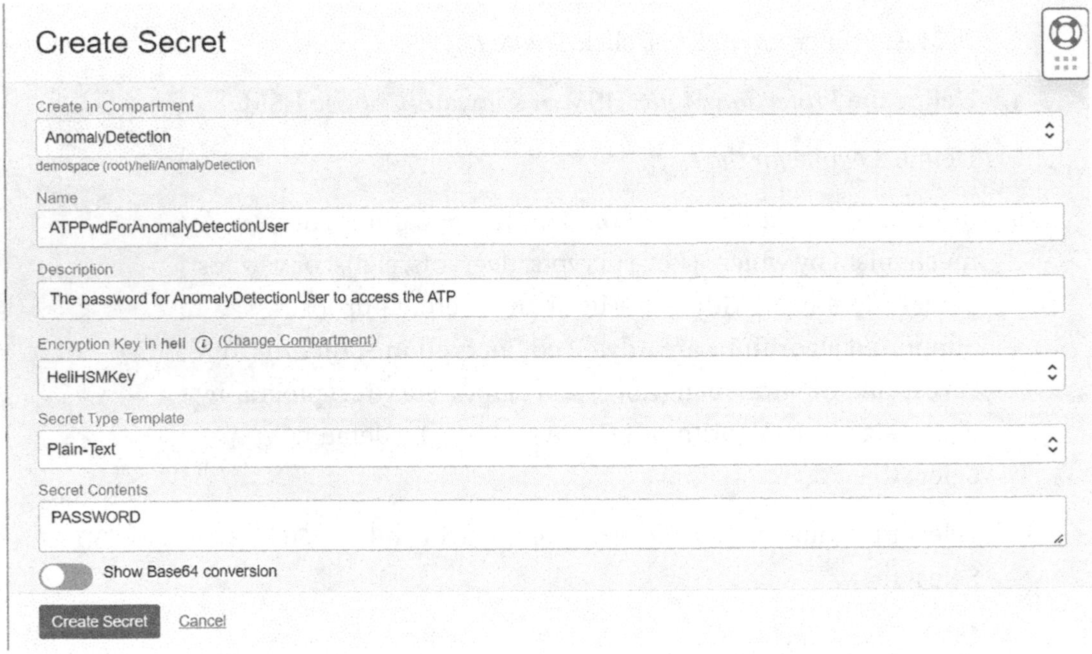

Create Secret

Create in Compartment

AnomalyDetection

demospace (root)/heli/AnomalyDetection

Name

ATPPwdForAnomalyDetectionUser

Description

The password for AnomalyDetectionUser to access the ATP

Encryption Key in heli (i) (Change Compartment)

HeliHSMKey

Secret Type Template

Plain-Text

Secret Contents

PASSWORD

Show Base64 conversion

Create Secret   Cancel

Figure 8-12. Creating a Secret

Now, the password for an anomaly detection user is stored in the OCI Vault and can be used from there when needed.

To be able to connect to an Autonomous Database, the username and password are not enough; you also need to define the *connection details*. The connection information can also be stored in the Vault as a Secret.

First, you need to get the *Wallet*. In OCI Console, select Oracle Database, Autonomous Database. Then select your database from the list of autonomous databases. In the Autonomous Database Details page (Figure 8-13), click *DB Connection*.

Figure 8-13. *Autonomous Database Details page*

Then, as seen in Figure 8-14, select *Instance Wallet* as Wallet type and click *Download wallet*.

Database Connection

If you are using TLS, you do not need to download the client credentials. The client credentials include a wallet and connection information, and are required for mTLS connections.

Download client credentials (Wallet)

To download your client credentials, select the wallet type, and click **Download wallet**. You then enter a password for the wallet. This client credential download only contains information for mTLS connections.

Wallet type ⓘ

| Instance Wallet | ⌄ |

| Download wallet | Rotate wallet |

Wallet last rotated: -

Connection Strings

Use the following connection strings or TNS names for your connections. See the documentation for details.

TLS Authentication

Close

Figure 8-14. *Downloading a Wallet*

The Wallet needs a password. Define the password as seen in Figure 8-15, and click *Download*. Save a ZIP file into a safe location. Click *Close*.

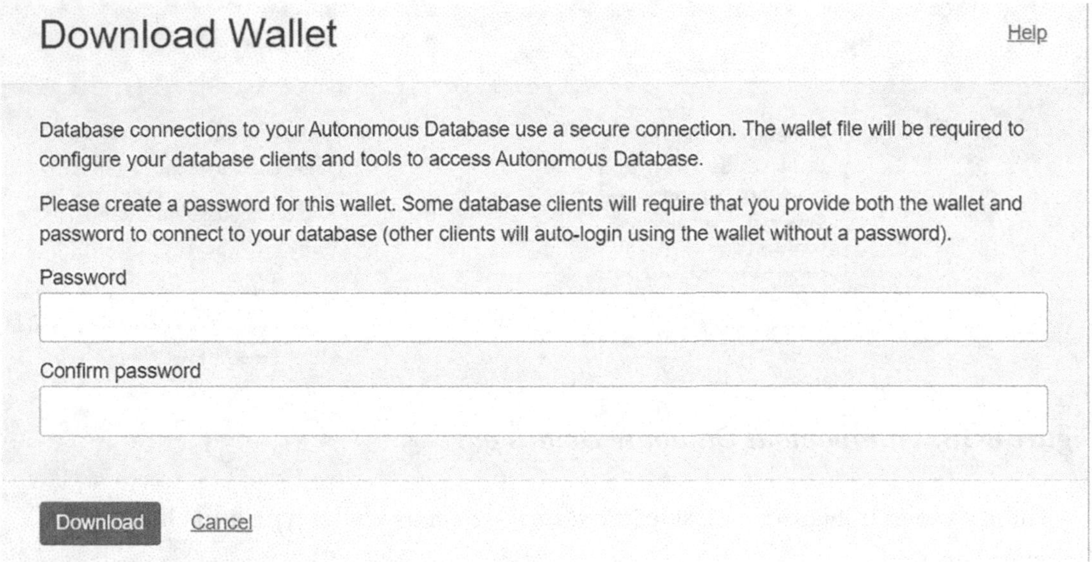

Download Wallet

Database connections to your Autonomous Database use a secure connection. The wallet file will be required to configure your database clients and tools to access Autonomous Database.

Please create a password for this wallet. Some database clients will require that you provide both the wallet and password to connect to your database (other clients will auto-login using the wallet without a password).

Password

Confirm password

Download   Cancel

Figure 8-15. *Defining a password for the Wallet*

Since the wallet consists of several files, we will base64 encode all of them. Extract the wallet.zip file to a folder on your local computer. You can use any Base64 encoder, for example, `www.base64encode.org/`. Drag and drop each file (except README.txt) at the time to the encoder, click ENCODE, and save the encoded file to a safe place. For example, drag and drop file cwallet.sso to the encoder, click ENCODE, download the encoded file, and save it, for example, as encoded_cwallet_sso.txt. When you have done this to all files in the wallet.zip file, your local folder should look similar to Figure 8-16.

Name

- cwallet.sso
- encoded_cwallet_sso
- encoded_ewallet
- encoded_keystore_jks
- encoded_ojdbc_properties
- encoded_sqlnet_ora
- encoded_tnsnames_ora
- encoded_truststore_jks
- ewallet
- keystore.jks
- ojdbc.properties
- README
- sqlnet.ora
- tnsnames.ora
- truststore.jks

Figure 8-16. *Wallet files and the encoded versions of them*

Then, create a *secret* for each file as seen in Figure 8-17:

1. In *Vault Details* page, navigate to *Secrets* in the *Resources*.

2. Click *Create Secret*.

3. Provide the information needed: Compartment, Name, Description, and Encryption Key.

4. Select *Base64* as the *Secret Type*.

5. Paste the content of the encoded file to the *Secret Content* field.

6. Click *Create Secret*.

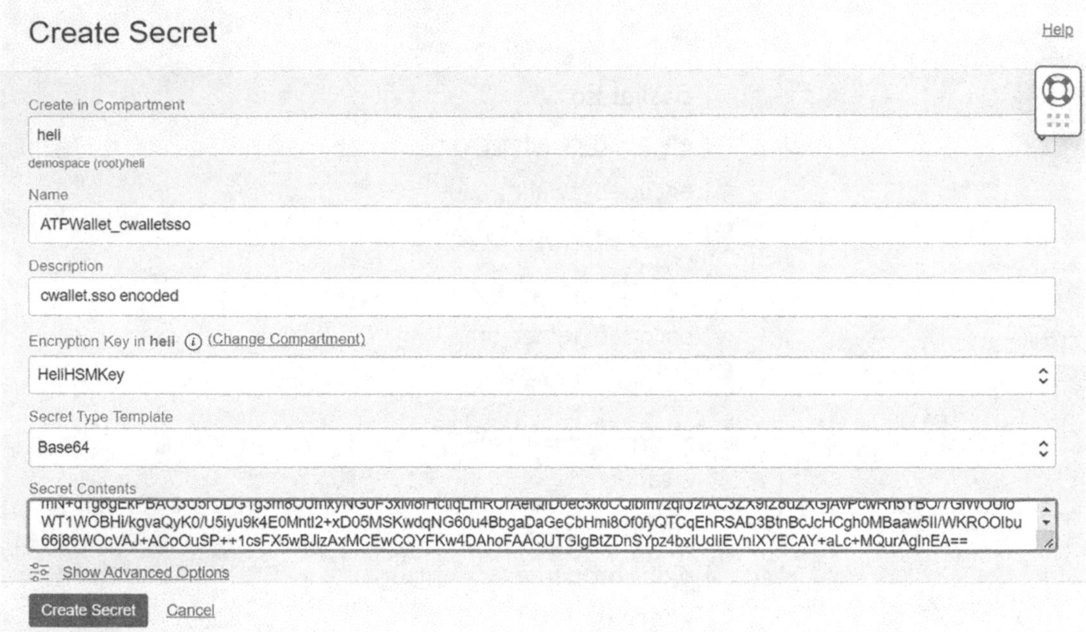

Create Secret

Create in Compartment

heli

demospace (root)/heli

Name

ATPWallet_cwalletsso

Description

cwallet.sso encoded

Encryption Key in **heli** ⓘ (Change Compartment)

HeliHSMKey

Secret Type Template

Base64

Secret Contents

rnN+dTg6gEKPBAO3U5fODG1g3m6OOfnxyNGUF3xlM8lHctIqLmROfAeIQfD0ec3k0CQIbIfff/2qfO2IAC3ZX9fZ8uZXGfAVPcWRf13YBO/7GfWOOlo
WT1WOBHi/kgvaQyK0/U5iyu9k4E0Mntl2+xD05MSKwdqNG60u4BbgaDaGeCbHmi8Of0fyQTCqEhRSAD3BtnBcJcHCgh0MBaaw5lI/WKROOIbu
66j86WOcVAJ+ACoOuSP++1csFX5wBJIzAxMCEwCQYFKw4DAhoFAAQUTGIgBtZDnSYpz4bxIUdIIEVnIXYECAY+aLc+MQurAgInEA==

⠿ Show Advanced Options

Create Secret   Cancel

Figure 8-17. *An example of creating a Secret for a Wallet file*

Follow the same procedure to create a secret for all the files in the wallet folder on your local computer.

When we created the Wallet, we defined a *password* for it. This password should be stored as a Secret too. Follow the same procedure as we did with the AnomalyDetectionUser's password earlier in this chapter and create a Secret.

Now, your list of secrets should look something like in Figure 8-18. Wait for all secrets to be in Active state to be available to use.

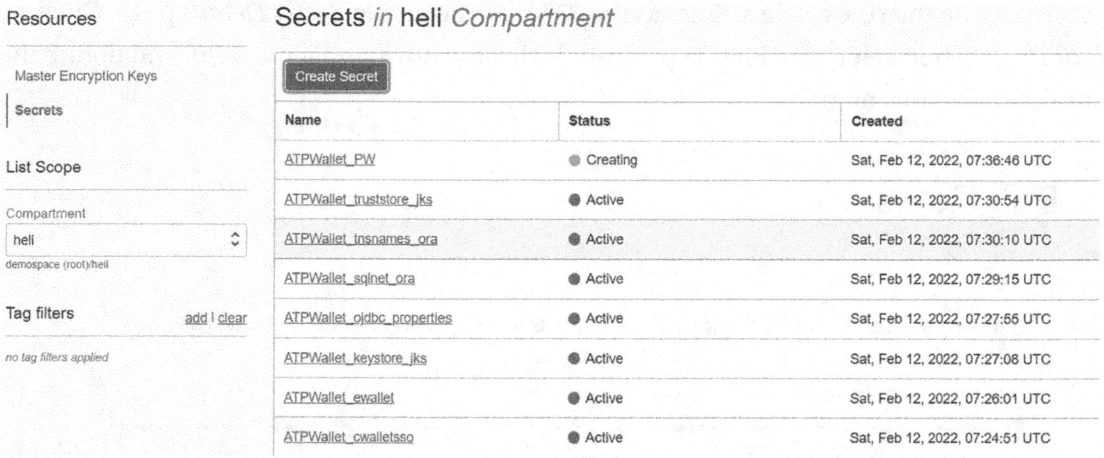

Figure 8-18. *List of Secrets*

A Secret can have *versions*. For example, if the password changes, you need to update the Secret too. That is done by creating a new version of the Secret. Select the Secret from the list of Secrets. In the *Secret Details* page, select *Version* from the *Table Scope* as seen in Figure 8-19. Click *Create Secret Version*. Update the data, for example, the password, and click *Create Secret Version*.

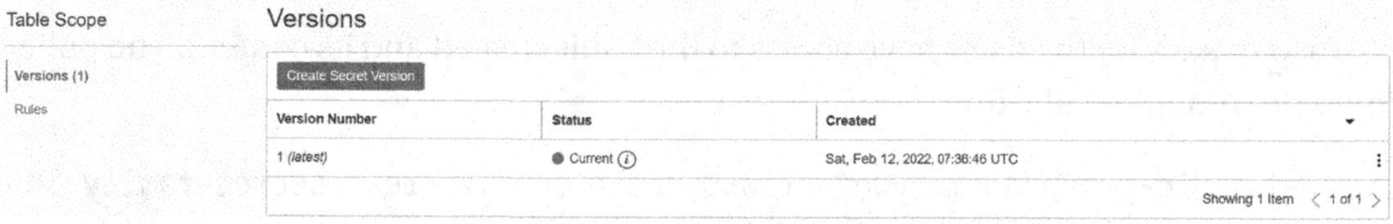

Figure 8-19. *Secret Details page showing the versions of the Secret*

You can also define rules for a Secret. There are two rule types:

1. *Secret Reuse Rule*: Prevents the reuse of secret contents across different versions of a secret. There are two configuration options: *Enforce on deleted secret versions* and *Don't enforce on deleted secret versions*.

2. *Secret Expiry*: Defines the expiry interval for a version and is the content retrieval blocked on expiry or not.

To define the rules, select *Rules* as the *Table Scope* on the *Secret Details* page. Click *Edit Rules*. Then select the Rule Type from the list as shown in Figure 8-20, and define the configuration for the rule.

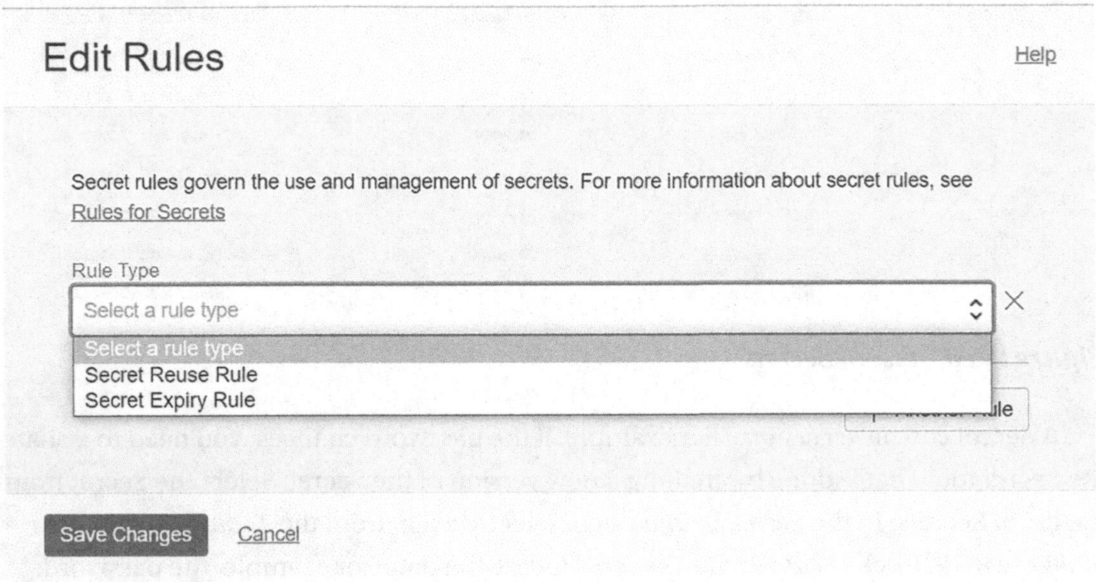

Figure 8-20. *Editing rules for a Secret*

Also make sure the users have access to the Vault created and its content. The policy could be something like this:

```
allow dynamic-group AnomalyDetectionDynamicGroup to read secret-family in
compartment Heli
```

In case your Autonomous Database is configured with *Private Endpoint*, you need to configure Private Endpoint for Anomaly Detection Service. Navigate to Private Endpoint in Anomaly Detection, as shown in Figure 8-21, click *Create Private Endpoint*, fill in the information needed, and click *Create*.

Anomaly Detection	Private Endpoints *in* heli *Compartment*		
Projects			
	Create Private Endpoint		
Private Endpoints			
	Name	**Status**	**Created**
List Scope		No items found.	
Compartment			

Figure 8-21. *A list of Private Endpoints and a button for creating a new Private Endpoint*

While creating different kinds of objects to OCI, you often need to choose the "correct" compartment. This decision is important since it affects, for example, the architecture, security, and maintainability of the cloud tenancy. In this example, we created the Secrets for general walled information to Compartment Heli and the anomaly detection–specific Secrets to AnomalyDetection Compartment. You might end up with a different solution.

Anomaly Detection Service

Anomaly Detection Service consists of *Projects, Models, Data Assets,* and *Detections. Projects* are workspaces for organizing data assets, models, and detections. A *Data Asset* is an abstracted data format that contains metadata of the actual dataset used for model training. A data asset can be created from data located in Oracle Object Storage, Oracle Autonomous Transaction Processing, or InfluxDB. A *Model* is a machine learning model that has been trained using the data asset to detect anomalies in time-series data. Most of the parameters are tuned by the service; just a few parameters are left for the user to define. When a model is trained successfully, it is automatically deployed into the cloud environment. The model can then be used to *detect* anomalies from a new set of data. A project can have multiple data assets and multiple models.

Requirements for the Data

There are strict requirements for the datasets, when using Anomaly Detection Service, since it is an automatized process for anomaly detection. These requirements make it possible for the model to learn what is "normal," a skill to be able to recognize abnormal data. The content of the dataset must be very good:

- The training dataset should not include anomalies.

- All of the different typical business scenarios should be included in the training dataset.

Anomaly Detection Service uses two types of machine learning kernels: *multivariate* and *univariate* kernels. The first one is for multivariate correlated signals and the latter for univariate independent signals. Univariate anomaly detection looks for anomalies in each individual metric, while multivariate anomaly detection builds a single model for all the metrics in the system. The univariate kernel only treats one signal at a time, so collective anomalies among multiple signals cannot be done.

The core algorithm of the Anomaly Detection Service uses Multivariate State Estimation Technique (MSET) and a multivariate anomaly detection algorithm called MSET2. This algorithm is created by Oracle Labs. The requirements for the dataset, when using MSET2 algorithm, is that the correlations between signals should be relatively high. The multivariate kernel excludes signals with lower correlations and changes to the univariate kernel building all univariate models. The univariate kernel uses a window-based feature engineering approach; therefore, to learn the patterns or inference anomalies, it requires an extra one window size of data before the actual training or detecting data. By default, the window size is 20 timestamps. The minimum total number of timestamps is 80. Univariate models will not detect anomalies from data pieces that are smaller than a window size, so the best result is obtained when the dataset size is a multiple of the window size. The univariate kernel cannot be invoked separately in Anomaly Detection service. It is only invoked by the multivariate kernel, automatically.

The Anomaly Detection service supports *CSV* and *JSON* file formats that contain *time series* data: timestamps and numeric attributes. The service also supports data from Autonomous Transaction Processing database and InfluxDB. These data sources have similar requirements in terms of content of the dataset. Each row in the dataset represents one *observation* of attributes at the given timestamp. Usually, the first column contains the timestamp and other numeric attributes following it. These other attributes are typically sensor or signal data.

Note   The attributes (except timestamp) can only contain *numerical* values. The algorithms used do not understand other data types. Possible Boolean flag values have to be converted to numeric values, if they are needed in the dataset.

The timestamp attribute is optional. But, if the timestamp is provided for one row, it must be provided for all the rows. The timestamp attribute must be named *timestamp* (all lowercase without any spaces), and it must be the first attribute of the dataset. The timestamps must be sorted in increasing order in the dataset and no duplicates are allowed. The timestamps can have different frequencies. For example, 100 000 observations in 1 hour and 10 observations in the next hour. Timestamps must follow the ISO 8601 format. The best practice is to use the precise time up to seconds or milliseconds.

There are some other requirements for the attributes in the dataset. The attribute names must be *unique*. The maximum number of attributes has been limited to 300. The value of an attribute can be missing, but in that case, it must be represented as null. The entire row can't have all the values as missing; at least one attribute has to have a value. None of the attributes can be named as MSET. It is also important that the attributes have been selected well for the dataset: they should cover the business scenarios with full value ranges on all attributes.

CSV formatted data must consist of comma-separated lines, with the first line as the header and other lines as data. Each column represents attribute data; the row represents an observation at a particular timestamp. The first column must be named as *timestamp* if timestamps are specified in data. Missing values are permitted with null, only numeric data type values are permitted, and the data is sorted by timestamp. The last line can't be a new line; it has to be an observation.

Similarly, *JSON-formatted data* must also contain timestamps and numeric attributes only. Use the following keys:

```
{ "requestType": "INLINE",
  "signalNames": ["sensor1", "sensor2", "sensor3", "sensor4", "sensor5",
"sensor6", "sensor7", "sensor8", "sensor9", "sensor10"],
  "data": [
      { "timestamp" : "2021-01-01T08:01:01.000Z", "values" : [1, 5.2, 6, 1,
      2.3, 4, 2, 3.2, null, 7] },
      { "timestamp" : "2021-01-02T08:01:02.000Z", "values" : [1, 2.2, 7, 1,
      3.2, 3, 1, 2.3, 5, null] }
  ]
}
```

Note   In JSON files, the missing value should be added as *null* without quotes.

In the model creation and training phase, the number of observations/rows in training data must be at least 8 × number of attributes or 80 whichever is greater. For example, with 100 attributes, the minimum rows required are Max (8 × 100, 80) = 800 rows. With 5 attributes, the minimum rows required are Max (8 × 5, 80) = 80 rows. If a new attribute is added to the dataset or the name of the attribute has changed, then the model has to be built again to include the new attribute to consider it during detection. If an attribute is detected to be a duplicate of another attribute during training, it is automatically dropped. When selecting the attributes for the dataset, select only attributes that are *related* to each other and are part of the *same system or process*. It is important that the attributes are somehow related to each other. If there are several systems or processes, build a separate model for each process using the dataset describing that process.

There is also another reason to select the attributes for the dataset carefully. As mentioned, the anomaly detection uses multivariate methods, and each added attribute introduces interactions between itself and all the other attributes. Therefore, the computational cost increases rapidly as the number of attributes increases.

When detecting anomalies from a new dataset, the maximum size of a detection payload is up to 300 attributes or maximum of 30,000 data points. Data points are counted as the number of attributes × the number of rows. This limitation might change, but bear in mind there might be a limitation for the payload.

For anomaly detection, it is important the data is of good quality, and the more data the better, as long as it is within the limits of the maximum allowed data.

Most of the time, if the model creation or the detection fails, the reason is that one or more of the requirements were not followed. For example, if the dataset is missing a header, you get an error message: "A header row comprising of signal labels is missing. Header row should include 'timestamp' (if exists) plus labels for each signal." If the dataset for testing has different headings than the training dataset, you get an error message: "An error occurred while rendering anomaly visualization due to [The detection data does not contain all signals that were used during training. Please provide the following signals: [temperature_1, temperature_2, temperature_3, temperature_4, temperature_5, pressure_1, pressure_2, pressure_3, pressure_4, pressure_5]], contact Support." If the header is missing or is different from the header in the training dataset, the model does not find any anomalies. "No anomalies detected for selected model type and detection data." Or, if the dataset does not contain enough rows, you get an error message: "[The number of rows in the training data is not enough!]. The error you will get if the dataset has too many data points is: An error occurred while rendering anomaly visualization due to [The number of total data points in the data exceeds the max number limitation! Please make sure entire number of data points in detection data is not more than 30000. The number of signal names does not match the number of signals. Please provide a name for each signal!], contact Support." Creating and training a model takes quite a long time, so it might be worth checking the data and make sure the dataset follows the requirements, before starting to create a model.

A user does not need to understand the kernels nor the process itself; the service automatically optimizes the outcome: a trained model. But the user *must* provide the process with datasets that meet the requirements.

Creating a Machine Learning Model and Detecting Anomalies

To start with Anomaly Detection, select *AI & Analytics* from the OCI Console navigation menu, and then select *Anomaly Detection* under *AI Services*. The *Projects* page opens up. Creating a model starts with either creating a Project or selecting an existing one. If you are not able to create a project and instead get an error message "! Error loading data," there are two possible explanations:

- You have selected the wrong compartment. Select the correct one.

- You do not have privileges to Anomaly Detection resources. Ask the Administrator to grant you privileges as explained earlier in this chapter.

To create a new project, select the correct compartment, and click *Create Project*, shown in Figure 8-22. If you want to create a Model under an existing Project, then select the Project name from the list of projects.

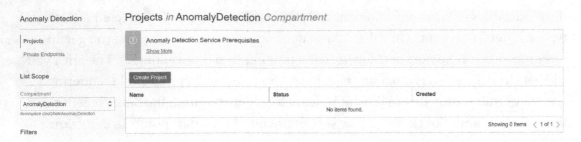

Figure 8-22. *A list of anomaly detection projects in a compartment and a button to create a new project*

Select the correct compartment from the list, insert a name and a description for the project, as shown in Figure 8-23. Then, click *Create*. The project appears on the list of projects.

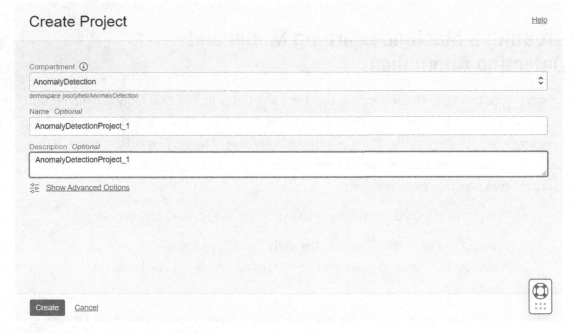

Figure 8-23. *Creating a new anomaly detection project*

Either click the project name, or click the three-dot menu on the right-hand side, and select *View Details*. The *Project Details* page opens (Figure 8-24). You can edit a project, move it to another compartment, add tags to it, or delete the project.

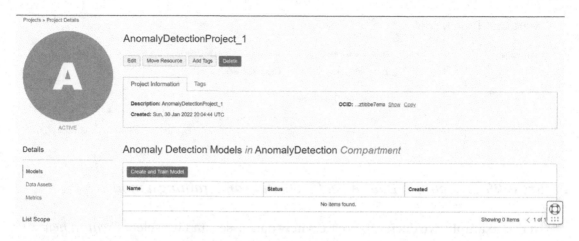

Figure 8-24. *Project Details page*

A project consists of *Models*, *Data Assets*, and *Metrics*, as shown in Figure 8-24. The first step is finding the data for the training process. Then, use that data to create a *Data Asset* that a model can use for training. The Data Asset can be created separately by selecting *Data Asset* from the *Project Details* page (Figure 8-24) and inserting the information needed. Or, it can be created while creating and training a model. To do that, click *Create and Train Model*.

The first step is to select the data asset used for the model creation and training.

Note   The data asset must include typical values; it should not include any anomalies, because this data asset is used to train the model to recognize normal data to be able to understand what is not normal.

You can either select an existing data asset from the list (Figure 8-25), or you can create a new data asset. Remember, a Data Asset is not just a data file for training; it also includes metadata for the model building. That's why the Data Asset must be created first.

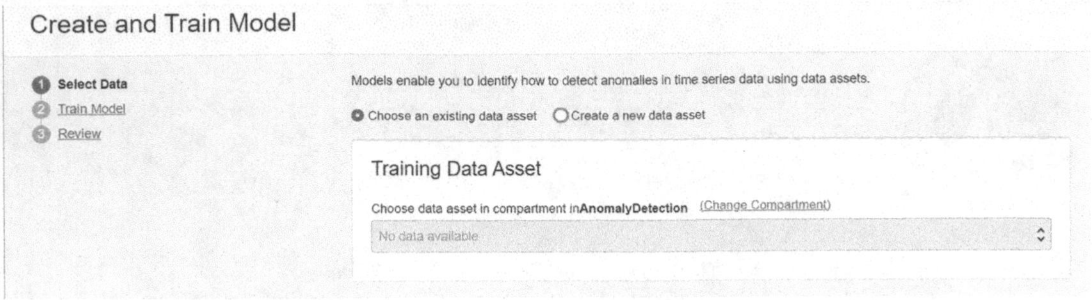

Create and Train Model

1 **Select Data**
2 Train Model
3 Review

Models enable you to identify how to detect anomalies in time series data using data assets.

◉ Choose an existing data asset   ◯ Create a new data asset

Training Data Asset

Choose data asset in compartment in**AnomalyDetection**   (Change Compartment)

No data available ⬍

Figure 8-25. *Selecting a Data Asset for creating and training a model*

In this example, we decide to create a new data asset, and we select *Create a new data asset*. Fill in the information needed on the *Create Data Asset* page (Figure 8-31): the compartment, name, and description of the data asset, and select the type of a data asset. The type can be Oracle Object Storage, Oracle Autonomous Transaction Processing database, or InfluxDB.

If you choose *Oracle Object Storage*, select the bucket and the training data file from that bucket (JSON, CSV). The namespace is also shown, but you are not able to change it.

If you choose *Oracle Autonomous Transaction Processing database* as the data source type, you should insert the following data:

- Database Name

- Table Name

- User Name

- Credentials

- Configuration

Insert the name of the database, the table containing the data, and the username you use for logging in. Add the credentials needed. In this context, Credentials does not mean just a username and a password. You need to have a Vault, an Encryption Key, and Secrets created for the compartment before you can use this service with an ATP data source. If you have not created them, then either create them as explained earlier in this chapter or ask an Administrator to do it for you. In Figure 8-26, you can see the information needed for the ATP database and in Figures 8-27 and 8-28 how the Secrets can be used to create the connection. In Figures 8-29 and 8-30, you can see how the configuration is done.

Create Data Asset
Help
AnomalyDetection
demospace (root)/heli/AnomalyDetection
Name Optional
DataAssetFromATP
Description Optional
A data asset created from a data from ATP
Type
Oracle Autonomous Transaction Processing
Database Name
BookATP
Table Name
DEMO_TRAINING_DATA
User Name
ANOMALYSDETECTIONUSER
Create
Cancel

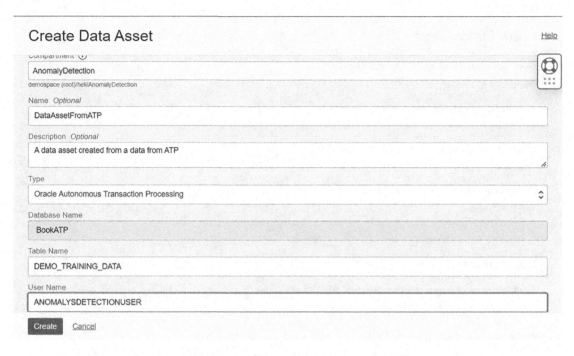

Figure 8-26. *Selecting ATP as the data source for a Data Asset*

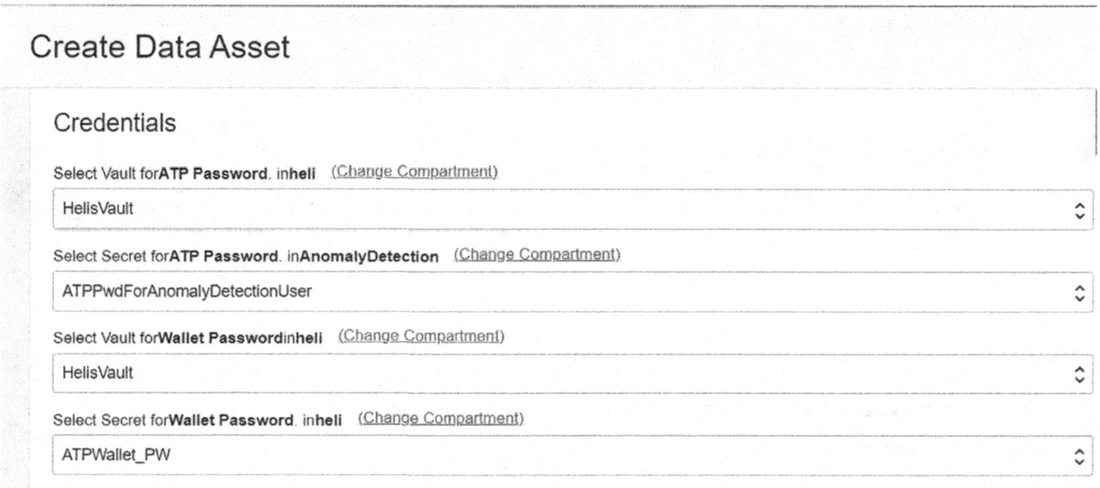

Create Data Asset
Credentials
Select Vault forATP Password. inheli (Change Compartment)
HelisVault
Select Secret forATP Password. inAnomalyDetection (Change Compartment)
ATPPwdForAnomalyDetectionUser
Select Vault forWallet Passwordinheli (Change Compartment)
HelisVault
Select Secret forWallet Password. inheli (Change Compartment)
ATPWallet_PW

Figure 8-27. *Defining the first set of credentials when creating a Data Asset from ATP*

Create Data Asset

Select Vault for **SSO Wallet**. inheli *(Change Compartment)*

> HelisVault ⌄

Select Secret for **SSO Wallet**. inheli *(Change Compartment)*

> ATPWallet_cwalletsso ⌄

Select Vault for **PKCS12 File**. inheli *(Change Compartment)*

> HelisVault ⌄

Select Secret for **PKCS12 file**. inheli *(Change Compartment)*

> ATPWallet_ewallet ⌄

Configuration

Select Vault for **Java Keystore**. in **AnomalyDetection** *(Change Compartment)*

> No data available ⌄

Create   Cancel

Figure 8-28. Defining the rest of the credentials when creating a Data Asset from ATP

Configuration

Select Vault for **Java Keystore**. inheli *(Change Compartment)*

> HelisVault ⌄

Select Secret for **Java keystore**. inheli *(Change Compartment)*

> ATPWallet_keystore_jks ⌄

Select Vault for **JDBC connection**. inheli *(Change Compartment)*

> HelisVault ⌄

Select Secret for **JDBC connection**. inheli *(Change Compartment)*

> ATPWallet_ojdbc_properties ⌄

Select Vault for **Network Configuration**. inheli *(Change Compartment)*

> HelisVault ⌄

Select Secret for **Network Configuration**. inheli *(Change Compartment)*

> ATPWallet_sqlnet_ora ⌄

Figure 8-29. Defining the first set of configurations for an ATP as a data source for Data Asset

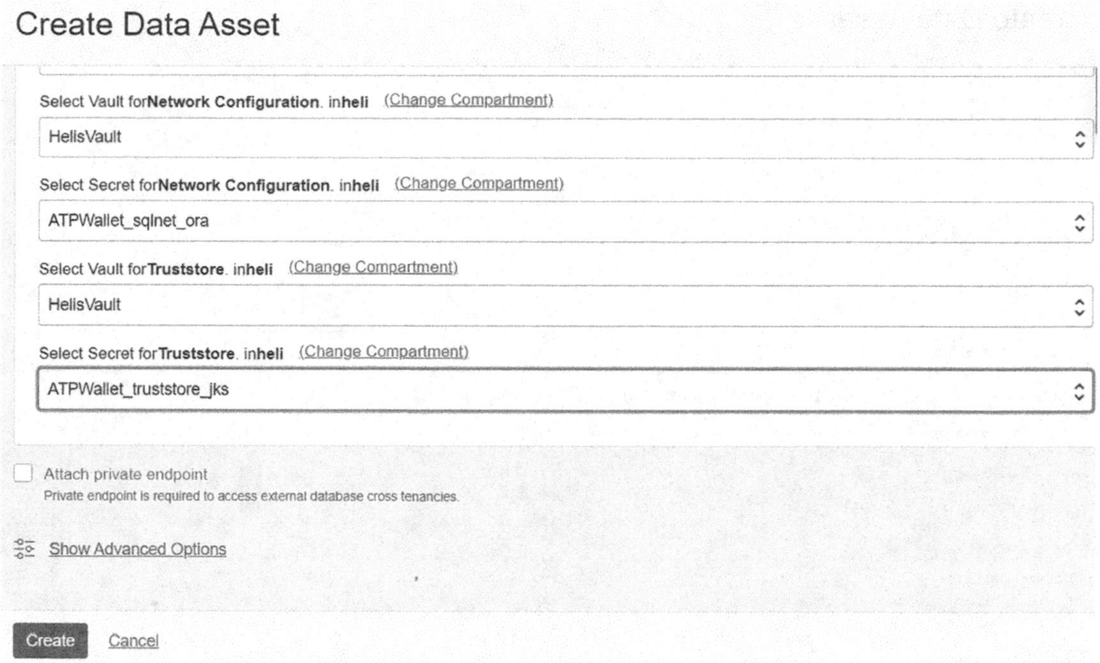

Create Data Asset

Select Vault for**Network Configuration**. inheli   (Change Compartment)

HelisVault

Select Secret for**Network Configuration**. inheli   (Change Compartment)

ATPWallet_sqlnet_ora

Select Vault for**Truststore**. inheli   (Change Compartment)

HelisVault

Select Secret for**Truststore**. inheli   (Change Compartment)

ATPWallet_truststore_jks

☐ Attach private endpoint
   Private endpoint is required to access external database cross tenancies.

Show Advanced Options

Create   Cancel

***Figure 8-30.** Defining the rest of configurations for an ATP as a data source for Data Asset*

You can also attach a private endpoint to access external database cross tenancies. In case you configured Private Endpoint, then enable *Attach private endpoint* and select it from the list of the private endpoints in the compartment.

If you choose *InfluxDB* as the data source type, insert the username, credentials, measurement name, and URL, and select the InfluxDB version from the list. If you need to access an external database, select Attach private endpoint to create a private endpoint.

In our example, we choose to use Oracle Object Storage (Figure 8-31) and select a csv file from the bucket. After selecting the training data, click *Create* to see that a data asset has been selected as shown in Figure 8-32.

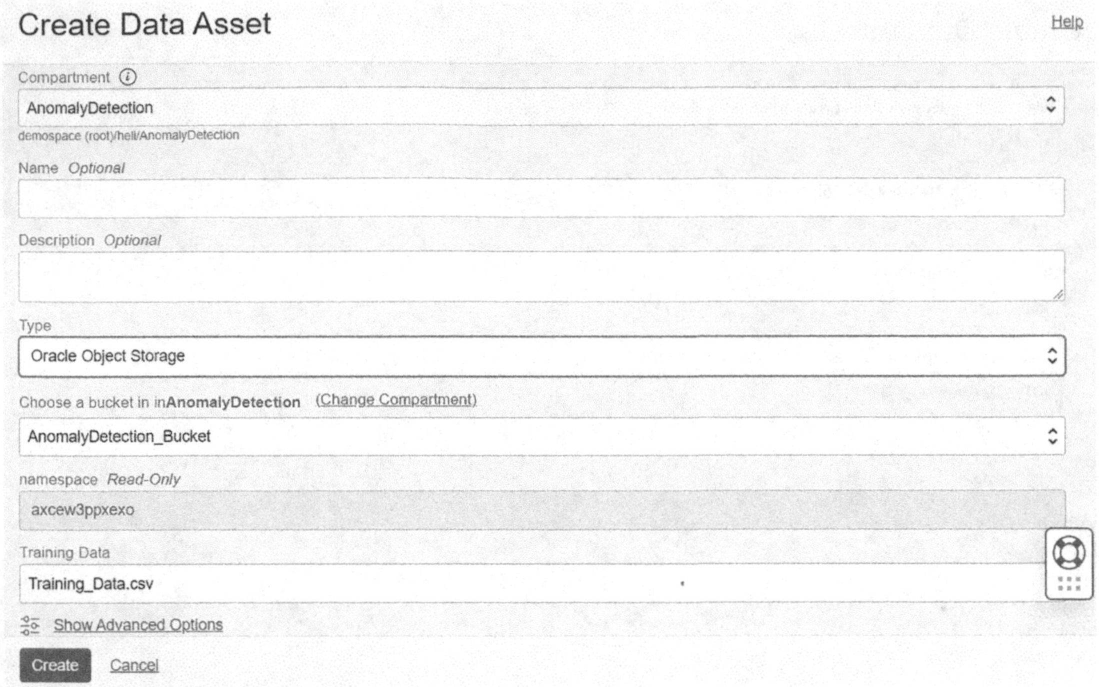

Create Data Asset

Help

Compartment ⓘ

AnomalyDetection

demospace (root)/hell/AnomalyDetection

Name *Optional*

Description *Optional*

Type

Oracle Object Storage

Choose a bucket in **AnomalyDetection**   (Change Compartment)

AnomalyDetection_Bucket

namespace *Read-Only*

axcew3ppxexo

Training Data

Training_Data.csv

Show Advanced Options

Create   Cancel

Figure 8-31. *Creating a Data Asset from a csv file stored in Oracle Object Storage*

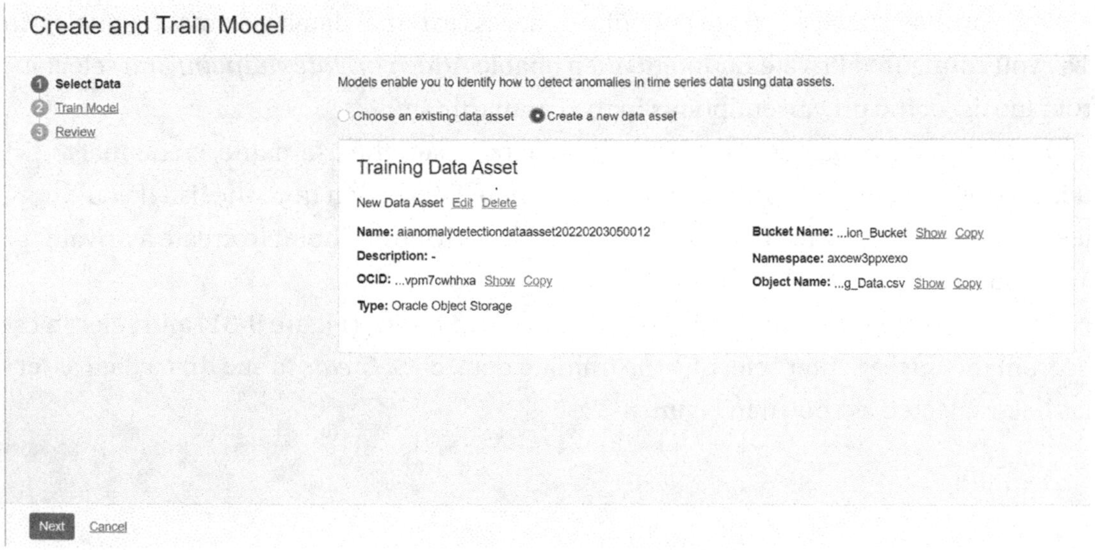

Create and Train Model

1 **Select Data**
2 Train Model
3 Review

Models enable you to identify how to detect anomalies in time series data using data assets.

○ Choose an existing data asset   ● Create a new data asset

Training Data Asset

New Data Asset Edit Delete

Name: aianomalydetectiondataasset20220203050012
Description: -
OCID: ...vpm7cwhhxa Show Copy
Type: Oracle Object Storage

Bucket Name: ...ion_Bucket Show Copy
Namespace: axcew3ppxexo
Object Name: ...g_Data.csv Show Copy

Next   Cancel

Figure 8-32. *Data Asset information to check before continuing the model creation and training*

Click *Next*. Now, we will create and train a model using the selected data asset.

Select the compartment, and define a name and a description for the model, as shown in Figure 8-33. Then, choose values for *Target False Alarm Probability* and *Training Fraction Ratio*. These are the only parameters for a user to define. The default values for these are 0.01 for Target False Alarm Probability and 0.7 for Training Fraction Ratio.

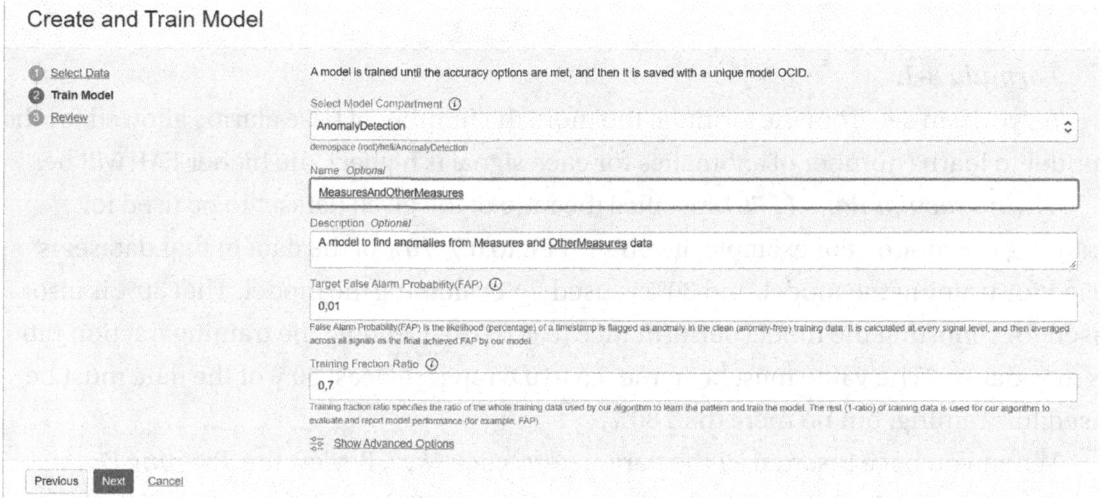

Figure 8-33. *Defining the parameters for model creation*

False Alarm Probability (FAP) defines the percentage of timestamps to be flagged as anomalies. FAP can be set to be at the same level of percentage of anomalies in real business scenarios if that level is known. The default value (0.01 or 1%) is seen as relatively appropriate for many scenarios. If you define FAP high, it means that the likelihood of false alarms is high. Also, be aware that the lower the FAP has been defined, the longer time it takes for the model to be trained with a risk it will never achieve to the target FAP. FAP is calculated at every signal level and then averaged across all signals as the final achieved FAP by the model. The FAB is calculated by summing up all the anomalies in every signal. That is divided by the amount of data points (number of signals multiplied by the number of timestamps). FAP = sum (number of anomalies in each signal)/(number of signals * number of timestamps). The formula is shown in Formula 8-1.

$$\frac{\sum_{i=1}^{NumberOf\,Signals} NumberOfAnomalies}{NumberOf\,Signals * NumberOfTimestamps}$$

Formula 8-1.

As you can see from the formula, the more the number of false alarms allowed for the model to learn (number of anomalies for each signal is higher), the higher FAP will be.

Train Fraction Ratio (TFR) specifies the ratio of the given dataset to be used for training the model. For example, if you set TFR to 0.7, 70% of the data in that dataset is used for training the model, and 30% is used for evaluating the model. That 30% is also used for reporting the model performance (e.g., FAP). Defining the training fraction ratio is mandatory. The value must be in the 0.5 to 0.8 range: at least 50% of the data must be used for training, but no more than 80%.

When you have inserted all the parameters, click *Next*. Review the *Training Data information* and the *Model Information* seen in Figure 8-34. If all is correct, click *Create* to create and train the model. If you need to fix something, click *Previous*.

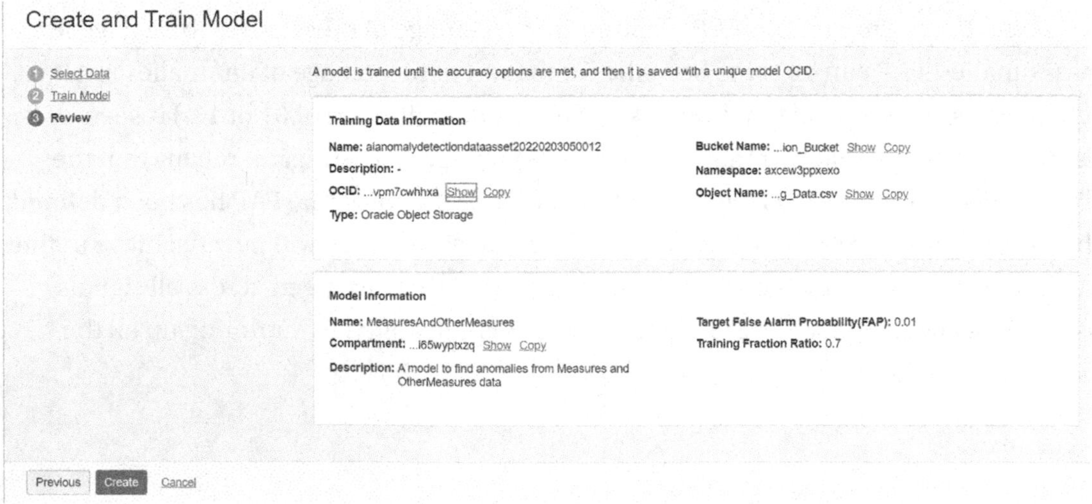

Figure 8-34. *Model information to be reviewed before creating the model*

It takes a while to create and train a model. During the process, you will see the model in the state *Creating*. When the process finishes, the state is updated to *Active*. Other possible states are *Deleting*, *Deleted*, and *Failed*.

The most common reason for a failure is that one or more of the requirements for the dataset were not followed as explained earlier in this chapter.

To investigate the model, either select the model from the model list by clicking its name, or select the three-dot menu on the right-hand side and select *View Details*. In the *Model Details* page, you can see the general information, model information, and tags defined for the model. *General information* (Figure 8-35) includes OCI-related information. You can change the name and description by clicking the *Edit* button and move the model to another compartment with the *Move Resource* button. You can delete the model with the *Delete* button.

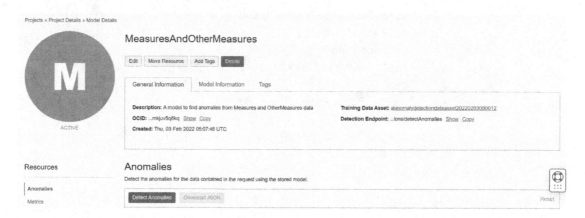

Figure 8-35. *Model Details page*

Model Information (Figure Model3) includes information about the model creation. It shows the values used for *Target False Alarm Probability* and *Training Fraction Ratio* while creating the model, as well as *Model False Alarm Probability* and *Multivariate False Alarm Probability* for the model. If you want to investigate the model details, click *Download* link next to *Model Details* to download the model details into a JSON file. This file is called details_result.json. You can see an excerpt of the file content in Figure 8-36.

```
{
    "rowReductionDetails": null,
    "signalDetails": [
        {
            "signalName": "IOT_3",
            "mviRatio": null,
            "isQuantized": false,
            "fap": 0.0023333333,
            "min": -4.6571,
            "max": 4.5794,
            "std": 1.88132,
            "status": "ACCEPTED",
            "details": null
        },
        {
            "signalName": "OtherMeasure_5",
            "mviRatio": null,
            "isQuantized": false,
            "fap": 0.0013333333,
            "min": -6.6104,
            "max": 7.0459,
            "std": 2.04693,
            "status": "ACCEPTED",
            "details": null
        },
    ],
    "warning": null
}
```

Figure 8-36. *An excerpt of the details_result.json file*

To investigate the tags, select the *Tags* tab (Figure 8-37). The model creation automatically adds two tags: CreatedBy and CreatedOn. You can add more Tags by clicking the *Add Tags* button.

Figure 8-37. *Model Information on Model Details page. Model Details page also includes tabs for General Information and Tags*

Now that the model has been created and trained successfully, it can be used with a new dataset to detect anomalies from it. To do that, click *Detect Anomalies*. Then select the file you want to check for possible anomalies either by dragging and dropping a file to the box, or clicking *Select File* and finding the correct file from your local folders (Figure 8-38). The file can be of format JSON or CSV. Then click *Detect*.

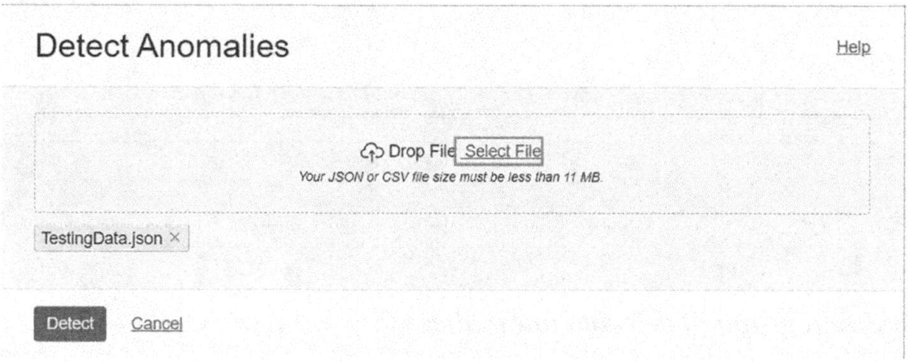

Detect Anomalies

Help

⌕ Drop File Select File

Your JSON or CSV file size must be less than 11 MB.

TestingData.json ✕

Detect   Cancel

Figure 8-38. *Detecting Anomalies using a JSON file*

Note   The data for anomaly detection must have exactly the same labels for the data in the heading as the training data had. In other words, the column names and the number of columns must match to the original training data, but the file can be of another file type.

Possible anomalies are shown as a graph. In the graph, the horizontal axis represents the timestamp or index, and the vertical axis represents signal values, measures. Each signal, or measure, is shown in its own subgraph. In each subgraph, the orange line indicates the actual input value of a signal, and the purple line indicates the estimated value the machine learning model has predicted. A red line highlights anomalies that have been detected at that timestamp. Anomaly has been detected and marked with red if the difference between the actual value and the predicted value is large enough. In Figure 8-39, you can see a possible anomaly in Measure_1 at one timestamp. Move your mouse over the graph to see how the actual value and estimated value at a certain timestamp are shown on the upper right corner of the graph. If the model detects an anomaly, it does not necessarily mean there is an anomaly. It is possible that the training dataset did not cover all normal situations of the process and therefore sees this situation as an anomaly. If this is the case, create a new training dataset containing also this situation, and train a model using the new dataset.

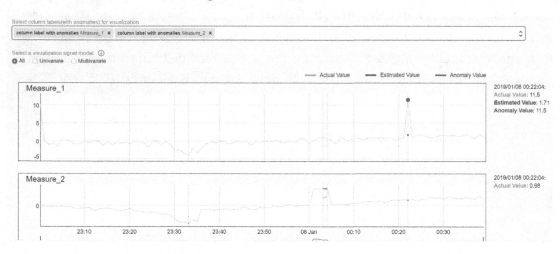

Figure 8-39. *A graph of detected anomalies*

In Figure 8-40, you can see an example of an estimated value being much higher than the actual value. Therefore, there is a possible anomaly on that timestamp.

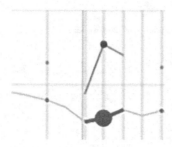

Figure 8-40. *A possible anomaly where the estimated value is much higher than the actual value*

In Figure 8-41, you can see an example where the actual value is much higher than the estimated value, and therefore, there is a possible anomaly on that data point.

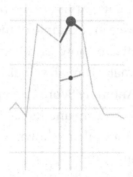

Figure 8-41. *A possible anomaly where the estimated value is much lower than the actual value*

By default, all variables are shown as a diagram, each variable on its own diagram. But, by selecting *Select column labels (with anomalies) for visualization* (Figure 8-42) and picking one or more of the variables, you can limit the diagrams to show only those variables that might have anomalies.

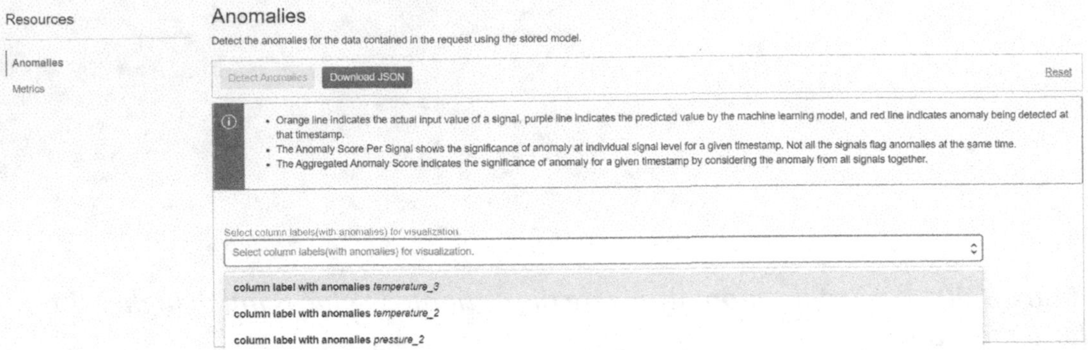

Resources

Metrics

Anomalies

Detect the anomalies for the data contained in the request using the stored model.

Detect Anomalies   Download JSON   Reset

ⓘ   • Orange line indicates the actual input value of a signal, purple line indicates the predicted value by the machine learning model, and red line indicates anomaly being detected at
        that timestamp.
    • The Anomaly Score Per Signal shows the significance of anomaly at individual signal level for a given timestamp. Not all the signals flag anomalies at the same time.
    • The Aggregated Anomaly Score indicates the significance of anomaly for a given timestamp by considering the anomaly from all signals together.

Select column labels(with anomalies) for visualization.

Select column labels(with anomalies) for visualization.   ⬍

column label with anomalies *temperature_3*

column label with anomalies *temperature_2*

column label with anomalies *pressure_2*

Figure 8-42. *Filtering column labels for anomaly visualization or downloading the detected anomalies into a JSON file*

The last two subgraphs in the set of graphs are *Aggregated Anomaly Score* and *Anomaly Score Per Signal*. You can see an example of these graphs in Figure 8-43. The Aggregated Anomaly Score indicates how significant the anomaly is in a given timestamp by considering the anomaly from all signals together. The higher the score is, the bigger the significance is. The Anomaly Score Per Signal indicates the significance of an individual signal at a given timestamp and its score. If several signals are having anomalies at the same timestamp, they all are shown with their score. Of course, not all the signals flag anomalies at the same time.

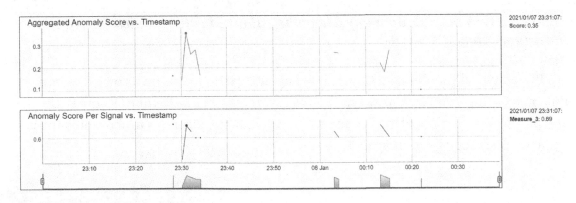

Figure 8-43. *Aggregated Anomaly Score and Anomaly Score Per Signal graphs*

You can also select the model visualized from *Select a visualization signal model*. The options are All, Univariate, and Multivariate. The default is All. If you select *Univariate* as in Figure 8-44, the anomalies found using univariate models are shown, and if you select *Multivariate*, those anomalies found using the multivariate models are shown.

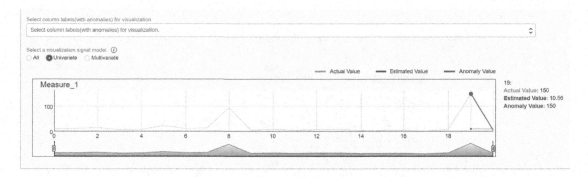

Figure 8-44. *Univariate signal mode selected for the graphs*

The anomalies are not saved forever and only one anomaly analysis is visible at a time. Creating the analysis for anomalies is very fast, so you can always create it again if needed. If you want to save the anomaly data into a file, download the results to a JSON file by clicking the *Download JSON* button shown in Figure 8-42. The file is called anomalies.json. You can see an excerpt of this JSON file in Figure 8-45. As you can see, the JSON file contains an array of anomalies grouped by timestamp. Each timestamp can have anomalies generated by a single signal or multiple signals. Anomaly generated by one signal contains a tuple of signal name, actual value, estimated value, and an anomaly score. The anomaly score indicates the significance of the anomaly. This score is within the range of 0 to 1. Each timestamp also has a normalized score that combines the significance scores across single or multiple alerted signals in that timestamp. This information can be very valuable for automating the business workflows to take immediate actions using anomaly scores. For example, the estimated value for each anomaly identified makes it possible to assess the severity of the anomaly occurrence. Or, a signal-specific anomaly score enables one to assess relative severity of anomalies across the signals. Or, aggregated scores of anomalies over time make it possible to see if the anomalies are becoming more severe over time.

```
[{
    "timestamp": "2021-01-07T21:00:08.000+00:00",
    "anomalies": [{
        "signalName": "Measure_1",
        "actualValue": 10.4738691915899,
        "estimatedValue": 1.0010240112850315,
        "anomalyScore": 0.6
    }],
    "score": 0.1267445569535895
}, {
    "timestamp": "2021-01-07T21:28:10.000+00:00",
    "anomalies": [{
        "signalName": "Measure_3",
        "actualValue": -2.3941492028804823,
        "estimatedValue": -1.3968646982447714,
        "anomalyScore": 0.6991412894058566
    }],
    "score": 0.17062950252017878
```

Figure 8-45. *An excerpt of this JSON file anomalies.json*

Metrics

You can find the *Metrics* from the *Project Details* page under *Resources* as seen in
Figure 8-24. You can also find *Metrics* as seen in Figure 8-46 on the *Model Details* page
under *Resources*. The difference between these two Metrics is that in Project Details, you
can see the Metris of the model training, while as in the Model Details page, you can see
the Metrics of the detection.

Figure 8-46. *Reviewing the Metrics for Projects and Models*

You can define the *Start time* and the *End time*. With the *Quick Selects* list, you can easily select, for example, *Last 7 days*. Then the Start time is automatically changed to seven days ago.

The Metrics shows five metrics of the Model: *Failed, Successful, Success Rate, Latency,* and *Total*. In each of these five metric panes, there is an i symbol for more information on the particular metric.

Also, in each of these panes, you can define the *Interval* and the *Statistic* method used. Interval can be Auto, one minute, five minutes, one hour, or one day. Statistics can be rate, sum, mean, min, max, count, P50, P90, P95, P99, or P99.9. You can hover the cursor on top of the screen to see the situation in all the metrics at one time point. In Figure 8-47, you can see an example of four of these metrics.

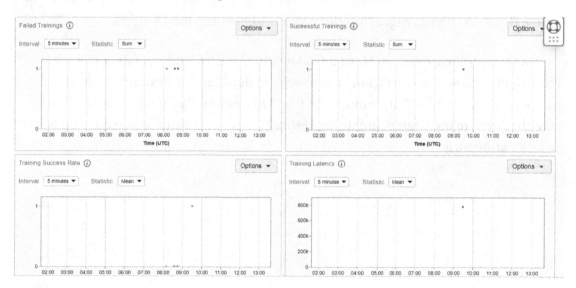

Figure 8-47. *Example of four metrics on model training*

If you click one of the metric panes, it opens up and you can investigate it in more detail. You can see an example of this in Figure 8-48. You can change the Interval or the Statistic, or you can use the *Adjust x-axis* bar to adjust the metrics on the timeline. Grab the end of the bar with a mouse and move the bar; the x axis adapts to that. From the *Options* list, you can select to *View Query in Metrics Explorer, Copy Chart URL, Copy Query (MQL), Create an Alarm on this Query,* or *Table View*.

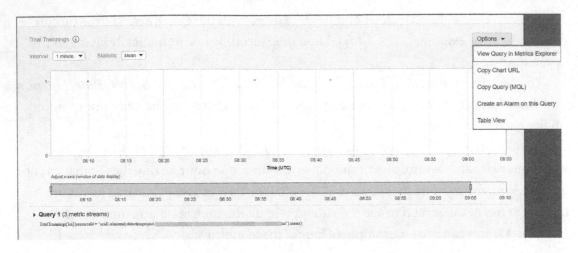

Figure 8-48. *A metric, adjusting the x axis and viewing the Options*

If you select *View Query in Metrics Explorer*, the Metrics Explorer (shown in Figure 8-49) opens. You can explore the metrics in detail and, for example, adjust the x and y axis. Or, you can edit the query with the *Query Editor*. Based on the editing, you can either update the chart or create an *Alarm*. You can also visualize the queries using the *OCI Dashboard*.

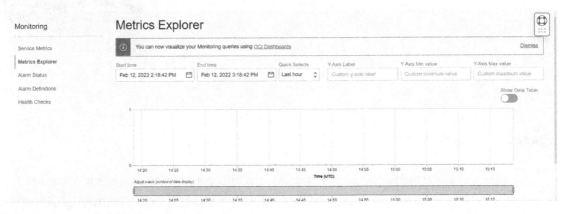

Figure 8-49. *Metric Explorer*

If you select the *Copy Chart URL*, the URL for the chart is copied to the memory and you can paste it wherever needed. *Copy Query (MQL)* copies the query so that you can paste it where needed.

Create an Alarm on this Query takes you to the *Create Alarm* page where you can create an alarm for the metric. *Table View* shows the same query result but as table data. To switch back to chart, select *Chart View* from the *Options*.

Metrics are only available for active models and users with the privileges. If you cannot see any metrics, you are probably missing the privileges. Create the appropriate policies to grant the privileges. It could be something like this:

```
allow group AnomalyDetectionGroup to use metrics in compartment Heli
```

Also note that to be able to see Alarms, you need privileges. The policy could be something like this:

```
allow group AnomalyDetectionGroup to use alarms in compartment Heli
```

But of course, the policy or policies defined depend on the need of privileges. Make sure to consider carefully that the privilege is really needed, and if so, define it in the right level.

Anomaly Detection with APEX Using the OCI API

Anomaly Detection API

Anomaly Detection API is on version /20210101 while writing this book. The Anomaly Detection API documentation can be found here:

```
https://docs.oracle.com/en-us/iaas/api/#/en/anomalydetection/20210101/
```

The documentation includes API references and all API endpoints available. The API references cover DataAsset, DataAssetCollection, Model, Project, WorkRequest, WorkRequestError, WorkRequestLogEntry, and Data Types. This is quite new service, so the API is also evolving.

Setting Up APEX for Anomaly Detection API

To start, create an IAM *user* in the OCI Console if you have not done that yet. Add the user to the *group* for Anomaly Detection, in our example AnomalyDetectionGroup. Then, go back to the user's detail page to make sure the user has *API Keys* selected. To do that, click *Edit User Capabilities* and check that API Keys is selected. To limit the user to interact with OCI resources only using API keys, deselect all the other options.

An API key pair is required to be able to work with the OCI REST APIs. To get the API key pair

1. Select *API Keys* from the left-hand side of the user details page.

2. Click *Add API Key*.

3. Select *Generate API Key Pair*.

4. Click *Download Private Key*.

5. Click Add.

The file you just downloaded is of type pem and looks something like this:

```
-----BEGIN PRIVATE KEY-----
MIIEvAIBADANBgkqhkiG9w0BAQEFAASCBKYwggSiAgEAAoIBAQCv2FWr73tHBsrA
VhqKE/WfOrzE6WzaYDzgAycr2SGOa3bQrkXx31uoOO9Rk2GHy71Zl+SzwFOQz3Bh
+HTDlaSC1FZSHZ/9DAUMidAjSpvMBnPAcIKGmmECgYASx9EM7tdWvhD3kpN9uBuc
r7ZBCU/O1mxeIm7eNlbCbLCfGsVhP4Q8v1HKQZz54y9YMRZW8eO3YEHtwwRJVegz
8n+yYWYa/IMLLq1i8ZRqhg==
-----END PRIVATE KEY-----
```

Remove the first (-----BEGIN PRIVATE KEY-----) and last line (-----END PRIVATE KEY-----), and then copy the content to a safe place. This is the *private key* you will use for Web Credentials. Check the *Configuration Preview* for the other details needed for creating Web Credentials in APEX. The information you will need is

- User OCID

- Fingerprint

- OCI Private key

- Tenancy OCID

- Compartment OCID

- Region of the tenancy

- Namespace

Then, log into APEX as the user you want to have access to Anomaly Detection APIs. Create a new Web Credential.

1. Go to *Workspace Utilities.*

2. Select *Web Credentials.*

3. Click *Create.*

4. Give the Web Credential a *Name*, and select *Oracle Cloud Infrastructure (OCI)* as the *Authentication Type.*

5. Paste the OCI userid (User OCID), OCI Private key, OCI Tenancy ID (Tenancy OCID), and OCI Public Key Fingerprint to correct fields.

6. Click *Create.*

Note   If you do not have all the information, you can always go back to the OCI Console and check the Identity & Security section, or you can ask the Administrator.

Using Anomaly Detection APIs with APEX

When you have created the *Web Credentials*, you are able to use the OCI API services. To use them, you can, for example, create a *REST Data Source*. We will create a data source for seeing all available Models in a Compartment.

1. In *APEX App builder*, select the application in which you want to create this REST Data Source.

2. Select *Shared Components.*

3. Navigate to *Data Sources* and select *REST Data Source.*

4. Click *Create.*

5. Select *From scratch* and click *Next.*

6. Select the *REST Data Source Type* as *Oracle Cloud Infrastructure (OCI).*

7. Give the REST Data Source a *Name.*

8. Define the URL Endpoint (check the Oracle documentation to find the correct Endpoint). In our example, the Endpoint is `https://anomalydetection.aiservice.us-phoenix-1.oci.oraclecloud.com`.

9. Click *Next*.

10. Select *Create New* as *Remote Server* (if you have already used the Anomaly Detection Service, select the Server from the list).

11. *Base URL* should point to the Endpoint selected in the previous screen.

12. Select the API service wanted for *Service URL Path*. In our example: /20210101/models/.

13. Click *Next*.

14. Enable *Authentication Required*.

15. Select the *Web Credential* from the list.

16. Click *Advanced*.

17. Select the *Query string* variable as *Parameter Type*, type CompartmentId as *Parameter Name*, and paste the OCID of the compartment to the *Value* field. Enable *Is Static*.

18. Click *Discover*.

19. If all was set correctly, the list shows all Models in that compartment.

20. Click *Create REST Data Source*.

Now you can create a page using the REST Data Source that lists all Models of the Anomaly Detection Service in this compartment. You can, for example, select the OCID of one Model and create an APEX application to use the model to detect anomalies from your data set.

In Figure 8-50, you can see an example of a very simple APEX application that takes the OCIDs of the compartment, project, and model as input as well as the file including the data. Clicking Detect calls the API to detect anomalies.

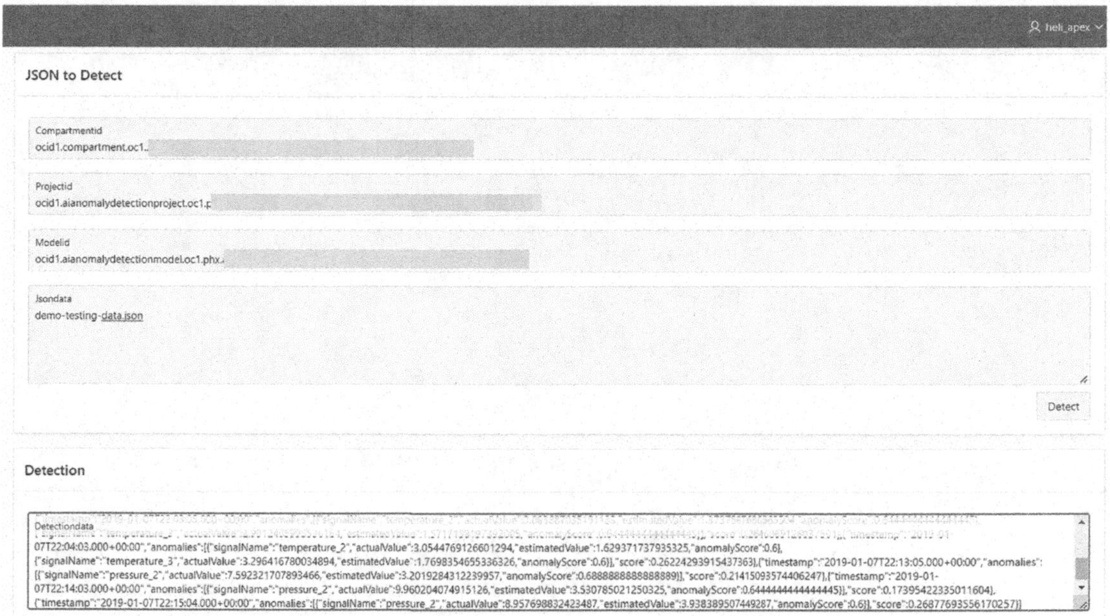

Figure 8-50. *An example of a simple APEX application calling the Anomaly Detection Service API to detect anomalies*

Summary

Anomaly detection is a machine learning method to identify unexpected events, observations, or items that differ significantly from the norm. Often machine learning and data science are seen as a very difficult field of expertise, and many developers feel uncomfortable starting all the studies on mathematics, statistics, algorithms, etc. Anomaly Detection Service makes it possible to use anomaly detection without data science expertise. Oracle Cloud Infrastructure (OCI) Anomaly Detection Service is a managed AI Service that enables users to easily build business-specific anomaly detection machine learning models that flag critical incidents and then use these models to identify anomalies in their business data. The sooner the incidents are detected, the sooner they can be fixed. The Anomaly Detection Service also has specialized APIs to use the services also outside the OCI Console. Limited resources are often the bottleneck with machine learning, especially when training a model. In the OCI, you have the possibility for scalability on demand.

CHAPTER 9

Language

Language is an AI Service for performing different kinds of text analysis using pretrained machine learning models. The service makes using machine learning easy and simple. You can use the Language Service for

- Language detection
- Text classification
- Key phrase extraction
- Named entity recognition
- Sentiment analysis

These pretrained models are frequently retrained and monitored by Oracle.

You can access the OCI Language Service using the OCI Console, REST API, SDKs, or CLI. At the moment, Language is not hosted in every region, so to be able to use it, make sure to check that it is hosted in the region you are planning to use it from. Currently, it is available only in commercial regions. The language detection model supports more than hundred languages; the other models support mainly English but are learning other languages every day.

The service does not check or fix grammar or spelling. Mistakes in grammar or spelling might result in bad model performance or unexpected results of the pretrained models.

Different Use Cases for Language Service

Natural Language Processing (NLP) is a subfield of AI and linguistics. It enables computers to understand, interpret, and manipulate human language. There are several applications for NLP, including the ones OCI Language Service is offering. The OCI Language Service is using NLP for written text only.

319

© Adrian Png and Heli Helskyaho 2022
A. Png and H. Helskyaho, *Extending Oracle Application Express with Oracle Cloud Features*,
https://doi.org/10.1007/978-1-4842-8170-3_9

There are five kinds of pretrained machine learning models available in Language Service: *language detection, text classification, key phrase extraction, named entity recognition*, and *sentiment analysis*.

On the OCI Console, they are all called automatically at the same time, and you can see the results of all of them. But, when using the API interface, you decide what of those services to call and in what order. You could just call one, or you could call several of those in a sequence. For example, when calling the Text classification service from the API, you need to have the language code. This means that you could call Language detection service first to find out the language of the text and then, using that information, call the Text classification.

Language Detection

Language detection detects the language of an input text and gives a confidence score for the detection. The range of the confidence score is 0–1; the closer it is to 1, the better the confidence. Language detection can be very useful in many business cases. It can be used to automate many business processes, for example, the customer feedback process. The first step of handling the feedback would be to detect the language, and based on that, the sentiment analysis can be done using that language, or the key phrase extraction of the language is used to detect the keywords of the feedback. And even the reply to the customer can be done in the correct language either automatically or manually. Because of the language detection step, we now know what language skill is required from the customer satisfaction employee who should be replying to the customer.

Another example is customer support interaction. In customer support interactions, it can be very valuable to be able to automatically detect the language the customer is using, then guiding the customer service process based on that knowledge. Being able to help the customer in the customer's own language can increase the customer satisfaction and also make the customer support process more efficient. A chatbot could switch automatically to the correct language, the user's manual is automatically given in the language the customer speaks, or the person at customer support, who speaks the language needed, is automatically selected to serve the customer. Some other possible use cases could be sorting documents automatically based on their language or routing incoming messages or customer support tickets to the localized team.

Text Classification

Text classification identifies the category and the subcategory of a document. It can identify more than 600 categories and is learning to identify more every day. Text classification can be used, for example, to automate business processes. It could be used to divide a set of data into categories invoices or food recipes. Or it could be used to automate processing of handling different kinds of financial documents. There is an example of text classification in Figure 9-1. The text is part of the description of a book *Machine Learning for Oracle Database Professionals: Deploying Model-Driven Applications and Automation Pipelines* written by Heli Helskyaho, Jean Yu, and Kai Yu. The text classification classifies it to be *Computer and Electronics/Programming* with confidence of 1.0000.

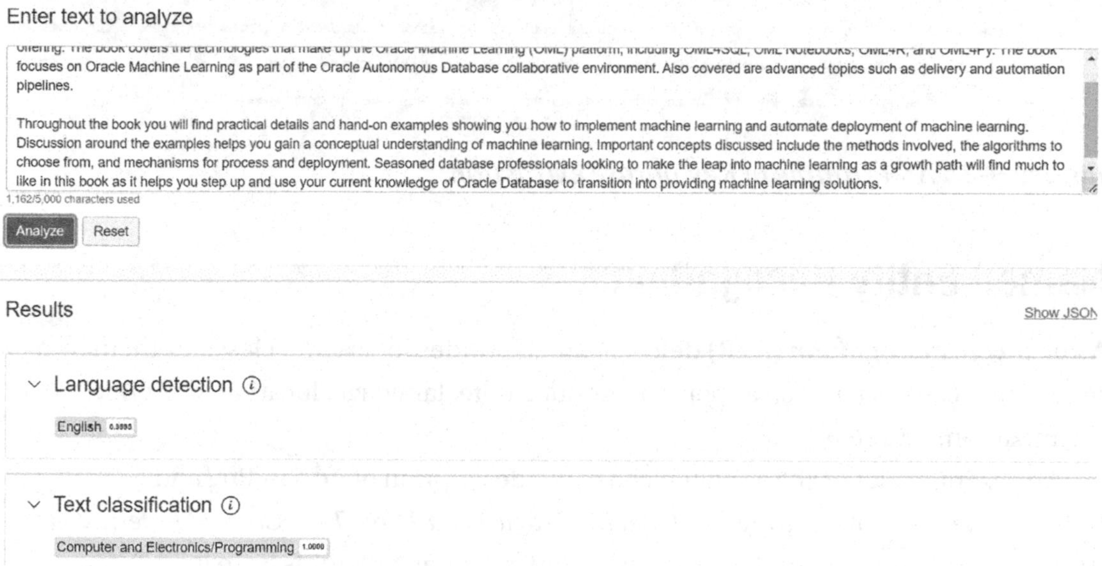

Figure 9-1. *An example of language detection and text classification*

Key Phrase Extraction

Key phrase extraction extracts the most relevant keywords or phrases from a text. It could be used to summarize the content of a text or recognize the main topics of it.

Key phrases consist of subjects and objects in the text. Any modifiers (adjectives) that are associated with these subjects or objects are also included as part of the candidate key phrases. Once candidates are initialized, the importance of each candidate is measured using statistics. Nonessential candidates are removed from the selected key phrases. Confidence scores for each key phrase signify how confident the process is about the key phrase. Confidence scores are a value from 0 to 1.

In Figure 9-2, you can see an example of key phase extraction. The text used is part of the description of a book *Machine Learning for Oracle Database Professionals: Deploying Model-Driven Applications and Automation Pipelines* written by Heli Helskyaho, Jean Yu, and Kai Yu.

The key phrase extraction finds several keywords or phrases from the text and is nearly 100% confident of all of them.

Figure 9-2.   An example of Key phrase extraction

Named Entity Recognition

Named entity recognition (NER) detects named entities in text and classifies them into predefined categories such as person, product, date, language, location, currency, organization, and so on.

For example, let's take a small piece of the description of Adrian Png and Luc Demanche book, *Getting Started with Oracle Cloud Free Tier: Create Modern Web Applications Using Always Free Resources*, and see what NER finds from it.

In Figure 9-3, you can see that it found several Products, Organizations, and one Quantity/Number element from the text. It defines the entity found with a color, for example, entities of Product category are marked with red, and the name of the entity category. It also shows how confident the decision was. For example, Oracle has been defined as a Product in one part of the text with confidence 0.5991 and as a Company in another part of the text with confidence 1.0000. This means that the service is not just using a list of words and based on the list defines the category; instead, it uses more complex algorithms to see the context of the word and makes more sophisticated categorizing. NER is not easy and mistakes happen often. For example, the grammar or misspelling can cause issues and misclassifications.

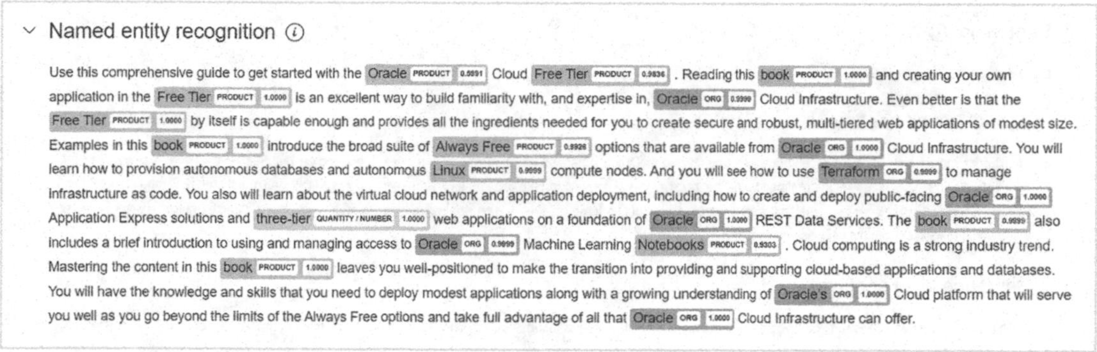

⌄ Named entity recognition ⓘ

Use this comprehensive guide to get started with the Oracle `PRODUCT` `0.9991` Cloud Free Tier `PRODUCT` `0.9836` . Reading this book `PRODUCT` `1.0000` and creating your own application in the Free Tier `PRODUCT` `1.0000` is an excellent way to build familiarity with, and expertise in, Oracle `ORG` `0.9999` Cloud Infrastructure. Even better is that the Free Tier `PRODUCT` `1.0000` by itself is capable enough and provides all the ingredients needed for you to create secure and robust, multi-tiered web applications of modest size. Examples in this book `PRODUCT` `1.0000` introduce the broad suite of Always Free `PRODUCT` `0.9926` options that are available from Oracle `ORG` `1.0000` Cloud Infrastructure. You will learn how to provision autonomous databases and autonomous Linux `PRODUCT` `0.9999` compute nodes. And you will see how to use Terraform `ORG` `0.9999` to manage infrastructure as code. You also will learn about the virtual cloud network and application deployment, including how to create and deploy public-facing Oracle `ORG` `1.0000` Application Express solutions and three-tier `QUANTITY / NUMBER` `1.0000` web applications on a foundation of Oracle `ORG` `1.0000` REST Data Services. The book `PRODUCT` `0.9999` also includes a brief introduction to using and managing access to Oracle `ORG` `0.9999` Machine Learning Notebooks `PRODUCT` `0.9203` . Cloud computing is a strong industry trend. Mastering the content in this book `PRODUCT` `1.0000` leaves you well-positioned to make the transition into providing and supporting cloud-based applications and databases. You will have the knowledge and skills that you need to deploy modest applications along with a growing understanding of Oracle's `ORG` `1.0000` Cloud platform that will serve you well as you go beyond the limits of the Always Free options and take full advantage of all that Oracle `ORG` `1.0000` Cloud Infrastructure can offer.

Figure 9-3. *An example of named entity recognition*

Sentiment Analysis

Sentiment analysis consists of *Aspect-Based Sentiment Analysis* (ABSA) and *Sentence Level Sentiment Analysis.* ABSA identifies aspects from the given text and classifies each aspect into positive, negative, mixed, or neutral polarity. It also defines a confidence score for each classification. The range of a confidence score for each class is between 0 and 1. The total sum of scores of all the four classes is one. The sentence-level sentiment analysis analyzes the whole sentence and gives confidence scores for each sentence in the text.

In Figure 9-4, you can see the sentiment analysis of a reader's review of *Real World SQL and PL/SQL: Advice from the Experts,* a book written by Nanda, Tierney, Helskyaho, Widlake, and Nuijten. The aspect-based sentiment analysis picks aspects from the text and defines a sentiment category for each of them. It also defines the confidence for each decision. Then, using those analysis, it defines the Document Sentiment and its confidence. In our example, this review has been defined to be *Mixed* with the confidence of 0.5680. The lower section of the Sentiment section classifies whole sentences in the text to categories. For example, the first sentence has been categorized as *Neutral* with the confidence 0.6251 and the last sentence as *Negative* with the confidence 0.7913.

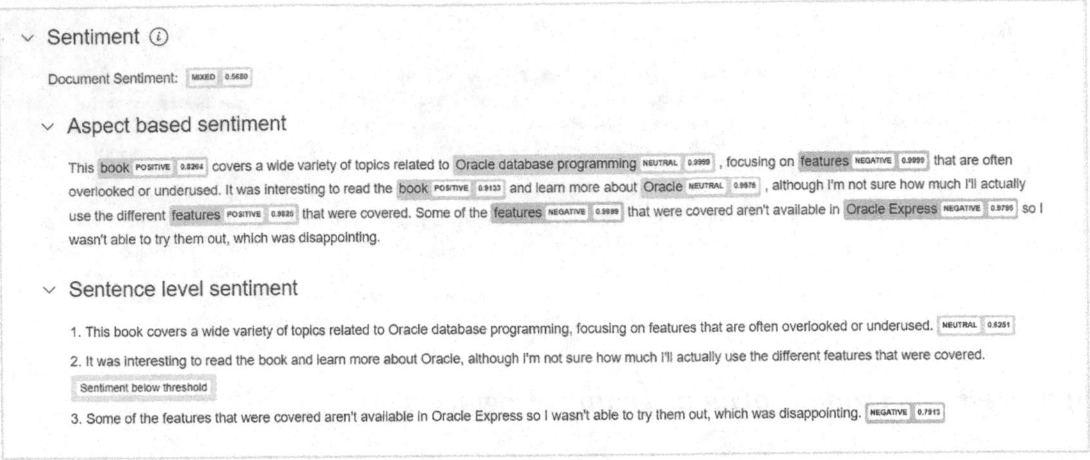

Figure 9-4. *An example of sentiment analysis*

Sentiment analysis is very useful for many business use cases. You can use sentiment analysis, for example, to follow social media and detect whether people are writing positive or negative comments about your product or brand. Or, you can automatically monitor the customer feedback. Then, based on the sentiment, route it to the correct team in your company attached with the priority needed.

Setting Up the Service

To start with the Language Service, you need an Oracle Cloud Infrastructure (OCI) account with Service Administrator role privileges, or somebody who can set up the service and grant you the privileges needed. You also need a supported browser. Please check the supported browsers from the OCI documentation.

If you have not created one yet, create an OCI user. The user can either be a Federated user or an IAM user. Federated user means that the user authentication is done by an *Identity Provider*. In this example, we create an IAM user.

Select *Identity & Security* from the OCI Console navigation menu, and then select *Users*. Click *Create User* and fill in the data needed as shown in Figure 9-5. Click *Create*. In this example, we create an IAM user called LanguageUser.

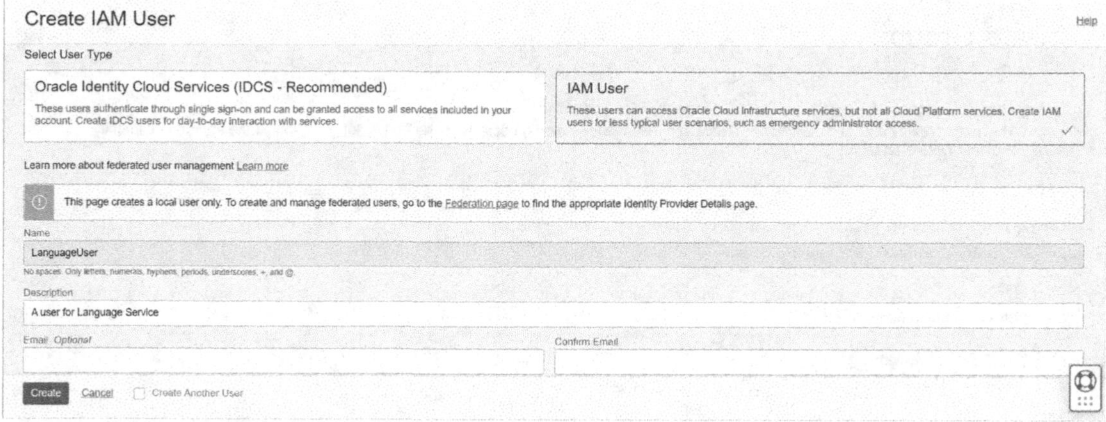

Create IAM User   Help

Select User Type

Oracle Identity Cloud Services (IDCS - Recommended)	IAM User
These users authenticate through single sign-on and can be granted access to all services included in your account. Create IDCS users for day-to-day interaction with services.	These users can access Oracle Cloud Infrastructure services, but not all Cloud Platform services. Create IAM users for less typical user scenarios, such as emergency administrator access. ✓

Learn more about federated user management Learn more

ⓘ This page creates a local user only. To create and manage federated users, go to the Federation page to find the appropriate Identity Provider Details page.

Name

LanguageUser

No spaces. Only letters, numerals, hyphens, periods, underscores, +, and @.

Description

A user for Language Service

Email Optional   Confirm Email

Create   Cancel   ☐ Create Another User

Figure 9-5. *Creating a user*

By default, only the users in the Administrators group have access to service resources. That also applies to Language Service resources. Therefore, you need to grant the newly created user privileges (policies) to resources needed. It is possible to add all policies directly to a user, but the best practice is to create a user group, assign the policies to that, and then add the user to the user group.

To follow that practice, create a *User Group*. Select *Groups* from the *Identity & Security* and click *Create Group*. Insert the Name of the group (e.g., LanguageGroup) and a Description as shown in Figure 9-6. Click *Create*.

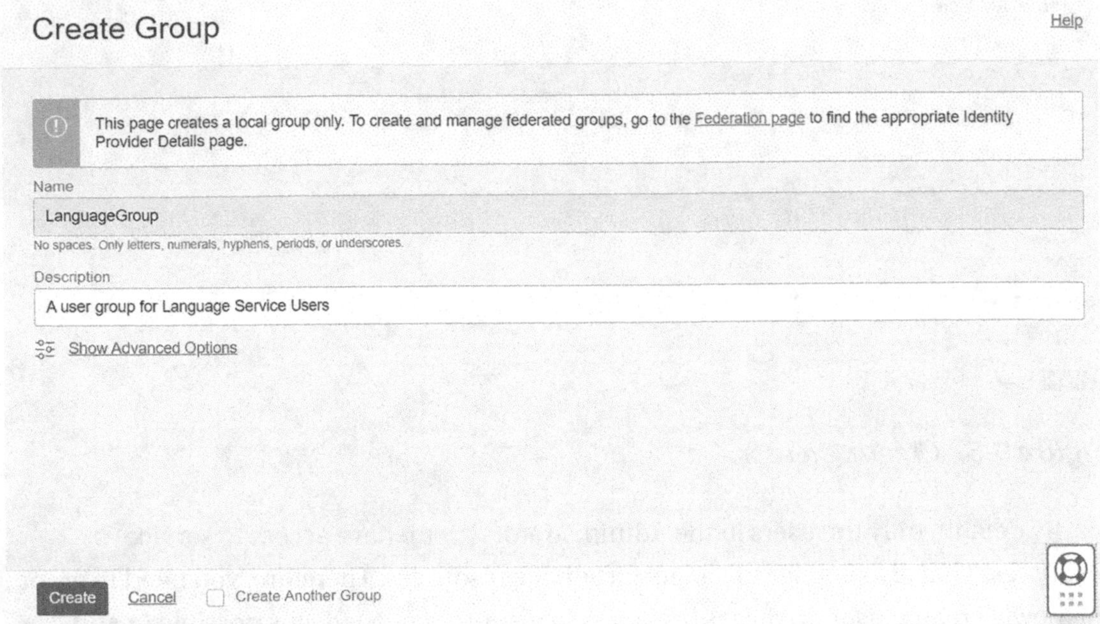

Create Group

(!) This page creates a local group only. To create and manage federated groups, go to the Federation page to find the appropriate Identity Provider Details page.

Name

LanguageGroup

No spaces. Only letters, numerals, hyphens, periods, or underscores.

Description

A user group for Language Service Users

⚌ Show Advanced Options

Create   Cancel   ☐ Create Another Group

Figure 9-6. *Creating a user group*

Note   If you are using an Identity Cloud Service Provider (IDCS Provider), for example, Oracle Identity Cloud Service (OICS), create the group and assign the users under Federation.

Then, add the User to the User Group. Select the Language user group from the list of Groups. In the *Group Details* page, navigate to the *Group Members* section and click *Add User to Group*. Select the user from the *Users* list (Figure 9-7) and click *Add*.

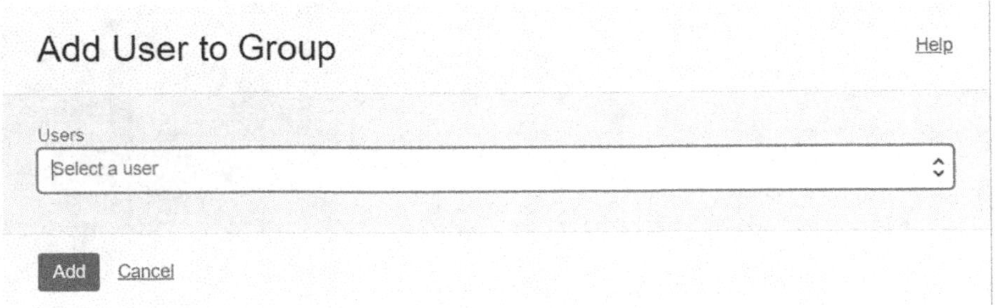

Add User to Group

Users

Select a user

Add   Cancel

Figure 9-7. *Adding a user to a user group*

The next step is to add the policies needed. There are two kinds of resource types: *aggregate* and *individual*. That means that you can either create the policy using the aggregate resource type to grant permission to all types of Language Services types at once, or you can use the individual resource types to limit the privileges to one or more types of Language Service types. To grant the privileges using the aggregate type, use resource type *ai-service-language-family*. The individual resource types are

- ai-service-language-entities
- ai-service-dominant-language
- ai-service-language-sentiments
- ai-service-language-keyphrases
- ai-service-language-text-classification

If you prefer permitting only the privileges needed, and not the aggregate privileges, you need to carefully select what individual resource types should be used. In Table 9-1, you can see each API operation and the resource type needed with *USE* permission to be able to call the API operation.

Table 9-1. *API operations and the resource type needed to perform the operation*

API Operation	Resource Type
BatchDetectDominantLanguage	ai-service-dominant-language
BatchDetectLanguageEntities	ai-service-language-entities
BatchDetectLanguageKeyPhrases	ai-service-language-keyphrases
BatchDetectLanguageSentiments	ai-service-language-sentiments
BatchDetectLanguageTextClassification	ai-service-language-text-classification
DetectDominantLanguage	ai-service-dominant-language
DetectLanguageEntities	ai-service-language-entities
DetectLanguageKeyPhrases	ai-service-language-keyphrases
DetectLanguageSentiments	ai-service-language-sentiments
DetectLanguageTextClassification	ai-service-language-text-classification

The syntax for an individual policy is

allow group <group-name> to use <resource type> in tenancy

For example:

allow group LanguageGroup to use ai-service-language-keyphrases   in tenancy

The syntax for aggregate policy is

allow group <group-name> to use ai-service-language-family in tenancy

In our example, we will create a policy as shown in Figure 9-8:

allow group LanguageGroup to use ai-service-language-family in tenancy

---

Note   Since the Language Service does not use resources in a particular Compartment, you need to create the policy on the **tenancy** level.

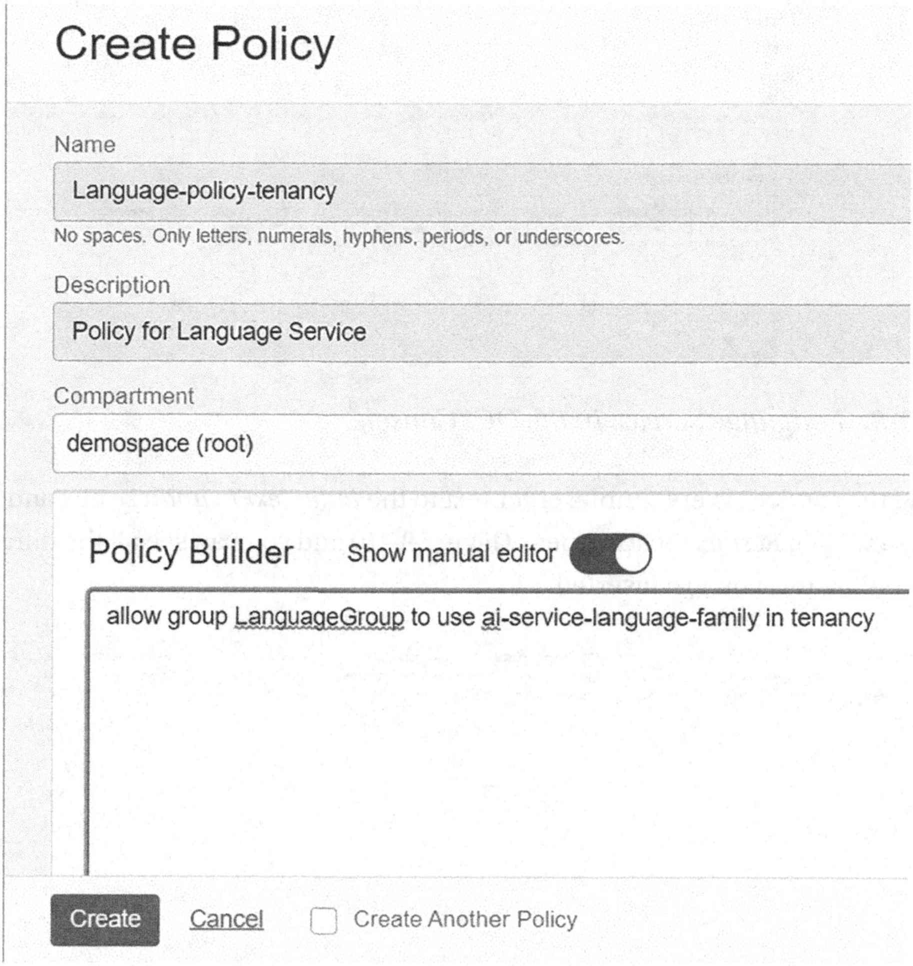

Create Policy

Name

Language-policy-tenancy

No spaces. Only letters, numerals, hyphens, periods, or underscores.

Description

Policy for Language Service

Compartment

demospace (root)

Policy Builder   Show manual editor ⬤◯

allow group LanguageGroup to use ai-service-language-family in tenancy

Create   Cancel   ☐ Create Another Policy

Figure 9-8. *Creating a policy for using the Language Service*

The user is now ready to use the Language Service.

Analyzing Text with the OCI Console

To start with the Language Service, select *Analytics & AI* from the OCI Console navigation menu. Then select *Language* under *AI Services*. When you enter the Language Service, you can see two selections: *Overview* and *Text Analytics* (Figure 9-9*)*. The Overview has lots of links to manuals, blogs, and other resources and general information about the service. This is a good place to learn more about the service. The service can be found by selecting Text Analytics.

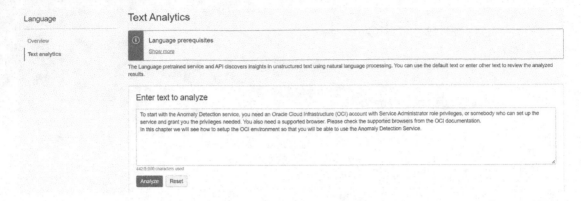

Figure 9-9. *Language Service in the OCI Console*

Using the service is very simple: enter text to the *Enter text to analyze* box and click *Analyze*. The *Results* section opens (Figure 9-10) and you can see all the different analyses on the text you just inserted.

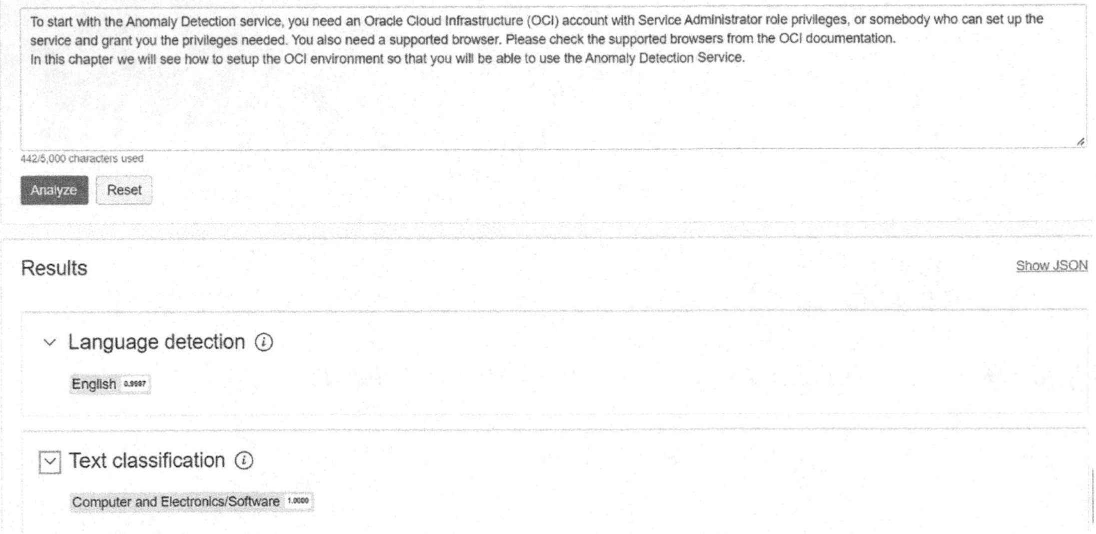

To start with the Anomaly Detection service, you need an Oracle Cloud Infrastructure (OCI) account with Service Administrator role privileges, or somebody who can set up the service and grant you the privileges needed. You also need a supported browser. Please check the supported browsers from the OCI documentation.
In this chapter we will see how to setup the OCI environment so that you will be able to use the Anomaly Detection Service.

442/5,000 characters used

Analyze   Reset

Results   Show JSON

⌄ Language detection ⓘ

English 0.9987

☑ Text classification ⓘ

Computer and Electronics/Software 1.0000

Figure 9-10. *Results of an analysis*

In our example (Figure 9-10), the Language detection detected the language being English with the confidence of 0.9987 and confidently (1.0000) classified it to be about "Computer and Electronics/Enterprise Software." The Named entity recognition service detected several entities from the text (Figure 9-11), and Key phrase extraction extracted several keywords from the text. Each entity or keyword recognition has the confidence attached to it.

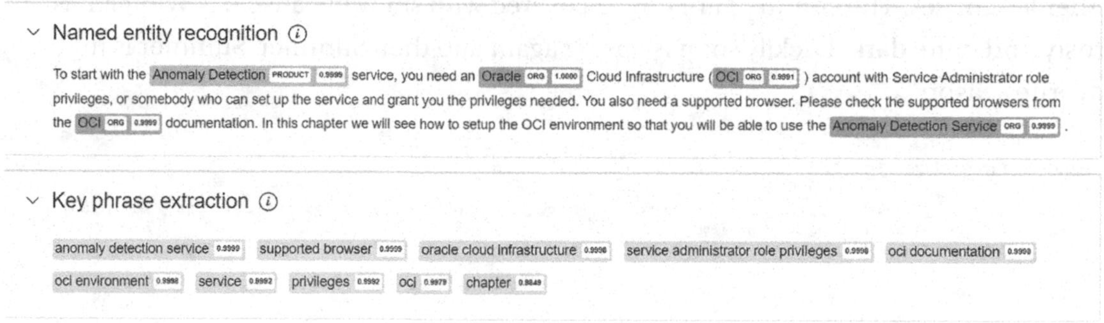

∨ Named entity recognition ⓘ

To start with the [Anomaly Detection PRODUCT 0.9999] service, you need an [Oracle ORG 1.0000] Cloud Infrastructure ([OCI ORG 0.9091]) account with Service Administrator role privileges, or somebody who can set up the service and grant you the privileges needed. You also need a supported browser. Please check the supported browsers from the [OCI ORG 0.9999] documentation. In this chapter we will see how to setup the OCI environment so that you will be able to use the [Anomaly Detection Service ORG 0.9999].

∨ Key phrase extraction ⓘ

[anomaly detection service 0.9999] [supported browser 0.9999] [oracle cloud infrastructure 0.9996] [service administrator role privileges 0.9996] [oci documentation 0.9999]
[oci environment 0.9998] [service 0.9992] [privileges 0.9992] [oci 0.9979] [chapter 0.9849]

Figure 9-11. *An example of named entity recognition and key phrase extraction using the OCI Console*

The sentiment analysis (Figure 9-12) first defines whether the text was generally positive, negative, mixed, or neutral. Then, it analyzes the sentiment based on aspects and each sentence. Funnily, in our example, the aspect-based sentiment analysis finds "Anomaly Detection service" negative.

∨ Sentiment ⓘ

Document Sentiment: [NEUTRAL 0.6998]

∨ Aspect based sentiment

To start with the [Anomaly Detection service NEGATIVE 0.7523], you need an [Oracle Cloud Infrastructure NEUTRAL 0.9999] (OCI) account with Service Administrator role privileges, or somebody who can set up the service and grant you the privileges needed. You also need a supported browser. Please check the supported browsers from the OCI documentation. In this chapter we will see how to setup the OCI environment so that you will be able to use the [Anomaly Detection Service NEUTRAL 0.5448].

☑ Sentence level sentiment

1. To start with the Anomaly Detection service, you need an Oracle Cloud Infrastructure (OCI) account with Service Administrator role privileges, or somebody who can set up the service and grant you the privileges needed. [NEUTRAL 0.7304]

2. You also need a supported browser. [NEUTRAL 0.6112]

3. Please check the supported browsers from the OCI documentation. [NEUTRAL 0.7698]

4. In this chapter we will see how to setup the OCI environment so that you will be able to use the Anomaly Detection Service. [NEUTRAL 0.6860]

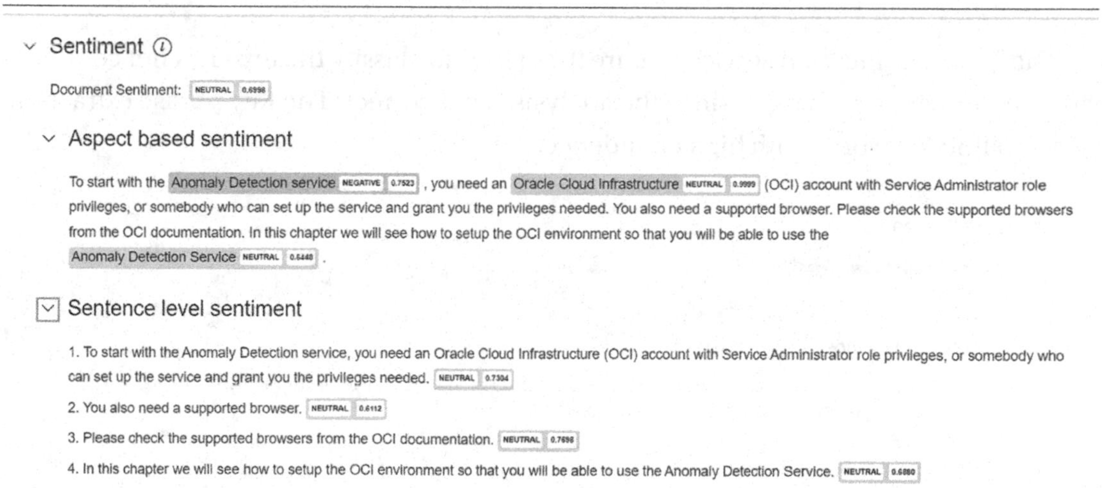

Figure 9-12. *An example of sentiment analysis using the OCI Console, including both aspect based and sentence-level sentiment*

This example was probably too easy for the service, so let's test it with a text in Finnish (a language spoken in Finland). In Figure 9-13, we have a text in Finnish and the service was very confident in recognizing the language. The text says something like this: "This text is in another language because I want to find out if this service understands other languages. The country I am now is covered with snow because it is Winter. It is frosty and quite dark. Luckily soon is Spring again and then Summer. Summer is my favorite season."

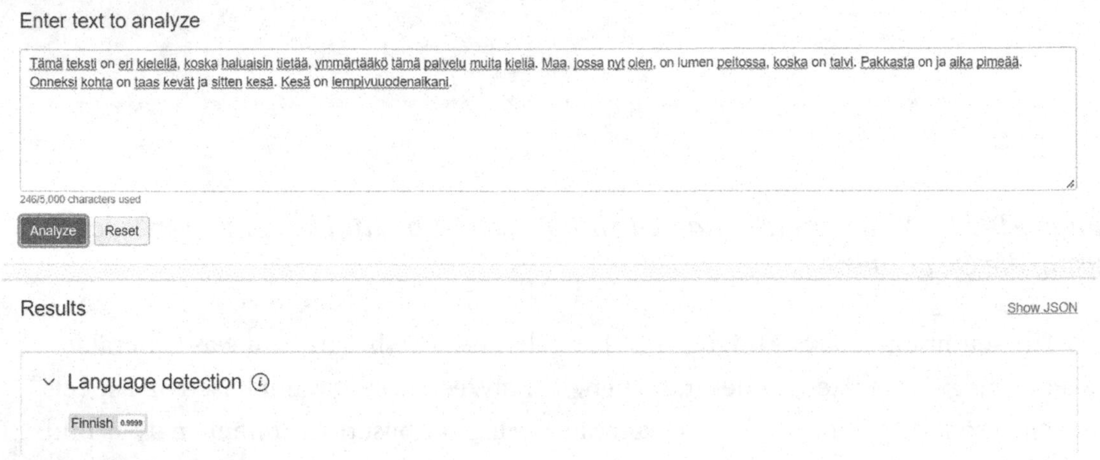

Enter text to analyze

Tämä teksti on eri kielellä, koska haluaisin tietää, ymmärtääkö tämä palvelu muita kieliä. Maa, jossa nyt olen, on lumen peitossa, koska on talvi. Pakkasta on ja aika pimeää. Onneksi kohta on taas kevät ja sitten kesä. Kesä on lempivuuodenaikani.

246/5,000 characters used

Analyze   Reset

Results   Show JSON

∨ Language detection ⓘ

   Finnish 0.9999

Figure 9-13. *Language detecting in Finnish*

The Text classification service (Figure 9-14) tries to classify the text. It is not confident with the decision and is right, since the analysis is not correct. The Key phrase extraction seems to find keywords with high confidence.

∨ Text classification ⓘ

   Health and Medical/Conditions and Disease 0.1283

∨ Named entity recognition ⓘ   No entity detected

   Tämä teksti on eri kielellä, koska haluaisin tietää, ymmärtääkö tämä palvelu muita kieliä. Maa, jossa nyt olen, on lumen peitossa, koska on talvi. Pakkasta on ja aika pimeää. Onneksi kohta on taas kevät ja sitten kesä. Kesä on lempivuuodenaikani.

∨ Key phrase extraction ⓘ

   ymmärtääkö tämä 0.9996   kieliä . maa 0.9996   nyt olen 0.9996   teksti 0.9992   kielellä 0.9992   tietää 0.9992   peitossa 0.9992   talvi 0.9992   pakkasta 0.9992   onneksi 0.9992
   kesä 0.9992

Figure 9-14. *Text classification, named entity recognition, and key phase extraction for text data in Finnish*

The sentiment analysis (Figure 9-15) finds the text neutral. It did not find any aspects, which is understandable because its Finnish skills are still limited. The Language Service is quite new and improves constantly.

∨ Sentiment ⓘ

Document Sentiment: [NEUTRAL] [0.5488]

∨ Aspect based sentiment [No aspect detected]

Tämä teksti on eri kielellä, koska haluaisin tietää, ymmärtääkö tämä palvelu muita kieliä. Maa, jossa nyt olen, on lumen peitossa, koska on talvi. Pakkasta on ja aika pimeää. Onneksi kohta on taas kevät ja sitten kesä. Kesä on lempivuodenaikani.

⊡ Sentence level sentiment

1. Tämä teksti on eri kielellä, koska haluaisin tietää, ymmärtääkö tämä palvelu muita kieliä. [NEUTRAL] [0.6884]
2. Maa, jossa nyt olen, on lumen peitossa, koska on talvi. [NEUTRAL] [0.6420]
3. Pakkasta on ja aika pimeää. [NEUTRAL] [0.6526]
4. Onneksi kohta on taas kevät ja sitten kesä. [NEUTRAL] [0.6453]
5. Kesä on lempivuodenaikani. [NEUTRAL] [0.6159]

Figure 9-15. *Sentiment analysis for a text written in Finnish*

You can show the results also as JSON by clicking *Show JSON* in the *Results* section. You can download the JSON file by clicking the *Download* link, or you can copy the JSON text by clicking the *Copy* link (Figure 9-16).

Enter text to analyze

To start with the Anomaly Detection service, you need an Oracle Cloud Infrastructure (OCI) account with Service Administrator role privileges, or somebody who can set up the service and grant you the privileges needed. You also need a supported browser. Please check the supported browsers from the OCI documentation.
In this chapter we will see how to setup the OCI environment so that you will be able to use the Anomaly Detection Service.

442/5,000 characters used

[Analyze] [Reset]

Results   [Show standard results]

Language detection

Copy Download

```
{
  "documents": [
    {
      "key": "1",
      "languages": [
        {
          "code": "en",
```

Figure 9-16. *Viewing the Language Service Results in JSON format. Copying it or downloading the content to a JSON file*

Analyzing Text with the OCI Language API and APEX

You can use the OCI Language API or the OCI command-line interface (CLI) to analyze input text. In this section, we discuss the OCI Language API and how it can be used from APEX.

Language API

The current version of the OCI Language API Reference and Endpoints can be found here: `https://docs.oracle.com/en-us/iaas/api/#/en/language/20210101/`.

When writing this book, the OCI Language Service API consists of the following POST requests for batch processing:

- BatchDetectDominantLanguage

- BatchDetectLanguageEntities

- BatchDetectLanguageKeyPhrases

- BatchDetectLanguageSentiments

- BatchDetectLanguageTextClassification

And, the following POST requests for individual document processing:

- DetectDominantLanguage

- DetectLanguageEntities

- DetectLanguageKeyPhrases

- DetectLanguageSentiments

- DetectLanguageTextClassification

The documentation describes them in detail, and under the *Data Types* section of the *OCI Language API Reference and Endpoints* documentation, you can find the references for each of these API calls. In the Data Types section, there is information about the attributes and an example of the requested JSON file.

There are some limitations to the service usage. Most of the limitations can be avoided by contacting Oracle. When writing this book, the limitation for characters in a request is 1000 and limit for concurrent requests per tenant is 5. Exceeding these limits results in a 400-API request error.

Setting Up APEX for Language API

To start, see that you have performed all the preliminary tasks explained in *Setting up the service* section.

An API key pair is required to be able to work with the OCI REST APIs. First, go and verify that the OCI user for Language Service has API Keys selected. Go to the *User Details* page (Figure 9-17) and click *Edit User Capabilities*. Verify that *API Keys* is checked as seen in Figure 9-18.

Figure 9-17. *The User Details page in the OCI Console*

Figure 9-18. *Editing user capabilities*

The next step is to get the API key pair:

1. Navigate to *API Keys* in *Resources* section (Figure 9-19) on the User Details page.

Figure 9-19. *API Keys in the User Details page*

2. Click *Add API Key.*

3. Select *Generate API Key Pair* (Figure 9-20).

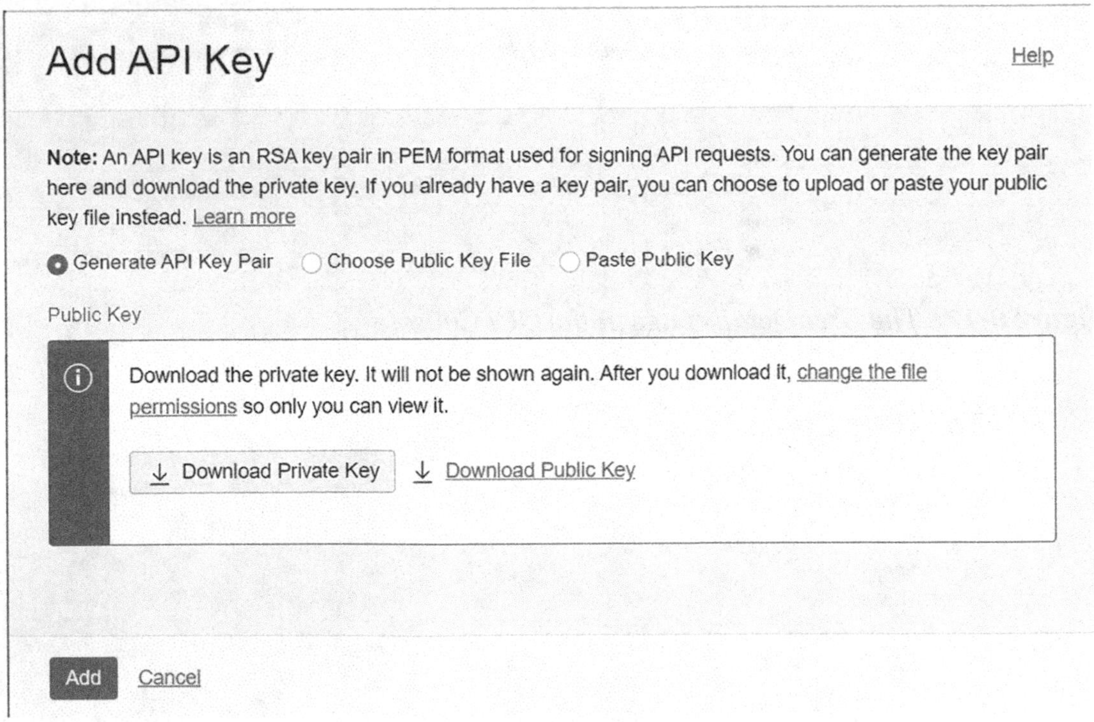

Add API Key   Help

Note: An API key is an RSA key pair in PEM format used for signing API requests. You can generate the key pair here and download the private key. If you already have a key pair, you can choose to upload or paste your public key file instead. Learn more

◉ Generate API Key Pair   ○ Choose Public Key File   ○ Paste Public Key

Public Key

> ⓘ   Download the private key. It will not be shown again. After you download it, change the file permissions so only you can view it.
>
>   ↓ Download Private Key   ↓ Download Public Key

Add   Cancel

Figure 9-20. *Adding an API Key and downloading the private key*

4. Click *Download Private Key*. You will not have access to this later, so make sure to save the pem file in a safe place.

5. Click *Add*.

6. A *Configuration File Preview* is shown. You will need this information later for creating the connection, but all this information can be found at any time.

The file you just downloaded is of type pem and looks something like this:

```
-----BEGIN PRIVATE KEY-----
MIIEvQIBADANBgkqhkiG9w0BAQEFAASCBKcwggSjAgEAAoIBAQCs1pNSW19iWdkx
4PvGo8PqfOOOpiQxAh5X7pe9WKOfmC44vTazvz8seO++DNs3Lz/oOuOkYLsmsPr1
fHQgXglEy7iF3y0VftYYnaaPT+qaI+Adahr6wZpjhmtk8lDoUZv1dTySbHu7nu5w
tyf+XmqkJ6Y7HbVWgsQEDcRKzlxfqV2mOR9XtBshwEEk2YCOPNERNb5KXDrHzOOT
ZIYOOSt7YGWEpDPA+Qc9IJO/GCJ1kxq4sTZWvflZNzfoSrhK7UHOLsX1sqACFTn6
y9K+Y7T+8Pwr45AJHY/8luz/ujfSth4mfyK8RJAGEd/ahYOZ6cGeBDGWCZZDrc53
5K
-----END PRIVATE KEY-----
```

Remove the first (-----BEGIN PRIVATE KEY-----) and last line (-----END PRIVATE KEY-----), and then copy the content to a safe place. This is the *private key* you will use for Web Credentials. Check the *Configuration Preview* for the other details needed for creating Web Credentials in APEX. The information you will need is

- User OCID
- Fingerprint
- OCI Private key
- Tenancy OCID
- Compartment OCID
- Region of the tenancy
- Namespace

If you already closed the *Configuration File Preview*, you can find the information from the *User Details* page by clicking the *View Configuration file* link (Figure 9-21).

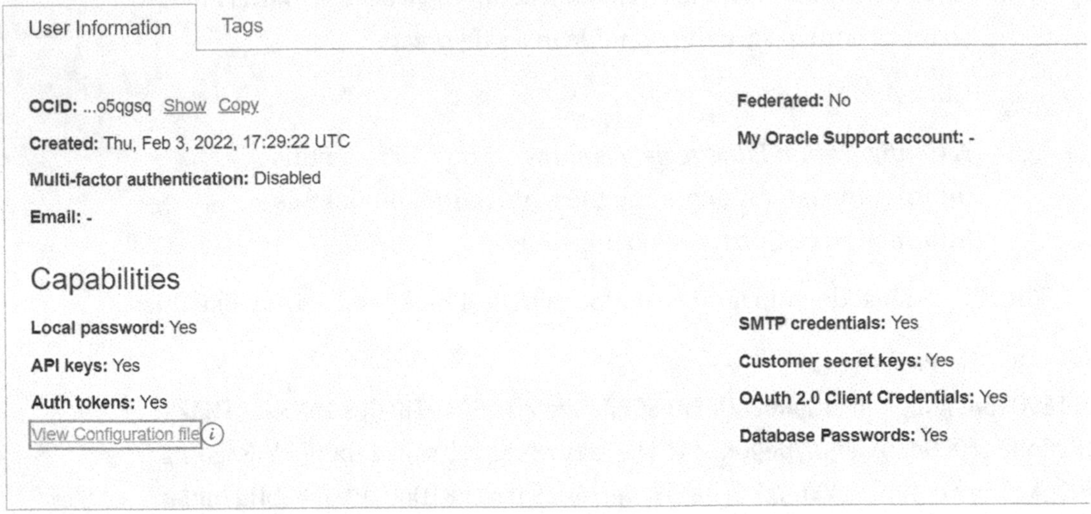

User Information   Tags

OCID: ...o5qgsq Show Copy   Federated: No

Created: Thu, Feb 3, 2022, 17:29:22 UTC   My Oracle Support account: -

Multi-factor authentication: Disabled

Email: -

Capabilities

Local password: Yes   SMTP credentials: Yes

API keys: Yes   Customer secret keys: Yes

Auth tokens: Yes   OAuth 2.0 Client Credentials: Yes

View Configuration file ⓘ   Database Passwords: Yes

Figure 9-21.   View Configuration file link on the User Details page

Then, log into APEX using the APEX user credentials.

Create a new Web Credential.

1. Go to *App Builder* and *Workspace Utilities*.

2. Select *Web Credentials*.

3. Click *Create*.

4. Give the Web Credential a *Name*, and select *Oracle Cloud Infrastructure (OCI)* as the *Authentication Type*.

5. Paste the OCI userid (User OCID), OCI Private key, OCI Tenancy ID (Tenancy OCID), and OCI Public Key Fingerprint to correct fields.

6. Click *Create*.

Note   If you do not have all the information, you can always go back to the OCI Console and check the Identity & Security section, or you can ask the Administrator.

Now, you have created a working connection to OCI from APEX.

Using Language API with APEX

When you have created the *Web Credentials*, you are able to use the OCI API services. To use an OCI API Service, you can, for example, create a *REST Data Source*. To create a REST Data Source

1. Go to *APEX App builder* and select the application in which you want to create this REST Data Source.

2. Select *Shared Components*.

3. Navigate to *Data Sources* and select *REST Data Source*.

4. Click *Create*.

5. Select *From scratch* and click *Next*.

6. Select *Oracle Cloud Infrastructure (OCI)* as the *REST Data Source Type* as shown in Figure 9-22.

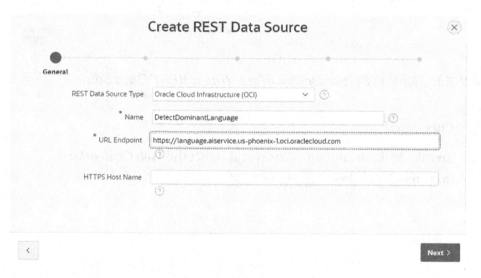

Figure 9-22. *General section of creating a REST Data Source*

7. Give the REST Data Source a *Name* and define the *URL Endpoint* (check the Oracle documentation to find the correct Endpoint). See Figure 9-22. In our example, the Endpoint is `https://language.aiservice.us-phoenix-1.oci.oraclecloud.com`.

8. Click *Next*.

9. Select *Create New* as *Remote Server* (if you have already used the Language Service, select the Server from the list). *Base URL* should point to the Endpoint selected in the previous screen. Type the API service wanted for *Service URL Path*. In our example: /20210101/actions/detectDominantLanguage. See Figure 9-23.

Figure 9-23. *Remote Server section of creating a REST Data Source*

10. Click *Next*.

11. Enable *Authentication Required* and select the *Web Credential* from the list as shown in Figure 9-24.

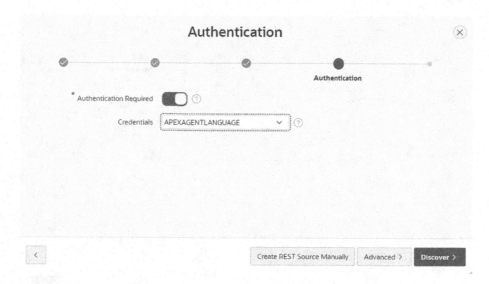

Figure 9-24. *Authentication section of creating a REST Data Source*

12.   Click *Advanced*.

13.   Select *Query string* variable as *Request / Response Body*, and
      type "text" as *Parameter Name*, as shown in Figure 9-25. Then,
      click the plus sign in the *Response Sample* field, and select a
      response sample JSON file. You can find it from the Oracle
      documentation pages.

Figure 9-25. *Parameters section of creating a REST Data Source*

14. Click *Discover*.

15. Check the details as seen in Figure 9-26.

Figure 9-26. *Preview Data section of creating a REST Data Source*

16.   Click *More details* button in Figure 9-27.

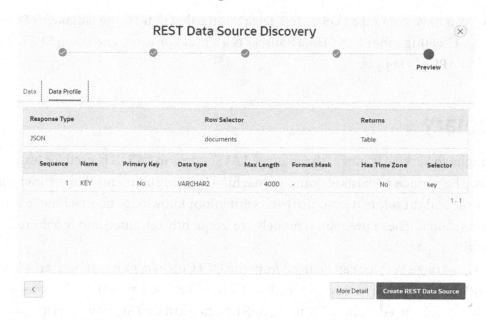

Figure 9-27. *Preview Data Profile section of creating a REST Data Source*

17.   Investigate all the tabs seen in Figure 9-28: Data Profile,
         Operations, Response Body, and Response Header.

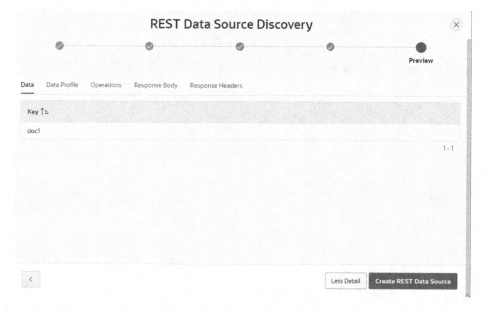

Figure 9-28. *Preview the REST Data Service before creating it*

18.   Click *Create REST Data Source*.

Now you have created a POST REST Data Source that detects the language of the given text. Creating other REST Data Sources is a similar process, and using REST Data Sources in APEX is simple.

Summary

OCI Language Service is part of the managed AI Services in OCI. It is used for text analysis. The service consists of complex machine learning elements that are invisible for the user and therefore easy to use even with minor knowledge on machine learning and data science. These pretrained models are frequently retrained and monitored by Oracle.

OCI Language Service can be used from the OCI Console, or it can be used with REST API, SDKs, or CLI. In this chapter, we saw how it is used from the OCI Console and how it can be used from APEX using REST Data Sources. Language Service can be used for language detection, text classification, key phrase extraction, named entity recognition, and sentiment analysis. It is quite a new service. It is improved all the time and more features are added.

CHAPTER 10

Vision

The ability for a human brain to process sight and sound allows us to interact with each other and the environment. Nearly every computing device – desktops, laptops, and mobile devices – has a display, microphone, and speaker that are used to interact with the human user, through their eyes, mouth, and ears. To date, they are the only two of the five human senses that have been artificially reproduced in machines. The remaining three – smell, taste, and touch – involve complex biochemical and physiochemical process that are not easily replicated given today's advancements in science and technology. Solutions exist but mostly only in experimental devices.

Today, the everyday computer is designed to accept and produce binary inputs and outputs. For example, to execute a command, the user types on a keyboard, an input device, that provides the instructions for a computer to process. The outcome of that process is then fed back to the user either through the display or sound device. The computer's response is generated digitally; however, when it leaves the device, it is delivered to the user using analog signals. The human eye and ears receive these analog inputs and then process them through the brain. The latter then makes decisions based on these processed signals. Could the computer, like the human, respond to sight and sounds? The answer is yes.

Image and speech recognition tasks are some of the most common applications of *artificial intelligence* (AI) and *machine learning* (ML). *Text-to-Speech* (TTS) software has been with us for quite a while and is commonly found in operating systems like *Microsoft Windows* and is used to improve accessibility of computers. Early examples of *computer vision* (CV) include image segmentation that is used to assist medical image diagnosis. However, these technologies were often proprietary, expensive, and not easily integrated into consumer applications.

Some of the early challenges in developing good ML models to perform these tasks include providing sufficient training data and computational power. However, the advancements in *Big Data* and *High-Performance Computing* (HPC) have vastly improved our ability to create robust, accurate, and generalized ML models.

For example, *ImageNet* (`https://image-net.org/`), a large-scale effort to amass a repository of labeled digital images, and the availability of *Graphics Processing Units* (GPU) have resulted in successes with training *Convolutional Neural Networks* (CNN) models. CNNs are a powerful variant of *Artificial Neural Networks* (ANNs) and commonly used in a subfield of AI called *deep learning*. CNN models are highly generalizable, but ML engineers can also use them to train them for specialized recognition tasks using a concept called *transfer learning*. These concepts are embodied in *Oracle Cloud Infrastructure* (OCI) *Vision* AI Service.

For a tool to be effective, it must also be easily incorporated into other systems like web applications. The OCI AI Services include well-defined REST APIs that allow developers to CV and TTS capabilities into web platforms like *Oracle Application Express* (APEX). In this chapter, we will introduce Vision, what is required, and how to utilize this service in your day-to-day APEX applications.

Working with OCI REST APIs

Oracle provides a comprehensive set of REST APIs that lets developers and administrators create, manage, and use OCI resources using the command-line interface (CLI) or custom applications/scripts. A software development kit (SDK) is also available for some of the more popular programming languages such as Java™, Go, and Node. JS™. There is also PL/SQL API, but, at the time of writing, is readily available on an Oracle Autonomous Database (ADB) only. As such, we will focus on working with the REST APIs directly using the APEX_WEB_SERVICE PL/SQL package, which will work regardless of where your Oracle Database is deployed.

To recap, use of the OCI REST APIs is governed by strict Identity and Access Management (IAM) policies. Permissions defined in IAM policies are assigned to IAM groups. An IAM user is created for the entity that wishes to use the API and is assigned to the relevant group(s).

After an IAM user is created, a set of private and public keys must be generated either using the OCI Console, OCI CLI, or the widely available OpenSSL application. The public key must be added to the user's account through the OCI Console. Once added, collect the required information as follows:

- Tenancy OCID
- User OCID
- User's API public key's fingerprint

As an added security layer, working with the OCI REST API requires all request to be cryptographically signed using the user's API keys. This can be a complex process that requires the client programming language to support RSA public-key cryptography. Fortunately, for APEX developers, we are shielded from this process by means of using the APEX *Web Credentials*. Creating and using a special OCI credential type will allow developers to call the APIs without needing to implement the request signing algorithm.

Instructions on how to create the necessary IAM groups, users, and policies, setting up the user's API keys, and creating an OCI Web Credential are detailed in Chapter 2.

OCI Object Storage

Using the Vision service involves the use of the OCI *Object Storage* to stage the image files for processing. Follow the instructions in Chapter 2 to create the following resources:

- IAM User: *demoapex*

- IAM groups: *DemoVisionGroup*

- Object Storage buckets: *ai-vision-demo*

The IAM user and group are required to access the OCI resources on behalf of the APEX application. Groups are entities that the OCI uses in IAM policies to define what they can or cannot do using policy statements. Assign the IAM user *demoapex* to the group *DemoVisionGroup*.

To allow the Vision demo application to access the Object Storage buckets and upload files, create a policy named *Demo-Object-Policy* and add the following statements:

```
Allow group DemoVisionGroup to read buckets in compartment adrian
Allow group DemoVisionGroup to manage objects in compartment adrian
```

To facilitate working with Object Storage, create a PL/SQL package in the APEX application's parsing schema with two procedures to upload and delete objects in the specified bucket. For example:

```
create or replace package pkg_oci_os_util
as
  gc_objectstorage_endpoint constant varchar2(500) :=
```

```
    'https://objectstorage.us-phoenix-1.oraclecloud.com';
  gc_namespace constant varchar2(30) := 'abcd1234xyz';
    gc_credential_static_id constant varchar2(50) :=
  'OCI_CREDENTIALS';

  procedure p_upload_object(
    p_bucket_name in varchar2
    , p_file_blob in blob
    , p_filename in varchar2
    , p_mime_type in varchar2
  );

  procedure p_delete_object(
    p_bucket_name in varchar2
    , p_filename in varchar2
  );
end pkg_oci_os_util;
```

Update the following package constants to suit your environment:

- **gc_objectstorage_endpoint**: Update the endpoint with the appropriate OCI region. In the example, the endpoint is for us-phoenix-1, the Phoenix region in the United States.

- **gc_namespace**: To obtain the tenancy's namespace string, click the profile button found on the top right of the OCI Console (see Figure 10-1). Click the tenancy link marked "A." The value you should enter can be found under the *Object Storage Settings* and is labeled "B."

- **gc_credential_static_id**: Replace the value or create an APEX Web Credential with the static ID OCI_CREDENTIALS. The credential should be of type *Oracle Cloud Infrastructure (OCI)*. An API key and the necessary information must be correctly filled out.

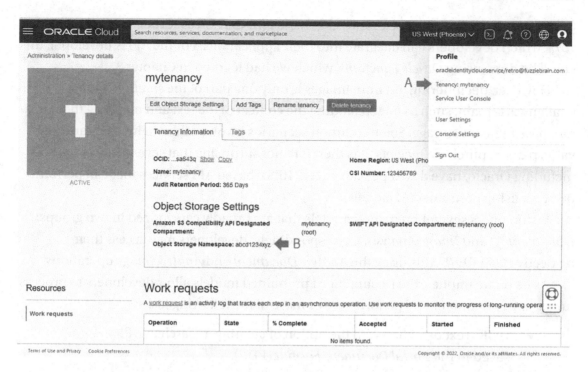

Figure 10-1. *Access the tenancy details to obtain the namespace string*

The complete code for the `pkg_oci_os_util` package specification and body is available in the chapter's source code directory.

OCI Vision

One of the challenges I have had with business (or personal) travel is consolidating receipts and potentially getting reimbursed for expenses made during the trip. Every receipt is different, and it can be a daunting task to enter them manually into the employer's account applications. You could buy a specialized scanner that comes with accompanying software to scan these receipts and enter them into an accounting application like *QuickBooks*®, but they can be costly solutions. These days, the software might even handle photographs of the receipts taken by mobile device, but what if your company has a custom application for managing expenses?

To process the images of the receipts, computers will have to perform optical character recognition (OCR) that involves processing and identifying text in a raster image. Machine learning is commonly used to perform such tasks, and there are several

OCR engines, such as the open sourced *Tesseract* (`https://tesseract-ocr.github.io/`), which developers can integrate into their applications. For the APEX developer, this could be done using *Oracle Functions*, which we had learned in Chapter 3.

However, deciphering text from images is only one part of the solution. Other challenges remain, such as understanding the context of the text and mapping them to a database table for storage. Some common scenarios involve tables in invoices and key-value pairs in purchase receipts. It is therefore not surprising that several cloud vendors, including Oracle, have developed advanced, REST-based API services that can perform this task using pretrained AI models.

Vision offers several pretrained models that are broadly categorized in two groups: *Document AI* and *Image Analysis*. Correspondingly, developers may access their respective OCI REST APIs using the *AnalyzeDocument* and *AnalyzeImage* operations.

As its name implies, the Document AI pretrained models allow developers to process images of a document and perform one or more of the following tasks:

- **OCR**: Text detection with the option of creating a searchable file saved in the *Portal Document Format* (PDF).

- **Document classification**: Analyzes and classifies the document type along with a confidence score.

- **Language classification**: Returns the three-letter language code based on the ISO-639-2 standard (`www.iso.org/standard/4767.html`), plus a confidence score. Supported languages include English, French, Simplified Chinese, and more.

- **Table extraction**: Identifies text written in a tabular format and extracts them in the same rows and columns.

- **Key-value extraction**: This pretrained model extracts key-value pairs from receipts, fields such as the merchant's location and contact information, and the items purchased, quantities, and prices.

And for Image Analysis, developers may request to perform the following tasks:

- **Object detection**: Identifies the objects, their category, and bounding boxes where the object was located.

- **Image classification**: Assigns and lists labels of all objects found in the image.

- **OCR:** Detects text in the image and provides bounding boxes where they are located.

Note   In addition to pretrained models for Image Analysis tasks, Vision also provides users the ability to create custom models. Developers can create Vision projects and, with the help of the *OCI Data Labeling* service, train a custom model for more specific computer vision tasks. The process involves using a concept called *transfer learning* that is beyond the scope of this chapter.

For our next application, we will code a *Travel Receipts* APEX application that allows users to snap and upload images and, then using Vision's key value extraction pretrained model, parse the fields in the receipt and render their values. Here's an outline of what happens when a user uploads and submits a scanned receipt through an APEX page.

1. Retrieve the image BLOB from the `APEX_APPLICATION_TEMP_FILES` tables.

2. Upload the BLOB to the *ai-vision-demo* Object Storage bucket using the `pkg_oci_os_util.p_upload_object` procedure.

3. Prepares and submits the Vision analyze document request using the `pkg_oci_vision_util.f_analyze_document` function and receives the JSON-formatted results.

4. Saves both the image and the document analysis results in a table.

Begin by creating a simple database table named *RECEIPT*, containing the following columns:

Column Name	Data Type	Purpose
RECEIPT_ID	NUMBER	Primary key
SCANNED_IMAGE	BLOB	For storing the scanned image
FILENAME	VARCHAR2(1000)	Filename of the uploaded image
MIME_TYPE	VARCHAR2(100)	MIME type of the uploaded image
RECEIPT_DATA	CLOB	For storing the results returned by Vision. Add a `is_json` check constraint

Next, create a PL/SQL package for working with the Vision API. The following code wraps the necessary steps for preparing and submitting the request to Vision's *AnalyzeDocument* REST endpoint:

```
create or replace package body pkg_oci_vision_util
as
  function f_analyze_document(
    p_bucket_name in varchar2
    , p_filename in varchar2
  ) return blob
  as
    c_path constant varchar2(100) :=
      '/20220125/actions/analyzeDocument';

    l_response blob;
  begin
    apex_web_service.g_request_headers(1).name := 'Content-Type';
    apex_web_service.g_request_headers(1).value :=
      'application/json';

    l_response := apex_web_service.make_rest_request_b(
      p_url => pkg_oci_vision_util.gc_vision_endpoint || c_path
      , p_http_method => 'POST'
      , p_body =>
          json_object(
            'document' value json_object(
              'source' value 'OBJECT_STORAGE'
              , 'namespaceName' value
                  pkg_oci_vision_util.gc_namespace
              , 'bucketName' value p_bucket_name
              , 'objectName' value p_filename
            )
            , 'features' value
                json_array(json_object('featureType' value
                  'KEY_VALUE_DETECTION') format json)
          )
```

```
    , p_credential_static_id =>
        pkg_oci_vision_util.gc_credential_static_id
  );

  if apex_web_service.g_status_code != 200 then
    raise_application_error(-20003, 'Analyze Document failed: '
      || apex_web_service.g_status_code);
    apex_debug.error('HTTP Status Code: ' ||
      apex_web_service.g_status_code);
    apex_debug.error(to_clob(l_response));
  end if;

  return l_response;
  end f_analyze_document;
end pkg_oci_vision_util;
```

The *AnalyzeDocument* endpoint is called using a POST method, and in the request body, developers must include a JSON payload containing details of the request. The request payload sent by the apex_web_service.make_rest_request that looks like this:

```
{
    "document": {
        "source": "OBJECT_STORAGE",
        "namespaceName": "abcd1234xyz",
        "bucketName": "ai-vision-demo",
        "objectName": "receipt01.png"
    },
    "features": [
        {
            "featureType": "KEY_VALUE_DETECTION"
        }
    ]
}
```

It includes the following key attributes:

- **Document**: We can submit the document either inline, where the document is embedded in the request payload, or as an Object Storage reference. If the document object source is OBJECT_STORAGE, then it must also contain the attributes that together specify the location of the object. These define the following:

  a.   Namespace name

  b.   Bucket name

  c.   Object name

- **Features**: This attribute accepts an array of feature types, which means developers could request to perform multiple analyses in a single REST call.

Before starting work on the APEX application, ensure that

1.   The IAM user and group for the application to access Object Storage and Vision have been created.

2.   An APEX Web Credential for OCI REST API access has been created in the workspace.

3.   The required IAM policies and statements have been defined to allow the IAM user to read and write to the target Object Storage bucket and can use the Vision services.

Earlier in the chapter, we had created the IAM user *demoapex* and assigned it to the group *DemoVisionGroup*. To allow the *demoapex* to use Vision, create a policy in the root compartment with the following statement:

```
allow group DemoVisionGroup to use ai-service-vision-family in tenancy
```

Create a new APEX application with three pages:

- **Page 1**: Home
- **Page 2**: Upload Document
- **Page 3**: View Receipt Details

On the home page, display a list of receipts that have been uploaded and analyzed. Create a classic report using the `RECEIPT` table as a source (Figure 10-2). It should display the `RECEIPT_ID`, `FILENAME`, and `MIME_TYPE` columns. The first report column should render a link to page 3 using the value of `RECEIPT_ID`. Also create a button to upload images and place it on the top-right corner of the report. It should redirect to page 2, a modal dialog page that we will create next.

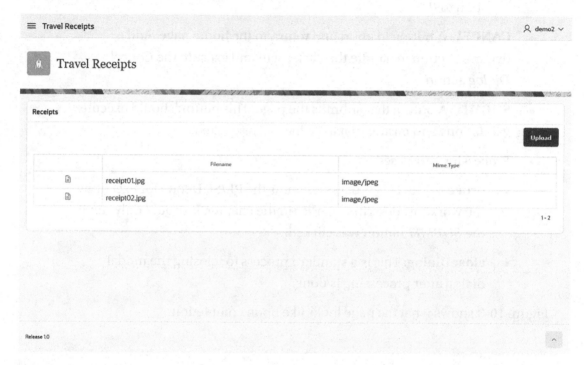

Figure 10-2. *The home page with an interactive report showing the uploaded receipts*

The second page for uploading images is where most of the action will occur. Add the following APEX components:

- **P2_FILE**: A page item of type *File Browse.*

  - Set the *Display As* value to *Block Dropzone* if the version of APEX you are using supports it.

  - Set the *Storage Type* to *Table APEX_APPLICATION_TEMP_FILES.*

  - Set the files in APEX_APPLICATION_TEMP_FILES to be purged at the end of the request.

- Set the accepted file types to *image/**.

- Set this as a required field.

- For the field's appearance, set the template to *Hidden*, and then through the template options, stretch the form item so that it will occupy all the horizontal space. Finally, set the label column span to *0*.

- **CANCEL**: A button to abort and return to the home page. Add a dynamic action to handle the click event and execute the *Cancel Dialog* action.

- **SUBMIT**: A button that submits the page. This button should execute validations and ensure that a file has been selected.

- Processing processes:

  - **processFile**: This process contains the PL/SQL code for executing the workflow described earlier in the chapter. It should only run if the *SUBMIT* button was clicked.

  - **closeDialog**: This is a standard process for closing the modal dialog after processing is done.

Figure 10-3 shows what the page looks like upon completion.

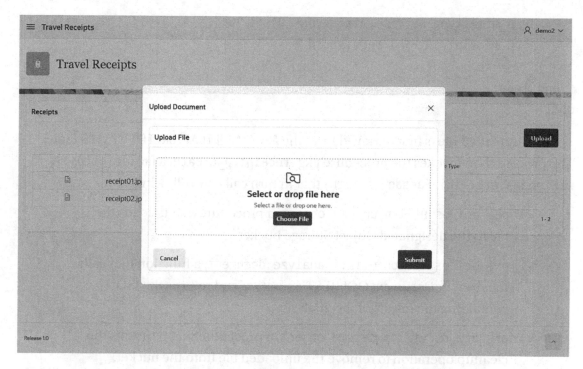

Figure 10-3. *A modal dialog page to handle file uploads and triggering the document analysis*

The user either selects or drops an image file in the designated space on the modal dialog and clicks the *SUBMIT* button. The *processFile* process is then triggered and executes the following PL/SQL code:

```
declare
  l_receipt_id receipt.receipt_id%type;
begin
  for file in (
    select * from apex_application_temp_files
    where name = :P2_FILE
  ) loop
    pkg_receipt.p_create(
      p_scanned_image => file.blob_content
      , p_filename => file.filename
```

```
            , p_mime_type => file.mime_type
            , p_receipt_id => l_receipt_id
        );
    end loop;
end;
```

The uploaded file is first retrieved from the APEX_APPLICATION_TEMP_FILES table. The process then invokes the procedure pkg_receipt.p_create, a façade (https:// wikipedia.org/wiki/Facade_pattern) that in turn calls the following:

- pkg_oci_os_util.p_upload_object, a procedure that uploads the file to the designated Object Storage bucket.

- pkg_oci_os_vision_util.f_analyze_document, a function that calls the *AnalyzeDocument* OCI REST operation and returns the JSON containing the results of the analysis.

- pkg_oci_os_util.p_delete_object, a procedure that performs the cleanup operation to remove the uploaded file from the bucket.

A final step then inserts both the uploaded file and the results returned by the pkg_oci_os_vision_util.f_analyze_document function. Storing the results allows us to query. The following JSON is a condensed version of a Document AI result:

```
{
  "documentMetadata" : {
    "pageCount" : 1,
    "mimeType" : "image/jpeg"
  },
  "pages" : [ {
    "pageNumber" : 1,
    "dimensions" : {
      "width" : 651.0,
      "height" : 868.0,
      "unit" : "PIXEL"
    },
    "detectedDocumentTypes" : null,
    "detectedLanguages" : null,
    "words" : [ ... ]
```

```
    "tables" : null,
    "documentFields" : [ ... ]
} ],
"detectedDocumentTypes" : null,
"detectedLanguages" : null,
"documentClassificationModelVersion" : null,
"languageClassificationModelVersion" : null,
"textDetectionModelVersion" : "1.2.87",
"keyValueDetectionModelVersion" : "1.2.87",
"tableDetectionModelVersion" : null,
"errors" : null,
"searchablePdf" : null
}
```

The content of the results is dependent on features listed in the request payload. For example, if one of the features added was TABLE_DETECTION, then the table array in a page object would contain an array of rows and cells for any table structures discovered during the analysis. In our example, we had only specified to detect key-value pairs found in receipts, and hence, we will find objects within the documentFields array, if any are found.

In the example application, we expect only receipts to be uploaded. These receipts would generally have the following types of information:

- Details on the merchant and summary information like total price of the items purchased in the transaction.

- A list of items purchased that include the item names, prices, and quantities.

Create the third page for viewing a record in the RECEIPT table. Include the following regions:

- **Scanned Image**: A *Static Content* region that contains two page items:

  - **P3_RECEIPT_ID**: A *Hidden* page item that stores the primary key of the record.

  - **P3_SCANNED_IMAGE**: A *Display Image* page item for rendering the scanned image that is stored as a BLOB in the RECEIPT table.

- **Parsed Data**: Another *Static Content* region that will serve as a container for the next two subregions. Display the parsed data alongside the scanned image and configure it to use the *Tabs Container* template.

- **Key Value Pairs**: Create this *Classic Report* region as a child of the *Parse Data* region.

- **Line Items**: Add a second *Classic Report* region under the *Parse Data* region.

- **Button Container**: Assign this *Static Content* region containing the buttons *CLOSE* and *DELETE* in the *Dialog Footer* position. These buttons will perform standard actions to close the modal dialog using a dynamic action and delete the record using a page process, respectively.

As mentioned earlier in the chapter, the key-value pairs are found in the `documentFields` array. The following snippet shows the first document field found in the sample receipt.

```
"documentFields" : [ {
  "fieldType" : "KEY_VALUE",
  "fieldLabel" : {
    "name" : "MerchantName",
    "confidence" : 0.9999982
  },
  "fieldName" : null,
  "fieldValue" : {
    "valueType" : "STRING",
    "text" : null,
    "confidence" : null,
    "boundingPolygon" : {
      "normalizedVertices" : [ {
        "x" : 0.1674347158218126,
        "y" : 0.12211981566820276
      }, {
        "x" : 0.6851611159364199,
```

```
        "y" : 0.12211981566820276
      }, {
        "x" : 0.6851611159364199,
        "y" : 0.1497695852534562
      }, {
        "x" : 0.1674347158218126,
        "y" : 0.1497695852534562
      } ]
    },
    "wordIndexes" : [ 0, 1, 2 ],
    "value" : "The Singapore Mint"
  },
  ...
]
```

Note   Every text value that Vision finds in the image has an associated bounding polygon/box and confidence score. These provide developers with the pixel coordinates in the image where the text was inferred from and a value between 0 and 1 with a probability that the predicted value is correct. The bounding box coordinates can be used, for example, to display and highlight where the terms were found, and the confidence scores can be used with a threshold to decide which predicted values are accepted or discarded.

Objects in this array may be of field type KEY_VALUE or LINE_ITEM_GROUP. Objects of KEY_VALUE type could contain values from predefined fields such as the merchant's name (MerchantName), phone number (MerchantPhoneNumber), the receipt's transaction date (TransactionDate), and total charges (Total).

To retrieve the key-value pairs found in a receipt, set the source for the *Key Value Pairs* region to use the following SQL query:

```
select
  data.field_name
  , data.field_value
from
  receipt r
```

```
    , json_table(
        r.receipt_data
        , '$.pages[*].documentFields[*]'
            columns(
                field_name varchar2(30) path '$.fieldLabel.name'
                , field_value varchar2(500) path '$.fieldValue.value'
                , field_type varchar2(30) path '$.fieldType'
            )
    ) data
where 1 = 1
    and receipt_id = :P3_RECEIPT_ID
    and data.field_type = 'KEY_VALUE'
```

Then, customize how the report is rendered. Select the region and then switch to the *Attributes* tab. Under the *Appearance* section, select *Value Attribute Pairs -Row* for the template. Figure 10-4 shows how the page should look like when completed.

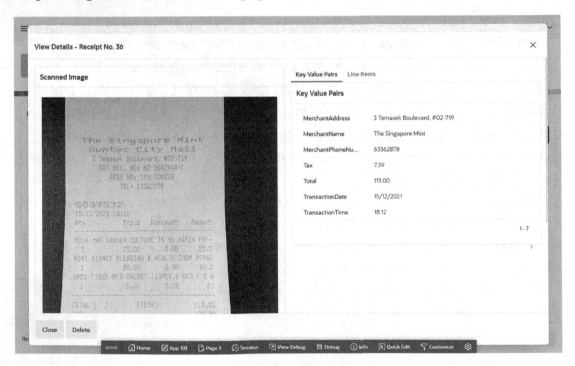

Figure 10-4. *Display the predefined documents found*

The list of items discovered in a receipt can be found in a document field of type LINE_ITEM_GROUP. Within this object is an items array that is a collection of objects that resembles the parent object. Each of these represents a line item (the field type would be LINE_ITEM). It in turn encapsulates an items array containing objects with the field type LINE_ITEM_FIELD. The elements of this array may contain the name, price, quantity, and total price of the line item. A sample of what these nested elements would look like is shown as follows:

```
{
  "fieldType" : "LINE_ITEM_GROUP",
    "fieldLabel" : {
      "name" : "line item group",
      "confidence" : null
    },
    "fieldName" : null,
    "fieldValue" : {
      "valueType" : "ARRAY",
      "text" : null,
      "confidence" : null,
      "boundingPolygon" : null,
      "wordIndexes" : null,
      "items" : [ {
        "fieldType" : "LINE_ITEM",
        "fieldLabel" : null,
        "fieldName" : null,
        "fieldValue" : {
          "valueType" : "ARRAY",
          "text" : null,
          "confidence" : null,
          "boundingPolygon" : null,
          "wordIndexes" : null,
          "items" : [ {
            "fieldType" : "LINE_ITEM_FIELD",
            "fieldLabel" : {
              "name" : "ItemTotalPrice",
              "confidence" : 0.9988584
            },
```

```
          "fieldName" : null,
          "fieldValue" : {
            "valueType" : "STRING",
            "text" : null,
            "confidence" : null,
            "boundingPolygon" : {
              "normalizedVertices" : [ {
                "x" : 0.6589861751152074,
                "y" : 0.4642857142857143
              }, {
                "x" : 0.728110599078341,
                "y" : 0.4642857142857143
              }, {
                "x" : 0.728110599078341,
                "y" : 0.49078341013824883
              }, {
                "x" : 0.6589861751152074,
                "y" : 0.49078341013824883
              } ]
            },
            "wordIndexes" : [ 37 ],
            "value" : "25.0"
          }
        },
        ...
      ]
    },
    ...
  ]
  }
}
```

To display the line items, configure the *Line Items* classic report region to display the results using the *Value Attribute Pairs -Row* template, and then set its source to use the following SQL query:

```
select
  data.field_name
  , data.field_value
from
  receipt r
  , json_table(
      r.receipt_data
    , '$.pages[*].documentFields[*].fieldValue.items[*]'
        columns(
            row_number for ordinality
          , nested path '$.fieldValue.items[*]' columns (
            field_name varchar2(30) path '$.fieldLabel.name'
          , field_value varchar2(500) path
                '$.fieldValue.value'
          , field_type varchar2(30) path '$.fieldType'
          )
        )
  ) data
where 1 = 1
  and receipt_id = :P3_RECEIPT_ID
  and data.field_type = 'LINE_ITEM_FIELD'
order by data.row_number
  , case data.field_name
      when 'ItemName' then 1
      when 'ItemPrice' then 2
      when 'ItemQuantity' then 3
      when 'ItemTotalPrice' then 4
      else null
    end nulls last
```

Clicking the *Line Items* will reveal what items were discovered in the submitted image (Figure 10-5).

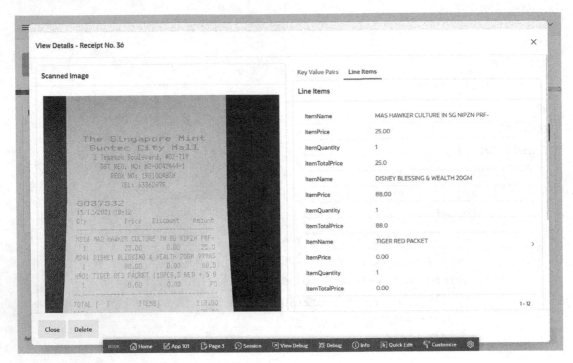

Figure 10-5. *The View Receipt Details page showing line items extracted from the receipt*

Summary

The goal of artificial intelligence and machine learning is to create computer systems and robots that can mimic human behavior. The human brain, the core of our decision-making processes, is highly reliant on the five senses including sight. The proliferation of digital capture devices, cheaper, more efficient data storage, and more powerful computer processing power have resulted in the advancement of computer vision technologies. Today, the OCI offers "AI as a Service" through its AI Services offerings including Vision. This makes it easier for APEX developers to include solutions involving image/object recognition, text extraction, and document classification capabilities. The sample application introduced in this chapter is just one area where AI can be applied, and I hope it has inspired you to create more intelligent web applications.

CHAPTER 11

Email Delivery Services

The *Email* is arguably one of the oldest and most used applications on the Internet and an indispensable tool for communication. It was first implemented for the Advanced Research Projects Agency Network (ARPANET) in the 1970s by a computer programmer, Ray Tomlinson. Email relies on client applications and a network of servers that accept, forward, deliver, and store messages using the Simple Mail Transfer Protocol (SMTP).

While emails were intended to provide multiway conversations between humans, it is also commonly used by software applications to send notifications, information, etc. Programming languages and frameworks implement APIs that communicate with email servers using SMTP, on behalf of the application. In *Oracle Application Express* (APEX) applications, the *APEX_MAIL* is a *PL/SQL* API that wraps the *UTL_SMTP* package in *Oracle Database*. However, the application is dependent on access to an email server or service to relay the message.

To send emails from applications, we can either utilize a managed service or provision a self-managed SMTP server. It is common these days for companies to rely on third-party, cloud-based services such as *Microsoft 365* for emails. The *Oracle Cloud Infrastructure* (OCI) also provides a managed service called *Email Delivery*. It is not included in the *Oracle Cloud Free Tier* offering and users will need to upgrade to a paid account to use it.

In this chapter, we will walk through the required steps to prepare your OCI tenancy for Email Delivery services. Once these have been provisioned, we will then configure an APEX instance to use the OCI's SMTP endpoint to send emails using the APEX_MAIL package. We will also examine various issues that might affect email deliverability, what actions can be taken to ensure that emails can be sent successfully, and what tools are available should difficulties arise.

© Adrian Png and Heli Helskyaho 2022
A. Png and H. Helskyaho, *Extending Oracle Application Express with Oracle Cloud Features*,
https://doi.org/10.1007/978-1-4842-8170-3_11

Setting Up OCI Resources

The Email Delivery service provides a SMTP server in most, if not all, OCI regions for posting emails. While it requires user authentication to access the service, there are no network restrictions for client connections. There are, however, additional layers of protection to prevent misuse. Create and configure the required OCI resources that together help secure the service and improve email deliverability.

Identity and Access Management

Security is at the heart of all OCI operations, and hence, like all other OCI services, Email Delivery requires that the necessary *Identity and Access Management* (IAM) resources and policies are created and configured. It is recommended that we use a separate IAM user for applications to send emails *via* the service. Begin by creating an IAM group to which an IAM policy will use to assign the necessary permissions.

1. Navigate to the Groups overview page by clicking the navigation menu, and then click *Identity & Security*, followed by *Groups*.

2. Click *Create Group*.

3. Enter a suitable name, for example, *EmailDeliveryAgents*, and provide a short description of its purpose (Figure 11-1).

4. Click *Create* to create the desired group.

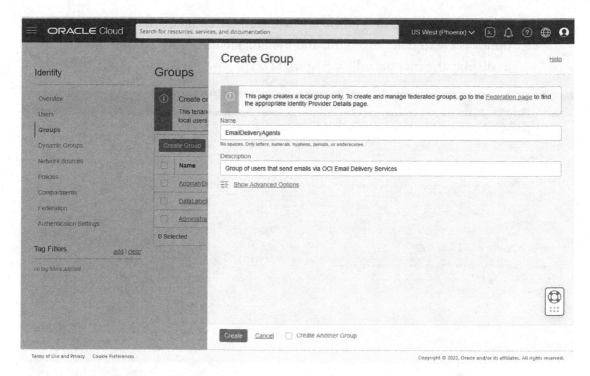

Figure 11-1. *Create an IAM group*

The next task involves creating an IAM policy and the required statements for this group to use the resources provided by the Email Delivery service.

1. Navigate to the Policies overview page by clicking the navigation menu, and then click *Identity & Security*, followed by *Policies*. Alternatively, if you are on the Groups overview page, then simply click the *Policies* link found on the menu on the left side of the page.

2. Once on the Policies overview page, select the compartment where this policy will be created in. We will create this in the tenant, so please select root compartment on the left side of the page, under the section *List Scope*.

3. Click Create Policy.

4. Enter the desired policy name and a description. Ensure that the policy is created in the tenant, and then toggle the *Policy Builder* to display the manual editor (Figure 11-2).

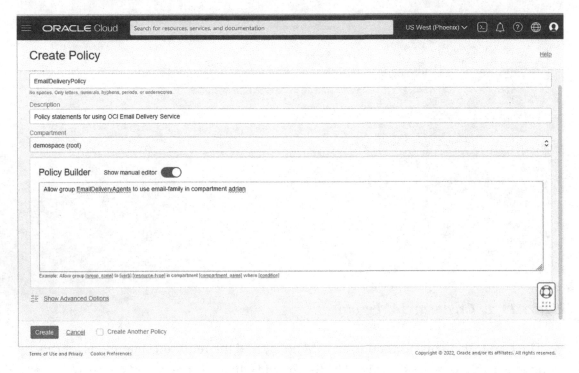

Figure 11-2. *Create a policy and add the required statements using the manual editor*

Note   The Policy Builder has templates only for creating statements to allow a group to manage the relevant OCI resources (Figure 11-3) and is not typically required for simply sending emails through the service.

Enter a policy statement using the following syntax:

```
Allow group <group name> to use email-family in compartment
<compartment name>
```

For example:

```
Allow group EmailDeliveryAgents to use email-family in compartment adrian
```

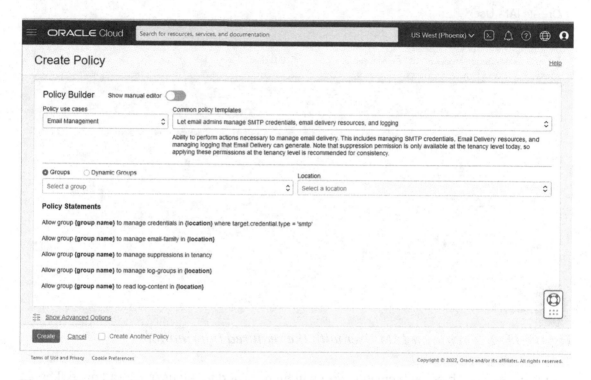

Figure 11-3. *Policy templates that generate statements for managing relevant OCI resources*

We will next create the IAM user *emailagent* and then assign it to the group *EmailDeliveryAgents*, thereby granting it the necessary permissions to use the service:

1. Navigate to the Policies overview page by clicking the navigation menu, and then click *Identity & Security*, followed by *Users*. Alternatively, if you are still on either the Groups or Policies overview page, then simply click the *Users* link found on the menu on the left side of the page.

2. Click *Create User*.

3. Select the user type *IAM User*.

4. Enter a suitable username and description, but leave the email fields blank as they are not required for this user (Figure 11-4).

5. Click *Create* to create the user.

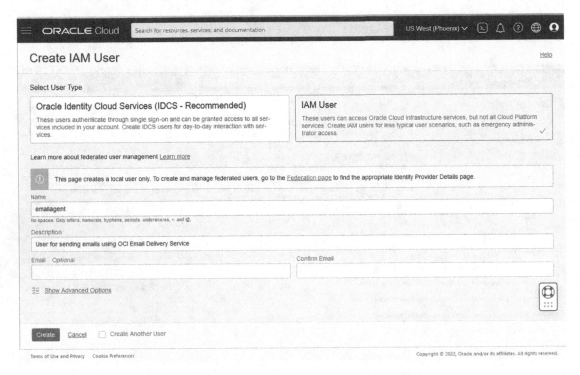

Figure 11-4. *Create an IAM User with the required information*

Once the user has been created, you will be returned to the user's detail page. There you will find several management actions that can be performed on the user. With the principle of least privilege in mind, we should limit what this IAM user can do on the OCI tenancy.

1. Click *Edit User Capabilities*.

2. By default, newly created users will have all the capabilities enabled. Limit this to only *SMTP Credentials* by unchecking all other options (Figure 11-5).

3. Click *Save Changes*.

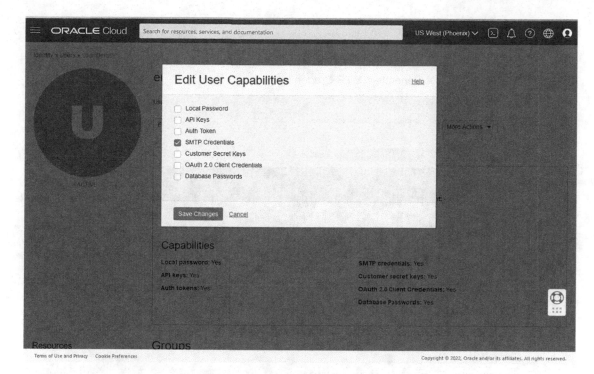

Figure 11-5. *Following the principle of least privileges, remove user capabilities that are not required for using the Email Delivery services*

At this point, the IAM user can only create *SMTP Credentials*. However, since it does not have the *Local Password* capability, you cannot log in to the OCI Console as that user to generate the username and password pair. Use your administrative user to do so instead.

1. On the user's details page, scroll down and under *Resources*, click the link *SMTP Credentials*.

2. Click *Generate SMTP Credentials*.

3. Enter a description that helps you recall what and/or where the credentials are used (Figure 11-6).

4. Click the *Generate SMTP Credentials* to generate the credentials.

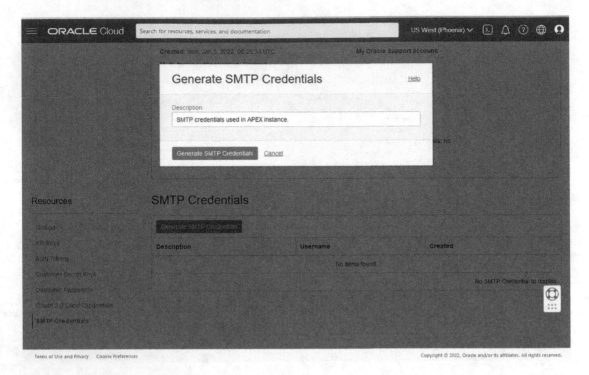

Figure 11-6. *Generate the SMTP Credentials and provide a useful description*

Note   Once the SMTP Credentials is created, a modal will display both the username and password (Figure 11-7). These are what you will use to connect to the OCI Email Delivery Service's SMTP servers. The latter is displayed **only once**, so please save these securely and immediately. If you lose the password, generate a new set of credentials.

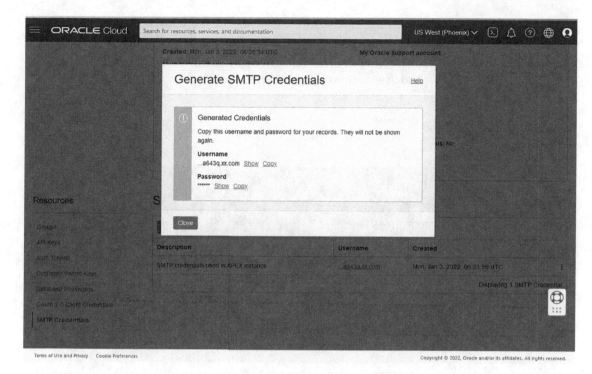

Figure 11-7. *The SMTP Credentials' password is displayed only once. Store it safely!*

The final step to perform is to assign the user to the relevant group (Figure 11-8):

1. On the user's details page, scroll down, and under *Resources*, click the link *Groups*.

2. Click *Add User to Group*.

3. Select the IAM group *EmailDeliveryAgents*.

4. Click *Add* to assign the user to the group.

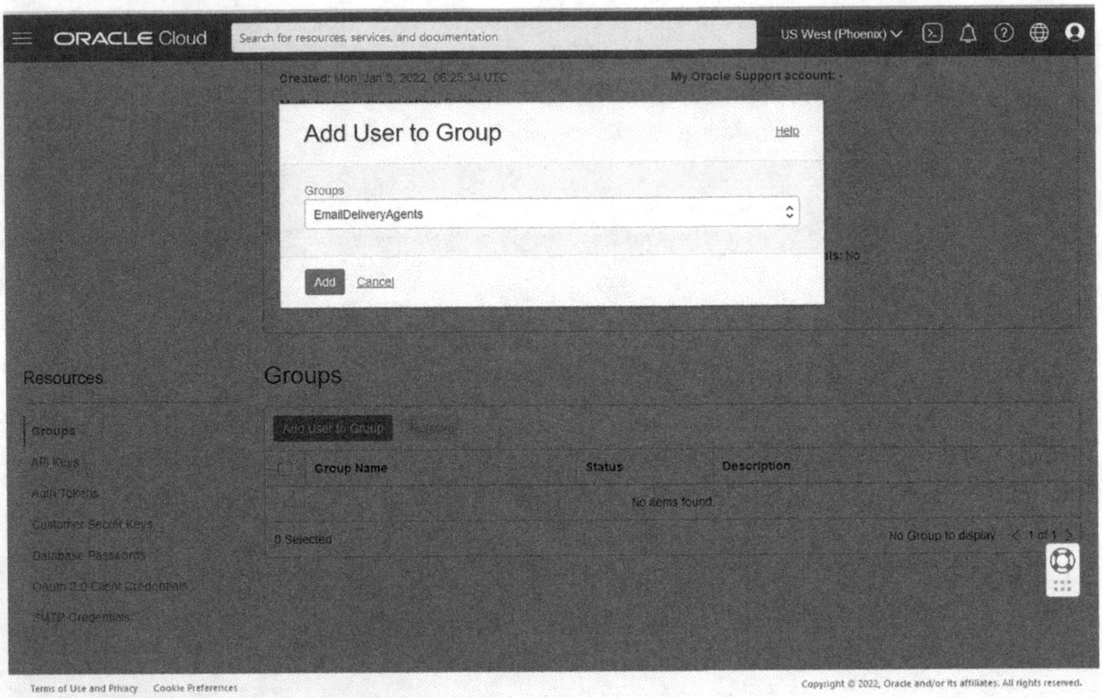

Figure 11-8. *Assign the IAM user to the appropriate group*

This completes the setup of IAM resources to facilitate the use of the Email Delivery services.

Regions, Availability, and Server Information

While OCI IAM resources are global, the resources associated with the Email Delivery services are not. These include

- The SMTP servers

- Email Domains

- Approved Senders

- Suppression List

When choosing a region for hosting your OCI resources, be sure to validate that it has all the required services. Use the matrix on this website (`www.oracle.com/cloud/data-regions/`) to guide your region selection. At the time of writing, it appears all OCI data regions support Email Delivery services.

To obtain the SMTP server information, first, select the desired region. Then, go to the navigation menu and click *Developer Services*. Under *Application Integration*, click *Email Delivery*. You should be redirected to the Configuration page; if not, click the link with the same name, under the *Email Delivery* section on the left side of the page. For example, the information for the Phoenix region in the United States is shown in Figure 11-9.

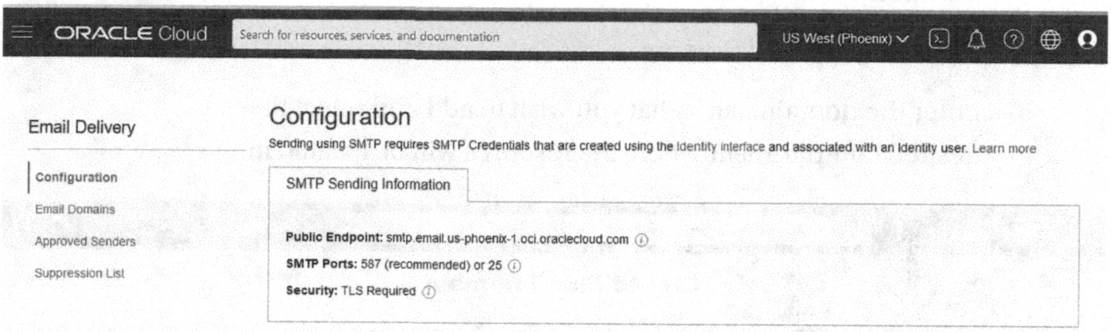

Figure 11-9. *SMTP server information for US Phoenix region*

Generally, the *Fully-Qualified Domain Name* (FQDN) for these servers follows this format:

```
smtp.email.<REGION_ID>.oci.oraclecloud.com
```

The `REGION_ID` can be obtained from the list here: `https://bit.ly/oci-docs-regions`.

Email Domains

Email Domains was a newer feature of the service that was introduced in the later half of 2021. One of its functionalities allows tenants to create *DomainKeys Identified Mail* (DKIM) signatures, an email security standard that allows the receiving client to validate that an email originated from a specific domain and was authorized by its owner. DKIM plays a role in ensuring email deliverability, which we will discuss later in the chapter. Prior to the release of this feature, OCI tenants must submit an Oracle Support *Technical Service Request* (SR) for a DKIM signature to be generated for a domain.

Before generating a DKIM signature, an email domain must be created (Figure 11-10):

1. Open the navigation menu on the top left of the OCI Console, and then click *Developer Services*.

2. Under *Application Integration*, click *Email Delivery* to get to the overview/configuration page.

3. On the left side of the page, under *Email Delivery*, click *Email Domains*.

4. Click *Create Email Domain*.

5. Enter the domain name that you wish to add and select the desired compartment where the resource will be located in.

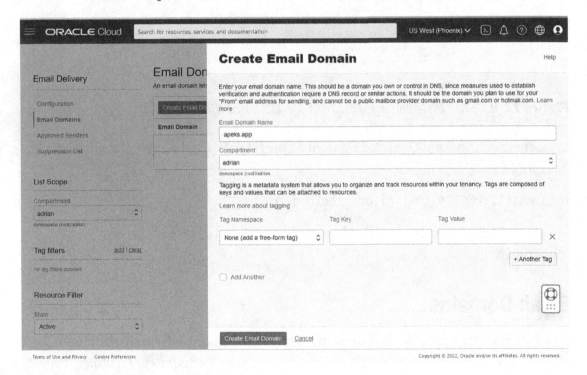

Figure 11-10. *Add your favorite domain to the Email Delivery service*

After creating the email domain, you will immediately be redirected to the domain's details page (Figure 11-11). Notice that both the *DKIM Signing* and *SPF Configured* properties have a warning icon next to them. These will turn into green-colored ticks by the end of this section.

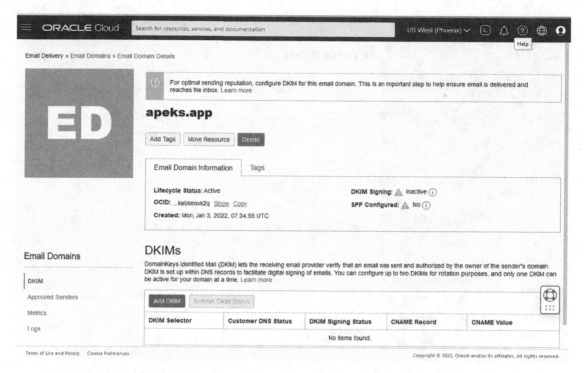

Figure 11-11. *Email Domain details page*

To generate a DKIM signature

1. Click *Add DKIM*.

2. Enter a DKIM Selector (Figure 11-12). This can be any value but, when concatenated with the domain, must be globally unique. It also must be no longer than 63 characters that may be any lowercased alphanumeric characters or a dash. Oracle recommends using the format: `<PREFIX>-<REGION_KEY>-<DATE>`. Where `PREFIX` can be something arbitrary like "email," `REGION_KEY` is the three-letter acronym for the region (see `https://bit.ly/oci-docs-regions`) that the domain was created in and the `DATE` in a suitable format, for example, 202201.

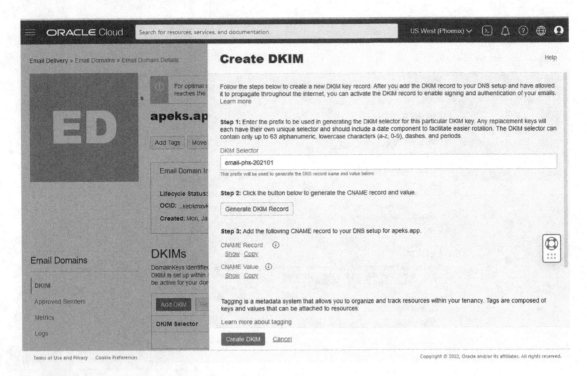

Figure 11-12. *Enter a valid DKIM Selector*

3. Click *Generate DKIM Record*.

4. This will generate two values: *CNAME Record* and *CNAME Value*
    (Figure 11-13). These will be used when creating the required
    DNS record.

5. Click *Create DKIM* to complete the process.

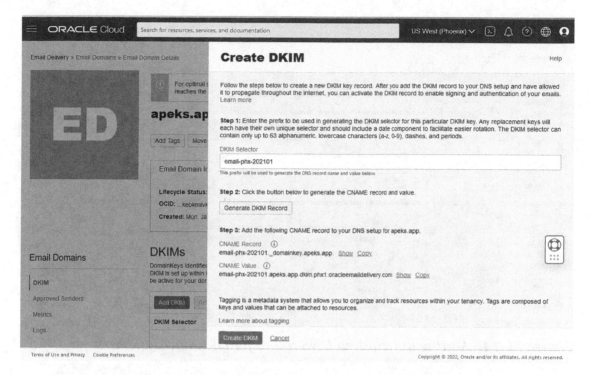

Figure 11-13. *Generate the required values for the DKIM DNS Record*

To activate DKIM signing, you must create the corresponding DNS record using the values provided. This is done through the DNS service for your organization's domain name. DNS service providers may have different user interfaces and methods for adding DNS records. The following steps are based on what *Cloudflare* (www.cloudflare.com/) provides (Figure 11-14), but generally, the procedure involves

1. Add a new DNS record of type *CNAME*.

2. Enter the *Name* and *Target* value as provided in the OCI Console.

3. Set a suitable Time to live (TTL) value.

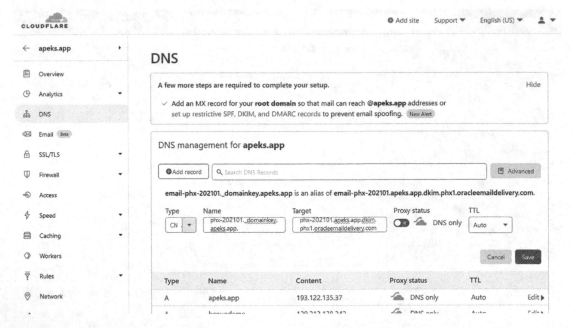

Figure 11-14. *Adding the required DNS record for DKIM in Cloudflare*

Wait for a few minutes and then return to the OCI Console and then click *Refresh DKIM Status* until the *DKIM Signing* status shows *Active* (Figure 11-15).

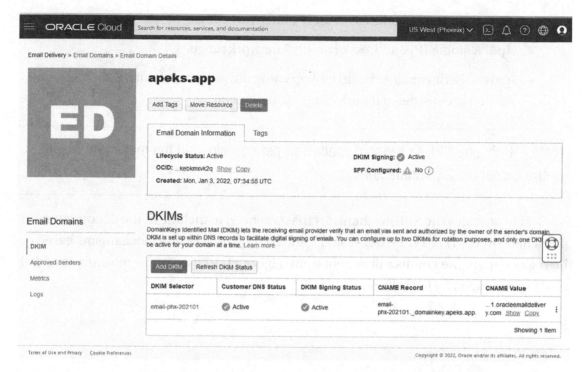

Figure 11-15. *Upon adding the required DNS record, the DKIM Signing status will indicate that it is active*

The other, and perhaps more well-known, DNS record involved in email authentication is the *Sender Policy Framework* (SPF) that is defined in RFC 7208 (see `https://tools.ietf.org/html/rfc7208`). It involves a single DNS *TXT* record that lists the mail servers that are permitted to send emails on behalf of a domain. It is associated with the domain name and a single string of text that always begins with `v=spf1` and ends with an "all" mechanism and its modifier. In between are a series of mechanisms that lists the authorized servers. These mechanisms can be a combination of any of the following:

- **include**: The SPF records of the specified domain are searched for a match. Typically used by email service providers like the OCI Email Delivery service.

- **a**: A DNS *A* record

- **mx**: All the A records for the domain's *MX* records.

- **ptr**: The client's IP looked up using a PTR query.

- **ip4**: A single IPv4 address or an IPv4 network range.

- **ip6**: A single IPv6 address or an IPv6 network range.

- **exists**: Perform an A record lookup using the provided domain. A match is considered if the lookup yields a result.

Note   Only one SPF TXT record is allowed per domain, and the maximum length of the content is 255 characters.

Oracle provides the SPF mechanisms that you need to include in the documentation found here: `https://bit.ly/oci-email-spf-config`. Include the mechanisms based on the region where the emails will be sent from. Figure 11-16 shows how the entry is added to a DNS managed by Cloudflare.

Figure 11-16. *Adding a SPF TXT record using Cloudflare's DNS management website*

It will take a while before DNS changes are propagated globally. You can validate that the SPF record exists using a tool like what Kitterman Technical Services, Inc. provides (Figure 11-17). You can access the site using the link: `www.kitterman.com/spf/validate.html`.

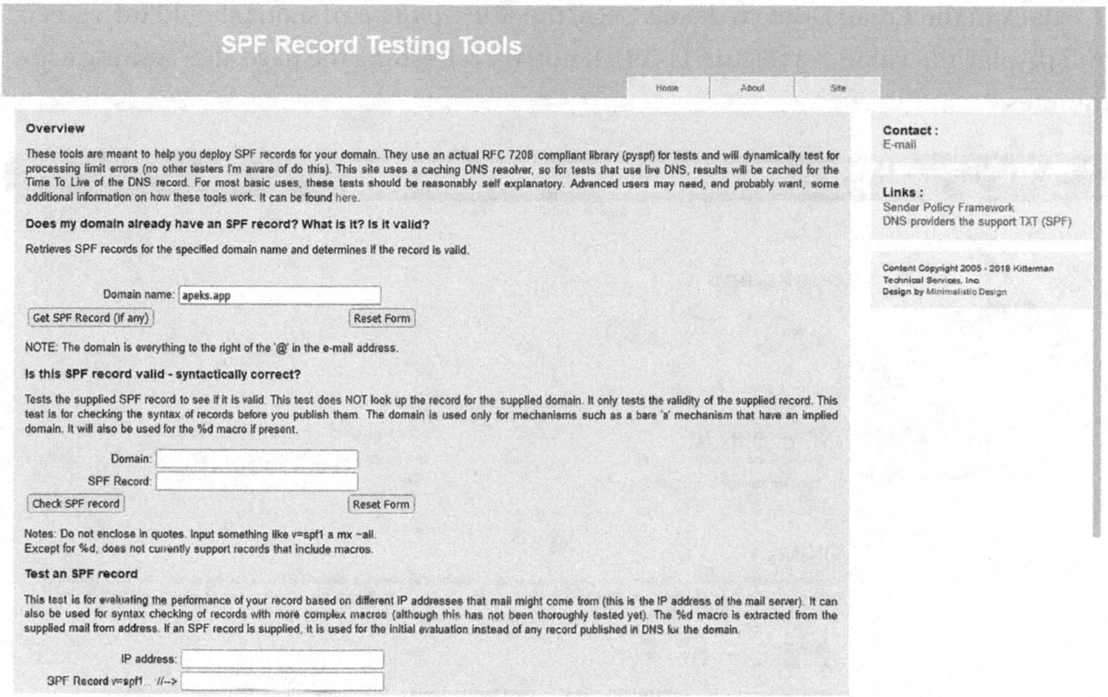

Figure 11-17. *A SPF Record Testing Tools*

Enter your domain in the first form and then click *Get SPF Record (if any)*. If the record is found, you will see a result like that in Figure 11-18.

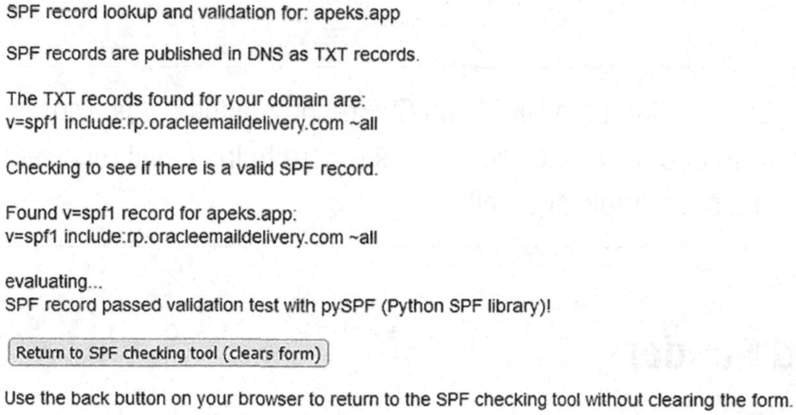

SPF record lookup and validation for: apeks.app

SPF records are published in DNS as TXT records.

The TXT records found for your domain are:
v=spf1 include:rp.oracleemaildelivery.com ~all

Checking to see if there is a valid SPF record.

Found v=spf1 record for apeks.app:
v=spf1 include:rp.oracleemaildelivery.com ~all

evaluating...
SPF record passed validation test with pySPF (Python SPF library)!

Return to SPF checking tool (clears form)

Use the back button on your browser to return to the SPF checking tool without clearing the form.

Figure 11-18. *Results of SPF record lookup*

Back in the Email Domain details page, the *SPF Configured* status should turn green and display the value *Yes* (Figure 11-19). If not, try refreshing the page after waiting a few minutes.

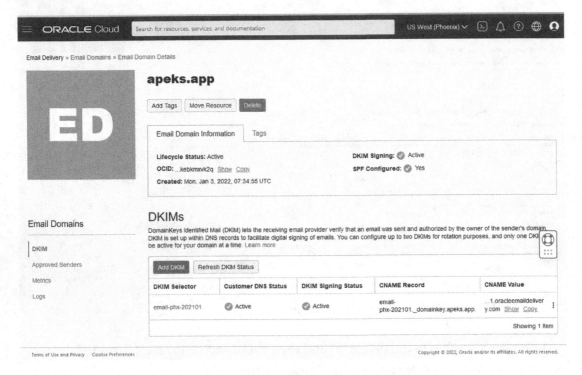

Figure 11-19. *A fully configured email domain*

Tip   Once you have both the DKIM and SPF records added, it is also recommended to add a *DMARC* record. This record helps email receivers decide how to handle a noncompliant email.

Approved Senders

The OCI Email Delivery servers will only accept and send emails where the "From" address has been added as an approved sender. These can be added without first creating an email domain. All email addresses in the "From" header must be an approved sender.

Approved senders are associated with an OCI compartment and must be added to each region where the target SMTP endpoint is located. For example, if the endpoint is *smtp.email.ca-toronto-1.oci.oraclecloud.com*, then create the approved senders in the Toronto data region. Adding them to any other regions, such as Montreal, will result in the email getting rejected. Also, add only email addresses that you own and/or manage as you will need to, at minimum, add a SPF record to avoid getting the emails classified as spam. Do not add or send from an email address provided by a public mailbox service provider such as Gmail, Hotmail, or Yahoo. These services have restrictive DNS rules that prohibit any servers that they do not manage, to send emails on their behalf.

Approved senders can be added through the OCI Console and REST APIs. The user that manages the approved senders must have the necessary rights to perform these tasks. If the user is not in the OCI administrators' group, then ensure that the group (e.g., *EmailManagers*) that the user belongs to has the following policy applied:

```
Allow group EmailManagers to manage email-family in tenancy
```

or

```
Allow group EmailManagers to manage approved-senders in compartment adrian
Allow group EmailManagers to inspect compartments in compartment adrian
```

To create an approved sender, please perform the following steps:

1. Open the navigation menu on the top left of the OCI Console, and then click *Developer Services*.

2. Under *Application Integration*, click *Email Delivery* to get to the overview/configuration page.

3. On the left side of the page, under *Email Delivery*, click *Approved Senders*.

4. Be sure to select the desired region and compartment for the new approved sender.

5. Click *Create Approved Sender*.

6. Enter the email address to approve (Figure 11-20), and then click *Create Approved Sender*.

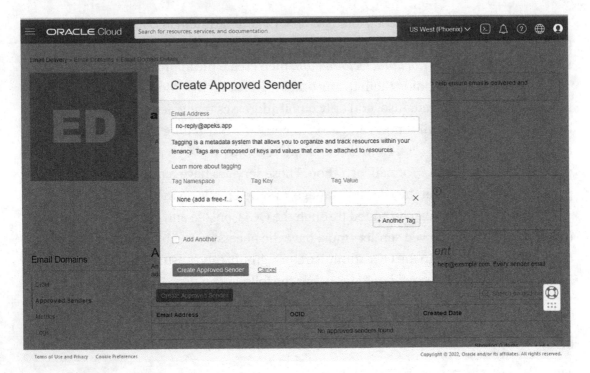

Figure 11-20. *Create an approved sender*

Suppression List

The role of the *Suppression List* is somewhat the opposite that of the Approved Senders. The Email Delivery service will not deliver any emails to addresses added to the list. These email addresses are assigned to at the tenancy level and not within compartments like we do with approved senders. They are added automatically by the service in situations where the service receives bounce codes indicating that there was a permanent failure in delivering the email or there has been a complaint. Example reasons for a reject email include hard bounces, too many soft bouncers, or a list-unsubscribe request was received.

To manage the suppression list manually, first ensure that the user has the appropriate permissions to manage the OCI resource involved. For example:

```
Allow group EmailManagers to manage suppressions in tenancy
```

Like the approved senders, entries can be managed either using the OCI Console or the REST APIs. To manage them using the OCI Console, perform the following steps:

1. Open the navigation menu on the top left of the OCI Console, and then click *Developer Services*.

2. Under *Application Integration*, click *Email Delivery* to get to the overview/configuration page.

3. On the left side of the page, under *Email Delivery*, click *Suppression List*.

4. Be sure to select the root compartment (tenancy).

5. Click *Add Suppression*.

6. Enter the email address to add to the list (Figure 11-21), and then click *Add*.

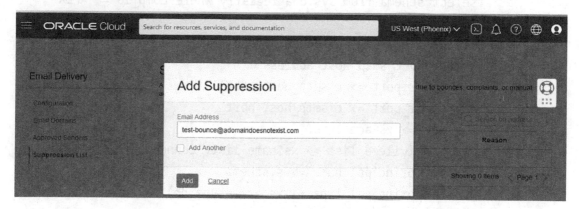

Figure 11-21. *Manually adding an email address to the Suppression List*

Configure APEX Instance for OCI Email Delivery Service

APEX is a *Rapid Application Development* (RAD) platform that shields developers from the need to implement "infrastructure-type" functionality like sending email. Once an instance is configured, developers simply use the APEX_MAIL PL/SQL API to send emails.

Typically, the database and/or instance administrator will perform the following tasks:

- Add the appropriate network *Access Control List* (ACL) that allows the database to communicate with the remote network resource successfully. The following is an example to allow connections to the OCI Email Delivery SMTP endpoint for the Phoenix region in the United States.

```
declare
  c_smtp_host_address constant varchar2(4000) :=
    'smtp.email.us-phoenix-1.oci.oraclecloud.com';
  c_smtp_host_port constant number := 587;
begin
  for s in (
    select schema from sys.dba_registry where comp_id = 'APEX'
  ) loop
    sys.dbms_network_acl_admin.append_host_ace(
      host => c_smtp_host_address
      , lower_port => c_smtp_host_port
      , upper_port => c_smtp_host_port
      , ace => xs$ace_type(
          privilege_list => xs$name_list('connect')
          , principal_name => s.schema
          , principal_type => xs_acl.ptype_db)
    );
    commit;
  end loop;
end;
/
```

- Create or add to an existing Oracle Wallet, the endpoint's root *Certificate Authority* (CA) certificate as a trusted certificate. Alternatively, if you have access to *orapki*, Oracle's command-line utility to manage the wallet, you may use a script (https://gist. github.com/fuzziebrain/202f902d8fc6d8de586da5097a501047) to generate an Oracle Wallet with all currently valid root CA certificates. For more details on this working with APEX and the Oracle Wallet, please refer to the following blog posts:

- `https://fuzziebrain.com/content/id/1720/`

- `https://fuzziebrain.com/content/id/1725/`

Important   The OCI Email Delivery service only allows connections and communications over *Transport Layer Security* (TLS) regardless of whether the port used is 25 or 587. Hence, setting up the Oracle Wallet is **required**!

- Configure the instance's Oracle Wallet configuration. The parameters to set include

  - Wallet path

  - Wallet password

Note   If the APEX instance is hosted on an *Oracle Autonomous Database* (ADB), then the network ACL and Oracle Wallet are already added and configured when the database was provisioned.

- Configure the instance's SMTP settings. The parameters to set include

  - Host Address

  - Host Port

  - TLS Mode (optional)

  - Username (optional)

  - Password (optional)

The SMTP settings for APEX can be configured using either the instance administration application (Figure 11-22) or using the APEX_INSTANCE_ADMIN API.

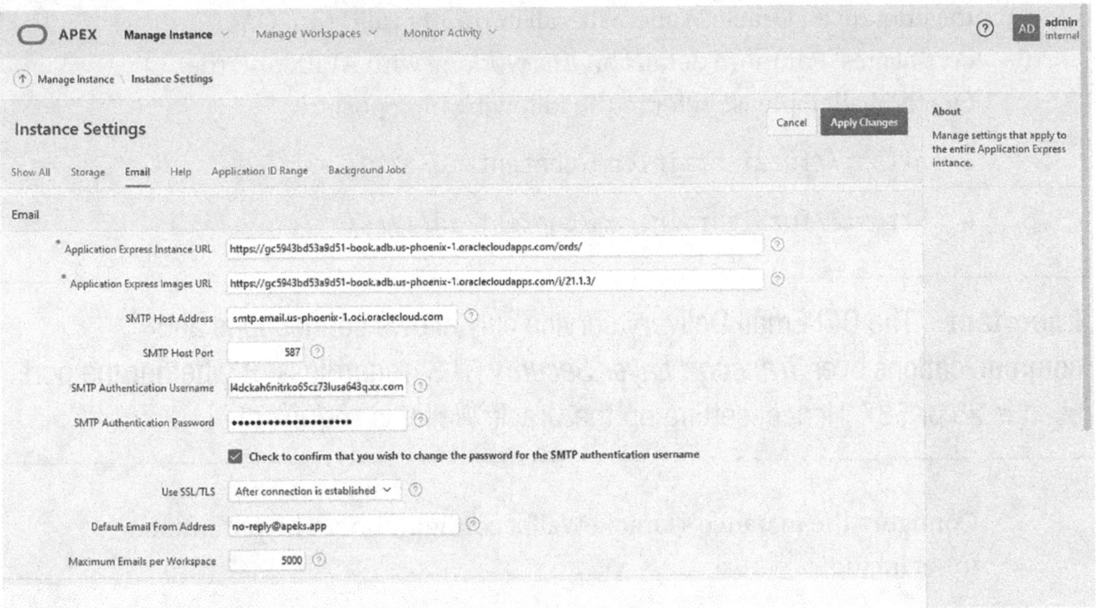

Figure 11-22. *Configuring the SMTP settings on an Oracle Autonomous Database using the instance administration application*

And the following is an example of how to configure the APEX instance using the PL/ SQL API:

```
declare
  c_smtp_host_address constant varchar2(4000) :=
    'smtp.email.us-phoenix-1.oci.oraclecloud.com';
  c_smtp_host_port constant number := 587;
  c_oci_smtp_credentials_username constant varchar2(4000) :=
    'ocid1.user.oc1..aaaaaaaab...truncated...43q.xx.com';
  c_oci_smtp_credentials_password constant varcahr2(4000) :=
    'somerandomalphanumericcharacters';
begin
  apex_instance_admin.set_parameter(
    p_parameter => 'SMTP_HOST_ADDRESS'
    , p_value => c_smtp_host_address);
  apex_instance_admin.set_parameter(
    'SMTP_HOST_PORT', c_smtp_host_port);
```

```
apex_instance_admin.set_parameter('SMTP_TLS_MODE', 'STARTTLS');
apex_instance_admin.set_parameter(
  'SMTP_USERNAME', c_oci_smtp_credentials_username);
apex_instance_admin.set_parameter(
  'SMTP_PASSWORD', c_oci_smtp_credentials_password);
commit;
end;
/
```

To verify that the values were set correctly, query the instance parameters using the following query:

```
select name, value
from apex_instance_parameters
where name like 'SMTP_%'
order by name;
```

Email Deliverability

It is not hard to set up an infrastructure and create an application to send emails. It is also not uncommon to find an unsecured SMTP server that is accessible over the Internet. Hence, receiving SPAM emails is a daily, if not minutely, occurrence. To combat unsolicited emails, organizations typically employ a combination of tools to reduce the chance of these unwanted messages landing in users' inboxes. These could include

- Server-based software that sieves and marks all incoming emails before they reach the mail servers, for example, Zerospam and Apache SpamAssassin

- Client-side plugins for or built-in features of common web or desktop email applications

If your outbound email sending environment is not configured correctly, the chances of having legitimate email flagged as SPAM are high. A more severe outcome is getting your sending domains added to a public SPAM database that SPAM filters often use. Removing you from the database is often a challenging process.

Testing Deliverability

Before starting to use the OCI Email Delivery extensively, I would recommend testing the deliverability of sending an email with the approved sender's address. There are several web-based tools that can perform this analysis. One such site is *mail-tester* (https://mail-tester.com). It is easy to use and very informative.

Whenever the website is loaded, a unique email address is generated (Figure 11-23). Send an email to the provided address and then click *Then check your score*.

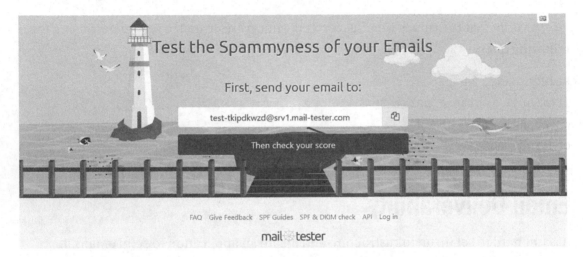

Figure 11-23. *mail-tester generates a unique email address that is used to send a test email for evaluation*

Next, write a simple PL/SQL anonymous procedure to send an email using the APEX_MAIL API. Specify the approved sender email address in the p_from parameter and the generated address from mail-tester in p_to. Here is a sample:

```
declare
  c_from varchar2(200) := 'no-reply@apeks.app';
  c_to varchar2(200) := 'test-tkipdkwzd@srv1.mail-tester.com';
begin
  apex_mail.send(
    p_to => c_to
    , p_from => c_from
    , p_body => 'Hello! Message delivered by OCI Email Delivery services.'
  );
```

```
  apex_mail.push_queue;
end;
/
```

Wait a few minutes and then check the results on mail-tester using the provided URL. The score and details of what contributed to the score will be displayed (Figure 11-24).

Figure 11-24. *The outcome of mail-tester's analysis of the test email sent*

If the DNS records were added correctly, then the score obtained should be a near-perfect score of 10. Mail-tester also provides details on where any scores are deducted to help users address issues and improve the deliverability of emails.

Troubleshooting Deliverability

A well-configured email sending infrastructure is no guarantee that an email will be sent or received successfully. When emails do not arrive as expected, developers will often want to know why. Besides deliverability, the APEX and OCI also provide tools for observability. These include the APEX_MAIL_QUEUE and APEX_MAIL_LOG views in APEX and OCI *Logging* for the Email Delivery services.

Most APEX developers would be familiar with the two views involved with APEX_MAIL. These can either be accessed through the APEX instance administration application or querying the views as a schema associated with the workspace using SQL. It will often provide the first clues as to why the email is not received. Common issues encountered include misconfigured SMTP settings in the APEX instance, an email address that is not on the approved senders list (Figure 11-25), a "To" email address that is on the suppression list, or an email payload that exceeded the service limits.

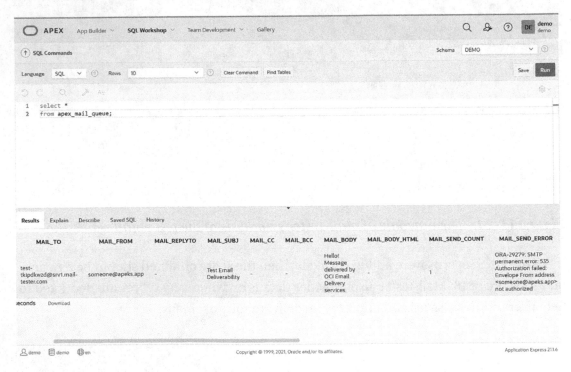

Figure 11-25. *Using the APEX_MAIL_QUEUE to identify any issues with outbound emails*

At times, APEX successfully sends the email and is verifiable using the APEX_MAIL_
LOG. To investigate if there are issues external to the instance, the best approach is to
enable logging for an email domain.

To enable the logs for an email domain, perform the following steps:

1. Open the navigation menu on the top left of the OCI Console, and
   then click *Developer Services*.

2. Under *Application Integration*, click *Email Delivery* to get to the
   overview/configuration page.

3. On the left side of the page, under *Email Delivery*, click *Email
   Domains*.

4. Be sure to select the compartment that the email domain is in.

5. Click the email domain to configure.

6. On the email domain's details page, under *Email Domains*,
   click *Logs*.

7. In the Logs table, click the toggle/switch to enable the desired
   event log. A modal will be opened for additional details to
   complete the process (Figure 11-26).

8. Click *Enable Log* to complete the process.

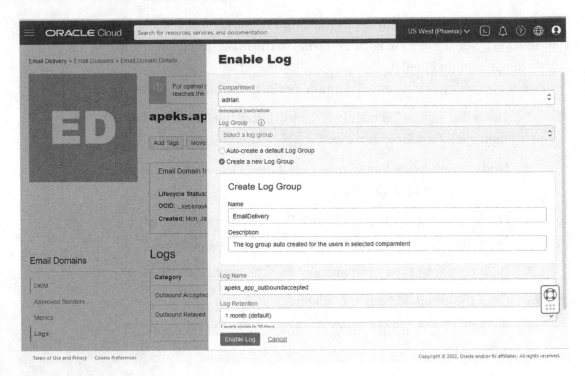

Figure 11-26. *Required details for enabling OCI Logging for the email domain*

There are two events that can be enabled for each email domain: *Outbound Accepted* and *Outbound Relayed*. For troubleshooting issues, I recommend enabling both. The first logs inbound requests and is used to validate if a request was successful or not. The latter logs successes and failures when the email is relayed by the service.

The logs can be viewed through the OCI Console and can be accessed *via* different paths and user interfaces. OCI Logging is available under the console's *Observability & Management* submenu. Either view individual logs or utilize the *Search* feature to view multiple logs at once. The latter is useful for troubleshooting as the events can be viewed collectively and in chronological order.

1. Open the navigation menu on the top left of the OCI Console, and then click *Observability & Management*.

2. Under *Logging*, click *Search*.

3. On the Search page, click the field *Select logs to search*. This opens a modal.

4. Manipulated to select all the logs to search (Figure 11-27).

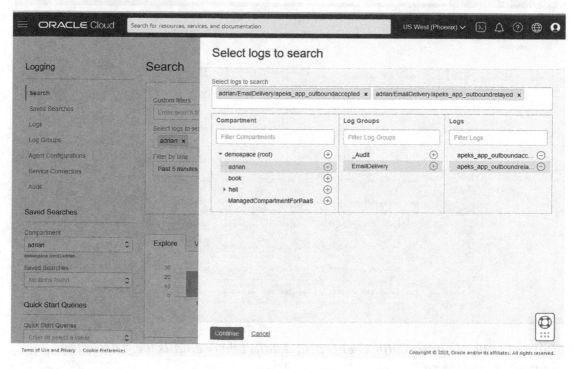

Figure 11-27. *Select the logs to search on*

5. Click *Continue*.

6. Change the time filter as needed. The table of log entries (Figure 11-28) should be refreshed automatically; if not, click *Search*.

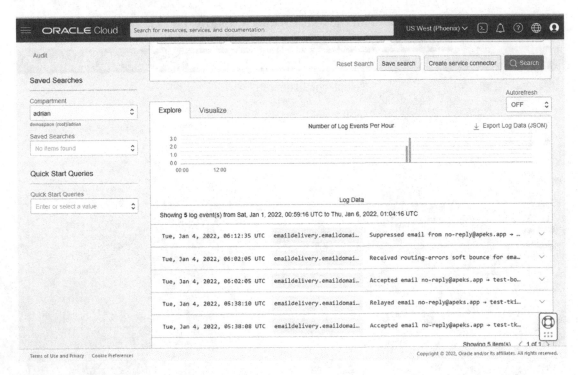

Figure 11-28. *Logs showing events and details where emails were accepted, relayed, or suppressed*

Note   Like all OCI resources, users will need the appropriate permissions applied through IAM policies. If you do not have the required access, please contact your OCI administrators.

Other Essentials

By now, we have gained a firm understanding of what is required to set up and use the OCI Email Delivery service with APEX to send emails. Perhaps the next important questions that we should consider are costs and are there any limits.

Today, Email Delivery services are priced at USD 0.085 per 1,000 emails sent per calendar month. As noted earlier in the chapter, this service is not included in the Oracle Cloud Free Tier, so the tenancy must be upgraded to a paid account before it can be used. Also, note that if the "To" address includes multiple email addresses, an email address is sent for each and will contribute to the usage and costs.

For most tenancies, the defaults for key service limits are

- A maximum of 200 emails or 2 MB chunk of data per day.

- A maximum sending rate of ten emails per minute.

- A maximum message size of 2 MB. This includes any required headers included in the email payload.

- A maximum of 2,000 approved senders.

OCI customers may submit requests to increase some of these service limits, for example, to allow email payloads larger than 2 MB but up to 60 MB. However, Oracle Support usually requires customers to provide details of how the organization is using the service and sending practices to meet anti-SPAM laws. You may also be required to set up email authentication methods like publishing SPF records and DKIM signing.

Summary

The OCI offers a managed service that can be used by APEX applications to send emails. It is a secure platform, implements best practices, and provides features to ensure email deliverability. In this chapter, we learned the necessary tasks to

1. Prepare the tenancy for the Email Delivery service.

2. Access the SMTP endpoints.

3. Configure a domain's DNS for maximum deliverability.

4. Configure an APEX instance to use the service.

5. Test email deliverability.

6. Configure the OCI for troubleshooting email deliverability issues.

Finally, we examined the costs and service limits when using the service.

Index

A

Access Control List (ACL), 390, 391
Advanced Research Projects Agency
      Network (ARPANET), 367
Aggregated Anomaly Score, 308
AnalyzeDocument, 350, 353, 358
Annotation class, 245, 251
Anomaly detection
    instrument error, 270
    MSET, 269
    normal data, 269
    real-time detection, 270
    SPRT, 269
    training data, 269
    unexpected events identification, 269
Anomaly Detection API
    APEX application, 316
    data source, 315, 316
    documentation, 313
    REST Data Source, 316
    setting up APEX, 313–315
AnomalyDetectionGroup, 275
Anomaly Detection service
    Alarm creation, 313
    compartment creation, 270–272
    dataset requirements, 289–293
    federated users, 279
    IAM user creation, 277–279
    login options, 273
    machine learning model, 293, 295
        (*see also* Machine learning model,
        Anomaly Detection)
    managed AI Service, 317
    metrics, 310–313
    OCI, 270
    policy creation, 275, 276
    user group creation, 273, 274
    Vault, Keys and Secrets, 280–289
    workspaces, 289
Anomaly Score Per Signal, 308
APEX application, 389
    BLOB object, 57
    conventional approach, 62
    digital photos table, 48–51
    external storage system, 62
    functions, 54
    Object Storage, 57–59, 61, 62
    procedures, 54
    retrieve tenancy
        namespace, 52, 53
    substitution strings, 54
    tasks, 48
    web credential for OCI, 51, 52
APEX_MAIL, 367
APEX Media Extension, 68
API Gateway
    APEX, 132, 133, 135, 136
    deployment, 112
    logging, 136–138
    OCI Events, 111
    OCI Object Storage, 111
    Oracle Functions, 112
    security, 136–138
    use case definition

© Adrian Png and Heli Helskyaho 2022
A. Png and H. Helskyaho, *Extending Oracle Application Express with Oracle Cloud Features*,
https://doi.org/10.1007/978-1-4842-8170-3

API Gateway (*cont.*)
APEX application, 112
architecture, 115
language translation engine, 115–122
language translation services, 114
language translation system, 123, 124
OCI services, 114
API keys, 45, 51, 76, 256, 258, 313–314, 335, 336, 347
API Management, 35, 126
API requests, 194, 261, 266, 268
Application Performance Monitoring (APM), 80–82
Application Programming Interface (API), 45, 68, 76, 182, 193, 255, 261, 313, 346
Artificial intelligence (AI), 345, 366
Artificial Neural Networks (ANNs), 346
Aspect-based sentiment analysis (ABSA), 323
Automated Machine Learning (AutoML), 167–177, 188
Automatic Data Preparation (ADP), 182, 188
Autonomous Database (ADB), 1, 147, 282
Autonomous Transaction Processing (ATP), 41
Availability domain (AD), 21

B

Big Data, 151, 345

C

Carriage Return and Line Feed (CRLF), 193
Center for Internet Security (CIS), 28, 29, 31
Certificate authority (CA), 24, 137, 200, 201, 390

Client Credential OAuth 2.0, 214
Cloud Native services, 35
Command-line interface (CLI), 334, 346
Compartment AnomalyDetection, 272
Computer vision (CV), 345, 346
Computing device, 345
Configuration File Preview, 258, 259, 337
Confusion Matrix, 172, 173
Convolutional Neural Networks (CNNs), 346
Cross-Origin Resource Sharing (CORS), 112, 130, 137
CSV formatted data, 291
Customer support interactions, 320

D

Data assets, 289, 295–301
Database service level, 169, 176, 199
Database system
load balancer, 21
Data Labeling API, 268
annotations, 255
with APEX
API request, 261
authentication, 263, 264
dataset request, 263
parameters, 264, 265
REST Data Source, 266, 267
Web Credentials, 261
APEX setting up, 257
API keys, 256–258
Configuration File Preview, 258, 259
IAM user creation, 255
View Configuration File, 260
Datalabelingdataset, 240
Data Labeling Management API, 255, 268
DataLabeling-non-tech-user-policy, 243

Data Labeling service
adding new records, 252
Administrators group, 237
APIs, 255 (*see also* Data Labeling API)
bucket creation, 236
compartment creation, 234, 235
data labeling errors, 252–254
datasets and records, 243–249
dynamic groups creation, 240, 241
labeling records, 249–252
new policies creation, 242
OCI, 233
resources, 233
user group creation, 238–240
users, 237
Data processing error, 269
Dataset Format, 244
Deep learning, 346
Demilitarized zone (DMZ), 11
Demo-Object-Policy, 347
DemoVisionGroup, 347
Digital Imaging and Communications in
Medicine (DICOM), 65
Distributed Denial of Service
(DDoS), 25, 138
Dockerfile, 86
Document AI, 350, 351
DomainKeys Identified Mail (DKIM),
377, 379–383
Dynamic Groups, 100

E

Email, 367, 388, 393, 397
Email deliverability, 367, 377
SPAM emails, 393
test, 394, 395
troubleshooting, 396–399

Email Delivery services
OCI, 367
SMTP, 367, 368
Email domains, 377–384, 386, 397, 398
Embedded Python Execution (EPE),
188–190, 196, 198–200, 213
Espressif Systems, 35
Event Service, 35

F

False Alarm Probability (FAP), 301–303
Federated users, 272, 274, 324
Filestack, 68
Fully qualified domain name
(FQDN), 24
Function Development Kit (FDK), 86, 103,
104, 123
FunctionsDevelopers, 79

G

General information, 303
GitHub, 4
Graphics Processing Units (GPU), 346

H

High-Performance Computing
(HPC), 345
Human error, 269
Hypertext Transfer Protocol (HTTP), 25,
51, 93, 112, 123, 130, 133,
193–195, 199

I

IAM user *demoapex*, 347
IDCS Group, 274, 275, 279

Identity and Access Management (IAM),
11, 38, 42, 74, 123, 346, 368, 369,
371–373, 375, 376
API keys, 76–79
Auth Tokens, 79
Groups, 79
policies, 79–82
users, 74, 75
ImageNet, 346
Image processing
client browser, 68
custom image processing REST API, 68
serverless technology, 67
third-party REST APIs, 68
Independent software providers (ISPs), 3
InfluxDB version, 289, 290, 296, 299
Infrastructure as a Service (IaaS), 2, 3, 36
Instance Principal Authentication, 100
Instance Wallet, 283
Interval method, 311

add user to group, 326
API operation and the resource
type, 327
create policy, 329
create user group, 326
key phrase extraction, 321, 322
language detection, 320, 321
NER, 322, 323
sentiment analysis, 323, 324
setting up, 324, 325, 327
text analytics with OCI Console,
329–331, 333
text classification, 321
user creation, 325
Language translation
API gateway, 125, 127–130, 132
IAM policy, 124
network security group, 125
Large objects (LOBs), 37
Line-delimited JSON (JSONL), 233, 268

J

Java Enterprise Edition (EE), 1
JavaScript, 67–69, 87, 88, 93, 111
JSON-format, 83, 197, 211, 291, 333

K

Key phrase extraction, 320–322, 330–332

L

Language
AI Service, 319
Language API, 334
Language detection, 319–321
Language Service

M

Machine learning (ML), 149, 345, 349, 366
kernels, 290
Machine learning model, Anomaly
Detection
anomalies.json, 309, 310
compartment selection, 301
configurations, 299
Create and Train Model, 295
creation and training, 301
Data Asset, 295, 296
data source, 297
defining credentials, 298
estimated value, 306, 307
FAP, 301
graphs, 308

JSON/CSV file, 305

Model Information, 303

OCI-related information, 303

Oracle Autonomous Transaction
Processing database, 296

Oracle Object Storage, 289, 296,
299, 300

parameters, 302

possible states, 303

private endpoint, 299

project creation, 293, 294

tags, 304, 305

TFR, 302

timestamp, 306, 309

training dataset, 306

variables, 307

Master Encryption Key, 280

Metrics, 310

Metrics Explorer, 312

Microsoft Windows, 345

Model False Alarm Probability, 303

Model information, 302

Model Metric, 169

Multilingual Engine (MLE), 67, 111

Multipurpose Internet Mail Extensions
(MIME type), 194

Multivariate False Alarm Probability, 303

Multivariate kernels, 290

Multivariate methods, 292

Multivariate State Estimation Technique
(MSET), 269, 290

Mutual-TLS (mTLS), 137

N

Named entity recognition (NER), 322,
323, 332

National Vulnerability Database (NVD), 28

Natural Language Processing (NLP),
113, 319

Network components

APEX instance, 2

Bastion, 11, 13–17

infrastructure issues, 3

network security groups, 7–11

PaaS service, 3

Virtual Cloud Network (VCN), 3–7

Network security group (NSGs), 9, 125

NsgPrivateDatabaseAccess, 24

NsgPrivateWebAccess, 10, 24

O

Object Storage, 245, 246

APEX web credentials, 46, 47

API keys, 45, 46

auto-tiering and life cycle
management policies, 37

Buckets, 40, 41

compartment, 39, 40

database, 35

groups, 42

IAM user, 44, 45

Oracle Autonomous
Database, 41, 42

Oracle Cloud Infrastructure, 36

policies, 43

services, 37

storing files, 37

Object Storage Demo, 48

Object Storage Settings, 348

OCI AI Services, 346

OCI Anomaly Detection Service, 269

OCI Console, 320, 344

OCI Container Registry (OCIR), 124

OCI Designer Toolkit (OKIT), 19

OCID (Oracle Cloud Resource
        Identifiers), 89
OCI Email Delivery services
    with APEX, 400
    approved senders, 386–388
    availability, 376, 377
    configure APEX instance, 389, 391–393
    email deliverability
        SPAM, 393
        test, 394, 395
        troubleshooting, 396–399
    email domains, 377–384, 386
    IAM, 368, 369, 371–373, 375, 376
    regions, 376, 377
    server information, 376, 377
    service limits, 401
    suppression list, 388, 389
OCI Language API Reference and
        Endpoints, 334
OCI Language Service, 319, 344
OCI Object Storage, 35, 347–349
OCI Public Key Fingerprint, 260
OCI REST APIs, 257
    APEX_WEB_SERVICE PL/SQL
        package, 346
    CLI, 346
    custom applications/scripts, 346
    IAM user, 346
    Oracle, 346
    SDK, 346
    security layer, 347
OCI vision
    AnalyzeDocument REST endpoint, 352
    APEX application, 354
    challenges, 350
    Document AI, 350, 351
    elements, 363
    features, 354, 359

home page, 355
Image Analysis, 350
JSON, 358
key-value pairs, 360, 361
KEY_VALUE type, 361
line items, 365, 366
LINE_ITEM_GROUP, 363
machine learning, 349
Oracle Functions, 350
QuickBooks®, 349
RECEIPT, 351, 359
Tesseract, 350
Travel Receipts, 351
uploading images, 355–357
value attribute pairs-row, 365
Vision's *AnalyzeDocument*
        endpoint, 353
OML4Spark, 151
OML REST services
    access token, 201–203
    APEX Application, 232
    APEX page, 229
    Application Item, 219
    AutoML Experiment, 210
    cognitive-text REST endpoint,
        205, 206
    Data Source, 216
    express solutions, 207
    Fetch Rows, 221
    GetToken Process, 226, 227
    Header parameters, 222
    HTTP request message, 207
    installing and setting up, 200, 201
    Interactive Report, 225
    OAuth2 token, 214
    OCI Database Service Console, 213
    OML4Py datastore, 210, 211, 213
    Oracle Cloud Infrastructure, 204

P15_TOPN field, 231
parameters, 215
Password Flow, 215
POST operation, 221
Python REST API, 208
Python script repository, 212
Region Query, 228
response message, 223
REST Data Source Operations, 219, 220, 230
sentence parameter, 224
Summary API endpoint, 220
TextList, 222
three-tier web applications, 207
TopN, 223
weight parameter, 224
Open Neural Networks Exchange (ONNX), 196
Open Vulnerability and Assessment Language (OVAL), 28
Operating system (OS), 89
Optical character recognition (OCR), 349
Oracle Application Express (APEX), 111, 346
    applications, 367
    autonomous database
        logs, metrics and alarms, 31–33
        private endpoint, 22–24
        secure APEX stack, 22
        vanity URL, 24, 25
        Vulnerability Scanning Service (VSS), 28–31
        web application firewall (WAF), 25–27
    database service, 1
    ML-powered algorithms, 1
    OCI Designer Toolkit (OKIT), 19

Resource Manager, 18
    Terraform, 18
Oracle Autonomous Database, 21, 111
Oracle Autonomous Linux, 20
Oracle Autonomous Transaction Processing, 289, 296
Oracle Cloud Functions
    development process, 69
    Fn Project, 69
    Fn Project CLI, 71, 72, 82–84
    ImageMagick, 69
    OCI CLI, 70
    OCI Object Storage, 65
    oracle cloud infrastructure container registry (OCIR), 85
    serverless technology, 69
    validate setup, 85
    virtual cloud network (VCN), 72, 73
Oracle Cloud Infrastructure Container Registry (OCIR), 85
Oracle Cloud Infrastructure (OCI), 2, 35, 51, 111, 233, 270, 317, 324, 348
Oracle Database (DB), 2, 65
Oracle Enterprise Linux, 20
Oracle Events, 97, 99
Oracle Functions, 111
Oracle Identity Cloud Server user, 277
Oracle Kubernetes Engine (OKE), 112
Oracle Machine Learning (OML)
    administration, 154–158
    APEX, 190
    Automated Machine Learning (AutoML), 167–177
    Autonomous Database, 139–145
    in-database machine learning, 190
    models, 177, 179–181
    notebooks, 158–167

Oracle Machine Learning (OML) (*cont.*)
  OML4SQL, 151
  Oracle Cloud Free Tier, 139
  URLs, 145, 146
  user
    administration, 147, 148
    Database Actions, 149, 150
  user interface, 151–154
Oracle Machine Learning for Python
    (OML4Py), 151, 184–190
Oracle Machine Learning
    Services, 196–198
Oracle Machine Learning for SQL
    (OML4SQL), 181–183
Oracle Multimedia (OMM), 65
Oracle Object Storage, 289

P

Password, 75, 152, 195, 284, 286
PhotosBucketManagers, 42, 45
PL/SQL API, 346, 367, 392
Pluggable databases (PDBs), 2
POST method, 353
Proof of concept (PoC), 114
Python script repository, 188, 189, 196,
    198, 208, 209, 212

Q

Query Editor, 312
QuickBooks, 349

R

Rapid Application Development
    (RAD), 389
Resource Manager, 4, 18

Resource Principal Authentication,
    100, 103
Resource Principals, 100–103, 240
REST APIs
  bearer token, 195
  Embedded Python Execution,
    198–200
  grant type, 196
  HTTP response status code, 195
  Oracle Machine Learning
    Services, 196–198
  sender-constrained token, 195
REST Data Source, 214, 216, 219, 225, 230,
    261, 262, 265–267, 315,
    316, 339–344

S

Sampling error, 269
Secrets, 281, 285–287
Sender Policy Framework
    (SPF), 383, 385
Sentence Level Sentiment Analysis,
    323, 331
Sentiment analysis, 197, 319, 320, 323,
    324, 331, 333
Sequential Probability Ratio Test
    (SPRT), 269
Simple Mail Transfer Protocol (SMTP),
    367, 368, 374, 377, 387, 390, 391,
    393, 396
Single Sign-On (SSO) login, 272
Software development kit (SDK),
    45, 91, 346
SPF Record Testing Tools, 385
Statistic method, 311
Supervised learning, 233
Suppression list, 388, 389, 396

T

Target False Alarm Probability, 301, 303

Terraform, 4, 18, 19, 36, 204

Test email deliverability, 394, 395

Text analysis with OCI Language API and APEX

  APEX user credentials, 338

  create REST Data Source, 339, 342

    authentication section, 341

    general section, 339

    parameters section, 342

    preview data profile section, 343

    preview data section, 342

    remote server section, 340

  data types, 334

  editing user capabilities, 335

  limitations, 334

  OCI Language API Reference and Endpoints, 334

  POST requests, 334

  POST REST Data Source, 344

  REST Data Source discovery, 343

  setting, 335, 337

  user details page, 335, 336

  web credentials, 339

Text classification, 319–321, 332

Text-to-Speech (TTS) software, 345, 346

Thumbnail generator function

  approach to development, 93–95, 97

  Cards Region, 108

  complete function and deploy, 103, 104

  configuration parameters, 97

  Docker build, 90

  execution environment, 87

  func.yaml file, 91

  JavaScript file, 87

  logging, 105, 106

  multiple programming languages, 86

  Node.js FDK, 88

  Object Storage, 107

  Oracle Function, 89, 92

  stock package.json file, 88

  photo collection, 110

  PhotosBucketAccessPolicy, 107

  resource principals, 100–102

  serverless function, 88

  triggering functions, 97, 99

  troubleshooting, 105, 106

  YAML, 86

Timestamp, 290–292, 301, 302, 306, 308, 309

Train Fraction Ratio (TFR), 302

Training Data information, 302

Training Fraction Ratio, 301, 303

Transfer learning, 346

Translate, 114

Transmission Control Protocol (TCP), 13

U

Univariate kernels, 290

Univariate models, 290, 308

User-defined functions (UDFs), 184, 189, 190, 198, 200

V

Vault, 280–282, 288, 296

VCN Wizard, 72

Virtual Cloud Network (VCN), 3–7, 72, 73, 112

Virtual Private Network
(VPN), 11, 118
Vision
OCI, 349 (*see also* OCI vision)
OCI Object Storage, 347–349
OCI REST APIs, 346, 347
Vulnerability Scanning Service
(VSS), 28–31

W, X, Y, Z

Wallet, 280, 282–286
Web application firewall (WAF), 25–27
Web Credentials, 46, 51, 214, 216, 259–261,
314, 315, 337–340
Windows Subsystem for Linux (WSL), 70
Work requests, 249–254

Printed in the United States
by Baker & Taylor Publisher Services